TOURISM

Concepts, Issues and Challenges

Editors

Prof. S.P. Bansal

Prof. Sandeep Kulshreshtha

Dr. Prashant Gautam

NEHA PUBLISHERS & DISTRIBUTORS

DELHI

Publisher
NEHA PUBLISHERS & DISTRIBUTORS
4832/24,Prahlad Lane,S-207 Ansari
Road, Daryaganj,Delhi-110002
Ph.: 43570976, 23278261

Edition: 2015

ISBN : 978-93-80318-57-8

Laser Typesetting
Jee-Vee Graphics, Delhi

Price : ₹ 1695.00

Printed in India

PREFACE

"...everything has a past. Everything – a person, an object, a word, everything. If you don't know the past, you can't understand the present and plan properly for the future."

— Chaim Potok, Davita's Harp

Over the decades, tourism has experienced continued growth and deepening diversification to become one of the fastest growing economic sectors in the world. Modern tourism is closely linked to development and encompasses growing number of new destinations. These dynamics have turned tourism into a key driver for socio-economic progress. Today, the business volume of tourism equals or even surpasses that of oil exports, food products or automobiles. Tourism has become one of the major players in international commerce, and represents at the same time one of the main income sources for many developing countries. This growth goes hand in hand with an increasing diversification and competition among destinations. This global spread of tourism in industrialised and developed states has produced economic and employment benefits in many related sectors – from construction to agriculture or telecommunications.

Globally, an ever increasing number of destinations have opened up and invested in tourism development, turning modern tourism into a key driver of socio-economic progress through the creation of jobs and enterprises, infrastructure development and the export revenues earned. As an internationally traded service, inbound tourism has become one of the world's major trade categories. Tourism exports account for as much as 30% of the world's exports of commercial services and 6% of overall exports of goods and services. Globally, as an export category, tourism ranks fourth after fuels, chemicals and automotive products. For many developing countries it is one of the main sources of foreign exchange income and the number one export category, creating much needed employment and opportunities for development2. In over 150 countries tourism is one of the five top export earners, and in 60 it is the number one export. It is the main source of foreign exchange for one – third of developing countries and one - half of each Least Developed Countries (LDCs), where it accounts for upto 40% of their GDP (UNWTO,2012).

Tourism Sector is a major generator of employment. As a highly labour intensive activity, tourism and tourism support activities create a high proportion of employment and career opportunities for low skilled and semi-skilled workers, particularly for poor, female and young workers. Women make up 70% of the labour force in tourism sector and half of all tourism workers are 25 years or under. The tourism sector can be an important source of employment for many of the unemployed youth and consequently reduces the poverty in the society (UNCTAD 2010).

According to UN World Tourism Organisation (UNWTO), the contribution of tourism to worldwide GDP is estimated to be in the region of 5%. For diversified economies, the contribution of tourism to national GDP ranges from 2 % for countries where tourism is comparatively a small sector, to over 10 % for countries where tourism is a main driver of the national economy. Tourism's contribution to employment is estimated to be 6 – 7 % of the overall number of jobs worldwide (direct and indirect)

Global market trends indicate that long-haul travel, neighboring country tourism, rural and ethnic tourism, wellness and health holidays, cultural tourism, spiritualism, ecotourism, sports and adventure holidays, and coastal tourism and cruises are a few emerging areas of tourist interest. From a geographic viewpoint, there has been a remarkable rise in Asian tourists, particularly from China and the East Asian countries. Further, the average age of an international tourist has also been reducing, representing a growing segment of young tourists who would typically travel to take a break from stressful professional lives. Continuing world prosperity, growing recognition of tourism's contribution to employment and economic growth, availability of better infrastructure, focused marketing and promotion efforts, liberalization of air transport, growing intraregional cooperation, and more effective Public-Private-Partnerships (PPPs) are seen as the key drivers for tourism in the next decade.

All countries throughout the globe are vying to secure the best shares of tourism for themselves, on realization of the benefits that this industry brings. But the mad blind rush for this sector, taken for granted at times has started showing its negative face in the shape of resultant impacts of the industry's very development. The growth of this industry has now raised a warning alarm for the developers and stakeholders, bringing forth concerns and dilemmas of future growth. A number of tourism related issues to be addressed by environmentalists, developers and local communities are constantly emerging and need serious thought.

With the growth in tourism there is also a growth in the understanding of the various dimensions involved in tourism, particularly the service dimension and the industry aspect. In this new understanding tourism has emerged as an extremely vital and strategic activity having immense potential for employment generation and earning foreign exchange – two core elements in a developing economy such as ours. At the same time we cannot ignore the fact that without proper monitoring tourism can be a double-edged sword. While it has the immense potential to be in the fore¬front of socio-economic development it can also put tremendous pressure on environment and socio culture ethos. Moreover new and socially untenable forms of tourism are also raising their ugly head. Thus the issue of cultural, social and economic sustainability of tourism also needs close and constant attention. Sustainability is recognized as one of the most important issue related to tourism development in the contemporary times. As developers and promoters of this industry, it is our key responsibility to ensure that a future for tourism will even exist for our coming generations too. To reap today, all benefits of this industry by exploiting and usurping our rich resources and putting at stake all assets, without having foresight to leave some rich reserves for the tourism for tomorrow, would be a conscious uncorrectable mistake made on our part. The continuous monitoring, identification and correction of our efforts in the direction of proper and sustained development is the issue that is presently demanding all our attention.

The present book 'Tourism: Concepts, Issues and Challenges' organised itself as per the spirit of the introductory quote of this preface. Editors are feeling very happy to bring this book on the occasion of '6th International Conference of Indian Tourism Congress' at Bali, Indonesia.

This book is a collection of assorted researches that addresses a large vista of tourism related issues. The research articles are all, in their own part, notable scholarly contributions documenting diverse aspects and studies related to the tourism. This book offers an inclusive glance into issues related with the status and development of tourism and hospitality industry. The tourism and hospitality industry is well on its way to becoming one of the most powerful growth engines in the coming time, thus these research studies are relevant for a number of stakeholders like governments, destinations, tour operators, travel agents, tourism workers, developers, tourism researchers, students and travellers themselves. This book seeks to fulfil the needs of planning for the industry.

Editors acknowledge the valuable research of the contributors and believe that this publication is a significant contribution towards future development and planning purposes not only for tourism industry but also for other tourism related activities and those who are interested in the tourism research. Editors sincerely believe in the standards of academic integrity and highest levels of scholastic conduct, thus declare that the respective authors would be responsible for any kind of plagiarism found in their contribution.

S.P. Bansal

Sandeep Kulshreshtha

Prashant Gautam

Bali, Indonesia

21.06.2014

LIST OF CONTRIBUTORS

Abhishek Sharma

Associate Professor, LBSIMT, Bareilly

Akshay Kulshrestha

Senior Supervisor (Tourism & Marketing), Maharajas' Express Indian Railway Catering & Tourism Corporation Ltd. (Ministry of Railways, Govt. of India) 3380, Old Ranjeet Nagar, South Patel Nagar, New Delhi

akshaykulshrestha@gmail.com

Ambar Vishal

Research Scholar,Deptt. of Travel & Tourism Management, Dr. B.R. Ambedka University, Agra, e-mail:ambarvishal@gmail.com

Anjali Khanna

Associate Dean, School of Hotel Management and Tourism, Lovely Professional University Phagwara, Punjab.

anjali.khanna@lpu.co.in

Anurag Agarwal

Associate Professor, Department Of Commerce S.S. PG College Shahjahanpur

Aparna Raj

Professor & Dean, Institute of Tourism & Hotel Management Bundelkhand University, Jhansi (U.P.) Institute of Tourism & Hotel Management Bundelkhand University, Jhansi

raj_aparnaraj@rediffmail.com

B Muniraja Sekhar

Associate Professor, K.M.M.Institute of Post Graduate Studies, Department of Management Studies, Tirupati-517502, bmrajasekhar@gmail.com

Balbir Singh

Research Scholar, HPUBS, Shimla

Binota Meinam

Associate Professor, Imphal College, Imphal, Manipur

meinambinota@gmail.com

Chandra Shekhar Barua

Indian Institute of Tourism and Travel Management (IITTM), Ministry of Tourism, Govt. of India, Govindpuri, Gwalior-474011, csbarua003@rediffmail.com

Charu Sheela Yadav

Indian Institute of Tourism and Travel Management, NOIDA

charupg@rediffmail.com

Charu Yadav

Assistant Professor, Jaipuria Institue of Management, Ghaziabad

Chithung Mary Thomas

Assistant Professor, D.M. College of Commerce, Imphal, Manipur

chithungmary@yahoo.com

Devinder Sharma

Associate Professor (Commerce), Himachal Pradesh University Centre for Evening Studies, Shimla.

Divya Khanna

Guest Faculty, Deptt. of Business Administration, MJP Rohilkhand University, Bareilly

G.B.Karthikeyan

Assistant Professor & Head, Department of International Business, Chikkanna Government Arts College, Tirupur.

G.G. Saxena

Executive Director, ICPB and

Former MD & CEO,

Delhi Tourism and Transportation Development Corporation (DTTDC)

ggsaxena@gmail.com

Gireesh Kumar

Guest Faculty, Deptt. of Business Administration, MJP Rohilkhand University, Bareilly

K.V.S.N. Jawahar Babu

Associate Professor, Department of Tourism, Nellore, Mobile: 9440494141, Email: sudhajaahar@gmail.com

Lalit K. Panwar

Secretary, Ministry of Minority, Govt. of India

Lipika K.Guliani

Assistant Professor, Panjab University, Chandigarh and Doctoral Candidate, PTU, Jalandhar lipika_b@yahoo.com

Lucy Jajo Shimray

Assoc. Prof. Dept. of Economic, DM College of Arts, Imphal. Affiliated to Manipur University(MU)

lucyjajo4@gmail.com

Manjula Chaudhary

Department of Tourism and Hotel Management, Kurukshetra Univesity, Kurukshetra,

manjulachaudhary@gmail.com

Mohit Chandra

Director , Amity School of Hospitality, Amity University Lucknow

Malhaur, Gomti Nagar Lucknow

hittsindia@gmail.com

N N Sharma

Associate Professor, Department of Commerce and Management, Govt. P.G. College Dharmshala, Himachal Pradesh (India)

nnsharma585@gmail.com

N. Lokendra Singh

Registrar, Manipur University, Email: lokendra_n@rediffmail.com

Naorem Sunita Devi

Project Fellow, Tribal Research Institute (TRI), Imphal, Manipur

sunitanaorem@gmail.com

Neelima Gaur

Vivek Khand 4/381, Gomti Nagar

neelimagaur@gmail.com

Nidhi Pathania

Research Scholar, School of Hospitality and Tourism Management, University of Jammu, Jammu and Kashmir, Email: nidhi_1_5@yahoo.com

Ninghorla Zimik

Assoc. Prof. Dept. of Political Science, Pettigrew College, Ukhrul, MED, Govt. of Manipur. Affiliated to Manipur University

ninghorzimik@gmail.com

Oinam Momoton Singh

Assistant Professor, Department of Sociology D.M. College of Arts, Imphal, Manipur,

momotonoinam@gmail.com

P.K. Yadav

Ex. Pro. V.C. Head and Dean Faculty of Management, M.J.P. Rohilkhand University, Bareilly

pkyadav_bly@yahoo.com

P.Premkanna

Associate Professor & Head, Department of Catering & Hotel Management, Hindusthan College of Arts & Science, Coimbatore. Tamilnadu.

premkannap@gmail.com

Pallavi Thakur

Assistant Professor, SoH&T, Bahra University

Parikshit Sharma

Research Scholar, SOTHSSM, IGNOU & Assistant Professor, SoH&T, Bahra University

parikshitsharma@live.com

Pawan Gupta

Indian Institute of Tourism and Travel Management, NOIDA

drpawan.gupta@yahoo.com

Pramendra Singh,

School of Tourism, Jiwalji University Gwalior, pramendra58@ gmail.com

Prashant Kumar Gautam

Assistant Professor

University Institute of Hotel Management and Tourism, Panjab University, Chandigarh

Prashant.k.gautam@gmail.com

Priya Sharma

Lecturer, IHM Kufri, Shimla

Promila Raita

Assistant Professor, Humanities, Maharaja Agrasen University, Baddi promila77raita@gmail.com

R.K. Tamphasana

Associate Professor, G.P. Women's College, Email: rktamphasana55@gmail.com

R.Nithiyanandam

Director, Sree Ramu College of Arts and Science, Pollachi, Coimbatore DT.Tamilnadu

directorsrc@yahoo.in

R.P.Nainta

Principal, Agriculture Cooperative Staff Training Institute, Sangti, Summerhill, Shimla

rpnainta@gmail.com

Rajendra Kshetri

Professor of Sociology, Nagaland (Central) University Lumami, Nagaland, aardhikshetri@gmail.com

Ravindra Singh

School of Tourism, Jiwalji University Gwalior, singhravindra007@gmail.com

S L Kaushal

HP University Business School, Shimla

kaushal.shyam@gmail.com

S.A. Rizwan

Assistant Professor

UIHMT, Panjab University, Chandigarh

syedahmadrizwan@gmail.com

S. Ismail Basha

Assistant Professor, K.M.M.Institute of Post Graduate Studies, Department of Management Studies, Tirupati-517502, sib.comp2011@gmail.com

S. Meera

Assistant Professor (International Business), Indian Institute Of Tourism and Travel Management (Under Ministry Of Tourism), Government of India, Nellore, Andra Pradesh

S.S. Narta

Professor, Deptt. Of Commerce and Director, UCBS, HPU, Shimla.

nartasshpu@rediffmail.com

Sandeep Dubey, School of Tourism, Jiwalji University Gwalior, sandeep.kanyakubj@gmail.com

Sandeep Kulshrestha

Director I/C, , Indian Institute of Tourism and Travel Management (IITTM), Ministry of Tourism, Govt. of India,

Sankul7@rediffmail.com

Sandeep Paatlan

Assistant Professor, School of Management, Maharaja Agrasen University, Baddi- sandeep_966@yahoo.com

Sandeep Walia

Assistant Professor

Maharaja Agrasen University, Baddi, Himachal Pradesh.

sndp.walia551@gmail.com

Sandeva Khajuria

Research Scholar, School of Hospitality and Tourism Management, University of Jammu, Jammu and Kashmir, Email: sandeva_khajuria@yahoo.co.in

Sanjay Mishra

Sr. Faculty Member, Department of Business Administration, MJP Rohilkhand University, Bareilly – 243006

Saurabh Dixit

Course Chairperson- PGDM (SS) and ANO, Indian Institute of Tourism and Travel Management (IITTM), Ministry of Tourism, Govt. of India, Govindpuri,

Gwalior-474011saurabhdixit246@gmail.com

Shakti Singh

Junior Research Fellow, Himachal Pradesh University Business School (HPUBS) Shimla (HP)

Shikha Sharma

Institute of Vocational Studies (MTA), H .P. University, Summer Hill, Shimla, Himachal Pradesh Email address: ssharma.shimla@gmail.com

Shweta Singh

Supervisor (Tourism), Maharajas' Express Indian Railway Catering & Tourism Corporation Ltd. (Ministry of Railways, Govt. of India) 12/1, Second Floor, East Patel Nagar, New Delhi

3shweta.s@gmail.com

Suneel Kumar

Assistant Professor, Department of Commerce, Shaheed Bhagat Singh College, University Of Delhi, India drsuneel.sbsc@gmail.com

Tanvi

Assistant Professor University Institute of Hotel Management & Tourism, Panjab University, Chandigarh, E-mail: tanubeniwal@yahoo.com

U.N Shukla

Associate Professor, Deptt. of Travel & Tourism Management, Dr. B.R.Ambedkar University, Agra, e-mail:shukla.ithm@gmail.com

Usha Agrawal

Head- Department of History and Tourism, Govt. P.G. College, MIG II 241, Kitiyani Colony, Mandsaur (M.P.) agrawalusha1@gmail.com

Vivek Mittal

Dean, Faculty of Management, CGC-Technical Campus, Mohali

Yashwant Gupta

Professor, Himachal Pradesh University Business School (HPUBS), Shimla (HP)

gupta_yashwant1@rediffmail.com

Ravinder Dogra

Assistant Professor, Indian Institute of Travel and Tourism Management, Gwalior

rdmtm9@gmail.com

Neelika Arora

Assistant Professor, Department of HRM and OB, Central University of Jammu

a_neelika@yahoo.com

Vishal Kumar

Associate Professor, Maharaja Agrasen School of Management, Maharaja Agrasen University, Baddi (H.P.)

vkfzr@hotmail.com

Savita

Assistant Professor in Commerce, Dev Samaj College for Women, Ferozepur City (PB)-152002

dhawansavita@hotmail.com

Prateek Agrawal

Associate Professor, Institute of Tourism & Hotel Management, Bundelkhand University

Jhansi (U.P.) – 284128, e-mail: prateek_ithm@yahoo.co.in

CONTENTS

ISSUES IN TOURISM DEVELOPMENT

CHALLENGES FOR TOURISM DEVELOPMENT

TOURISM CONCEPTS

TOURISM CONCEPTS

This introductory section of the book is presenting its readers a kaleidoscopic view of the length and breadth of the industry. The first chapter of the section 'Agra Wings More than Taj Mahal: a Study of Alternative Tourist Attractions in Agra' by Akshay Kulshrestha and Shweta Singh talks about the potential of Agra other than the famous Taj Mehal. In this chapter authors have given a very comprehensive overview of tourism expansions in Agra. In chapter 'Community Based Homestays – A New Concept in Orchha (M.P.)' authored by Aparna Raj concluded that homestay tourism is a rapidly growing niche market, utilized by an increasing number of domestic and international tourists.In the chapter author has presented a case study of Orcha.

Binota Meinam, Chithung Mary Thomas and Naorem Sunita Devi in the chapter 'Economics of Tourism: an Empirical Study of "Andro-Santhei-Park", Imphal through Leibensteine's Critical Minimum Effort Theory' have concluded that the success of any tourism scheme (whether public or private ownership) concerning expansion and preservation of modern values and traditional values needs people's participation.

Chapter 'Bed and Breakfast Accommodation in Delhi Region - a Step towards conserving Natural Resources' by G.G. Saxena, Lalit K. Panwar, Manjula Chaudhary and Sandeep Kulshreshtha discusses the need of bed and breakfast units for creation of additional tourism infrastructure , coping the shortage of requisite hotel rooms, opportunity to the tourists to experience family warmth , feel of Indian customs and traditions , authentic home cooked food, cheaper accommodation as well as ultimately contributing for conservation of natural resources.

Lipika K.Guliani in the chapter 'Exploring Chandigarh as Tourist Destination: an Analytical Study' aims to assess the determining factors that influence tourists' satisfaction and to estimate the tourist satisfaction index in Chandigarh, important tourism destination in India.

In the chapter 'Pukreila: A Driving force for Community Based Tourism Initiatives (Opportunities & Challenges)' by Lucy Jajo Shimray and Ninghorla Zimik, authors have tried to put forwards the proofs for counting on community based tourism. Chapter is a humble attempt to highlight how Pukreila can be the driving force to explore the vast opportunities of natural and cultural resources of the region.

Parikshit Sharma, Pallavi Thakur and Priya Sharma in the chapter 'Shimla: a Study of the Change in Preferences from Traditional to Modern Food Habits of the Local Community' is attempt to showcase the changing preferences of tourists.

The main aim of chapter Bhimbetka, India's Rock Art Heritage Site: Protection, Promotion and Management by Usha Agrawal is to measure the potential of tourism at Bhimbetka and related challenges and opportunities. Today, at the site, there is need of protection, promotion and management related steps to be taken in order of sustainable development of the site.

The chapter 'Dargah for Tourist's Consumption: A Study' by Sandeep Walia and S.A. Rizwan tries to look into the monastic order in Islam. This monastic order has become prevalent as Sufism and has ritualised to an extent where it can be offered as a product in the tourism market. Chapter 'Tourist vis a vis Tour Guide' by Sandeep Kulshreshtha, Saurabh Dixit and Chandra Shekhar Barua will give readers an idea about a tour guide and its role in the industry in a very basic language. Chapter 'Tourism and Hospitality Marketing' by B Muniraja Sekhar, K.V.S.N. Jawahar Babu and S.Ismail Basha is an aim to peep into the concept of marketing of tourism and hospitality,

Shikha Sharma in the chapter 'Heritage Tourism: a Study on Jaivillas Palace' has concluded that The museums are considered as places where tourist comes to know about its culture. But with the changing time the concept of the traditional museum is changing to modern one. The museums are now considered as places which should also incorporate some fun element along with learning experiences. The museum provide the visitor respect as being a part of the same culture, choice and variety of artefacts, involvement and active and varied learning experiences, involvement and a contemporary experiences.

Chapter 'Community Based Eco-Village Tourism in Manipur Hills : Lessons from the States of Sikkim and Nagaland' by R.K. Tamphasana and N. Lokendra Singh concluded that eco-village tourism can become as one of the most effective socio-economic tool for combating hill areas development and opens an avenue for young/women unemployed and entrepreneurs in the near future.

In the chapter 'Tourism in India: A 360 Degree Boon' by P.K.Yadav, Sanjay Mishra, Abhishek Sharma and Charu Yadav, authors have tried to understand the interactivity between economics of tourism industry and complementary industries with various stakeholders. The quest for alternative tourism or newer forms of tourism like health tourism, rural tourism is also examined, briefly in the chapter.

AGRA WINGS MORE THAN TAJ MAHAL: A STUDY OF ALTERNATIVE TOURIST ATTRACTIONS IN AGRA

Akshay Kulshrestha

Senior Supervisor (Tourism & Marketing), Maharajas' Express Indian Railway Catering & Tourism Corporation Ltd. (Ministry of Railways, Govt. of India) 3380, Old Ranjeet Nagar, South Patel Nagar, New Delhi

akshaykulshrestha@gmail.com

Shweta Singh

Supervisor (Tourism), Maharajas' Express Indian Railway Catering & Tourism Corporation Ltd. (Ministry of Railways, Govt. of India) 12/1, Second Floor, East Patel Nagar, New Delhi

3shweta.s@gmail.com

Abstract

Agra has held a place for itself as the tourism Icon of India and is eminent on World Tourist Map owing to the presence of the Taj Mahal, a UNESCO World Heritage Site and one of the Wonders of the World. As per the calculations of World Travel & Tourism Council, tourism generated INR 6.4 trillion or 6.6% of the nation's GDP in 2012. However, it's worth making a note that these tourist arrivals occur in specific pockets only. If we go by recently published statistics available from Ministry of Tourism, in 2011,

Uttar Pradesh contributed 19.6% and 9.4% of domestic and foreign tourist arrivals in the country. Based on these numbers, U.P. was ranked number 2 in terms of domestic tourist arrivals while in terms of foreign tourist arrivals, it ranked at number 4. Remarkably, more than 60% of the foreign tourist arrivals to UP were to the Agra (Taj Mahal, Agra Fort, and Fatehpur Sikri). Not to be surprised, every year more than three million tourists visit Taj Mahal. Though, Agra have been the fourth most visited cities of India by foreign tourists during the year 2011 and was ranked 65 Worldwide yet it's not very lucky with the length of overnight stays, the average length of stay being only 0.8 days.

The purpose of this study is to examine the alternative tourist attractions in Agra other than Taj Mahal so as to promote Agra as a complete destination to International as well as Domestic Tourists and to increase the length of overnight stays. There are more than 200 buildings of historical importance in and around Agra for both domestic and foreign tourist. Taj Mahal, Agra Fort, Fatehpur Sikri, Itmad-ud-Daulah, Akbar's Tomb (Sikandra), Jama Masjid, Chinika Rauza, Ram Bagh and Keetham Lake are few of them. Fatehpur Sikri, located at a distance of 37 km from the city too is an UNESCO World Heritage site. Dara Shikoh's library, MirzaGhalib's birthplace, Swami Bagh- the headquarters of the Radhasoami faith, Mariam Tomb, Roman Catholic Cemetery (Red Taj), the ancient Manka Meshwar Shiva temple, the Jama Masjid, and churches of different Christian sects, St. Patrick's Junior College - Asia's oldest convent and the Akbar Church are few of the 'un heard of' attractions that can be used to tap niche sectors of tourism such as pilgrimage, cultural, heritage, study tour, Golf tourism, shopping etc. The handicrafts, cuisines, and less popular sites can hold tourists to stay for 2-3 days. Apart from a selection of historical monuments and blend of cultural and religious assortment, Agra can also be promoted for Themed events, like concerts on the banks of River Yamuna overlooking Taj Mahal and fascinatingly as a theme wedding destination, of course with support from the forest department and agriculture administration.

Key Words: Taj Mahal, Niche Tourism, MICE, PPP, SOC Analysis.

We have also devoted a small segment of this study in understanding the advantages & challenges of promoting Agra as a wide-ranging destination along with the benefits to the local community in terms of more employment, infrastructure, social and financial enrichment.

"We travel, some of us forever, to seek other states, other lives, other souls."

From elite hobby to mass tourism, tourism in modern times has come a long way. Historically, tourism can be traced in the narrative of MarcoPolo in the 13th century and the "grand tour" of the British aristocracy to Europe in the 18th century as early tourism. However, we regard Thomas Cook as the founder of organized tours for introducing first chartered train tour in 1841 from Loughborough to Leicester, but in true terms, tourism can be recognized for as long as the human race has been wandering. The ancient man traveled to fulfil his/her basic needs of food, shelter and safety of family but gradually having developed an understanding he advanced in the hierarchy of needs (Maslow's hierarchy of needs) and hence kept on cultivating various motives and modes of travel. He started to travel for leisure, learning and happiness. Today, we recognize travel as 'Tourism' which is more organized with integrated components of transportation, accommodation, safety, amenities and ancillary services. Over decades tourism has taken a vast shift in Domestic as well as International tourism owing to improved standard of life style, education, growth in disposable income & leisure time and technological advancements.

India has always charmed foreign tourists for its historically rich monuments, mystical call of its mountains and lakes, romance of its beaches and the religious fervor that it evokes. In modern times tourism has evolved with newfound focus.It not only provides for bread & butter of millions directly/indirectly but is also major source of nation's foreign exchange earnings and hence is acknowledged as an industry of vast potential.

Tourism in Agra

Agra has held a place for itself as the tourism Icon of India and is eminent on World Tourist Map owing to the presence of the Taj Mahal, a UNESCO World Heritage Site and one of the Wonders of the World. As per the calculations of World Travel & Tourism

Council, tourism generated INR 6.4 trillion or 6.6% of the nation's GDP in 2012. However, it's worth making a note that these tourist arrivals occur in specific pockets only. If we go by recently published statistics available from Ministry of Tourism, in 2010, Uttar Pradesh contributed 19.6% and 9.4% of domestic and foreign tourist arrivals in the country. Based on these numbers, U.P. was ranked number 2 in terms of domestic tourist arrivals while in terms of foreign tourist arrivals, it ranked 4.

Tourists Visiting Taj Mahal, Agra:

Tourist Statistics of Taj Mahal (Statistics is based on ticket sales of Taj Mahal)

Year	Indian	Foreign	Total
2008	2635284	591560	3226844
2009	2585560	491554	3077114
2010	4081426	647428	4728854
2011	4604603	692332	5296935
2012 (upto Aug 2012)	3373615	418606	3792221
*Children below 15 are not ticketed.			

Source: Uttar Pradesh Tourism Directorate.

STATISTICS FOR 10 MOST POPULAR CENTRALLY PROTECTED & TICKETED ASI MONUMENTS DURING 2010:

Domestic Visitors			Foreign Visitors		
Rank	**Monument**	**Visitors**	**Rank**	**Monument**	**Visitors**
1	Taj Mahal	4081426	1	Taj Mahal	647428
2	Qutabminar	2498907	2	Agra Fort, Agra	381479
3	Red Fort, Delhi	2262810	3	Qutabminar, Delhi	298180
4	Sun Temple, Konark	1929690	4	Humayun Tomb, Delhi	228914
5	Charminar, Hyderabad	1609666	5	Fatehpursikri, Agra	210450
6	Agra Fort, Agra	1417641	6	Keshhva Temple	181078

7	Golconda Fort, Hyderabad	1373170	7	Red Fort, Delhi	142029
8	Elora Caves, Aurangabad	1187432	8	Mattancherry Palace Museum, Kochi	128753
9	Bibi Ka Makabra, Aurangabad	1100088	9	Western Group of Monuments	90721
10	Gol Gumbaj,Bijapur	1011341	10	Group of Monuments, Mamallapuram	69758

***Source:** Archaeological Survey of India.

Agra is the host of most popular tourist destination both for domestic as well as foreign tourists. It has the most visited site by both the domestic as well the foreign tourists - The Taj Mahal, and 6th most popular site for domestic visitors – the Agra Fort, which is also the second most popular site for foreign visitors.Remarkably, more than 60% of the foreign tourist arrivals to UP were to the Agra (Taj Mahal, Agra Fort, FatehpurSikri). Significantly, every year more than 3 million tourists visit Taj Mahal.

Though, Agra has been the fourth most visited cities of India by foreign tourists during the year 2011 and was ranked 65th Worldwide yet the duration of tourist stay in Agra is dismal, the average length of stay being only 0.8 days.

Objectives of The Study

This study principally targets to the following objectives:

- To explore the alternative tourist attractions in Agra other than Taj Mahal.
- To examine prospectof promoting Agra as a complete destination to International as well as Domestic Tourists.
- To observe a range of already existing attractions and new activities that can be developed and further promoted to make tourists spend alonger time (days) in Agra and to increase the length of overnight stays.
- To study key challenges and to suggest important Strategy for overcoming those challenges.

◈ To understand the advantages of promoting Agra as a wide-ranging destination in terms of the welfare of the local community.

Overview of Methodology adopted:

i. To achieve the desired result the study was based on tested methods of surveys and interviews of the various constituents of the tourism industry including the tourists. Surveys had been conducted with purposefully and meticulously designed questionnaires, and interview methods. Proper analysis of the government policies and the data of tourists' arrivals and receipts in Agra will also help in deriving conclusions in the research. Information was gathered from the state tourism department and the data available on the internet from standard sources.

ii. Study is conducted with a combination of secondary as well as primary research methods. The broad methodology is as follows:

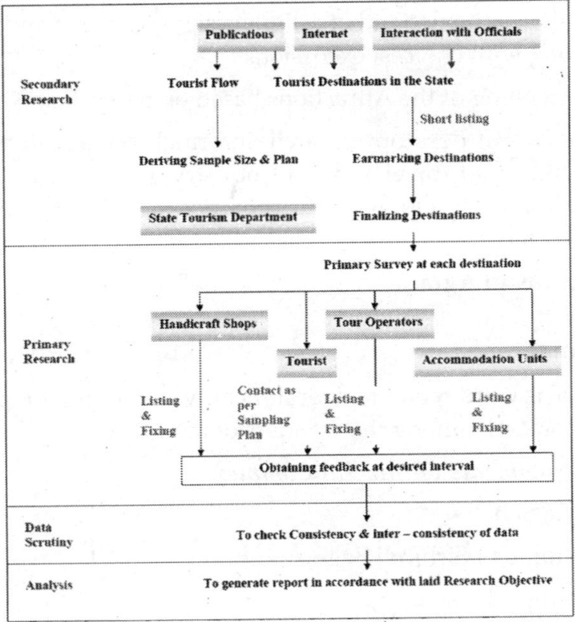

Fig. 1 Research Methodology

Tourism Potential of AGRA:

The city of Agra is known worldwide for Taj Mahal and a million of tourists from all over the world visit every year to experience varied flavors of this glorious monument of love. Agra was a seat of the Mughal rulers for years and hence it has a number of Mughal historical monuments in and around the city and numerous other rulers also contributed to the rich past of this city. FatehpurSikri, the deserted city of red sandstone, was built by Emperor Akbar near Agra.

The city of Agra is situated on the west bank of the river Yamuna. It is very well connected by railway and road-way with major cities of India and is imperative component of famous tourist circuits like Golden Triangle of Delhi- Jaipur- Agra and the popular route of Delhi-Agra-Khajurao-Varanasi. With the inception of new Yamuna Express way, the city is now easily and comfortably accessible from the capital city of Delhi by road.

Although the beauty and grandeur of the Taj Mahal is impeccable and beyond compare yet there are numerous more buildings of historical prominence and of religious significance in and around Agra along with choicest excursions.

Initial Screening of the Attractions based on Secondary Research:

On the basis of desktop research, informal interaction with the local members of travel and tour industry in the state as well as State Tourism Development Corporation, following attractions were identified:

Monuments in Agra:

Taj Mahal

Taj Mahal is word renowned for its beauty and grandeur and hold a place for itself among the wonders of the world.

Other Monuments within Taj Complex

1. Rauza Saheli
2. The tomb of Sirhindi Begum
3. Fatehpuri Masjid
4. Mumtazabad (Taj Ganj)

Agra Fort

Built by Akbar in Red Sandstone when he was through with the consolidation of his power after accession to power in 1654, Agra Fort worked both as a military strategic point as well as the royal residence. Many of the palaces inside the fort were later added by next generations of Mughal Emperors like Jahangir and Shahjahan.

Buildings Inside the Agra Fort

1. Jehangir Mahal
2. Jodha Bai's Palace
3. Delhi Gate
4. Amar Singh Gate
5. Akbari Mahal
6. Shah Jehani Mahal
7. Khas Mahal
8. Shish Mahal
9. Anguri Bagh
10. Muthamman Burj
11. Mina Masjid
12. Diwan – I - Khas
13. Nagina Masjid
14. Machchhi Bhawan
15. Moti Masjid
16. Diwan – I - Am

FatehpurSikri

16 kms from the city of Agra, stands the deserted city of FatehpurSikri. FatehpurSikri, once the capital of Mughal Empire, is one of the finest examples of Mughal architecture. Though the city is in ruins, it is a good excursion for those travelling to Agra. It need to be promoted as a place where one should spend a day with sunset over the ruins.

The Main Attractions

Diwani – I - Am, Diwani – I - Khas, Jodhabai's Palace, Friday Mosque, Salim Chisti's Mausoleum

Sikandara

This monument is only 13 km. from the Agra Fort and is the mausoleumof Akbar who ruled over the Mughal Empire from 1556 to 1605. Akbar began building his mausoleum in the spartan style of Timurid architecture. The mausoleum was completed by his son, the next Mughal Emperor, Jahangir, who added more decorative elements to the design of Akbar's tomb in Sikandra.

The entrance to Akbar's tomb in Sikandra is under a huge arched gateway, similar to the BulandDarwaza at FatehpurSikri. There are beautiful calligraphic inscriptions on the white marble front of the gate. As you enter the gate you will see a formal garden in the charbagh tradition, and the tomb of Akbar situated at the center. Within the same complex is another sober tomb made of red sandstone, which contains the grave of Akbar's wife Mariam, the mother of Jahangir.

As the monument hold great historical importance to the foreign tourists, it can also be promoted as a family picnic spot among the domestic as well as local tourists.

Itmad-ud-Daula

It is the tomb of Mirza Ghiyas Beg, a Persian who had obtained service in Akbar's court. The tomb set a startling precedent as the first Mughal building to be face with white inlaid marble and contrasting stones. Unlike the Taj it is small, intimate and, since it is less frequented, has a gentle serenity.

Chini Ka Rauza

It is one of the lesser-known monuments of Agra. It is the tomb known as the Chini ka Rauza, which is situated 1 Kilometer north of Itimad ud Daulah's Tomb. The Chini ka Rauza was built in 1635 and is the tomb of Allama Afzal Khan Mullah of Shiraz, a scholar and poet who was the Prime Minister of the Mughal Emperor Shah Jahan. The tomb gets its name from the colorful tiles (chini) that cover the walls of the tomb. The tomb is built in a rectangular shape and is topped with a globulardome.

The SoamiBagh

Samadh is the mausoleum of Huzur Soamiji Maharaj (Shri Shiv Dayal Singh) in the Dayalbagh section in the outskirts of the city. He was the founder of the Radhasoami Faith and the Samadh is sacred to its followers. Construction began in 1908, and it is believed that construction will never end. It is often seen as the "next Taj Mahal". The carvings in stone, using a combination of colored marble, are life-like and not seen anywhere else in India.

Other Monuments of Agra:

1. Kanch Mahal (Glass Palace)
2. Tomb of Itibar Khan
3. Guru -ka-Tal
4. Sarai NurJehan
5. Humayun 's Mosque Kachhpura
6. Tomb of Sadiq Khan Mir-Bakhshi
7. Tomb of Salabat Khan Mir-Bakhshi 'Roshan-Zamir'
8. Battis Khambah
9. Jami Masjid and the Muthamman Chowk
10. Chhatri Rani Hada
11. Tomb of Firuz Khan Khwaja Sara
12. Tomb of Sheikh Ibrahim (Nephew of Salim Chishti)

Tourist Attractions of Historical Importance:

Mehtab Bagh is situated on the river bank, facing the Taj Mahal. Also known as "The Moonlight Garden", this garden offers a majestic view of the Taj Mahal from behind across the river Yamuna. The Garden is now a ticketed monument under Archeological Survey of India (ASI).

Ram bagh holds its importance as the oldest Mughal Garden in India.Originally built by the Mughal Emperor Babur in 1528, this garden is located about five kilometers northeast of the Taj Mahal. Colossal walls enclose the garden with corner towers crowned by pillared pavilions. The agarden is divided into quarters by stone paved pathways. On the north- eastern side of this building, there exists another terrace, from which steps leads to a Hammam. Immediately north side of this garden, there is a row of ruined houses with a gateway, built of red sandstone at each end (Source-Archeological Survey of India).

Tajganj is an area encircling the Taj Mahal is called as Tajganj. Tajganj initially accommodated the artists and architects who worked on building the Taj and the generations of these artists still living in this area. Tajganj can be the place to experience the hustle and bustle of the town and can be targeted to be developed more prominentlyfor budget travelers and backpackers.

Barah Khamba and Chattries on the Yamuna bank form a photogenic view across the river Yamuna.

Promoting Agra beyond Taj Mahal

Agra- As a destination for Niche segment:

Niche tourism refers to how a specific tourism product can be tailored to meet the needs of a particular audience/market segment. Locations with specific niche products are able to establish and position themselves, as niche tourism destinations. Niche tourism, through image creation, helps destinations to differentiate their tourism products and compete in an increasingly competitive and cluttered tourism environment (Prabakaran & Panchanatham, 2013).Niche Tourism and the special interest tours are gaining popularity in western world and Agra with all its assets holds capability to facilitate various segments of the tourism sector in this one city.

Pilgrimage, Cultural, Heritage Study Tours:

In addition to the above listed places of historical importance, Dara Shikoh's library, Mirza Ghalib's birthplace, Swami Bagh- the headquarters of the Radhasoami faith, Mariam Tomb, Roman Catholic Cemetery (Red Taj), the ancient Manka Meshwar Shiva temple, the Jama Masjid, and churches of different Christian sects, St. Patrick's Junior College - Asia's oldest convent and the Akbar Church are few of the historical and cultural attractions that can be used to tap niche sectors of tourism such as pilgrimage, cultural, heritage, study tour, etc.

Wildlife Tourism:

Soor Sarovar Bird Sanctuary is approximately 15 km from Agra, on Agra-Mathura highway and is a house of more than150 species of birds. This Sanctuary also supports a substantial number of Rock Python.

The Keoladeo Ghana National Park or the Bharatpur Bird Sanctuary is located at a distance of 105Kms from Agra. Some 377 species are spotted at Bharatpur Sanctuary, making it one of the most inviting destinations in India for ornithologists, amateurs and nature lovers. Both the Sanctuaries can be clubbed together and be promoted as a package to tourists interested in bird watching. This excursion will surely make the tourists to stay in the city for atleast another night. This can also be utilized as a plank for promoting 2-3 days Photography tours that is a new and promising initiative in Wildlife tourism.

Golf Tourism in Agra: Agra Club Golf Course With the mesmerizing view of Taj Mahal, Agra Club Golf Course assures a pleasant golfing experience for the golf lovers. Developed in 1904, this nine-hole course has some of the holes providing a breath taking view of the Taj Mahal. This golf course can be developed into a world class golf course and designated as a place for some of the important golf championships. This will be helpful in encouraging sports tourism in Agra.

Rural Tourism: Barara Tourist Village While visiting a foreign country a tourist wants to see the real side of that place as well. As it is said the real India still resides in its villages. Taking tourists to the villages doesn't only enhances the experience for the tourists but also gives exposure to the villagers and an opportunity in form of economic benefits. The Barara village is at 12 Kms from Agra on Agra- Fatehpur road which gives it a hand-on advantage. The village has been host to IFYE (International Farm Youth Exchange) delegates from USA since 1964 and some of the villagers are well versed with English. Barara village is just an example of rural tourism. Other nearby villages can be identified and developed as model villages for village safari tours and Agri-tours.

Medical Tourism Prospective:

Medical tourism is defined as an act of traveling to other places or countries for medical surgery or treatment (usually due to either lower costs or specialized facilities) combined with a short stay or holiday. Medical tourism: With global revenues of approximately US$ 20 Billion (2005), the medical tourism industry is one of the world's largest industries. India's cost effective treatment makes it an important player in this industry. Seeing the huge potential in the sector of medical tourism, the government has also started issuing M (medical) visa to the medical patients, and MX visas to the spouse accompanying them, which are valid for a year. Around 2 lakh medical tourists visited India last year and the figure is expected to grow by 50% this year. Agra has all the modern Medical facilities and best Medical practices at way cheaper prices than the west and the other parts of the country.

There are some prerequisites of developing Agra for medical tourism such as:

1. Upgradation of basic amenities and hospital infrastructure
2. Co-ordination between the healthcare and tourism sectors
3. Creating a resource pool of highly skilled and cordial manpower
4. Standardization of services and accreditation of hospitals

Same day excursions from Agra:

Planning and promoting itineraries keeping Agra as a base for night stays and adding same-day excursions to nearby places is a good strategy to encourage number of night stays in the city. The following places have been shortlisted for the purpose:

Bharatpur: 105 Kms from Agra is the historic town of Bharatpur. Bharatpur has its own legendary stories of bravery of Jat Kingdom against Mughals and British rulers. The area not only houses the forts, palaces of the Mughal and Rajput architecture but also contains a vibe of rich Rajasthani Culture.

Mathura and Vrindavan: Just 56 Kms from Agra lies the Holy and colorful city of Mathura, which literally means 'city of gods', an epithet that matches its tranquil atmosphere. Mathura is famous among the domestic as well as foreign tourists as the home of

Lord Krishna. During Holy (festival of colors) and Janmashtami (Birthday of Lord Krishna), the city is swamped with pilgrims and tourists.

In the same district lies the town of Vrindavan, The land of Shri Krishna where he spent his youth as a cowherd boy and hence holds religious importance to the devotees.

Chambal Safari: Mere 70 kms from Agra is The National Chambal Sanctuary (NCS). It is a 400 km stretch of the river Chambal and a 6 km wide swathe of the ravines on both sides of the river, covering an area of 1235 sq. km. This sanctuary provides protection for 1200 Gharials & 300 Marsh Crocodiles and is a home to 8 species of Turtles and some smooth coated Otters.

Activity Based Attractions:

Outdoor Activities in Agra include exploring the forts and museums. Tonga ride to the Taj Mahal ora stroll around in the markets have been the only activities available to the guests for ages. However with the changing time a few activities have been developed and are welcomed by the guests. "Taj Nature Walk" and "Hot air Balloon safari" are greeted positively by the tourists but it is yet not being promoted on a larger scale and not many tourists coming to Agra are aware of such activities. Such activities need to be promoted on a generic scale while other engaging activities need to be developed. Few other suggested activities are:

- Promotion of places like Bateshwar, Shiva Temple and the MahaAarti held in the evening at the Ghats of river Yamuna.
- Boat cruise in river Yamuna with a mesmerizing view of Taj Mahal and the Agra Fort.

Agra as an International center for MICE

MICE segment or the Meeting, Incentives, Conferences and Events is one of the fastest growing segment of Tourism and Hospitality industry and is an excellent tool to overcome off-season and low-season challenges for both the industries.

The project may be directed towards capturing MICE segment flow towards North India because of its easy connectivity and proximity with Delhi. Conventions must be supplemented with exhibitions and events as events tend to attract more media coverage and hence greater exposure to Agra as a destination. Agra could strongly compete with other south Asian countries for international events like Music Concerts, Beauty pageants, Award Ceremonies etc.

Destination Weddings

The wedding industry is a multi-billion dollar market.Indian weddings is approximately $40 billion Industry and is growing at over 25 per cent annually. Destination weddings are picking up popularity at a rapid pace in this big fat wedding world.

Destination wedding is defined as a wedding that takes place at an exotic location atleast 100 miles from where the bride lives. Wedding is hosted at a location to which most of the invited guests must travel and often stay for several days.Home to the symbol of love, the Taj Mahal, would be the most desired place to tie-a-knot all over the world.The Oberoi Amarvilas, Trident, Agra, Radisson Blu Agra, Jaypee Palace Hotel are some the hotels accomplished for hosting a royal and opulent wedding. State Tourism may develop the choicest locations with view of Taj Mahal for events like such.

Assesment & Analysis

A) Infrastructure Assessment

A.1 Accommodation

Accommodation, in a wide range of price level, is available in Agra.Rooms are available in varied range: in five star hotels -1165, four star hotels -156, three star- 349. Besides, there are several budget hotels, guest houses and tourist bungalows in the city.

A.2 Local Transportation

The main mode of transportation is auto rikshaws, cycle rikshaws and private taxis. However, the public buses have been introduced but point-to-point tourist bus services (Hop-on buses) should be launched. Auto rikshaws may also be upgraded to provide a good experience.

A.3 Human Resources

Agra lacks trained manpower to handle the niche segments of tourism.

A.4 Parking at heritage monuments

Parking availability for tourist vehicles is a major problem. Sites with high tourist inflow such as Taj Mahal, Agra Fort and Sikandra are facing serious problem primarily due to lack of land availability. Multi-level parking is a good solution that optimizes space.

A.5 Promotional Issues

There is a need to promote few lesser-known monuments that are located near the main attractions but still deprived tourist attention. After the conservation of these monuments, they can also be clubbed in the list of "must see" sites. There is also a need to develop some good shopping places/activities by utilizing locally available resources so that tourist stays back at least for a day (night halt).

A.6 Infrastructure improvement at lesser known monuments

Basic facilities are required at lesser-known monuments. Restoration of these monuments is also required.

A.7 Lack of basic infrastructure facilities for tourists at destinations

To facilitate tourist in the city, Tourist Information Centres (TICs) are required at major locations. Facility of safe drinking water is also required.

A.8 Security issues

Due to omnipresence of the hawkers and local guides chase tourist from the parking itself which leaves a very wrong impression among tourists. Because of these touts and nasty behavior of some local people, tourists (especially foreign) generally don't spend much time at starting and ending points (entrance to monument stretch). It actually hampers income generation at local level. This issue needs to be regulated by authorities effectively.

B. Assessment of Challenges:

The key challenges towards developing Agra as a complete destination are:

(a) Lack of quality infrastructure,

(b) Skill development,

(c) Conducive policy framework,

(d) Coordination among various authorities.

The important Strategy for overcoming the above challenges can be:

- Adopting PPP model to address infrastructure constraints: expertise of private sectorshould be used in implementing larger tourism projects such as integrated tourismdestinations / Theme Parks, Eco tourism etc.
- Involving local community.
- Conducive Policy frame work for tourism development.
- Leveraging Technology: pan India travel currency cards, on line travel and hotelbookings, timely information exchange between stakeholders, availability ofmultilingual web sites, focused internet advertising campaigns and effective use ofsocial media can enable greater tourist inflows and seam less travel to Agra.

C. Advantages of developing Agra as a complete destination

C.1 Benefits to the Host Community

- Direct/ indirect quality employment opportunity.
- Longer stays of tourists deliver greater spending into local economy.
- Maintenance and improvement of the public area including the development of infrastructure, facilities, and improvements to cleanliness, safety and amenities.
- Contributes to the feasibility of local services and facilities that are essential for host communities.
- Encourages the protection of community assets and preservation of the natural and built environment.
- Contributes to maintaining and enhancing cultural and heritage assets.
- Adds substance to local traditions, festivals, cultural events, crafts.

- Creating and sustaining employment, providing a stability to community life
- The encouragement of local and civic pride, enhancing the sense of community and creating "social capital".

C.2 Supply of Hotel Rooms at all levels

Agra has a problem with limited overnight stays that can be addressed by developing new segments like MICE. International statistics suggest that an average Meeting/Convention duration is 3days.

C.3 Benefits to the Guest Community

- Greater satisfaction and experience of a life time.
- Better services at all levels.
- A complete experience that entrusts a feeling of "value for money" and hence "Happy Holidays".
- A catalyst for change, fresh ideas, new opportunities in a changing world.
- An awareness and appreciation of other people and cultures and encouragement to learn new skills, languages, etc

D. Market Opportunity Analysis

The market assessment was carried out through detailed interview of various industry experts along with a bunch of ground level facilitators (travel agents/ Tour operators/ Tour guides/ Hoteliers etc.) and on the basis of outcome the following have been established:

Primary Market Interests:

- Strong historical and cultural focus with Taj Mahal as the main focal attraction.
- Red fort is the second most famous destination after Taj Mahal followed by Fatehpur Sikri and then others.
- Strong interface between Delhi and neighboring states. Also a strong link of the circuit connecting Khajuraho and Varanasi via Gwalior.

Key Marketing Linkages:

- Delhi is the gateway for International and most Domestic travel.

- Uttar Pradesh itself doesn't have any other significant entry or exit.
- Agra and Varanasi is considered unique in the world with no effective competitor but Agra is the most dominant attraction with primary linkage to Jaipur, Gwalior, Jhansi, Orchha, khajuraho.

Conclusion

Conclusion on the marketing opportunity is derived after strength, opportunity and constraints (SOC) analysis.

Strength:

- Agra is a world class unique destination and is a known name worldwide for the presence of Taj Mahal.
- The primary connotation about Agra in people's mind is that of a rich historical / Cultural heritage and of sacredness i.e. Agra already holds a good image in the eyes of global tourism.
- Agra is very well connected to the capital and the major cities/ states via rail and road network.
- Agra has a great number of accommodation options available ranging from five star luxury hotels to the budget class accommodations.
- Local population of Agra is already sensitized towards the presence of foreign tourists.
- Agra proudly houses some of the most polished tour guides in the trade and has ample handicraft shops for those interested in shopping.

Opportunities:

- Agra is a house of numerous monuments of historical and cultural importance. These must be developed and incorporated in further development project planning.
- Primary linkage to the capital city of Delhi facilitates the opportunity to develop Agra as a destination for world class conferences and conventions.
- The rich agricultural affluence of villages surrounding Agra

must be utilized by developing selected villages for Agri-tourism and Rural Tourism.

- The Romantic presence of the monument of love makes Agra most suited destination to be offered for destination weddings and Music events.
- Advanced Medical sector of Agra must be tapped for promoting Agra for Medical Tourism.
- Promoting additional one-day excursions is a good way of increasing number of night stays in the city.
- More accommodations under BnB scheme and the home stay concept may be encouraged for duel advantage to the tourist as well as the local community.
- No. of room nights should be increased for any tourists.

Constraints:

- Most of the monuments are in hostile condition and require major restoration.
- Accessibility to various attractions within the city is a major deterrent factor given the poor traffic condition and the miserable status of the roads which calls for greater need of superior urban infrastructure and cleanliness.
- There is limited provision of the organized sector.
- There is paucity of parking space and even of basic amenities like drinking water and hygienic lavatories at destinations.
- There is need of greater activity based tourism development with major focus on evening activities.
- Safety is yet another major issue.

Having analyzed the vast potential of Agra as a tourist destination it is evident that the Government must draft policies to overcome constraints and to minimize the challenges. Same can be effectively achieved by adopting PPP Model for development of Agra as a complete destination. The government, the tourism department, travel and hotel industries, Forest Department, organizations for environment protection and home ministry must work together step by step towards developing Agra, as such changes aren't brought overnight and one department can't pull it all by itself.

State tourism department should encourage and assist various travel agents and tour operators to plan and promote niche tour packages such as medical, golf, rural and wild life. Same day excursions must be included and highlighted to encourage tourists to stay longer in the city. This may be promoted by India Tourism as a part of their marketing campaign and be publicized in the international tourist magazines and in-flight magazines. This will boost tourism even in off-seasons. It is important to exclusively market Agra as a destination with a rich assortment of attractions to choose from with special emphasis on increasing number of night stays in the city.

The motive of this study is not just to suggest a process to earn profit from the vast tourism potential of Agra, but it also puts emphasizes on the sustainable development and conservation of resources which is the most important need of today's world.

References

Tourism Statistics (2005 to 2012).

Uttar Pradesh Tourism Directorate.

Archaeological Survey of India; www.asi.nic.in

Tourism Department Uttar Pradesh. (2004 to 2012). ke karya kalap publication: Tourism Department; Lucknow (Uttar Pradesh), India.

Tourism Policy. (2011, 2012). Published by Tourism Department, New Delhi, India.

Incredible India. (August, 2006). Designed for the Market Research Division, Ministry of Tourism, Government of India, New Delhi, India.

World Tourism Organization, Year Book of Tourism Statistics.

Edensor, T. (1998). Tourists at the Taj (International Library of Sociology) (Paperback), 1st edition, Routledge.

Dr. A.K .Malviya, Tapping the neglected and hidden Potential of tourism in Uttar Pradesh, Conference on Tourism in India – Challenges Ahead, 15-17 May 2008, IIMK.

IL&FS Infrastructure Development Corporation Ltd (IL&FS IDC), appointed as the National Level Consultant (NLC) by Ministry of Tourism (February– 2012); Identification of Tourism Circuits across India, Interim Report submitted to Ministry of Tourism, Government of India.

Rohan Gawande and Sudhir Dethe (2008); Branding Indian Tourism: Entering Second Phase; Conference on Tourism in India – Challenges Ahead, 15-17 May 2008, IIMK

Prabakaran & Panchanatham; Niche Tourism Products of India; Abasyn Journal of Social Sciences Vol. 6 No. 1

www.incredibleindia.org

www.tourism.nic.in

www.wttc.org

www.up-tourism.com

COMMUNITY BASED HOMESTAYS – A NEW CONCEPT IN ORCHHA (M.P.)

Aparna Raj

Professor & Dean, Institute of Tourism & Hotel Management Bundelkhand University, Jhansi (U.P.) Institute of Tourism & Hotel Management Bundelkhand University, Jhansi raj_aparnaraj@ rediffmail.com

Abstract

Homestay tourism is a rapidly growing niche market, utilized by an increasing number of domestic and international tourists. Homestay refers to a visit to somebody's home in a foreign country which allows visitors to rent a room from a local family in order to learn local culture, lifestyle, or language. Orchha, a small town near Jhansi gets a small portion of the Khajuraho bound traffic, though the place is extremely rich in Natural as well as Historical heritage.. Friends of Orchha is a registered non-profit organisation working in Madhya Pradesh, India on creating livelihoods linked to tourism, preserving the environment of heritage sites like Orchha and promoting cultural exchange between visitors and locals. Friends of Orchha took the initiative to start homestays in Orchha, a concept which was absolutely new to the local families, and has seen the transformation in the families which took part in this initiative. This paper goes on to explore the importance of homestays in Tourism with special reference to the homestays at Orchha (M.P.)

Key words: Homestays, tourism, community tourism

Introduction

Community-based homestay tourism is a form of tourism that is closely related to nature, culture and local custom and is intended to attract a certain segment of the tourist market that desires authentic experiences. In 1996, holidays involving staying with an ordinary family in a private home were identified as a tourism product with the potential to grow in popularity (Swarbrooke and Horner, 2007).

Homestay is an alternative tourism product that has the potential to attract tourists due to a marked increase in international demand for tourism that enhances tourist knowledge by allowing them to observe, experience and learn about the way of life of the local residents of their destinations.

The homestay which refers to a stay at a residence by a traveler or a visiting foreign student is viewed as a means of culture and heritage tourism emerging with traditional houses and culture of residents achieving two goals at the same time: increasing the income of host country families and encouraging them to preserve their cultural heritage by presenting their traditional houses (Wang, 2007). Many tourists believe that the homestays they participate in represent a unique living in a new culture. Tourists seek authentic experience and architecture of the host culture. Homestays could provide the cultural experience and the sense of being at home. This allows them to behave more freely and feel comfortable and relaxed in a foreign culture. The search for an authentic experience among travelers also increases the construction of cultural and heritage based tourism in order to provide a more authentic encounter for tourists. Through homestays, these cultural attributes often provide participants - with such staged authenticity and acceptable satisfaction while hosts seek to offer tourists a genuine connection to the community. Residents desire tourists to visit their houses because travellers bring economic benefits to their community while they still maintain their traditional culture and heritage (Cole, 2007).

Culture and heritage tourism trends have particular relevance for rural areas when they are accompanied by abundant natural resources. Traditional ways of earning on stocks provide the primary source of income. But, to stimulate rural economies, it has become unavoidable for rural regions to seek alternative uses for local resources (Liu, 2006). Cultural heritage tourism is an option for enhancing rural lifestyles and distributing income in the region. As a result, tourism has become the priority tool of rural orthodoxy (Augustyn, 1998). Homestay programs play the main role in cultural tourism and are the fastest growing segments of the tourism market (Wang, 2007). The culture and heritage that has been preserved in a location causes the local people's everyday lives to infiltrate the everyday lives of travelers and thus, makes a homestay more attractive. Because of this, homestay tourism is a rapidly growing niche market, utilized by an increasing number of domestic and international tourists. As an attraction, it also continues to grow due to word-of-mouth. Therefore, to expand this market, the desirable cultural and heritage attributes should be considered in order to raise the number of travelers and thus, increase the local resident income. In addition, operators need to regard which attributes influence tourist satisfaction and their destination choice in order to formulate the strategies that attract and better satisfy customers.

Defining a Homestay

Homestay refers to a visit to somebody's home in a foreign country which allows visitors to rent a room from a local family in order to learn local culture, lifestyle, or language. It is a living arrangement offered by a host or host family that involves staying in their furnished house or suite. The guest of a homestay would be staying in home-like accommodation with shared living spaces, facilities, and amenities. Utilities and meals are usually included and the length of stay could be daily, weekly, monthly, or unlimited unless specified otherwise by the host (Rivers, 1998). Frederick (2003) also defined the homestay as a stay by a tourists or a visiting foreign student who is hosted by a local family. Homestay can occur in any destination worldwide; residents of homestay countries encourage homestays in order to develop their tourism industry. The concept of the home may be perceived to distinguish homestay establishments from other forms of accommodation. Rhodri (2004) stated that the distinction between homestay and hotel is boundaries of private area. The private space of homestay is opened to visitors that would not fall under the term of hotel. In other words, it may refer to a sector of homestay accommodation to distinguish the accommodation from other types which do not share all the characteristics to the same degree.

Homestay accommodation is a term with specific cultural associations such as private homes, interaction with a host or host-family, sharing of space which thereby becomes public (Lynch & MacWhannell, 2000). The associations of homestay establishments which link to the concept of the home can be distinguished from other forms of accommodation. In homestay accommodations, the boundaries of private homes are opened to public space, distinguishing from other accommodations with private space open to staff only (Lynch, 2000b). Thus, one may refer to the sector of homestay accommodations to distinguish the accommodation from other types which do not share all characteristics to visitors. Homestay accommodation types include farmstay accommodation, some small hotels, host families, and bed and breakfasts. It is used to refer to types of accommodation where tourists or guests pay directly or indirectly to stay in private homes (Lashley & Morrison, 2000). Lynch (2000a) studied networking in the homestay sector which found the particular nature of the homestay was the interaction between guests and hosts/family. The family has a key role to play in setting the norms of behavior which impact the guest while staying in the home.

Homestays are outstanding attractions which pull for the attention from operators. Moreover, homestay activities develop communities and increase community income while still maintaining the culture and environment of the local area. Simple lifestyles of local residents have become an important attraction which gains the attention of tourists.

Homestays are viewed as culture and heritage tourism, which emerged with the culture of local residents. Homestay tourists believe that the homestay represent a unique way of living in a new culture. They need an authentic experience, to see the architecture of the host culture and a sense of being at home. Understanding motivation is therefore a starting point to understand homestay tourists and how they satisfy their needs.

Home stay host/family

The associations between visitors and hosts may be described as linked by the concept of the home which may be perceived to distinguish homestay establishments from other forms of accommodation. Host of homestay is described as family who live on the premises, sharing their space which becomes public while other forms of accommodation, such as hotels where the host's (the manager or staff) private home is not on the premises and the boundaries of the private space are open to staff only (Lynch, 2003).

Culture and Heritage Attributes

A destination attribute is an important factor for evaluating tourists' satisfaction of a destination. To satisfy guests, accommodation providers need to understand their guests in terms of the experiences they seek. It is important to evaluate the experiences provided, both tangible and intangible, by mainstream accommodations in contrast to homestays (Howell, Moreo, & De Micco, 1993). Previous studies have shown an increased demand for accommodations in private homes or hosted accommodations, especially homestays or nature lodges, which represent a rapidly growing sector of the tourism industry (Morrision et al., 1996). Therefore, it is important for homestay providers to understand which attributes satisfy guests in order to develop better business strategies and gain the attraction of more customers.

Socio Economic Impacts of Homestays

A research by Kadir (1993; 1995) found that the tourism industry has contributed to the creation of employment opportunities for local people and increase their income. The study by Amran (2003) claimed that the homestay programme can improve self-satisfaction, healthy living and changing socio-economic level of the participants. The growth of this homestay programme will not only increase revenue and infrastructure but also change the mindset of the local culture to realize the importance of safeguarding and preserving cultural heritage to be shared and developed together with the global community (Yahaya et al, 2009). Studies by Hall (2001), found that the homestay programme also contributed to the preservation and conservation of the environment through the control of logging activities that may affect the river water pollution.

Orchha – A Destination rich in history, religion and nature

Orchha, meaning a "hidden place", certainly lives up to its name. Languishing amid a tangle of scrubby dhak forest, 18 km southeast of Jhansi, the former capital of the Bundela dynasty gets only a small portion of the Khajuraho bound traffic. Architectural gems, however, abound in this town. Orchha was founded in the 16th century by the Bundela Rajput chieftain Rudra Pratap Singh, it is a city frozen in time, on the banks of river Betwa. The city of Orchha consists of several buildings constructed at different times. In the times of Bharati Chand (1531 - 54), the Ramji Mandir Palace and the city walls were completed. During the reign of Madhukar Shah (1554 - 92) Orchha saw a long period of peaceful prosperity, when the early Bundela paintings were painted on the walls of the palaces. One of the other notable rulers of Orchha was Raja Bir Singh Ju Deo (1605 –27) who built the exquisite Jehangir Mahal, Hardaul Mandir & Chatturbhuj Temple. Other than the scenic beauty of the river Betawa, Orchha has a number of notable places of Tourist interest, some of these are, Jehangir Mahal, Raj Mahal, Rai Praveen Mahal, Ram Raja Temple, Chaturbhuj Temple, Laxminarayan temple, Phool Bagh, Chhatries and Shahid Smarak. Founded in 1501, Orchha boasts magnificent temple and fortress ruins, in its bustling downtown and along the Betwa River. Here, Rama, the Hindu lord of virtue, is revered as a god and a king, due to a strange series of events in which a palace was "transformed" into a temple. A nightly sound-and-light show inside these fortress walls helps illuminate the tale and the city's rise to glory.

Friends of Orchha – Homestays

Friends of Orchha is a registered non-profit organisation working in Madhya Pradesh, India on creating livelihoods linked to tourism, preserving the environment of heritage sites like Orchha and promoting cultural exchange between visitors and locals.

Interaction with a group of women from a poor neighbourhood of Orchha was the spark that led to the creation of Orchha Home-stay, a social enterprise that creates incomes and assets for families below poverty line while providing a rich cultural experience for both visitors and hosts.

The activities of the organisation are financed by the members of its international branch and by a few other development aid agencies. Friends of Orchha, India is guided by a Managing Committee of seven persons while the international section has four volunteers based in Geneva at its helm.

The organisation was founded in 2006 by Indian-born sociologist Asha D'Souza and her Dutch husband, anthropologist and documentary film-maker Louk Vreeswijk, just as Orchha was emerging from a terrible drought. Those fortunate enough to be living in the heart of town could benefit from the growing tourist economy, but too many in poor neighborhoods on the periphery struggled below the poverty line, with very few options available. This social enterprise creates incomes and assets for families below poverty line while providing a rich cultural experience for both visitors and hosts.

D'Souza and Vreeswijk gathered together a core group of poverty-plagued women. After numerous meetings they agreed to create a new home-stay program, which would not only offer income for participating families, but would also provide a rich opportunity for cultural exchange for both villagers and their guests.

The activities of the NGO are funded through individual contributions of the members of Friends of Orchha.. The German Consulate in Mumbai also gave a small grant in 2007 for improving water supply and sanitation, also the Swiss Commune of Vandoeuvres and the Josephina Stichting in the Netherlands that have helped the NGO in investing in the construction and furnishing of the home-stay. The 1% for Development Fund in Geneva supported its efforts to improve public health in the Ganj neighbourhood through the construction of toilets and bathrooms for the twenty poorest families.

In a relatively short time, Friends of Orchha has grown to six houses, with eight homestays. Using a revolving loan fund, participating families build guest houses using green building techniques that vastly reduce energy consumption. They install state-of-the-art composting toilets. These need no water source, and composted waste provides high-quality natural fertilizer, as well as bio-gas to replace wood for cooking (reducing deforestation).

The Orchha Home-stay links responsible tourism with community development. It offers not just board and lodging but an intercultural experience. What better way to discover India than to stay with an Indian family - not a privileged one, but a family of farmers, artisans and labourers who represent the majority of Indians.

The rooms are tiled ones that are well adapted to the local climate, clean and comfortable. The rooms are equipped with lights, a fan and mosquito nets and furnished with wooden beds or charpoys, natural cane chairs and a table. Each of these houses has a newly built bathroom and toilet that is shared with the family. Three houses have Indian-style, composting toilets and two have a Western toilet. As water is scarce in the region, it has been chosen to build dry toilets that produce good compost and to filter the waste water so that it can be used for irrigation.

The host families provide tasty, hygienically prepared meals and adjust the amount of spices according to the taste of the guests. Guests always enjoy sharing a meal with them and find it a heart-warming experience.

The loan repayment process is designed to succeed. For each night a guest stays, the home-stay family earns 20% of the room rate directly. Another 20% pays for housekeeping, booking and management. The remaining 60% automatically pays off the zero-interest construction loan. If the rooms are unoccupied, loan payments simply stop until more guests show up. Besides, the family gets the whole amount charged for meals. The economic benefits of the home-stay enterprise have been spectacular, all the host families have more than doubled their incomes. The extra cash has served to repair leaking roofs, keep their kids in school & set up other small businesses. During the tourist season, which lasts from October to March, families often earn Rs. 25,000-30,000 per month.

Friends of Orchha supports a number of other community services, too: a youth center which merges education, sports, theater and activities to combat caste discrimination; local entrepreneurial development (including the training of local women to make paper bags from handmade paper to replace the scourge of plastic, which currently despoils the countryside); and plans for a municipal waste facility to compost, recycle and vastly reduce solid-waste landfill.

Problems being addressed through the Homestay concept

1. Poverty and unemployment: After four years of drought (2002 – 2006) in the region, farmers and herdsmen could not eke out a living from the land. They were in search of daily wage labour to earn a livelihood. The innovation allowed them to add value to the resources they had to make a living.
2. Caste and gender discrimination: Most of the host families belong to lower castes with whom others would not share a meal. Being able to receive foreigners and Indians from big cities in their homes has boosted their self-image. Women were confined to the home without any decision-making powers. Now they have assumed an economic and social role that has improved their status in the family and community.
3. Lack of sanitation: Open defecation was the norm in this area. Most families did not have toilets and women could relieve themselves only before sunrise and after sunset, risking snake bites and even sexual harassment. Having to bathe in the open with their clothes on, skin infections and boils were frequent. Availing of a toilet and bathroom has had a positive impact on their health and personal hygiene.
4. Almost no general knowledge: Illiteracy is high particularly among the women. Even those who have been to school have little knowledge of geography or current events. Living with people from other cultures and finding out about life elsewhere has been a 'window on the world' for people who have so far lived in closed societies.

Uniqueness of the Homestays

The homestays have had quite a few guests who intended to stay just a few days and have ended up staying for weeks with one of the host families. They were able to discover India from within, to experience the life of a family of small farmers, herdsmen or artisans in this picturesque town of Orchha. It's been a discovery for the host families too – they had never had a chance to get to know foreigners and are full of questions about what life is like in those faraway places that they've just learned to locate on a map. By providing accommodation and meals for about 15 days a month, eight months per year, the families have been able to double their incomes. The extra money has been used to repair a leaking roof or get a proper electricity connection. Besides, they now have an additional room in their houses and a nice, tiled toilet and bathroom that the family shares with their guests. Other families of this poor, low-caste neighbourhood also earn through providing services such as laundry, transport or selling their handicrafts to the guests. Ecological techniques have been used for building that make the community conscious of the need to recycle waste and save water.

The Homestays have allowed a section of the population that was excluded from the economic and cultural opportunities that tourism engenders to access them. They now have food security even when they don't find work, can pay for their children's education, meet their medical expenses, undertake much needed home improvements The women in particular needed to be able to contribute to family income without going out to work. Their spontaneous hospitality have charmed the guests many of whom have spread the word to other tourists they meet. The cultural impact of the Orchha home-stay on the local community has been tremendous. People no longer regard foreigners as persons to extract money from by any means. They have grown to appreciate them as friends and have learned about their countries, cultures and values. This includes seeing that women can be independent, can choose their own life partners, etc. While opening their minds to other cultures, this interaction convinces local people of the value of their traditions in housing, food and handicrafts, traditions that are adapted to the climate and now even have market value.

Environmental consciousness has grown too. The importance of cleanliness for guests has got host families to adopt more hygienic practices in their homes with regard to cooking, cleaning and dealing with waste. The need for water conservation and waste recycling is demonstrated through the new toilets and bathrooms that recycle water for irrigation and produce compost and biogas. Visitors have realised that they can choose forms of tourism that help alleviate poverty and protect the environment. At the same time, they have discovered how the majority of Indians live and gone away with a much more positive impression of India than commercial tourism gives.

Volunteers

The organisation works with the help of volunteers. In 2009, Marine Gueltas and Ludivine Mouton who had specialised in Eco-tourism from the Business school in Rennes spent five months in Orchha helping it to market the home-stay accommodation. Delphine Douçot, a young Swiss engineer offered her services in mapping solid waste generation in Orchha. She developed a plan for ecological waste management that has been submitted to the municipality. Marisa Perrier, otherwise known as the 'lady in red', came over for a month from Australia in January 2010 to teach English to young people at the Youth Centre and to the home-stay families. Virginie Lemasson arrived in Orchha on her bicycle intending to stay a couple of weeks but ended up staying a couple of months with one of the home-stay families. She helped a great deal in preparing the documents for the Home-stay and she was the star of the Women's Day celebration in Ganj. Simon and Enzo helped the organisation in managing the reservations on line with a Google calendar. They were followed by two young Finnish girls, Aniina and Satu, engaged in Development studies in Helsinki. They worked on the database that helped the organisation keep track of occupancy rates and the earning of the host families. Emmanuel, continued this work. Céline spent a month with the homestay and made computer wizards of several children in Orchha.

The Main Barriers

According to Mrs Asha D'Souza, there have been two big challenges:

First, they work with the poor, or rather the economically poor because they are culturally rich. They cannot afford to take the risks that business demands. And that's what distinguishes their social enterprise from others - one has to take the burden of risk off their shoulders during the first few years.

Second, is finding the human resources who would be willing to work in this very small town. One has to identify motivated persons and then train them. As they lack experience, constant guidance is necessary.

The Final Word

The effects of homestays are very evient on the family, one tends to see happier and more welcoming faces. The houses are cleaner and more hygienically kept. Some homestays even provide bicycles for the guests to roam around Orchha during their visit. More families are interested in joining the homestays, but as of now the Friends of Orchha are unable to take them in due to the investment needed, they need more volunteers and financial contributions to make homestays viable in more homes in Orchha. Guests get first hand experience of Indian weddings, Indian festivals and Indian Food while on their stay at the homestay. Some guests have recommended that it would be nice if a trained guide would also be available in the homestay. Homestays are here to stay it seems in Orchha, people of Orchha have welcomed this new and innovative practice and with the guidance and help provided to them they can proceed further in this direction.

References

Augustyn, M. (1998). National strategies for rural tourism development and sustainability: The Polish experience. Journal of Sustainable Tourism, 6(3), 191-209.

Cole, S. (2007). Beyond authenticity and co modification. Annals of Tourism Research, 34(4), 943-960.

Frederick, C.M. (2003), Merriam-Webster's collegiate dictionary. Merriam-Webster. 595.

Howell, R. A., P.J. Moreo, & F.J. De Micco. (1993). A Qualitative Analysis of Hotel Services Desired by Female Business Travelers. Journal of Travel and Tourism Marketing, 1(4), 115-132.

http://greentravelerguides.com/orchha-green-home-stays-hotels/

http://www.changemakers.com/socialbusiness/entries/orchha-home-stay-linking-tourism-and-development

Lashley, C. & Morrison, A. (2000). In Search of Hospitality: Theoretical Perspectives and Debates, Oxford: Butterworth-Heinemann.

Li Liu (2006), Quality of Life as a Social Representation in China: A Qualitative Study, Social Indicators Research, 75(2), pp 217-240.

Liu, A. (2006). Tourism in rural areas: Kedah, Malaysia. Tourism Management, 27(5), 878-889.

Lynch, P. (2003). Homestay Accommodation Sector. LTSN Hospitality, Leisure, Sport & Tourism, 1-6.

Lynch, P.A. & MacWhannell, D. (2000). Home and Commercialised Hospitality. In Search of Hospitality: Theoretical Perspectives and Debates, Oxford: Butterworth_Heinemann, 100-117.

Lynch, P.A. (2000a). Networking in the Homestay Sector. The service Industries Journal, 20(3), 95-115.

Lynch, P.A. (2000b). Setting and its Significance in the Homestay Sector: Explorations. Proceedings of CHME 9th Annual Hospitality Research Conference, Huddersfield, 319-333.

Morrison, A.M., Pearce, P.L., Moscardo, G. Nadkarni, N. & O'Leary, J.T. (1996). Specialist Accommodation: Definition, Markets Served, and Roles in Tourism Development. Journal of Travel Research, 35(1), 18-26.

Rhodri, T. (2004). Small firms in tourism: international perspectives. Boston: Elsevier.

Rivers, W. P. (1998). Is Being There Enough? The Effects of Homestay Placement on Language Gain During Study Abroad. Foreign Language Annals, 31(4), 492-500.

Swarbrooke J and Horner S (2007) Consumer Behaviour in Tourism. Oxford: Butterworth-Heinemann

Wang, Y. (2007). Customized authenticity begins at home. Annals of Tourism Research, 34(3), 789-804.

Wang, Y. (2007). Customized authenticity begins at home. Annals of Tourism Research, 34(3), 789-804. www.orchha.org

ECONOMICS OF TOURISM: AN EMPIRICAL STUDY OF "ANDRO-SANTHEI-PARK", IMPHAL THROUGH LEIBENSTEINE'S CRITICAL MINIMUM EFFORT THEORY

Binota Meinam
Associate Professor, Imphal College, Imphal, Manipur
meinambinota@gmail.com
Chithung Mary Thomas
Assistant Professor, D.M. College of Commerce, Imphal, Manipur
chithungmary@yahoo.com
Naorem Sunita Devi
Project Fellow, Tribal Research Institute (TRI), Imphal, Manipur
sunitanaorem@gmail.com

INTRODUCTION:

Tourism as a Growth Agent of Community Development

Tourism plays a significant role in economic development of a community and state. Community based tourism has brought several socio-economic & ecological changes in the region. Andro Santhei Park has offered better life to the Andro community through various ways out. This community based effort has benefitted to local community to earn income by providing / preserving scenic beauty, ethnic cuisine & beverage, historical heritage site, cultural values of ethnic community on commercial basis and selling of local products (particularly, local beverage, meal & pottery products). Not only having economic benefit it also increases cultural harmony with different ethnic groups and it increases the national integration. Community Based Tourism (CBT) is an approach of shared leadership, emphasizing community well being over individual profit, balances of power within communities and fosters traditional values & culture, conservation of natural resources and responsible stewardship of land (Naycander, E., 2010). Fostering community enterprises is the most effective means of achieving true participation & active involvement of communities.

Here, an attempt is therefore made to examine the theory of Critical Minimum Effort (CME) propounded by Harvey Leibenstein (Leibenstein, H. 1957) in the progress of community growth of the Andro (Ckakpa) Community in the behest of Santhei-Park (Eco-Park) development since 2000. The present research study keeps the following hypotheses that:

1. Tourism development can give more income to the community.
2. Community themselves create income increasing forces.
3. It made decreasing income depressing forces.
4. Tourism development gives new horizon to community to develop their own socio-economic infrastructures in the area with/without support of government.
5. Entrepreneurial skills are developed.
6. The community expands their outlook into global level.

Methodology:

Target Population: The whole enterprising units of pottery (i.e. 14 units) and 6% of the total brewing industries of Andro Households (i.e. 105 brewing units).

Data Source: Both primary and secondary data have been used for the present analysis. For primary data source a semi-structured written questionnaire is used to elicit the primary data.

Analysis:

At the given backdrop, it is worth mentioning that the backward communities (SC/ST/OBC/Minorities) are characterized by the vicious circle of poverty that keeps them around a low per capita income equilibrium state. In order to achieve the transition from the level of backwardness to the more developed state we need to have a certain "Critical Minimum Efforts" which would raise the per capita income to a level at which sustainable development could be maintained. The rational of the Critical Minimum Effort theory rests on the existence of certain favourable economic conditions so that both the income increasing forces and the income-depressing forces expand. In the development process such conditions are created by the expansion of the 'growth agents'. They are the quantum of capacities residing in the members of community (within) to carry out growth contributing activities. The given contributing factors have been seen in the Andro Eco-Park. It can be examined with the help of following Chart 1. The growth agents are small entrepreneurs, the investors, the savers, the innovators. It results in the creation of entrepreneurship, the increase in the s tock of knowledge, the expansion of productive skills of the community population and increase the rate of saving and investment.

Proposed Model:

Chart-1

Destination Attraction Factor of Andro-Eco-Park

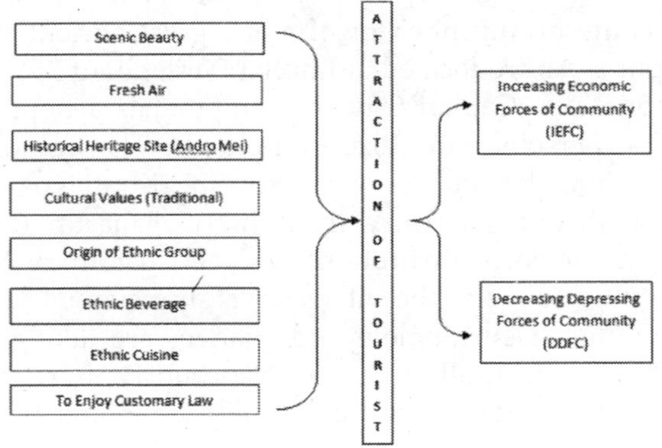

Chart – 2

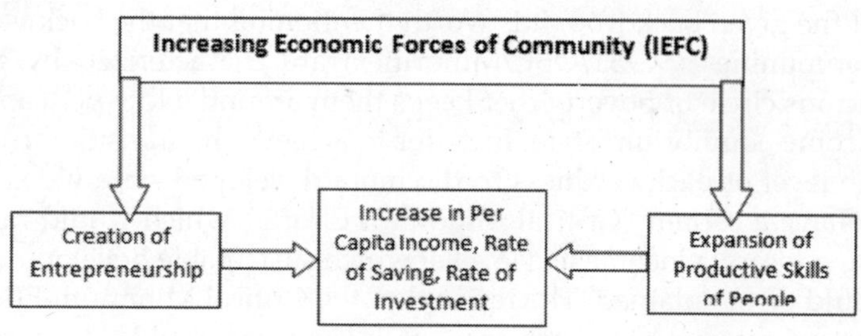

Chart – 3

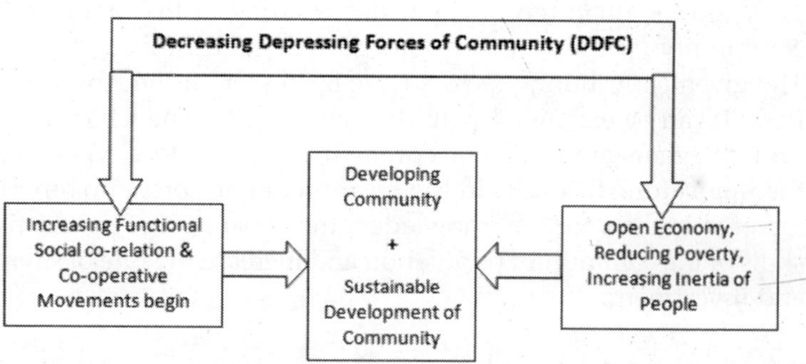

Sustainable Development of the Andro-Park Community Based Tourism through CME Theory:

Andro Ethnic Community (Chakpa), one of the major original villages is the proud inheritor of many great ancient traditions of Manipuris. Andro located at Imphal West, about 25 kms away from Imphal, the Capital City of Manipur has a population of about 9758 persons with 1626 households. The age old social institutions of the village chieftainship, Khullakpa Ahallup Pana Sang (Senior Advisory Institution), Naharup Pana sang (Young Labour Force Institution), Village Customary Laws are still very much alive at the village level. Indigenous Religion is still continuing. Development and changes are taking place in co-operation with Ahallup Pana & Naharup Pana, with ancient traditions and customs are preserved & promoted in order to protect social identity.

Andro-Santhei-Park is the true existence of their co-operative movement. Their customary laws & traditional cuisine are the major attraction of domestic & foreign tourist. Andro (and other Chakpa inhabited areas) is the only one place where tourist can enjoy 'Waiyu' (local wine) beyond the dry state laws. 'Waiyu', 'Kalei', 'Atingba' (Pukyu) are the famous local beverage (made from Rice). Every household of Andro are mandatory to brew wine. It is included in their staple food which is restricted in other major parts of the State population. Further, the community is reputed for their pottery skill too. Many of the pottery artisans are found dedicated to promote their traditional skill of pottery in addition to the economic achievement.

Table – 1

Ethnic Beverage Sale Progress in the last three years (2011-2013)*

Year	Sale Progress per day (in Litre)	Cost of Materials per Litre (in Rs.)	Total cost per Litre (in Rs.)	Surplus Income per day	Surplus Income in a Month
2010-11	20-30	20	40	500	15,000
2011-12	30-40 (28.6)	30	60	1050	31,500
2012-13	40-50 (44.4)	40	70	1350	40,000

Note: Figures in the parentheses indicate the rate of increase.

*SI = (TC – CM) X AS

Where, SI = Surplus Income per day,

TC = Total Cost per litre,

CM = Cost of Material per litre, and

AS = Average No. of litres sold per day.

Table – 2

Cost-benefit Analysis of Ethnic Pottery by Women Entrepreneurs of the Andro Community

Year	No. of Entre-pre-neurs	No. of Gener-ated Em-ploy-ment	In-come of the Entre-pre-neur (in Rs.)	Cost of Mate-rials per month (in Rs.)	Eco-nomic Ben-efit per month (in Rs.)	Socio-Cul-tural Benefit
2000-05	7	35	1800	300	1500	100%*
2005-10	12 (41.7)	120	2400	400	2000	100%*
2010-14	14 (50.0)	305	3000	500	2500	100%*

Note: Figures in the parentheses indicate the rate of increase.

*100% = Fully satisfied and wants to preserve the cultural heritage of Pottery.

The rationale behind the primary data which has been collected for the present research work is of these small enterprises that has functional relationship between beverage brewing & pottery. For brewing 'Waiyu' they need to have these 'Kharungs' (big pots-capacity 7 kg. of rice). Without these pots the brewing sector cannot produce quality final products. In the process of brewing good quality 'Waiyu' they have to use this particular kharung. (Few entrepreneurs use metal pots but maximum of the entrepreneurs don't prefer metallic pots). They believed that if they don't use the traditional kharung they won't harvest the good quality beverage. Therefore, the people of Andro still keep their traditional values alive even though there are many alternatives. However, in this area of quality products further research is suggested. Further, researchers need to identify the grey areas of this factor analysis by using scientific methods.

From the above table 2 it is clearly observed that after the creation of tourist destination of Andro-Eco-Park, the number of employment has been increased (from 35 in 2011 to 308 in 2013).

Most of the pottery works are done only by women folks. It is because of the fact that the maximum numbers of pottery artisans are illiterate, very few of them have educational level below matriculation (77 out of 105, table 3).

Table - 3

Type of Entre-preneur	Total No. of Entre-preneur	Level of Education			
		Below Matricu-lation	**10 + 2**	**Gradu-ate**	**Illiterate**
Bever-age	105	26	2	0	77
Pottery	14	3	0	0	11

Traditionally, in Andro maximum brewing and pottery has been done by the women folks. Very few men folks are involved in brewing & pottery. Most of the menfolks are involved in Agricultural sectors. From the above table 3 it is observed that maximum number of pottery artisans and traditional brewers are illiterate. Very few of them have read & write knowledge only.

Table - 4

Consumer Profile of the Andro-Eco-Park

Age Group (in Years)	No. of Domestic Tourist (per day)	Tourist Items Consumed Most	Picnic Spot (per day)	Relaxation (in person)	Study Tour (per bus)
20-30	400	Scenic beauty & beverage	10-20 groups	0	2-3
30-40	200	Scenic beauty, beverage & traditional culture	5-10 groups	0	0
40-50	100	Scenic beauty & traditional culture	1-2 groups	5-10	0

Age Group (in Years)	No. of Domestic Tourist (per day)	Tourist Items Consumed Most	Picnic Spot (per day)	Relaxation (in person)	Study Tour (per bus)
Above 50	10-20	Scenic beauty & traditional culture	0	5-10	0

Photo 1: A view of Andro-Santhei-Park

Photo 3: Andro Kharung and different pottery items.

Photo 3: A Carved Pillar at Museum, Andro.

Photo 4: Brewing of Waiyu.

Photo 5: Hamei used for brewing.

Photo 6: Entrepreneur Sharubam Thermomala Devi with Research Team.

Findings of The Research Study:

As a result of the increasing economic forces of the community the sale progress of the ethnic brewing industry has increased from 28.6 percent in 2012 to 44.4 percent in 2013. Similarly, due to the decreasing depressing forces of community the entrepreneurial units in the community has expanded at a rate of 41.7 percent in the year 2012 to 50.0 percent in 2013. That is, the number of pottery unit has increased from 7 to 14 during the year 2011-2013. This shows the increasing functional relationship between the brewing and pottery industries in the community due to the development of the Andro-Eco-Park since 2000. Thus, the major findings of the present research study can be summarized as:

- Expansion of Andro-Eco-Park is the result of critical minimum efforts of the Andro Community.
- It is totally private community based tourism destination development scheme under the supervision of social institutions (i.e. Ahallup Pana & Naharup Pana).
- It gives an eminent reputation of traditional values & cultural preservations.
- 100% beneficiaries are belonged to the community itself. The income of the community has increased (from Rs. 15,000 pm (in 2011) to Rs. 40,500 pm (in 2013).
- The number of employment has increased. (i.e. From 35 to 308 employment during last three years, 2011-2013)
- The community itself creates various income creating economic forces. (i.e. Parking fees, toilet fees, nontraditional artisans, food cuisine, etc.).
- The development of CBT in the Andro area made to reduce the income depressing forces (i.e. increasing inertia of the people, increasing functional co-relationship, less idle hour, co-operative movements begin).
- It gives new hopes and new knowledge of work culture by facing new demands of tourists' necessities.
- It breaks the inertia of idle and ignorance mind of the community.
- It contributes the social benefits to others.
- It promotes the traditional & cultural values of the community.

Conclusion:

Tourism, as a multi-facet sector industry has multiple benefit to the consumers, service providers and state. Success of any tourism scheme (whether public or private ownership) concerning expansion and preservation of modern values and traditional values needs people's participation. However, in case of Andro-Santhei-Park, the maximum number of entrepreneurs are Illiterate or below matriculation level. Therefore, it seems to have slow progress in the tourism development. There is lack of professional touch to various tourism related activities. There is lack of professional manpower and marketing strategist in the area. Poor maintenance is big issue in most of the tourist destination in the state. The rich culture and unique tourism products excels the tourism potential of the state. So, for a comprehensive expansion of tourism sector in the state, the knowledge of VICE (Visitors, Industry, Communities, and Environment) Model is necessary. To go through the Model we need to have an Academic Institution of Tourism of Excel in the state as a mandatory device.

References:

Ellis, Sotear (2012) "Community Tourism in Cambodia" Doctoral Thesis, Edith Cowan University, Combodia.

Kohli, Indrajit, Nirvikar (1989) Exports and Growth: Critical Minimum effort and diminishing returns. Journal of Development Economics, Volume 30, Issue 2, April 1989, Pp. 391-400, www. Sciencedirect.com/science/article/pii/030438788900114 Retrieved May 23, 2014.

Kulshreshtha, Ruchika et al (2014) Impact of Festival Tourism in Promoting Destination Image: A Case Study with Special Reference to Mathura region. In Binota, Meinam et al (2014) Strategic Interventions in Tourism Development: Regional Perspective, New delhi,: Bharti Publications, Pp. 69-76.

Leibenstein, Harvey (1957) Economic Backwardness and Economic Growth – Studies in the theory of Economic Development.

Naycander, E. (2010) 'CBT development in Rupununi – A Bluprint". Conservation International Foundation, Guyana Inc.

BED AND BREAKFAST ACCOMMODATION IN DELHI REGION - A STEP TOWARDS CONSERVING NATURAL RESOURCES

G.G. Saxena
Executive Director, ICPB and
Former MD & CEO,
Delhi Tourism and Transportation Development Corporation (DTTDC)
ggsaxena@gmail.com
Lalit K. Panwar,
Secretary, Ministry of Minority, Govt. of India
Manjula Chaudhary
Department of Tourism and Hotel Management, Kurukshetra Univesity, Kurukshetra,
manjulachaudhary@gmail.com
Sandeep Kulshreshtha
Director I/C, Indian Institute of Tourism and Travel Management,
sankul7@rediffmail.com

Abstract

Running any industry causes depletion of natural resources. It is estimated that consumption of natural resources has become five times more than what it was 50 years ago. As compared to other sectors like manufacturing, oil-excavation, coal and mining etc., tourism and hospitality sector is relatively more cleaner and environment friendly due to Eco-tourism, green tourism etc. Accommodation part of hospitality sector is responsible for consuming huge electricity, water & other natural resources. However only about 18 % and 23 % of total expenditure is incurred by domestic and foreign tourist respectively towards accommodation out of total money spent on travel, transport, food, shopping, recreation and leisure, accommodation etc. Commercial hotels which solely fall in the construction sector are main source of accommodation and therefore could be partly blamed for depleting of natural resources. This paper discusses the need of bed and breakfast units for creation of additional tourism infrastructure , coping the shortage of requisite hotel rooms, opportunity to the tourists to experience family warmth, feel of Indian customs and traditions , authentic home cooked food, cheaper accommodation as well as ultimately contributing for conservation of natural resources.

Keywords: Bed & Breakfast, Hotels, Accommodation, Tourism

Hospitality sector in India

Hospitality is an ancient tradition of India. Innovations in Indian hospitality reveal that options of accommodation are very diverse, ranging from cosy homestays and tribal huts to stunning heritage mansions and royal palaces of erstwhile Royalty/ maharajas. The Bed & Breakfast accommodation is one such innovative homestay option of Indian hospitality. The B&B accommodation is a blend of a luxury hotel and a private home, embodying the best of both worlds. The owners live on site and interact with travellers as if they were invited guests rather than anonymous occupants of a certain room number. Of course, there is the luxury of breakfast, a sumptuous home cooked repast, which comes with the price of the room and is served every morning in a common dining area.

The B&B accommodation or home stays are very popular amongst tourists in countries which attract a large number of visitors like USA, Germany, UK and other European & South American countries besides Australia, New Zealand, and Japan. In India it is in nascent stage inspite of its huge advantages as compared to regular hotels and motels. The B&B scheme started in India in the year 2006 under the "Incredible India" Scheme of the Ministry of Tourism, Government of India. Despite a shortage of budget accommodation in Indian cities, the scheme was not viable for the owners and failed to attract adequate number of tourists in almost all Indian cities. In Delhi also there is not significant increase in last four years(Table 1 and Graph 1) in bed and breakfast units.

Table 1: Details of Registered Bed And Breakfast Units in Delhi

Registered as on	Premises			Number of Rooms		
	GOLD	SILVER	TOTAL	GOLD	SILVER	TOTAL
1.4.2010	45	316	361	208	955	1163
1.4.2011	70	429	499	259	1357	1616
1.1.2012	62	400	462	233	1335	1568
1.1.2013	46	314	360	171	1018	1185
1.4.2013	48	282	330	178	967	1145
30.4.2013	49	277	326	188	958	1146

(**Source** DELHI TOURISM DEPTT. GOVT.OF NCT OF DELHI)

Graph 1 Bed and Breakfast Units in Delhi

The B&B Scheme in India has many advantages over regular hotels, i.e., (a) B&B Scheme presents the essence of Indian hospitality. It provides an opportunity to the traveller from outside to stay with an Indian family and experience family warmth as well as get a feel of Indian customs and traditions besides relishing authentic home cooked Indian food; (b) room tariff is cheaper by about 20% to 30% as compared to commercial hotel rooms due to applicability of levy of taxes and fees by the local Governments at lower domestic rates instead of higher commercial rates for; (c) hotel business is purely a commercial activity giving benefits to only a few owners while B&B business distributes income amongst the amateur entrepreneurs who are owners of individual homes. and therefore it focuses on social aspect in the developing country like India; (d) It helps in saving huge additional infrastructure costs towards construction of hotels, recycling of waste water, electricity generation, cutting of trees and other materials required for creating additional facilities for accommodation (e) it has better potential to attract tourists with disability or medical tourists. The rate of growth of medical tourists in Delhi is more than 25%

as observed in the research work on " Tapping Accessible and Medical Tourism by B&B Establishments in Delhi" (Bansal et. al., Saxena G.G., 2013 p.495)

Running any industry causes depletion of natural resources. Mega trend of growing industrialisation is,therefore 'over-consumption' of resources and the curse of excess which is the key trend of 'so called' development and same needs to be curtailed for the future generation and earth, the beautiful planet. Mr. Nakul Anand, President, Hotel Association of India and Executive Director, ITC Hotel while, recently delivering a key note address on general trend of depleting of natural resources 'due to over-industrialisation in developed and developing countries, as published in the article dated 26th June, 2013, Travel Trends Today, has estimated that over-consumption has become five times more than what it was 50 years ago. In the last five years, there has been an 800 percent increase in water consumption in the industrial nations where population during the period has only tripled, while humanity has used benefits of conquering the sky, moon & space, all of these have come with a price tag and that is green house emissions which are on rise since last quarter of the century. Present scenario on global warming is that there is an ecological overdraft, which takes the earth one year and four months to regenerate what is being consumed in a single year. Mr.Anand suggested that 'the way forward' is to live off the interest of our planet's resources, i.e., sunshine and biological richness rather than the capital, that is, non-renewable resource as published in Travel Trends Today T3 (June, 2013).

Accommodation Factor in Hospitality Sector

As compared to other sectors like manufacturing, oil-excavation, coal and mining etc., tourism and hospitality sector is relatively more cleaner and environment friendly. The leaders in this sector always gave weightage to utilise local resources like solar and wind energy, biological waste and other regenerating resources in the form of ecofriendly tourism and green tourism thereby utilising local resources and converting waste into utility fuel. It is, however, a fact that accommodation part of hospitality sector is responsible for consuming huge electricity, water & other natural resources. . Commercial hotels which solely fall in the construction sector, are main source of accommodation. A five star hotel in Delhi alone consumes 15 million litres of water daily and generates 10 million of litres of sewage. Nevertheless,, hospitality sector can, at the most, be attributed towards depletion of resources by only about 18 % and 23 % of total expenditure incurred by a domestic and a foreign tourist respectively towards accommodation out of total money spent on travel, transport, food, shopping, recreation and leisure, accommodation etc as mentioned in (MoT, Market Pulse Report, 2011 p.56-58,)

Exploiting tourism potential or conserve resources

The luxury industry is worth approx £ 77 billion and is now truly global. Despite this boom, the current trends of over civilisation casts a shadow on tourism industry too and there are warning signals of a coming impasse. Sometimes, questions are being raised about ethics & adverse impact of tourism on ecology & environment. Perception of success is sometimes different from actual success. Stay in Five Star hotels have become symbol of elite class. Over-consumption is becoming a mark of exhibitionism and it is being replaced from conspicuous to conscientious consumption. With the rupee rate fluctuating, tourists have begun weighing all options but even the most price sensitive travelers will continue to travel, though they may shift to short haul destinations. Commercial establishments, in general, will need to re-look at products and so will be the hotels with new service and other offerings. The ITC Group and other hotels have started making their products more eco-friendly. However, there is dilemma before stakeholders of Indian luxury industry whether to compete with global players particularly from countries contributing to high volume tourism or to focuses on conservation of resources. It is ,in fact, a difficult proposition in view of tremendous potential in augmenting inbound tourism because India will become the fourth largest passenger airline market in the world by 2016 behind only the US, China and Brazil. As per India Tourism data 2011 (MOT, Statistics, 2011 p60-63) foreign exchange earnings due to foreign tourists are 16564 million US dollars while number of days of stay of foreign tourists in India is about 22 days. Number of foreign tourists arrival in 2011 was 6.29 million so one foreign tourists brings a foreign exchange of about 120 US dollars per day and as per Planning Commission of Government of India Report , an investment of every ten lakh rupees creates maximum employment to the extent of 78 jobs in tourism sector. Therefore, growing links generate jobs and underpins economic growth in all economies but exploiting growth will require value with policies that do not stifle innovation, tax regimes that do not punish success and investment to enable infrastructure to keep up with growth (IATA, 2012)

Tourism potential in India

India has everything for inbound foreign tourists and also for domestic tourists. It has sea, sun, snow, sand, mountains, flora and fauna, rivers and monuments. It has 27 world heritage sites, 7500 km. of coastline as well as 9000 years of history, civilization and heritage. India is also recognized for her wisdom, knowledge and thought. In India, the ancient and the modern co-exist simultaneously. As regards diversity, India is the birthplace of four religions namely Hinduism, Buddhism, Jainism, and Sikhism. It has the second largest Muslim population after Indonesia. The oldest Jewish Synagogues and their communities have lived in India while Christianity has existed here for the last 2000 years. With all these unique attributes three Muslim Presidents and a female President were elected under the Indian governmental system.

Tourism sector in India has a vast potential as there are large number of places to visit with all the imaginable varieties for attracting travelers. There are 55,000 km. of lakes, streams and rivers. India is also a well known rich culinary heritage destination. It has 70 million hectares of forest, over 147 dance forms and 5000 years of experience in Ayurveda and Yoga. For inbound tourists, the variety is fascinating as 22 languages with 1542 dialects are spoken in India. There are a large number of "Tea Estates" totaling 1641 in India. Around 60% of the world's tiger population exists here. There are 60 national parks, 400 wild life sanctuaries, 476 forts and palaces and 80237 registered newspapers. There are many rare varieties that are to be found only in India. It is said that Indians and Chinese will dominate "in spending" in future and the world's two most populous nations will drive tourist numbers. They will also wield enormous clout with their money power by the year 2030 in the Asia Pacific Region. At present, India has the money power to spend 13.3 billion US dollars against China's 50.8 billion US dollars. However, this will increase to 91.2 billion US dollars against China's corresponding increase to 199 billion US dollars. Other nations like Korea, Indonesia and Japan will be far behind India and China though at this stage Japan has money power of 13.3 billion US Dollars and Korea of 20 Billion US Dollars.

Importance of B&B accommodation

Coming back to the issue at (d) above, i.e. innovating the ways to fight against depleting of natural resources, stakeholders in this luxury industry never neglect environmental issues. Even tourists intend to find alternative source of accommodation as against stand-alone infrastructure in the form of regular hotels. The concept of Bed and Breakfast (B&B) accommodation is a viable alternative to conscious consumer who appreciates the concern of depleting resources. . It is an answer to utilize existing spare accommodation in the houses reducing pressure on adding buildings in form of hotels. B&B stay option has other advantages, too, as mentioned in (a) to (e) above.

The 'B&B stay' concept helps in saving huge additional infrastructure costs towards construction of hotels, recycling of waste water, electricity generation, cutting of trees etc. and other materials required for creating additional facilities for accommodation. In a country like India, additional land for constructing more hotels is made available by shrinking of forest land, cutting of trees, generation of more electricity and water etc. In Indian cities, there is always a shortage of accommodation particularly in budget category during the period of various festivals, carnivals, conventions, functions, national and international conferences etc. These events are generally planned from September to March every year where large number of foreign and domestic tourists arrive in various cities thereby increasing the demand for more accommodation.

As per figures of foreign tourist arrival as mentioned in (MoT, Statistics at a Glance, 2012), in countries like France (8.02%), USA (6.3%), China (5.57%), Spain (5.57%), Italy (4.48%) where maximum percentage of foreign tourists arrive every year the shortage of regular commercial accommodation is met by the B&B stays prevalent in these countries but in different modes. In tourism business, requirement of accommodation is not same throughout the year as there is a heavy pressure for requirement of rooms during yearly or half yearly conferences, conventions and exhibitions in the city. The Bed and Breakfast Scheme is an excellent alternative to cope up with seasonal requirement of accommodation besides having its own regular business throughout the year.

Tourist is required to be engaged with the human touch which can contribute to the total experience of tourist. In this regard experience of tourist living with Indian families can bring him closer to Indian culture and human bondings. In many cases the foreign tourist has stayed back as they liked Indian families so much. B&B can create authentic experience for guest to understand uniqueness of Indian culture and hospitality tradition. The owners can go an extra mile to suit needs of guests both in expressed and unexpressed way and tailor their services to meet expectation of guests. The development of hospitality resources is perhaps the most important factors in tourism. The finest physical facilities will be worthless if the tourist feels unwelcome. Recent research has shown an increased demand for specialist accommodation in private homes or "hosted" accommodation, in contrast to mainstream accommodation facilities such as hotels and motels, as found in (Morrison et al., 1996 p.18); Warnick and Klar, 1991 p.17).

There is some evidence that guest' motives for staying in bed and breakfast accommodation centre on the desire to "have a relationship with local people" as written in (Johnston-Walker, 1999); (Lynch and Tucker, 2003); (Stringer, 1981).

Concept of B&B stay is equally important from the point of view of 'Impact of private accommodation on economic development of tourist destination' as mentioned in issue number (c) above. There is an interesting research paper by author Ana Portplan, on "The impact of private accommodation on Economic development of Tourist destination. The Case of Dubrovnik-Neretva County http://hrcak.srce.hr/file/12394 concludes that hotels in Republic of Croatia are mostly in foreign ownership and the income realized in this form is mostly withdrawn from Croatia. Therefore, the importance of private accommodation like B&B is even bigger. The consumption by guest in B&B stay is mostly on indigenous products and therefore helps in increase of purchasing power of resident population. Though, this analogy is only partially applicable in India, there is no doubt that the B&B scheme helps in avoiding additional burden of creation of infrastructure and distribution of income amongst individual owners of the property.

It is evident from above that the concept of B&B scheme is developed on the basis of generation of income for distribution amongst masses rather than income going into a few hands. The scheme works on the doctrine of personal relationship and care. It may work towards social development also. Human relationship is a binding force for human society. The whole world is now converging as "Vasudev Kutumbakam" or a global family. So this is a new horizon which is being developed through B&B scheme. At micro-level of economics, the wealth created through B&B business is distributed in a homogenous manner in the society. One cannot become rich by earning through B&B income while commercial hotels are mainly run on "profit earning" concept. In other words, concept of B&B scheme is a step towards community income and a sign of democratic process as on the other hand commercial hotels concept is like the "capitalism" process. Promotion of B&B concept can prove to be a more acceptable social norm. In the Bed & Breakfast system, on the other hand income is distributed amongst the larger strata of society. Such additional income to a family is more useful for maintaining the standard of living for host and also used for expenditures like higher education for children, etc

Limitations of B&B Scheme in India

But all positive points in favour B&B concept, particularly in India, do not make the concept readily acceptable to inbound tourists. A research was conducted on this topic in Delhi recently; This research was based on field survey of 48 B&B owners conducted by Delhi Tourism and Transportation Development Corporation (DTTDC) during January 2012 and June 2012 (DTTDC file survey, 2013). As per findings of the research work, "average income of Rs 23150/- per month was computed by a Delhi B&B unit as against possible potential of earning Rs 77085 per month by such B&B units. So, there is a huge gap in actual vis-à-vis maximum possible income". These findings were published in paper entitled "Economics of Bed and Breakfast scheme of Delhi" (Saxena G.G., 2013 p.157). Now, the question arises whether incoming tourists prefer B&B stay over the conventional accommodation available in regular hotels? A survey was conducted between june to December 2012 by DTTDC on this aspect too. Response from 210 foreign & domestic tourists was received & analysis was done by the authors in the research paper "Tourists and B&B scheme of Delhi" accepted by Indian Journal of International Tourism and Hospitality Research (Saxena G.G., 2013). Important findings were that 27% of surveyed tourists were not satisfied with service offered at the place of stay in Delhi but none of 13 tourists staying in B&B units felt agrieved on any issue related to stay. As many as 23% tourists desired friendly welcome & homely care."

Survey also revealed that, on an average, the tourists coming to Delhi prefer to spend upto Rs 4045/- per night for an average stay of 3 to 4 days and they expect good services with "a home away from home" feeling, personal caring, emotional atmosphere, delicious home cooked food including taste of local culture and traditions. All these desirable elements will certainly be available in a B&B accommodation. An added advantage of B&B stay, nevertheless, is that tourists get similar facilities as are available in regular hotels in tariff range which is approximately 25% to 30% cheaper because there is exemption from levy of Luxury tax and applicability of commercial rates on electricity & water bills in B&B accommodation. It is noticeable that there are very high rates of luxury tax and service tax to the extent of 25% applicable on tariff of rooms in metropolitan city hotels. The surveyed tourists who were ready to spend on an average ◎4045/- per night will be required to pay on an average ◎2742/- per night only in a B&B unit with similar facilities which are available in such a regular hotel. During such survey from tourists, it was revealed that most of the tourists staying in regular hotels particularly all 16 foreign tourist staying in paharganj hotels, had no knowledge about locations or other details of B&B units in Delhi. Therefore, all these tourists expect on-line reservation and payment system to be available in B&B units. If all such issues are addressed by B&B owners and the State Government, the B&B units will become a viable alternative for large group of tourists who are in search of enjoying home stays in tourist places. in view to exploit the potential and avail the benefits of B&B system, Ministry of Tourism Government of India and the State Governments are expected to proide extra incentive for promotion and marketing of the B&B scheme asthe problem of shortage of budget accommodation could be solved without any further acquisition of land and development of infrastructure and draining out non-renewable resources of energy, thereby earning "carbon credit" by India.

References

Bansal, S.P., Kulshreshtha, S, Gautam, P. "Tourism Towards New Horizons – Status, Issues & Perspectives", 2013 Tapping Accessible & Medical Tourism by B&B Establishments in Delhi, (Saxena.G.G, Chapter- 44), Kanishka Publishers, Distributors , New Delhi, p.495-5

DTTDC File No. DTTDC/B&B/32/2012-13/Survey of B&B owners and tourists conducted (2013)

Dubrovnik-Neretva County, Coatia, viewed 12 November 2013 http://hrcak.srce.hr/file/12394

IATA Press release no 50, Date 6th December, 2012

http://www.iata.org/pressroom/pr/pages/2012-12-06-01.aspx

Johnston-Walker, R. (1999). "The Accommodation Motivations and Ac-commodation Usage Patterns of International Independent Pleasure Travellers."Pacific Tourism Review, 3: p.143-50

Lynch, P. A., and H. Tucker (2003). "Quality Homes, Quality People: The Challenge of Quality Grading and Assurance in Small Accommodation Enterprises." In Small Firms in Tourism: International Perspectives, edited by R. Thomas. Oxford: Pergamon

Morrison, A. M., P. L. Pearce, G. Moscardo, N. Nadkarni, and J. T. O'Leary (1996). "Specialist Accommodation: Definition, Markets Served, and Roles in Tourism Development."Journal of Travel Research, 35 (1): p.18-26.

Ministry of Tourism, Govt. of India, "Tourism survey in the State of Delhi" Chapter 9.9 Table 42 – Market Pulse (2011) p.56-58 http://tourism.gov.in/writereaddata/CMSPagePicture/file/marketresearch/New/Delhi.pdf

Ministry of Tourism, Government of India, India Tourism Statistics 2011, Chapter 2,

Inbound Tourism- Foreign Tourist Arrivals in India, p.60-63, viewed 12 November 2013 http://tourism.gov.in/writereaddata/CMSPagePicture/file/Primary%20Content/MR/pub-OR-statistics/2011statisticsenglish.pdf

Ministry of Tourism, Government of India, India Tourism Statistics at Glance 2011, 1-4 viewed 12 November 2013

http://tourism.gov.in/writereaddata/CMSPagePicture/file/marketresearch/

INDIATOURISMSTATICS%28ENGLISH%29.pdf

Saxena GG, "Economics of Bed and Breakfast Scheme in Delhi", South Asia Journal of Tourism & Hospitality, July, 2013 p.157.

Saxena, G.G., "Tourists and B&B scheme of Delhi" Indian Journal of International Tourism & Hospitality Research, August 2013 issue Kurukshetra University (Accepted Paper) p.157

Stringer, P. (1981). "Hosts and Guests: The Bed and Breakfast Phenome-non."Annals of Tourism Research, 8 (3): 357-76.

Shayan Mallick (26th June, 2013)_"Overconsumption of Resources Discussed as Hai E-Conclave - Nakul Anand, Travel Trends Today

http://www.traveltrendstoday.in/news/2013/06/26/overconsumption-of-resources-discussed-at-hai-e-conclave

Warnick, R. B., and L. R. Klar (1991). "The Bed and Breakfast and Small Inn Industry of the Commonwealth of Massachusetts: An Exploratory Survey."Journal of Travel Research, 29 (Winter): p.17-25.

EXPLORING CHANDIGARH AS TOURIST DESTINATION: AN ANALYTICAL STUDY

Lipika K.Guliani

Assistant Professor, Panjab University, Chandigarh and Doctoral Candidate, PTU, Jalandhar lipika_b@yahoo.com

Abstract

Tourism has been one of the world's fastest growing industries, and there are large societies entirely dependent upon the visitor for their provisions. India's rich history and its cultural and geographical diversity make its international tourism appeal large and diverse. It presents heritage and cultural tourism along with medical, business, educational and sports tourism. Chandigarh is one of the famous and favorite destination among the tourists. The paper tries to look into the statistical records of tourists arrived in Chandigarh during the last few years and their view with respect to Chandigarh as tourist destination. This study aims to assess the determining factors that influence tourists' satisfaction and to estimate the tourist satisfaction index in Chandigarh, important tourism destination in India. To meet the objectives of this study, a set of questionnaire was used as an instrument to collect the primary data from tourists who visit Chandigarh. There were 100 questionnaire consists of 7 categories and 21 items pertaining services provided in Chandigarh and tourist's impression about Chandigarh as a tourism destination. The 8 categories are 1) Transportation Services 2) Accommodation Services 3) Food and Beverage Service 4) Emporiums/shopping arcades 5) Travel Agents 6) Safety and security 7)Destination attractiveness. Information on specific and general satisfaction levels with regard to each item and socio-demographic profiles of tourists were also collected. Data was analysed using the Statistical Package for Social Sciences (SPSS).

Keywords:-Tourists, tourists destination, satisfaction

Introduction

Tourism has a direct impact on the national revenue for all touristic countries, it creates work opportunities, industries, and several investments to serve and raise nations performance and cultures, also distributes their history, civilization, and traditions. As per the UNWTO World Tourism Barometer, December 2013, India's rank in the World Tourism Receipts during 2012 was 16th and rank in international tourist arrivals was 41. The rank of India was 7th among Asia and the Pacific Region in terms of tourism receipts during 2012.

Tourists' evaluation of destination attributes and their satisfaction levels have received considerable academic interest with much emphasis on image assessments prior to visitation, during visitation and/or post trip evaluations. The present paper is going to investigate all the three aspects by taking Chandigarh as tourist destination. Chandigarh is one of the major tourism destinations in Punjab, which is known for its amazing colonial buildings, manicured gardens, parks, serene lakes, lively markets and vibrant culture. Chandigarh is the best-planned city in India, with architecture which is world-renowned, and a quality of life, which is unparalleled.

This paper intends to explore the various dimensions of 'Chandigarh' from the tourists point of view and rank it as holiday destination. The basic factors that the tourist destinations must provide includes the accessibility for the mass market, various visitor attractions, ample shopping facilities, information services regarding tourism and most importantly affordable and luxurious accommodation and catering facilitates. All these factors were analyzed throughout the paper with the help of survey in relation with the tourist choice in chandigarh. A qualitative and quantitative approach is used to analyse the data. The target population for this study was adults and all types of tourists who come to Chandigarh for the purpose of leisure, medical, business and recreational etc. The tourist population is 100 in this research study. The purpose of this paper is to assess the factors that influence tourist satisfaction and to measure the satisfaction index with regard to Chandigarh.

Literature Review

The UNWTO (2002) defines a local tourism destination as "a physical space that includes tourism products such as support services and attractions and tourism resource .However, the influence of destination image on evaluative factors such as service quality, trip quality, perceived value and future behavioural intentions has only recently galvanised some scholarly attention. Specifically, the effect of image on future behaviour has been described as an area of neglect in destination image theory (Chen and Tsai 2007; Taxi and Gartner 2007). Existingstudies (Bigne et al. 2001; Petrick 2004; Chen and Tsai 2007; Chi and Qu 2008) confirm that a positive relationship exists between destination image, satisfaction and future behaviour. However, these findings need to be extended to different destination settings to broaden the understanding of these relationships and their impact on customer loyalty (Lee et al. 2005). Nonetheless, it seems that favourable perceptions of destination attributes have a positive influence on tourist satisfaction, which in turn has a positive impact on future behaviour, while other variables such as service quality and perceived value tend to have a moderating effect. Understanding the performance of a destination and satisfaction levels are of paramount importance given that they influence destination competitiveness and visitor loyalty. Conventional marketing wisdom suggests that customer loyalty, as an indicator of customer retention, has a direct link with a company's profitability. In tourism research, loyalty has been measured using two main indicators: willingness to recommend or word-of-mouth, and likelihood of return (Bigne et al. 2001; Chen and Gursoy 2001; Baloglu et al.2003; Petrick 2004). It is likely that satisfied visitors will come back and will tell others about their favourable or unfavourable experiences (Kozak 2001). In fact, customer loyalty is regarded as a better predictor of actual behaviour than customer satisfaction and many existing customer loyalty indices are behaviour based (Chi and Qu 2008).Also, there are limited studies devoted to how certain perception of an image attribute is more or less significant than other attributes (Boo and Busser2005), and their relative impact On constructs such as satisfaction, intention to revisit and likelihood to recommend (Kozak 2001,2003). Researching whether specific cognitive or affective images have relatively more or less influence on future behavioural intentions can have a number of implications. First, it can reveal additional strengths and weaknesses of destinations by assessing their individual performance levels and the feedback received from their customers (Kozak 2001). Second, it can better equipped tourism managers to alter their product/service offerings and their marketing efforts to maximize the use of limited resources (Petrick 2004).

Customer satisfaction is defined as a "psychological concept that involves the feeling of well-being and pleasure that results from obtaining what one hopes for and expects from an appealing product and/or service" (WTO, 1985). Customer satisfaction reflects the perceived quality of products that are actually delivered to customers

Meaning of Destination

A destination consists of a mix of five elements which are interdependent to produce a satisfying holiday experience to the visitors and these elements are: attractions, facilities, infrastructure, transportation and hospitality and quality of service. Destinations may be primary or secondary. A primary destination is attractive enough to be the primary motivation for tourism visits and is aimed mainly at satisfying tourists for several days or longer periods. On the other hand, a secondary destination also known as a stopover destination is one either an interesting or necessary place to visit on the way to the primary destination.

About Chandigarh

Chandigarh, the dream city of India's first Prime Minister, Sh. Jawahar Lal Nehru, was planned by the famous French architect

Le Corbusier. Picturesquely located at the foothills of Shivaliks, it is known as one of the best experiments in urban planning and modern architecture in the twentieth century in India. As the capital of the states of Punjab and Haryana, and the Union Territory of Chandigarh it is a prestigious city. Serenity and a city are two diametrically opposite concepts, which however, get belied in the 'City Beautiful'. Chandigarh is a rare epitome of modernization co-existing with nature's preservation. It is here that the trees and plants are as much a part of the construction plans as the buildings and the roads. India's first planned city, is a rich, prosperous, spic and span, green city rightly called " THE CITY BEAUTIFUL ". Chandigarh derives its name from the temple of "Chandi Mandir" located in the vicinity of the site selected for the city. The deity 'Chandi', the goddess of power and a fort of 'garh' laying beyond the temple gave the city its name "Chandigarh-The City Beautiful".

World Renowned Places of Tourist Interest in Chandigarh

Chandigarh, is one of the most popular tourist destinations of India. However, unlike most of the other places, the city is famous for the modern architectures and the exotic landscape, rather than the ancient historical monuments. Be it the magnificent Capitol Complex or the unique Rock Garden, the tourist attractions of Chandigarh are quite unusual in their very nature. Of all the major tourist places in the beautiful city, we have provided information on the most popular ones, in the lines below

RockGarden

Rock Garden is a unique attraction as Chandigarh, in its being a magnificent gallery of artistic works made out of industrial and urban wastes. The raw materials have been molded to form lively images of animals, human beings, trees, etc. Founded by Nek Chand, a government official, in 1957, the garden preserves a special collection of artistry found nowhere else in the world.

Sukhna Lake

Sukhna Lake is a popular artificial lake in Chandigarh, made at the foothills of the Shivalik hills. It was created by Le Corbusier, in the year 1958. It is an ideal place for exercises like walking, jogging, strolling and even organizing picnics. The lake is rich in natural beauty and serves as the shelter for several migratory birds as well.

Capitol Complex

Capitol Complex is Le Corbsier's most spectacular work in the Chandigarh city. He had conceived the master plan of Chandigarh as analogous to the parts of the human body, in which Capitol Complex was supposed to be the heart. It consists of three architectural Government buildings, High Court, Secretariat, and Legislative Assembly. In the middle stands The Open Hand, the official emblem of the city, signifying the city's credo of "open to be given, open to receive".

Leisure Valley

Le Corbusier planned lots of greenery in Chandigarh, by constructing a series of parks and gardens, collectively called the Leisure Valley. The valley consists of gardens extending from Sector 53 in the Southern edge to the Sector 1 in the North. Some of the gardens and parks are Rajendra Park, Bougainvillea Garden, Fitness Trails, Rose Garden, Children Traffic Park, Botanical Garden and Smriti Upavan & Topiary Park.

International Dolls Museum

A wide collection of fascinating dolls and marionettes under a single roof is the main feature of the International Dolls Museum in Chandigarh. Situated at the Bal Bhavan, this museum is functioning under the guidance of the Indian Council of Child Welfare, Chandigarh. International Dolls Museum is situated in Bal Bhawan, in Sector 23 of Chandigarh. It contains more than 300 dolls from nearly every country in the world. It was inaugurated on 24th December, 1985. The museum was established by Chandigarh administration, in alliance with Rotary Club of Chandigarh, for the purpose of entertaining the children. It is a must-visit if you're visiting the city with your kids.

Government Museum And Art Gallery

Government Museum & Art Gallery is located in Sector 10 of Chandigarh and has a fine collection of stone sculptures belonging to the Gandhara School of Art. It also displays fossils and artifacts belonging to the prehistoric times and works of modern art and miniature paintings. This square building (165 feet by 165 feet) is a splendid display of architecture by none another than Le Corbusier himself.

Chhatbir Zoo

If there's one animal that you would want to see, it is the Royal Bengal White Tiger. A thrill sets down upon your spine when you take pictures standing really close to the Tiger. It has now developed into a zoological park of prominence. Visitors are taken to the tiger's sanctuaries in the caged motor vehicle while the animals roam freely in their reserved areas. There are also a large species of birds. Mondays are a holiday at this place.

Pinjore Gardens

Pinjore Gardens, also called Yadavindra Gardens, are 20 km (12 mi) from Chandigarh on the Chandigarh Shimla road. Taxis and buses ply regularly between Pinjore and Chandigarh. Pinjore lies on the foothills of the lower Shivalik ranges. The fascinating gardens in the Mughal style are one of the most popular picnic spots in the region. A mini zoo, plant nursery and Japanese garden, as well historic palaces and picnic lawns await tourists.

Chandi Mandir

Chandi Mandir is a temple located in the northern border of the city. Devoted to the Mother Goddess of power, Chandi, it is considered as one of the twelve Shakti Peethas for Hindus. The name Chandigarh is derived from this shrine only. There is an aura surrounded to this temple and if you are in search of divinity and tranquility, there is no better place for you than this temple. It is also one of the oldest temples of the area, claimed by many to date back to era of Mahabharata.

Cactus Graden

Cactus Garden is the largest succulent botanical garden of Asia. It is located at a distance of about 8 kms from the city of gardens. Situated in the heart of the city of Panchkula, it covers a total area of 7 acres. Cactus garden is known for its rare & endangered species of Indian succulents. You can spot nearly 3500 different kinds of species over there. Chandigarh Cactus Garden was set up in the year 1987. This unique garden consists of three green houses. It has been drawing more and more crowds every year, consisting not just of tourists, but botanists.

Religious Places In Chandigarh

In addition to the various tourist spots, Chandigarh has lots to offer to the people seeking religious visits. Right from temples to the gurdwaras, the religious places in the city offer a wide variety. In fact, it has a plethora of worship places not only within, but also near its bounds. For instance, there is Chandi Mandir, after which Chandigarh has been named. Then, there is Nada Sahib Gurdwara, which witnesses a huge rush of devotees - Sikhs, Hindus, Jains, and so on, every Sunday.

The Tower of Shadows & Other Attractions

Situated between the High Court and the Parliament, the Tower of Shadows stands like "a monument of shadows". It presents an interesting study of the movement of the sun. The tower is an incredible demonstration of architecture and excellence of Le Corbusier. Other important attractions of the place are Geometric Hill, Martyr's Memorial, and Museum of Evolution of Life.

TRENDS IN TOURIST ARRIVALS IN CHANDIGARH

Tourist Arrival Statics in Chandigarh 2014

Month	Domestic	Foreign
January	88081	2074
February	90883	3140
March	91184	3331

(**Source**:chandigarhtourism.gov.in)

Tourist Arrival Statics in Chandigarh from January, 2013 to December, 2013

Month	Domestic	Foreign
January	78,463	2,677
February	77813	2,629
March	68,520	4,223
April	80,460	4,284
May	72,534	3689
June	82,718	2466
July	76,284	1764
August	72,156	2,602
September	81,841	3,433
October	79,884	4158
November	79,243	4,089
December	87,006	4,113
Total	9,36,922	40,124

(**Source**:chandigarhtourism.gov.in)

Tourist Arrival Statics in Chandigarh from January, 2012 to December, 2012

Month	Domestic	Foreign
January	77,1617	2,472
February	77,892	3,094
March	74,339	3,901
April	78,488	5,719
May	83,860	2,462
June	75,915	1,563
July	84,433	2,055
August	72,087	2,210
September	74,364	2,216
October	78,861	3,014
November	76,514	2,423

December	76,219	3,001
Total	9,24,589	34,130

(**Source:**chandigarhtourism.gov.in)

Chandigarh City: Location Advantage

Picturesquely located at the foothills of Shivaliks, the Union territory of Chandigarh serves as the capital of Punjab and Haryana. Known internationally for its architecture and urban planning, Chandigarh is home to numerous architectural projects of Le Corbusier, Pierre Jeanneret, Matthew Nowicki, and Albert Mayer. Some of the many tourist attractions in the city include the Famous Rock Garden, an international dolls museum and a number of garden and parks. The city can also be used as a base to make excursions to nearby Kasauli, Chail, Solan and Shimla. Chandigarh is the gateway to Himachal Pradesh, an acknowledged tourist haven. Shimla, just 110 km by road. Kasauli, only one hour drive. It is a hill station not very far from the city. If one is lucky, in clear weather it offers a staggering view of Chandigarh from the Himalayan Foothills. The foreign visitors will need to present a valid passport to gain entrance.Other Himachal hill stations such as Kullu and Manali, a gateway city to Himachal Pradesh. A trip by road to Kullu takes about 12 h by bus or 6-7 hours by taxi. Dharamsala, home of the Dalai Lama and top Himachal hill station. One can visit Pinjore Gardens that are within a range of 15-20 km from Chandigarh on the way to Shimla.

Research Methodology

A qualitative and quantitative approach was used in this study to fulfill objective of research. The target population for this study was adults and all types of tourists who come to Chandigarh for the purpose of leisure, medical, business and recreational etc. The tourist population was 100 in my research study.

In this research there are two type of data use as one is primary data and secondary data. Primary data: Primary research involves collecting new data which has been collected exclusively for the research and for which the researcher is the primary user. In this research primary source of data is questionnaire. Secondary data:

Secondary research is based on material and research formerly collected by other researchers for some purpose other than that of the researcher. In this research use secondary source of data is pdf files. The data is collected from 100 tourists who have visited Chandigarh for the purpose of leisure, medical, business and re-creational etc.

Our choice of sampling technique is a non-probability choice. Our choice is made through convenience which means that we contacted people that we found available. Convenience choice means that the respondents are chosen because they are available (Bryman & Bell, 2005). And the required data for the research was collected through convenient random sampling method, with a prepared set of questions.

Data Analysis

Standard deviations are used to measure dispersion of data around the mean. To be able to analyze the different answer options we gave each option different points, this method is called Likert scale. The expectations and perceptions are evaluated through 7 statements and the answer options are rated through five point Likert scale. The result showed mapping service quality of tourism industry in Chandigarh. SPSS software was used for all the analysis from the questionnaires into diagrams and tables that are easier to facilitate.

The measurement of all items was done by asking the respondents to rate the level of importance attached to all items separately. The Likert scale used was;

1= Strongly Disagree 2= Disagree 3= Neutral

4=Agree 5=Strongly Agree

Table 1: Personal Profile of tourists

Personal Profile		Number	%
Gender	Male	70	70
	Female	30	30

Personal Profile		Number	%
Age	20-30 years	50	50
	31-40 years	42	42
	41-50 years	8	8
	50 years and above	0	0
Marital Status	Married	67	67
	Single	33	33
Education	High school	12	12
	Secondary school	8	8
	Graduate	40	40
	Post graduate	38	38
	Other	2	2
Occupations	Service	38	38
	Business	17	17
	Self Employed	10	10
	Professional	22	22
	Housewife	8	8
	Student	5	5
Family Monthly Income	Less than Rs. 25,000	5	5
	Rs. 25,001-50,000	12	12
	Rs. 50,001-750,00	45	45
	Rs. 75,001-100,000	20	20
	Above Rs.100,000	18	18

Source: Primary Survey

Table 1 show the number and percentage of the tourist. And also show the gender, age, marital status, education, occupation and family monthly income of tourist.

Table 2: Show the variable of transportation service.

Transportation		Strongly Agree	Agree	Neutral	Disagree	Strongly Disagree
Local transport facility (taxi/buses/ auto etc) is accessible in the city	Number	55	35	10	0	0
	%	55	35	10	0	0
The driver and staff of transport were reliable and responsible	Number	35	45	20	0	0
	%	35	45	20	0	0
Transport facility was available on reasonable charges	Number	43	42	15	0	0
	%	42	42	15	0	0
Transport staff was trustworthy	Number	30	35	32	3	0
	%	30	35	32	3	0

Source: Primary Survey

Table 2 shows the number and percentage of the tourist who come to Chandigarh and use service how much they satisfied with each service of transportation 55% tourist strongly agree with the Local transport facility (taxi/buses/auto etc) is accessible in the city, 45% tourist agree with the driver and staff of transport were reliable and responsible, 43% tourist strongly agree and agree with the Transport facility was available on reasonable charges, and 35% tourist agree with the Transport staff was trustworthy.

Table3: Show the variable of Accommodation service.

Accommodation		Strongly Agree	Agree	Natural	Disagree	Strongly Disagree
The location of hotels was easier to reach	Number	43	42	15	0	0
	%	43	42	15	0	0
Rooms are available on fair prices	Number	20	58	20	2	0
	%	20	58	20	2	0
There was good facility of food, information, phone and internet etc	Number	30	43	27	0	0
	%	30	43	27	0	0

Source: Primary Survey

Table 3 shows the number and percentage of the tourist who come to Chandigarh and use service how much they satisfied with each service of Accommodation 43% tourist strongly agree with the location of hotels was easier to reach, 58% tourist strongly agree with the rooms are available on fair prices, 43% tourist strongly agree with hotels have good facility of food, information, phone and internet etc.

Table 4: Show the variable Food and Beverage service.

Food And Beverage		Strongly Agree	Agree	Natural	Disagree	Strongly Disagree
The price of food was reasonable	Number	20	63	17	0	0
	%	20	63	17	0	0

Food And Beverage		Strongly Agree	Agree	Natural	Disagree	Strongly Disagree
The quality of food was good and hygienic	Number	40	40	20	0	0
	%	40	40	20	0	0
Food and service delivery on time	Number	47	30	20	3	0
	%	47	30	20	3	0

Source: Primary Survey

Table 4 shows the number and percentage of the tourist who come to Chandigarh and use service how much they satisfied with each service of Food And Beverage 63% tourist agree with the price of food was reasonable, 40 % tourist strongly agree and agree with the quality of food was good and hygienic, and 47% tourist strongly agree with the Food and service delivery on time.

Table: 5 Show the variable of emporiums/ shopping arcades service

Emporiums/ Shopping Arcades		Strongly Agree	Agree	Natural	Disagree	Strongly Disagree
Accessibility to the emporiums is easier	Number	25	52	23	0	0
	%	25	52	23	0	0
Products are available on reasonable prices	Number	32	43	25	0	0
	%	32	43	25	0	0
The sales persons respond to request quickly	Number	37	45	18	0	0
	%	37	45	18	0	0

Source: Primary Survey

Table 5 shows the number and percentage of the tourist who come to Chandigarh and use service how much they satisfied with each service of Emporiums/ Shopping Arcades 52% tourist agree with the accessibility to the emporiums is easier to reach, 43% tourist agree with the products are available on reasonable prices, 45% tourist strongly agree with the sales persons respond to request quickly.

Table: 6 Show the variable of Travel agents/ Guides.

Travel Agents/ Guides		Strongly Agree	Agree	Natural	Disagree	Strongly Disagree
The staff was very courteous and polite	Number	15	10	75	0	0
	%	15	10	75	0	0
Travel agent staff was trustworthy	Number	5	8	87	0	0
	%	5	8	87	0	0
The charges are affordable and reasonable	Number	3	20	77	0	0
	%	3	20	77	0	0

Source: Primary Survey

Table 6 shows the number and percentage of the tourist who come to Chandigarh and use service how much they satisfied with each service of travel agents/ guides provided to the tourist by tourism industry 75% tourist neutral with the staff was very courteous and polite, 87% tourist neutral with the travel agent staff was trustworthy, 77 % tourist neutral with the charges are affordable and reasonable.

Table: 7 Show the variable of Safety and Security.

Safety and Security		Strongly Agree	Agree	Natural	Disagree	Strongly Disagree
It was safe to visit in Chandigarh	Number	57	30	10	3	0
	%	57	30	10	3	0
There are satisfactory arrangements for safety and security	Number	47	40	13	0	0
	%	47	40	13	0	0
Police is reliable	Number	35	40	17	8	0
	%	35	40	17	8	0
Police solved problems quickly	Number	33	39	20	8	0
	%	33	39	20	8	0

Safety and Security		Strongly Agree	Agree	Natural	Disagree	Strongly Disagree
Police solved problems quickly	Number	30	40	15	15	0
	%	30	40	15	15	0

Source: Primary Survey

Table 7 shows the number and percentage of the tourist who come to Chandigarh and use service how much they satisfied with each service of Safety and Security 57 % tourist strongly agree with the it was safe to visit in Chandigarh, 47% tourist strongly agree with the satisfactory arrangements for safety and security, 40% tourist agree with the Chandigarh police is reliable, 39% tourist agree with the police solved problems quickly, and 40% tourist agree with the police solved problems quickly.

Table: 8 Show the variable of Destination.

Destination		Strongly Agree	Agree	Natural	Disagree	Strongly Disagree
Destinations are visually aesthetically attractive	Number	58	32	10	0	0
	%	58	32	10	0	0
Comfortable climate in Chandigarh	Number	57	33	10	0	0
	%	57	33	10	0	0
Chandigarh is exciting place to visit	Number	60	32	8	0	0
	%	60	32	8	0	0
I would recommend Chandigarh to other to seek my advice	Number	40	37	23	0	0
	%	40	37	23	0	0
I would like to visit Chandigarh again	Number	57	32	11	0	0
	%	57	32	11	0	0

Source: Primary Survey

Table 8 shows the number and percentage of the tourist who come to Chandigarh and how much they satisfied with Chandigarh as tourist destination 58 % tourist strongly agree with the destinations are visually aesthetically attractive, 57 % tourist strongly agree with the comfortable climate in Chandigarh, 60% tourist strongly agree with the Chandigarh is exciting place to visit, 40% tourist strongly agree with the they recommend Chandigarh to other to seek my advice, and 57 % tourist strongly agree with they like to visit Chandigarh again.

Table 9 shows the relations between transportation, accommodation, food and beverages, emporiums/shopping arcades, travel agents and guides, safety and security and destination.

Table-9: Show the correlation

Correlations

		Average score of transportation	Average score of accommodation	Average score of food and beverages	Average score of emporiums/shopping arcades	Average score of travel agents and guides	Average score of safety and security	Average score of destination
Average score of transportation	Pearson Correlation	1	.231	.077	.236	.112	.271	-.119
	Sig. (2-tailed)		.152	.639	.143	.492	.090	.463
Average score of accommodation	Pearson Correlation	.231	1	.049	.488**	-.209	.237	.077
	Sig. (2-tailed)	.152		.762	.001	.196	.141	.636
Average score of food and beverages	Pearson Correlation	.077	.049	1	.271	.160	.316*	.089
	Sig. (2-tailed)	.639	.762		.091	.325	.047	.584
Average score of emporiums/shopping arcades	Pearson Correlation	.236	.488**	.271	1	-.216	.385*	.173
	Sig. (2-tailed)	.143	.001	.091		.181	.014	.284
Average score of travel agents and guides	Pearson Correlation	.112	-.209	.160	-.216	1	.118	-.216
	Sig. (2-tailed)	.492	.196	.325	.181		.470	.181

		Average score of transportation	Average score of accommodation	Average score of food and beverages	Average score of emporiums/ shopping arcades	Average score of travel agents and guides	Average score of safety and security	Average score of destination
Average score of safety and security	Pearson Correlation	.271	.237	.316*	.385*	.118	1	.357*
	Sig. (2-tailed)	.090	.141	.047	.014	.470		.024
Average score of destination	Pearson Correlation	-.119	.077	.089	.173	-.216	.357*	1
	Sig. (2-tailed)	.463	.636	.584	.284	.181	.024	

Discussions

The broad tourism industry aspects included in the study were (i) transportation (ii) accommodation, (iii) food and beverages, (iv) emporiums/ shopping arcades, (v) travel agent/ guides, (vi) safety and security, and (vii) tourist places each having several sub-dimensions. The study reveals that tourists were indifferent regarding the transportation, accommodation, food and beverages, emporiums/ shopping arcades, travel agents/ guides etc. It means tourist are highest level of satisfied with the services quality provide by the tourism industry in Chandigarh. The safety and security provide by Chandigarh as a tourist destination is good. Additionally, this research also finds the service quality is also a way of thinking about how much satisfy with service that they hold positive attitudes toward the service they have received by tourism industry and revisit in destnation. The results from the study showed that such dimensions as quality of accessibility, accommodation, safety and security, travel agents/ guides and their components have significant, direct and positive relationship with satisfaction of tourists .

Conclusion

The key purpose of this research was to study the role of Chandigarh as tourist destination. The dimensions which reveal the high level of tourists' satisfaction are: transportation, accommodation, food and beverage, emporiums/ shopping arcades, travel agents/guides, safety and security. The survey was based on a limited number of respondents. The results of the study exposed that most of the tourists which arrive in Chandigarh are males from service class with monthly income more than 50,000 p.m. Most of the tourists found that in Chandigarh there is good quality of accessibility of transportation, accommodation, safety and security, travel agents/ guides and their components. It is proved that all the components have significant, direct and positive relationship with satisfaction of tourists. Moreover, the present study shows that Chandigarh is a popular destination among tourists and most of the tourists are satisfied with the transportation, food, security, shopping arcades, the role of travel agents and are willing to visit again.

References

Baloglu,S.,Pekcan, A,, Chen, S.L and Santos,J.(2003).The Relationship Between Destination Per-formance, Overall Satisfaction, and Behavioural Intention for Distinct Segments,JournalOf Quality Assurance in Hospitality& Tourism,4(3/4): 149-165

Bigne J.E, Sanchez, M.1 and Sanchez,J.(2001). Tourism Image, Evaluation Variables and After Purchase Behaviour: Inter-Relationship,Tourism Management,22(6): 607-616

Chen, C. and Tsai,D.(2007). How Destination Image and Evaluative Factors Affect Behavioral Intentions, Tourism Management,28(4): 1115-1122

Chen,J.and Gursoy, D.(2001).An Investigation of Tourists' Destination Loyalty and Preferences,International Journal of Contemporary Hospitality Management,13: 79-86

Chi, C.G.Q and Qu, H. (2008). Examining the Structural Relationships of Destination Image,Tourist Satisfaction and Destination Loyalty: An Integrated Approach,Tourism Management,29(4): 624-636

Essays, UK. (November 2013). A Literature Review On Tourism Destination Tourism Essay. Retrieved from http://www.ukessays.com/essays/tourism/a-literature-review-on-tourism-destination-tourism-essay.php?cref=1

Kozak, M. (2003). Measuring Tourist Satisfaction with Multiple Destination Attributes,

Kozak,M.(2001).Repeaters' Behaviour at Two Distinct Destinations, Annals Of Tourism Research,28(3):784-807

Lee, C.K., Lee, Y.K. and Lee, B.K. (2005). Korea's Destination Image Formed by the2002WorldCup, Annuls of Tourism Research,32(4): 839-858

Petrick,J.F.(2004). The Roles of Quality, Value, and Satisfaction in Predicting Cruise Passengers'Behavioural Intentions,Journal of Travel Research,42(4): 397-407

Prayag Girish (2008).Image, satisfaction and loyalty-The case of cape town, Anatolia : An International Journal Of Tourism and Hospitality Research, volume 19,Number 2: 205-224

Tourism Analysis,7(3/4):229-240

PUKREILA: A DRIVING FORCE FOR COMMUNITY BASED TOURISM INITIATIVES (OPPORTUNITIES & CHALLENGES)

Lucy Jajo Shimray

Assoc. Prof. Dept. of Economic, DM College of Arts, Imphal. Affiliated to Manipur University(MU)

lucyjajo4@gmail.com

Ninghorla Zimik

Assoc. Prof. Dept. of Political Science, Pettigrew College, Ukhrul, MED, Govt. of Manipur. Affiliated to Manipur University

ninghorzimik@gmail.com

Abstract

In the last few decades, Community Based Tourism (CBT) has gained much popularity as one viable alternative for mainstream tourism. CBT can be defined as Tourism owned and managed by the local community which delivers equal benefits to the community concerned. The present study was undertaken on 'Pukreila' as key factor for CBT initiatives as tourism always has a link with women. Pukreila are the married women not to be harmed by anyone according to the Naga tribal customary laws. She acts as negotiator of peace in times of war and inter-village feuds. Whereas mass tourism claims that it employs more women than men and are often seen as the face os tourism quite literally as they appear in the travel brochures as the ambiquitous image of warmth, welcome and hospitality(equations,2009). The paper is a humble attempt to highlight how Pukreila can be the driving force to explore the vast opportunities of natural and cultural resources of the region. It further attempts to identify the various challenges and henceforth bring a viable solution both for sound economic management and social responsibility to the local community with a humble suggestion that forming of Village Tourism Committee (VTC) comprising only womenfolk can be initiated. This will ensure safety measures from the adverse impact of CBT that may arise in the long run.

Keywords: Pukreila, CBT, Unique, Naga, Community.

Introduction

Tourism ever since its creation in 1961 under Mr Bernard Lance(oecd/94,49) has blossomed and prosper as a fast growing activity and has indeed perceived as a significant factor for economic growth in the countries it has developed and a driving force for social development. Gopal(2008) has rightly stated that Community-Based Tourism(CBT) is closely related to the traditional and romantic ideas of good old days, pure and simple, intact nature and perfect integration of man in his natural environment. The present paper has taken into account a new concept of intermingling Pukreila with CBT initiative as the main driving force in tourism Industry from a regional context with the sole objective of bringing the community's participation to the forefront collectively. Whereas CBT is based on the active participation of the local community while at the same time creating a good relationship between the local community and the tourist is very important. The Pukreilas are awefully great and honourable women in the true spirit of the traditional Naga Customary Laws and even from the modern concept of her acumen.

CBT initiative has common threads to see tourism as means to achieving development goals depending much on its accessibility on regional, national and international level. In Tourism industry women are often seen as face of tourism quite literally as they appear in travel brochures and also as the ambiguitious image of warmth, welcome and hospitality (equations,2009). CBT exist to strengthen the wellbeing of the community. It shares knowledge and expertise with local communities so that they make good decisions by providing access to accurate and timely information on the best practices, regional trends and the changing environment in the place where they lived and worked in. Therefore the CBT initiative could be initiated to link communities together so that by collaborating as a team and build a regional response to an issue and sets a stronger region for everyone to see. The paper intends to focus and promote Pukreila on various opportunities and challenges of CBT initiative that may be quite contextual in its analysis though theoretically on the local priorities and issues, bringing peace together around key issues and supporting planning CBT in delivering benefits to the residents.

The main concern therefore in the present paper is – Who is Pukreila? What is CBT initiative in understanding the growth of tourism?. To what extend Pukreila can break gender injustices and empowered women's participation in tourism successfully?. To study the various opportunities and challenges the observation and insights are being derived from more general contexts in addressing the regional core issues. CBT provides visitors with an opportunity to appreciate the traditional cultures and places of significance owned partly or wholly by the tribal community /indigenous people encompassing a wide range of products and services including cultural heritage and nature based tours, educational programmes, arts and crafts, events accommodations, transport and hospitality (Frania, Kanara Zygadlo,2003)

Who is Pukreila?

Pukreila is an honourable name given to those women who are married to the man of another community or another village or outside the community. However, in the modern context, Pukreila can be related to both married and unmarried women in the society. The literal meaning of Pukreila means peace maker(negotiator of peace), a great lady and a neutral lady.Though in Naga tribal society women were not treated equally with men, yet, she hold a place of high esteem as none other male can do about especially in times of inter-village feuds and war, Pukreila plays a great role in defusing the war and conflicts between the two parties. No man can lay a hand on her once she raise her Zeithing (Metal staff).

When two villages failed to settled a dispute or conclude a war, the last word comes from woman herself. Such a high prerogative honour has never been given to men (Y.K Shimray).

The bravery of Naga Pukreila can also be narrated to a story when the case of factional feuds between the two factions of NSCM(IM) and NSCN(K) in Nagaland when the internal feuds were at its peak, some brave Naga Pukreilas stepped forward and interposed between the the two parties lifting up their hands and averted a warlike situations. Though she is not the head of the family yet her rights are equally honoured in the Naga society/community. Lifting up of hand is a sign of peace and none dares to challenge her.

The most latest initiative taken by Pukreila can be noted by the Shirui Seige' on 10th Jan'2009.When the Indian Army laid siege of the village with jawans surrounding the entire NSCN(IM) camp of Khusumung Battalion and the Naga village and ordered the NSCN group to surrender within 24 hours. Instead of surrounding the latter instead sent a message saying they would retaliate in case they are attacked. At this extreme juncture, the Pukreilas of the shirui village and the neighbouring villages from the district headquater(Ukhrul) assembled and reacted swiftly by keeping strict vigil despite the freezing cold and chilling winter nights. More than 2000 women too part under the initiative of Pukreilas in the vigil braving the cold nights and forsaking their homes and children. The love of mothers and sisters demonstrated in their action move the hearts of both the warring groups and so defused the tensions and ended the Shirui Seige on 21st Feb'2009. Such is the noble and brave initiative taken by the Tangkhul Naga Pukreilas and girls.(Free press, Sangai 19th-3rd march,2009).

By nature women has a heart softer than men that yearns for peace and harmony in the family and community. Though she is not directly the decision maker yet she controls the family and society/community indirectly through her wisdom and tolerance. In the present trends the role of Pukreila is still continuing in tandem with the changing situations and scenario. However, the paper is not bias to the extend that she is an angel but admits that she too makes mistakes at times but is taken care off and corrected to the maximum.

Understanding CBT initiatives & related Issues:-

With the concept of sustainability alongside the economic reforms in developing economics the need for having small self sustained business models appeared as the most feasible approach to preserve the integrity or rural systems that is agrarian or otherwise, a sustainable self sustenance structure in themselves(Wikipedia). This concept grow around the 1980. As a fallout, CBT grew for providing alternative sources of income for supplementing the agricultural practices. And at the same time it tries to preserve their cultural identity and conserve the environment from further degradation.

Mention may be made that CBT model initially emerge i countries like Australia and New Zealand upon the indigenous Aborigines and Maori populations respectively(Pran Nath,2003). By 1990 (SIGA) the utility of CBT model wass well established and later replicated across Africa and South East Asia and started gaining momentum as a tool for inclusive growth in the field of Tourism potentiality with Academic development. However as Harrold Goodwin has aptly pointed out that while many projects being funded in developing countries on CBT, the success of these projects have not been properly monitored as a result the actual benefits to the local communities still remain a dream or unsatisfactory and unquantified. In a developing countries like India and North East Region(NER) where agriculture is the mainstay of livelihood, the concept of of promoting CBT initiative has to be at the cost of significant opportunity cost(Keynes). However, agriculture being the backbone and the foundation for any economic development has to be improved side by side and cannot be sidelined. Therefore, understanding CBT initiative has to be understood within the domain of a community's participation as a subsistence income for supplementing their income and economic lifestyle comfortably with little or low cost infrastructure. This has to be understood at the grassroot level for CBT initiatives.

CBT methods of development are based on participatory approach and ultimately emerge as a result to both the conservation and development approaches widely practice by organisations bound by their linking environmental conservation and socio-economic development i.e. reducing the poverty level mostly in an around the protected areas. Meantime, the success of CBT initiatives have been quoted by Wheeler as:

" The traveller is preferred to the tourist, the individual to the group,specialist operators rather than large firms, indigenous accommodation to multi-national hotels, small not large-essentially good versus bad.... perhaps the true situation is best expressed as the good guises versus the bad guys" What a statement !.

Mann (2000) has beautifully define the concept of CBT and its initiatives so broadly that it appears to include almost all forms of tourism which involve community members and benefit them and anything that involves genuine community participation and benefits. CBT initiatives has to be managed and owned collectively by the community taking into account its environmental, social and cultural sustainability so that it enables the visitors to increase the awareness about the local community and learn more about the ways of local life(cbt-i.org.accessed) as rightly define by the Thailand Community Based Tourism Institute. An example of Landirejo village can be used to suit the needs of Regional context. In 2002, there were only 10 home-stays, 15 transports, and two restaurants. By 2004, it increases to 22 homestays,22local transport and 6 restaurants in which were all the poor people have the potential to involve either as part time or full time in the tourism sector through the co-operatives called Koperasi. Here all income and profits earned were shared equally coming from fees collection, handicrafts, sales, accommodation services, meals etc. and part of the revenues were used to maintain to improve village hygiene by ensuring equitable distribution of benefits to all the community members. Over the years now, this particular village is established as tourism village.(Wikipedia)

Mountain Shepherd Initiatives (MSI) in Uttarakhand can be one example of CBT initiatives for better understanding inaugurated in the vicinity of Nanda Devi Biosphere in the year 2006 as projected under reviewed literature.(Equations,2009). It marked the first women Trek into the tourism business as a challenging task for establishing community and environmental degradation. Girls are being trained in mountaineering and tourist guide as men does. Apart from their traditional roles of carers within the family, CBT initiative relies on women's traditional skills in carpet weaving, upgrading their knowledge and skills into the tourism loop. In the MSI since the youth were mostly taking care of the tourist as guides yet, the very payment by the tourists in home-stays were paid to the women land lady. So revenues were collected and manage by women. In short, MSI has taken firm step in guiding the community about the roles where women may have opportunity and has created a space for discussion as to what roles she should feel comfortable and not absorbed into vulnerability to exploitation by tourists. This can be a good reference for CBT initiatives that is progressing.

The most common example can be taken. in the case of Shirui village Tourism Committee in Ukhrul district of Manipur. This survey was taken during the course of the Ph.D research by the author. As Shirui village is famous for its unique flower Shirui-Lily known as the state flower of Manipur where thousands of people came to visit the peak every year. The village youth organised among themselves as guides to tourist and even provide stay-home at times with limited amount ranging from rupees200 to 250 per night. The entrance fees were collected @10 rupees per member. Besides, a guest house is also under construction under the funding of IFAD an International Funding Agency nearing for completion. During the month of May, Shirui-Lily Week is being observed every year since its inception in the year 2011-12 by the village tourism committee. Cultural folk dances, songs, and various items are showcased as part of tourism activities. Notably women takes a great role in this activities as a CBT initiatives but the only thing is the local community need more education and managerial skills to impart the CBT initiatives successfully. Here Pukreila take a major role in Tourism activities indirectly otherwise in terms of hospitality to visitors and travellers. All handloom and handicrafts are exhibited by the local women. A few foreigners who could visit were charmed and attracted by the indigenous products such as men's waist coat, necktie, muffler etc. Many self help groups are taking initiatives either individually or with NGO's support. Notably more women participation is notice. But to what extent they are successful depends upon different self-help groups.

Another example of effective CBT initiatives can be traced back to the initiatives undertaken by the Khonoma village in Nagaland under Khonoma Green Village Project started in 2003 as a source of revenue generation with the main objectives of training the local people , exploring options of alternatives technologies, value addition to the village properties and better management in tourism under the innovative experiment of communitization in 2002-03 following the enactment of Nagaland Communitization Act on Public Institutions and Services. The communitization was based on triple 'T' approach of Trust, Train and Transfer and was found to be successful. The Nagaland Government was therefore recognise for its innovative uses of social capital for the United Nations public Service awards in 2008 for communitization programmes.

CBT is one of the most effective ways of redistributing wealth by moving money into local economies to a community that would otherwise not be earned. It brings communities together for a more harmonious understanding and even reach out the message of warmth and hospitality from the community within to outside tourist.

Main objectives of the paper:-

- It attempt to bring a new concept by promoting 'Pukreila' as key driver in CBT initiatives to improve environmental conditions and socio-economic life of the rural community.
- It aim to analyse the various opportunities and Challenges of CBT initiatives from generalisation to the regional/local context.

Opportunities:

Social benefits:

A positive sense of community identity can be reinforce and tourism can encourage local communities to maintain their traditions and identities.The pride and community identity can be generated through tourism and its CBT initiatives. The local community can organise fairs and festival and showcase their traditional/indigenous folk dances, songs and sports. This will help the tourist to better understand the ground reality about their way of life. In so doing the community themselves can earn revenues as alternate incomes. It will even build better understanding for more sustainable tourism development. Mention may be made here that Ukhrul district is dominated by Tangkhul Naga community.It also belongs to few eminent personalities of the state of Manipur. Shri Rishang Keishing, Lt. Shri Yangmaso Shaiza. Lt. Shri R. Khathing,belongs to this community. Interestingly during election times when there was intense conflict between the civil organisation/politicians and the underground outfits, it was the women (Pukreila) who always take the initiative in bringing peace and amicable solutions in the district. Even during Child trafficking protest pukreila including all the women took the initiative in nailing the culprits and brought the children back home safe and sound.Pukreila are more accountable to the community's wellbeing and social development.The rich cultural resources can be promoted by empowering women to the maximum through fairs, festivals, events, exhibitions(Handloom&handicrafts) etc. Thus CBT initiative should be encourage to promote tourism side by side so that through educating tourism knowledge they will be empowered as a partaker in the community's decision making.

Economic benefits:-

The popularity of farmer markets is increasingly becoming a key driver of economic development in Regional areas. Some of the benefits that the community can earn may include:

-Showcasing local produce and products such as indigenous cuisines,,traditional handloom and handicrafts,indigenous Nungpi Ceramic. Nungpi village in Ukhrul is famous for its indigenous pottery made out of blackish clay and has earn many accolades at the national level.

The CBT initiatives can be projected to various regional and local areas of unique beauties and natural surroundings.

It will allow community's events to be incorporated and provides distribution and opportunities for small businesses, example various self help groups can take up joint restaurant, eatery shop, etc collectively and earn revenues for themselves.

The CBT initiatives can help the local community in building infrastructure including roads, parks and other public places. Here both men and women and even women alone can take the initiatives.

Environmental benefits:

Under the CBT initiatives, conservation of local environment and natural resources will enhance the reputation of any tourism business.. CBT initiatives particularly in the eco-tourism can place a greater focus on the conservation of natural resources through the recognition of their importance to visitors experiences and their economic value to the local community. CBT is also a powerful opportunity to impact and change the minds of tourists. In order to achieve the targeted aims and objectives of CBT, involvement and active participation of the tourist as partners in the process in which they could be enabled to facilitate to do so are important issues. Tourism revenues is to a large extent safe from external exigencies, but is a possible step towards ensuring national integrity. Special case may be mention where there are large unique natural settings historical places of importance in the district of Manipur such as the Shirui peak, Sihai Peak, Khangkhui Mangsor cave that needs preservation through CBT initiatives where the community can collectively take care of the sites and protect the environment from degradation.

Relation between Resources and Actions in Community Based Tourism (MI, 2010)

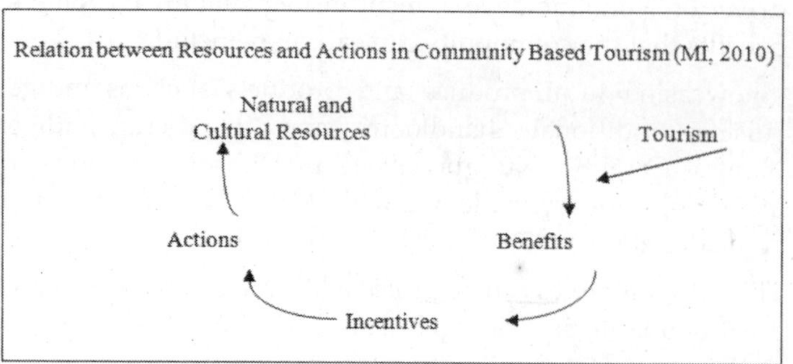

Source: SIGA.2012.

In Ukhrul district of Manipur, there is a particular NGO under the Caption of Ukhrul District Community Resouces Management Society(UDCRMS) in collaboration with the International Funding Agency known as IFAD which is operating successfully with many self help groups(SHP's) from different villages of the district as CBT initiatives. Under this project many creative and innovative schemes are implemented especially for community development. Some of the schemes are bakery shop, poultry farm, piggery, weaving, arts and crafts, horticulture etc. this has indeed added extra income to the family management. The revenues so collected are jointly manage by the group leader of each SHG and annually gave audit in the form of account statement to the project manager which is managed by a lady. Such kind of initiatives has enable the local community to come together for more meaningful enriching experience. This could be also translated as Endogenous Tourism Project (ETP) which we shall deal more in the challenges aspects of CBT initiatives as follows:

Challenges:

It is a challenge to emphasise on the importance of the women (Pukreila) especially to break the traditional social norms as growth engine of CBT initiatives. To make the CBT initiatives more successful women themselves can form a Village Tourism Committee (VTC) comprising of only women as we called Pukreila including all the girls to properly initiate CBT related activities in the community development processes. In the post independence continuosly an effort are being made to find a balance between tradition and globalisation so that this pose a serious question with respect and sustainability as well. Despite living in abundance of resources, the tribal population has not been able to capitalize on its natural bounty due o lack education and training which again brings us back to the vicious circle of external ownership and internal leakages. Therefore, the right mix of agriculture and tourism based activities can actually be an effective counter solution as well. Based on this concept, the paper intends to promote Pukreila because as a man's goal is to achieve and rule, a woman's goal is to achieve and live with peace and comforts. A sustainable community development is the prime objective of CBT initiative in which Women/Pukreila can take the task alongside the policy planners in the tourism Industry. Some of the challenging factors may be analyse to understand CBT initiatives more deeply.

- ◈ Cohesive Marketing that reflects on Provincial Territorial Realities:

India's cultural, geographical and language landscape makes the country a highly appealing tourist destination. Diversity is the major differentiating characteristics and capitalizing on it must become a tourism planning priority. The level of maturity in tourism varies among different states or territories or villages. While some are emerging destinations, other areas are better established with thriving tourism businesses and yet some areas are still yet to explore its potentiality. Thus product development and marketing opportunities vary among rural and urban areas. However, there is the need to keep developing collaborative approaches to increase the cohesion, effectiveness and efficiency of national initiatives while recognising the different needs of all provinces and territories.. Strengthening the collaboration of tourism marketing between the different communities and he world tourism Corporation will serve better coordinate existing initiatives and will improve their complimentarily, potentially leading to innovative partners. It needs Research initiative to identify growth opportunities for all territories and improve overall marketing strategies to capitalize on new emerging opportunities both domestically and internationally.

Attracting and Retaining a Workforce:

The tourism labour market is characterised as a seasonal, fragmental, multi – faceted service industry. The seasonal nature of tourism industry is contributing to the development of dual labour markets, comprise of core workers and peripheral ones.

In light of potential labour shortages, it is important to enhance the quality of jobs in the Tourism Industry and facilitates new entry of those who are under-represented in the labour force. It needs to study the various challenges other countries are doing, address the grievances. eg; OCED(organisation for Economic operation and development) are taking efforts to enhance the employability of foreign worker. So that it can redress how the host community can adjust the current immigration policies to better reflects the Tourism Industry's needs. It needs wide range of long term career opportunities and prospects that tourism offers, attractions, hotel, airlines, auto rental and entertainment are few areas that could offer long term career.

Industry in Tourism Infrastructure:

Enjoyment and success of tourism experience needs public infrastructure. All Govt. should work collaboratively. Significance of tourism interests in infrastructure project must continue to be communicated to the various jurisdictions responsible for infrastructure development.Those preservation of museums, cultural institutions, heritage sites and parks are examples.

Ensuring Efficient Transportation System:

The vast diversity and diverse geography poses an ongoing transportation challenges for cost initiatives. Recent shift and growth in the low cost career segment of the airline industry is helping the domestic tourism market with flexible price structure. So that it can attract more people to travel with affordable accesses for many pioneers countries that were otherwise considered too costly to serve.

Thus, there is need to seek opportunities to ensure accessibility, affordability, affordability and service quality by a liberalized International Air policy so that tourists entry into the host community is not impeded. Example, A liberalization of open Skies bilateral agreement between Canada and USA is one such example. Tourism should be initiated with the help of broad based input that involves all stake holders, including the community where development is taking place. Education and training programmes should be conducted to improve and manage the heritage and natural resources should be established.

The Endogenous Tourism Project(ETP) which is a joint project of Govt. of India- A Ministry of Tourism and United Nations Development Programme (GOI-UNDP) to support CBT initiatives for sustainable livelihood opportunities among low income communities is one common example in the context of development and social justice, ethics, sustainable human development, elimination of poverty, addressing inequalities and inequities. The study of Equations reveals that when women were empowered in decision making through tourism studies and allowed to take greater responsibility and role in the midst of the traditional and conservative societies it challenges the superior role creating tensions. However in most of the tribal dominated areas like Chhatisgarh, Nagaland and even Manipur women takes a leadership role in implementing various projects under CBT initiatives. In Sikkim, Raghurajpur near Orissa-Puri the Village Tourism Committee is completely devoid of Women in any form of decision making(Equations). Against this backdrop the paper intends to mobilise the participation of women as Pukreila for community development. Pukreila can be promoted as a new venture in CBT initiatives for stronger capacity building, enhancing skills and management in various projects of ETP. Setting them free from the bondage of male dictatorship and dominancy by given them freedom to exercise their potentiality will enable the tourism go a long way in the modern era where globalization is gaining its recognition world over.

To make CBT initiatives more successful it should ensure that the planning process are transparent, accountable and participatory taking into account the views, aspirations, experiences realities and concerns about the tourism's benefits and impacts particularly the impacts on local communities. Tourism plan model need to look into the local dynamics in terms of their social infrastructure capital of the local context as well as the political realities into account especially the environmental, social, cultural and economic.CBT initiative should be initiated not for exploitation but for sustainable tourism

Conclusion:

With world increasingly coming into the grip of sustainability driven frame of mind, empowering small and rural communities, enabling them to preserve their traditional lifestyles is the baseline of every long term growth strategy. Thus the policy time frame from bottom-top rather than from top-bottom would prove beneficial for inclusive growth development. The paper therefore suggest that Pukreila can play the part as key factor to the attainment of the goal in a way that will be both acceptable and adaptable sustainable CBT initiatives. Whereas the power of man lies in ruling the whole universe under his thumb a woman's power lies in saving the whole world with love and care for the whole community. The present paper therefore suggest that definitely CBT initiatives can be taken as a good indicator alongside the Pukreila as the catalyst of growth engine in tourism industry, not a yardstick for few individuals but for the whole communities. Forming of Village Tourism Committee (VTC)may prove effective. The study under the present findings conducted reveals that CBT initiatives which involves more women participation excels more successfully than those which has lesser women involvement in community development programmes.

References

Equations,(2009);'Nature,Markets,Tourism':Exploring Toutism'claimsto Conservation in India.

Equations (2010);'Envisioning Tourism in India'

Frania Kanara Zygadlo, A.M.(2003); Maori Tourism Concepts, Characteristics and definition. Lincoln University.

Harorld Goodwin &Rosa Santilli,(2009)' Community = Based Tourism: A Success? ICRT occasional paper 11.

Mann, M,(2000); 'The Community Tourism Guide Earth Scan:18

Strategic Initiative &Govt. Advisory (SIGA)Team(2012);'Emerging Dimensions & New Products in Indigenous Tourism'

Stephen Angkang- Hao(Tangkhul) Customary Laws,199,Imphal.

Wheeler,B,(1992)'Is Progressive Tourism Appropriate? Tourism Management vol.-5 (Wikipedia).

WTO,(2006) "Poverty Alleviation through Tourism' A compilation of good practices WTO. retrieved 2014.

.(www.ic.gc.ca/..//00 040;Challenges &opportunities facing Canada's Tourism Industry.

Y.K Shimray (Manuscript);-Tangkhul Cultural Life.

Zehol,Lucy(1998); 'Women in Naga Society' a Regency Publications, New Delhi.

Imphal Free press;19th-3rd March 2009, Imphal Manipur.

The Sangai Express;19th-3rd March 2009 Imphal Manipur

SHIMLA: A STUDY OF THE CHANGE IN PREFERENCES FROM TRADITIONAL TO MODERN FOOD HABITS OF THE LOCAL COMMUNITY

Parikshit Sharma

Research Scholar, SOTHSSM, IGNOU & Assistant Professor, SoH&T, Bahra University

parikshitsharma@live.com

Pallavi Thakur

Assistant Professor, SoH&T, Bahra University

Priya Sharma

Lecturer, IHM Kufri, Shimla

Abstract

"Dev Bhoomi Himachal", is the apt name coined for Himachal Pradesh, being the land of gods, goddesses and local deities governing the local life and customs of the people in the state. The state has varied culture, climatic zones, demography and geography. The people here are down to earth and helping, promoting the tagline of tourism, "AtithiDevoBhava" to its core. With its varied culture, flora and fauna, food is an integral part of the state. The North Indian food is mostly popular with the food from Punjab, Haryana and Jammu & Kashmir. The food from Himachal Pradesh has not been popularized, with only a few cookbooks and researches done in this area. Himachal Pradesh has a rich cultural heritage and gastronomy. The study examines the eating habits of people in Shimla, the state capital. The prime focus is on the liking of the people for the traditional versus modern food, dining out habits, preferred dining outlets, and cooking styles preferred. This paper is an attempt to explore various aspects of the eating habits of people in Shimla. Participatory interview, with structured questionnaire were conducted with 150 respondents (households) of Shimla using simple random sampling technique.

Key words: Food Habits, Shimla people, Traditional, Modern, Food.

Introduction

Himachal Pradesh,predominantly a part of the Punjab State, came into existence as a full-fledged state on 25th January, 1971, being the 18th state of the Indian republic. Since then, it has been flourishing with its agrarian economy. With a territorial spread of 55,670 km2, it shares its boundaries with Jammu and Kashmir on the north, Punjab on the west and south-west, Haryana and Uttarakhand on the south-east and by the Tibet Autonomous Region on the east.

With the third fastest growing economy, it ranks fourth in the list of highest per capita income of Indian states.

Agriculture, Tourism, and Hydroelectric power generation are the three dominant sources of the state's economy. The contribution of agriculture is approximately 45% to the net state domestic product. It is the main source of income as well as employment in Himachal. About 93% of the state population depends directly upon agriculture.

The regular diet of Himachalis is quite similar as compared to the rest of north India but bears it'sexclusiveness for its taste and ingredients used. Having lentil, vegetables and non – vegetarian dishes as the main food, it is accompanied with the roti (breads) made of available flours like wheat, maize and barley along with the rice variations. Some of the specialties of the Himachali cuisine include Madra, Maahni, Bhaat, Mitha,Bhujju, Saag, Palda, Redhu, chamba chuk, siddu/bathooru, chutney, Wadi, khatti dal, laute, poode, kachauri, etc.

With the above facts in view, an attempt has been made in this research paper toinvestigate the eating/food habits of the people of Shimla.

Objectives of Research

This research focuses on exploring the food habits of people in Shimla, which includes: -

1. Their liking for Traditional vs.Modern food,
2. Dining out habits,
3. Preferred dining outlets, and
4. Cooking styles preferred.

Literature Review

In the research conducted by RituAnand on "Determinants impacting the consumers food choice withreference to fast food consumption in India" it was understood that the key elements laying the impact on the consumers food choice were passion for dining out, socialize, ambience and the taste. In a study conducted inthe year 2007 on "Feeding the family in India: An approach to household food consumption" by MadhuNagla, it was discovered that at the household level's consumption pattern is shifting, green leafyvegetable are often excluded from the diet because of time consumed during the preparation process, viz. cleaning, washing, chopping, and finally, the cooking. The method of preparation and cooking of food is alsochanging with the advances in the method, equipment, fuel used."The Indian Cuisine" Krishna Gopal Dubey (2011) highlights in his book the different aspects of Indian cuisine and the basic features of the Indian cooking. Indian History has a great influence on cuisine of country from the Mughals, British, and Portugueseas they have introduced their own cooking styles and range of ingredients. With an impact by the westerners, the basic meal still consists of lentils, vegetables, pickles, chutneys, rice, bread,and the non – vegetarian delights. Even with so much of the advancements, people in India like relishing their food with hands and the meals are generally brought to an end with a sweet dish, pan or nuts and tea to wash the palate.

Research Methodology:

The paper has qualitative as well as quantitative aspects of research. Primary and secondary data have been gathered havingresponse from Participatory interviews and structuredquestionnaire from 150 respondents (households of Shimla) on random basis. Secondary data has been collected from books, journals, magazines available.

Analysis:

Table 1.1

Type of Food Prefered

FOOD TYPE	PREFERED BY (OUT OF 150)	PERCENTAGE (%)
Traditional Food	41	27.33 %
Modern Food	109	72.66 %

Figure 1.1

Type of Food Prefered Percentage

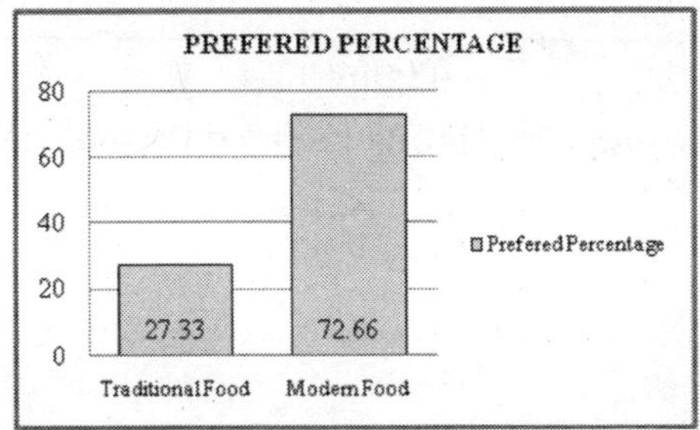

As per the survey, with a sample size of 150 residents of Shimla for their preference of food type between Traditional and Modern food, it was found that only 27.33 percentpreferred traditional food, whereas, 72.66 percent of the population surveyed showed their likings towards the Modern food types. Therefore, it may be asserted that the there is a paradigm shift in the liking of the population from traditional to modern food. The reason may be presumed to be: -

1. The preparation time required for the modern food is quite less as compared to the traditional food preparations on routine basis.
2. The change of palate over the years has shifted from traditional to the modern day food. The reason for which is presumed by the researcher to be the shift in tastes and liking of the next generation from the previous generation.
3. The advertisement plays a major role.
4. Easy and door – to door availability of the cooked food.
5. Lifestyle changes

Table 1.2

Dining out Habits

DINING OUT HABITS	PREFERED BY (out of 150)	PERCENTAGE (%)
ONCE A WEEK	99	66
TWICE A WEEK	27	18
THRICE A WEEK	19	12.66
MORE THAN THREE TIMES	5	3.34

Figure 1.2

Dining Out Habits Prefered Percentage

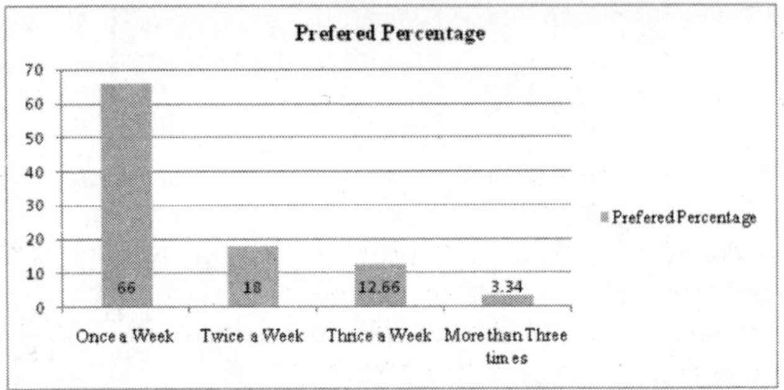

According to the survey conducted, 66% of the total population preferred to dine out once a week, 18 % preferred twice a week, 12.66% preferred eating out thrice a week and only 3.34 % were interested in having their food more than three times outside their routine.

The possible reasons for this may be:-

1. Increase in the Discretionary Income (Average Spending Power of the population).
2. Proximity of the restaurants/ dhabas/ hotels.
3. Lifestyle factor (Hectic schedule, Working spouse, Odd shift timings)
4. Status – cum – Prestige factors

Table 1.3

PREFERED FOOD OUTLETS

Preference	PREFERED BY (OUT OF 150)	PERCENTAGE (%)
RESTAURANT / HOTELS	30	20
DHABA	25	16.67
FAST FOOD OUTLETS	45	30
HOME	50	33.33

Figure 1.3

Prefered Percentage for Food Outlets

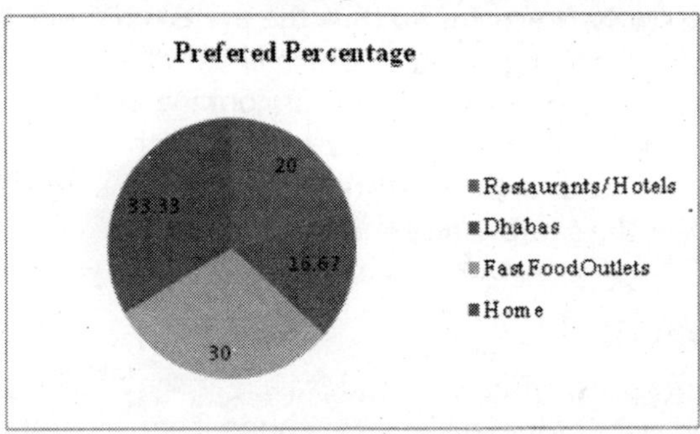

As the study indicates, people of Shimla preferred eating at home with 33.33% of the total population, Fast food outlets come second to home with 30 %, followed by Restaurant/ Hotel and Dhaba, with 20 and 16.67 % respectively.

Table 1.4

Prefered Method of Cooking

Preference	PREFERED BY (OUT OF 150)	PERCENTAGE (%)
Traditional	30	20
Modern	80	53.34
Combination of both	40	26.66

Figure 1.4

Prefered Percentage For Method Of Cooking

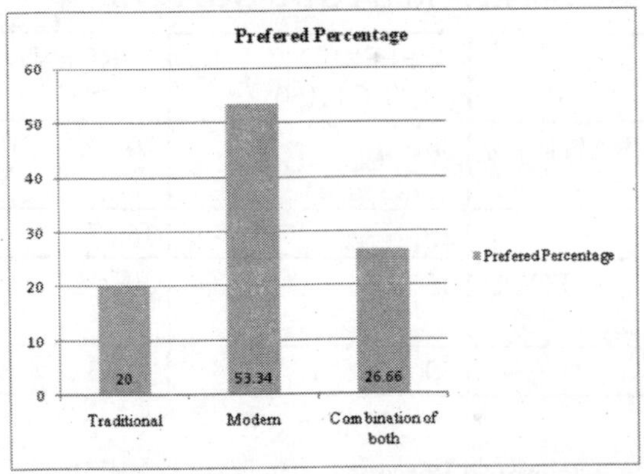

As per the study, it was found that, the preferred mode of cooking is the modern cooking method, which is 53.34% of the total sample size. The second preferred mode of cooking is the combination of both, traditional and modern methods with 26.66%. The least preferred method is the Traditional method of cooking having only 20 % of the sample response.

Conclusion

Over the decades, Himachal Pradesh has arisen as an economically developed state of India, since Statehood from 25th January, 1971. Since then, Himachal is growing at a very fast pace with its deep roots in its culture and the agrarian economy. Himachali cuisine has awide variety of food making it charming and a matter of delight for the residents.

Shimla, being the capital, has different people and is inhabited by people from different parts of the State as well as the Nation. The food culture is also varied. The residents prefer Traditional as well as the modern food, with more inclination towards the modern food. The possible reasons for this shift from the traditional to modern could be:-

1. The preparation time required for the modern food is quite less as compared to the traditional food preparations on routine basis.
2. The change of palate over the years has shifted from traditional to the modern day food. The reason for which is presumed by the researcher to be the shift in tastes and liking of the next generation from the previous generation.
3. The advertisement plays a major role.
4. Easy and door – to door availability of the cooked food.
5. Lifestyle changes

In lieu of this, the dining out habits has also shifted from eating at home to eating out in restaurants/ hotels, dhabas and others. The possible reasons for this may be:-

1. Increase in the Discretionary Income (Average Spending Power of the population).
2. Proximity of the restaurants/ dhabas/ hotels.
3. Lifestyle factor (Hectic schedule, Working spouse, Odd shift timings)
4. Status – cum – Prestige factors

In comparison of the modern and traditional cooking methods, it was found that the majority of the population has an inclination towards the modern methods of cooking food with 53.34% as compared to the traditional method of 20%. The reasons are:-

1. Convenience of cooking
2. Less time and labor intensive
3. Availability of equipment's and raw material

Therefore, it may be concluded that the people have shifted their likings from the traditional to the modern food and cooking methods due to the non-availability of the time required for the preparation of the food. The change has also been registered due to the Life style changes and the duality of the income in the households.

Recommendations

With the above study and the findings, the conclusions thus made, it may be recommended that: -

1. The State Tourism Department must take more initiatives to promote the traditional food in order to keep its sanctity and the taste in the palate of the people.
2. The locals of Shimla must devote time in order to keep their ancestral wealth intact by cooking the traditional food using the traditional methods wherever possible.

References

Malik G., Kadyan A., Balyan V. (2013): "Food Habits of people in Haryana", International Journal of Research in IT & Management, Vol. 3, Issue 7, pp. 16-21.

Anand, Ritu. "A study of determinants impacting consumers food choice with referenceto the fast food consumption in India", Society and Business Review, Vol. 6,pp. 176-187.

Dubey, Krishna Gopal.(2007), "The Indian Cuisine", ISBN- 978-81-203-4170-8

Nagla, Madhu.(2007), "Feeding the family in India: An approach to household foodconsumption", International Journal of Consumer Studies, Vol.31, Issue 3, pp. 295-302

Nagla, Madhu.(2011), "Leisure, Food and Health: Practices and Attitudes of rural andurban people in India", World Leisure Journal, Vol. 47, pp. 24-31.

G. Nanda, P. Vijeta (2010): Vyanjan, IHM Kufri, Shimla Websites of Himachal Pradesh Tourism Development Corporation and other blogs were also referred to, during the literature review.

DARGAH FOR TOURIST'S CONSUMPTION: A STUDY

Sandeep Walia
Assistant Professor
Maharaja Agrasen University, Baddi, Himachal Pradesh.
sndp.walia551@gmail.com
S.A. Rizwan
Assistant Professor
UIHMT, Panjab University, Chandigarh
syedahmadrizwan@gmail.com

Abstract

The paper tries to look into the monastic order in Islam. This monastic order has become prevalent as Sufism and has ritualised to an extent where it can be offered as a product in the tourism market. This paper attempts to visit these dargahs from an eye of a tourist product developer and propose the offering of dargahs as a tourists product and rate it in the market for the global tourists.

Keywords: Islam, Sufism, Dargahs, Wellness, Spirituality.

Introduction

Islam like Christianity developed its monastic order later and saints the underlying basis, of which is the mystic interpretation of the religious life known as Sufism. Sufism can be described as the interiorization and intensification of Islamic faith and practice.

The original sense of 'Sufi' seems to have been 'one who wears wool' because in the eight century word was applied to muslims whose ascetic inclination led them to wear coarse and uncomfortable woollen garments. Gradually it came to designate a group who differentiated themselves from others by emphasis on certain 'sunnahs' or traditional way and life of prophet. By the ninth century of gerund form 'tasawwu' literally 'being a Sufi' or 'Sufism' was adopted. (Badlick 1989).

Sufi is described the great Muslims achieved the goal of human life, nearness to God and their typical genre was hagiography, which aims at bringing out the extraordinary human qualities of those who achieve divine nearness. Muslim opponents of Sufism have been anxious to show that Sufism is a distortion of Islam, and they have happily seized on any opportunity to associated Sufism with unbelief and moral laxity (Carl 1985).

Given the difficulty of providing an exact definition of Sufism, it is not easy to discern, which muslims have been Sufis, and which have not. Being a Sufi certainly has nothing to do with the Suuni/ Shi'i split nor with the schools of jurisprudence. It has no special connection with geography, though it has played a greater role in some locations than in others. There is no necessary correlation with family. Both men and (less commonly) women become Sufis, and even children participate in Sufi ritual activities, though they are seldom accepted as full-fledged members before puberty Sufism has nothing to do with social class, although some Sufi organizations may be more or less class specific.

Ajmer's Dargah: Chishti's Epitome in India

The oldest of the darwish fraternities in India is the Chishti order, which traces its origin to Khwajah Abu Abdal Chisti, who died A.D. 966. It was introduced into India by Khwajah Muin-ud-Din Chisti, of Sistan, a southern district of Afghanistan, where he was born A.D.1142.

He in 1192 A.D. with the army of Shihab-du-Din Ghuri came to Delhi, where he stayed for a time. At the age of fifty-two year (A.D.1195), he went to Ajmer, which henceforth became his permanent residence, until his death in A.D.1236. (Jarret 1984).

His tomb, in the famous dargah of the Khwajah Sahib, Ajmir, is the center of attraction for tens of thousands of Muslims and even

Hindus, who annually visit the city on the occasion of the 'urs' or festival, which celebrates the anniversary of the death of the saint. On this occasion two enormous kettles are filled with rice, at the expense of wealthy Muslims who thereby seek to win merit. The contents are distributed in portions to any of the people present who may desire some. In connection with the dargah mosque, which was built by Akbar, there is a flourishing madrasah. Akbar's connexion with the Chisti tomb of Ajmer forms a very important chapter in the history of the life of the Emperor as well as that of the tomb connexion with his campaign against Chittor, and a view related to birth of Jahangir in 1567 A.D. (Douglas 1893).

The spiritual descendants of Khwajah Mu in-du-Din Chisti have been among the most famous saints of India.

The most noted of the above list of Chisti saints would include Khwajaj Qutb-ud-Din, Bakhtyar Kaki, of Ush, near Baghdad, who is buried near the Qutub Minar, at Delhi for whom, it is said this great column was named.

Shaykh Farid-ud-din Bhakarganj, better known as Baba Farid, whom died in A.D. 1265, and whose tomb is at Pak Pattan, in the Punjab is known throughout India. The crowd that each year attends his urs on the fifth of the month of Muharram is enormous, and includes Hindus as well as Muslims. He was succeeded by two famous disciples. Hadrat Nizarm-ud-Din Awliya, of Delhi and Hazrat Makhdum Ala-ud-Din Ali Ahmad Sabir.

Nizam-ud-Din Awliya, whose name was Muhammad bin Ahmad bin Daniyal al-Bukhari, was native of Budaun, U.P., where he was born in A.D. 1238, was nominated by Baba Farid to be his khalifah (successor) when he was only twenty years of age, seven years before the death of Fariduddin.

The most noted of his disciples were the poets Amir Khusru and Amir Hasan Dihlawi, and the historian Diya-ud-Din Barani. He died in the year A.D. 1325 and his tomb in the Delhi, surrounded a large mausoleum is still visited by devout pilgrims form near and far.

Hadrat Makhdum Ala-ud-Din Ali Ahmad Sabir, the second disciple of Farid-ud-Din who became his successor, likewise acquired a great reputation for piety before his death in A.D. 1291. His tomb is just north of Rurki, at a spot called Piran Kalir, where there is a large gathering every year on the occasion of the saint's 'urs'. His followers are called Sabiris.

Nizam-ud-Din Awliya left as his khalifah Nasir-ud-Din Muhammad, the Lamp of Delhi (Chirag-i-Dihli), who died in A.D. 1356. One of the most important of Chishti saints was Shaykh Salim chishti. He exerted a potent influence in the lives of the Mughal emperors and the royal families of his time. The emperor Jahangir was born in his house, and the saint himself lies buried in a beautiful tomb at Fatehpur Sikri. The followers of the saint, Nizam-ud-Din Awliya, and his successors are called Nizamis.

Towards the close of 18th century a revival of the order throughout the Punjab and Sind was led by Khwajah Nur Muhammad Qiblah-i-Alam, who was by ancestry a Rajput, and not of Sayyid origin, as had been the case of the former great leaders of the fraternity. Therefore, 'it would seem that in a sense the modern rise of the Chishti sect marks an indigenous revival of Islam, under religious leaders of local tribes, instead of the older Sayyid families'. (Rose, 1920).

The names of titles given to the holy men of the religious orders, such as Sabir and Shakarganj and so on, are very interesting in the matter of their origin.

It will be noted that the name usually reveals some special spiritual characteristic, or some special ability. The title given to Ala-ud-Din Ali Ahmad is, thus, explained in the Gular Sabiri: 'One day Baba Farid, 'Ali Ahmad's spiritual director and material uncle, bade him to give food and alms on his behalf to the poor. This he did, and, though stationed at the kitchen (langar khanah) night and day, he did not quit it to take his food at his own house. As he got weaker day by day, mother asked him the reason and he replied that he had taken no food for several days as his leader's orders bade him to distribute it to others, but did not authorize him to take any himself. Also as he required to be present at the kitchen, he could not leave it. For this he received the name Sabir (the patient one)'. (Yasin 1910).

Mystic Experience or Modified Wellness

Wellness is not all about body but encompasses spiritual health too. What we anticipate in our destinations in not holiness or divine visions, but something even more miraculous – the opportunity to feel different from the way we feel at home. It is as if the act of traveling to a certain place in the world entitles us to feel happier and more alive (Chaline 2002 : 67).

Wellness can be defined in various ways. The concept of 'wellness is relatively young and it was coursed by Dr. H.L. Dunn (1961) who combined 'well being' and 'fitness' and promoted it in a variety of settings. Sweeney and Witiner (1991) saw wellness as an interplay between sex life tasks: spirituality, self-direction, work, leisure, love and friendship and seven life forces: family, community, religion, education, government, media and business/industry.

The two key features of wellness are personal authenticity and transcendence. Islamic Sufism has to be delved into to understand the concept and relate it. One more support that dargah has garnered over a period of time is that unlike other Islamic products for example masjid is for Muslims, but a dargah is open for all (Afsar quoted in Sharma 2012). One of the features that would attract dargahs as a potential product is that it is synonymous with unity where people from all faith visit it (Burman 2002).

The Pir/Sufi/Holy man buried in the dargah is considered to have immense power. Anthropologist has compared it to peripatetic hindu ascetics. The figure of the saint may be highly ambiguous and locals fear an irrational outbreak of his anger. There is obscurity hovering over many a saint which can be a pull factor. They are considered as carriers of qualities that are not genuine to normal residents of this world and are often excessive and inassimilable to instrument usage. The element of existence of invisible and extraordinary forces is believed to manifest themselves at such sites. The dargahs are products of collective expectations and hopes by local population that seeks help in everyday matters and protection from harm (Deces 2011).

Understood as Islam's life-giving core Sufism is co–extensive with Islam. Wherever there have been Muslims, there have been Sufis. If there was no phenomenon called 'Sufism' at the time of the Prophet, neither was there anything called 'fiqh' or 'kalam' in the later senses of these terms. All these names that came to be applied to various dimensions of Islam after the tradition became diversified and elaborated. If one wants to call the Sufi dimension 'mysticism' then one needs an exceedingly broad description of the role that mysticism plays in religion, such as that provided by Louis Dupre, who writes that religions 'retain their vitality only as long as their members continue to believe in a transcendent reality with which they can in some way communicate by direct experience') DŪPRE (1987).

In order to describe the psychological accompaniments of these two emphases, the Sufis offer various sets of terms, such as 'intoxication' (sukr) and 'sobriety' (sahw) or 'annihilation' (fana') and 'subsistence' (baqa'). Intoxication follows upon being overcome by the presence of God: the Sufi sees God in all things and loses the ability to discriminate among creatures. Intoxication is associated with intimacy (uns) the sense of God's loving nearness, and this in turn is associated with the divine names that assert that God is close and caring. Sobriety is connected with awe (haybah) the sense that God is majestic, mighty, wrathful and distant, far beyond the petty concerns of human beings. God's distance and aloofness allow for a clear view of the difference between servant and Lord, but his nearness blinds the discerning powers of reason. Perfect vision of the nature of things necessitates a balance between reason and imaginal unveiling.

Dargah and Internet

The newest technology in the marketing of the dargah is the marketing of the dargah on the internet. The websites have been classified into three categories:

1) Website for/by tourists which promote dargah as an important historical site which tourist should visit.
2) Websites aimed at religious travellers or pilgrims
3) Religious or philosophical sites that mention the dargah in a religious context.

These sites have their specific objectives. Tourism websites promote and reflect on the dargah as an important historical and cultural site. Religious and philosophical websites are primarily interested in sharing their religious beliefs and practices. The categories overlap and do not have watertight objectives (Henderson and Weisgrau 2007). Among all these the travel websites outnumber those that attempt to record or analyse. They are frequently visited due to the secular approach that they follow.

THE STUDY

A questionnaire based study was conducted at Ajmer, a major dargah destination of India. The sample size comprised of International passengers and due to visit of lesser number of tourist only a sample size of '30' (thirty) tourist could be attained. It was a supervised, self administered survey. Structured questionnaire was used and survey was based on random sampling basis.

The sample consisted of 40 per cent women and 60 per cent men below 25 years of age, 70 per cent between 25 and 50 years of age and 10 per cent above 50 years. To gauge their financial condition an indirect way of judging their spending capabilities was tried to be judged but most of the visitors were sceptical in disclosing their annual income. The maximum respondents were from the European market.

TABLE4.1

On a Scale of 10 Rate Dargah and Mausoleum on the Basis of their Attraction (1 being minimum 10 begin maximum).

Scale	1	2	3	4	5	6	7	8	9	10
No. of Respondents	Nil	Nil	3	6	3	6	9	3	Nil	Nil

Source: Primary Survey

The response was quite encouraging 60 per cent of the respondent rated it above point 5 on a scale of ten 30 per cent of them ranking it at a point of seven. This was all the more motivating as it is at present, presented as a raw product to the tourist market.

It was further asked, what was the most attractive thing at a Dargah?. This would have helped to design marketing tools especially advertising for such a product.

TABLE 4.2

What do you find most attractive in context with Dargah and Mausoleum.

Architecture	3
Cultural significance	12

Religious significance	15
Spiritual significance	9
Historical significance	3
Curiosity	9
Others	-
	51

Source: Primary Survey

The sample size was same 30. But many respondents wanted to go in for more than one choice without rating their choice, as rating would have been an hindrance to the lesser educated tourist. Religious significance topped all the options standing at 29.4 per cent. Even a product for the every hungry cultural market can be offered as this option was supported by 19.9 per cent of the respondent. Curiosity element and spiritual significance fought to be next option. Architectural significance and historical significance placed them as the last option.

The host's attitude often defines the success of product and definitely has a say. The study gauged the attitude of the locals, which included the caretakers of the Dargah and people present there in the eye of the tourist.

TABLE 4.3

The Attitude of Local People at Dargah can be Best Described as

Extremely Friendly	Friendly	Casual	Hostile
NIL	9	18	3

Source: Primary Survey

60 per cent of the tourist found it casual. Neither were they welcomed nor feel they were unwelcomed. Rather their presence was ineffective on the host's behavior and there wasn't any special behavioral change or any other thing significant to be noted. 30 per cent of the tourist found it friendly. These tourists were of Middle East origin and South Asian origin probably their understanding of the atmosphere helped them to enjoy a friendly interaction 10 per cent found it to be hostile. These were generally youngsters not very properly dressed as on eastern standards.

To assess their level of participation it was seen whether they participated and performed the rituals.

TABLE 4.4

Did you Made Any wish or performed any Ritual.

YES	18
NO	12
Total	30

Source: Primary Survey.

60 per cent of the tourist performed a ritual 40 per cent replied in negative. Among the 40 per cent some of them were not allowed to go very near to the main nucleus of the Dargah.

Tourist were asked to rate the facilities at Dargah. It was expected that at least satisfactory range can be attained as pilgrims already visit these places in hordes. Already the pilgrim and tourist, who were at extremities, were tuning themselves at a point to attain a proper fusion point where the terms could be interchangeably used. As 'tourismization' of pilgrim has started to take place and 'pilgrimization' of tourist is taking placed.

TABLE 4.5

Where Do You Rate Facilities at the Dargah.

Excellent	Good	Satisfactory	Unsatisfactory
NIL	6	18	6

Source: Primary Survey

60 per cent of the tourist found it satisfactory. Only 20 per cent found it unsatisfactory and same percentage as good. There wasn't a single respondent going in for excellent as a response.

The respondents were further probed for the motivation to Dargah.

TABLE 4.6

You visited Dargah Because

It is a part of your package	12
Due to religious reasons	9
Recommended by friends and relatives	6

To make a wish	3
Others	NI L

Source: Primary Survey

40 per cent of the visitors were visited as they bought a package which had Dargah as a package's constituent. 30 per cent visited it due to religious reasons. This option included these people also who were interested in witnessing the religious aspect. It has being proved from time in time that mouth to mouth publicity is the best mode of promotion. 20 per cent of the visitors were coaxed by their friends and relatives to visit the place. 10 per cent of the tourist had come to make a wish. There were no takers for the 'others' option.

To assess the mode of publicity which can be used to promote this product the respondent were probed to recognise the promotional element.

TABLE 4.7

First your came to know about Dargah through

Guide	News-paper	Maga-zine	Elec-tronic media	Internet	Friends	Travel Agent	Others
3	6	3	NIL	NIL	9	9	NIL

Source: Primary Survey

Options of 'Friends' and 'Travel Agents' fought to be at top slot with 30 per cent of the respondents supporting it respectively. 20 per cent were enlighted through articles in newspaper the giant mode in print media. Guides and magazines were at 10% respectively.

Economics guide the tourist's choice so the respondents were quizzed on the economic feasibility of their money spent in and around dargah.

TABLE 4.8

The Standards of Services Provided by Shops, Restaurants. In and Around Dargahs Are:

Very expensive	6
Expensive	12

Economical	9
Very Economical	3

Source: Primary Survey

40% found it expensive. 20 per cent found the services very expensive. 30 per cent found it 'economical'. The respondents were divided as much depends upon their earning capacity. This was qualitative and comparative to the salary of the respondent.

TABLE 4.9

Is This Your First Visit to a Dargah

YES	30
NO	NIL
TOTAL	30

Source: Primary Survey

All of the respondents were first time visitors. The sample remained homogeneous in this regards.

The next question asked about the problems faced by the visitors. As it was an open ended question, answers were varied lack of sanitation, congestion poor crowd management beggars, extortion, lack of clean food units and drinking water were re-occurring problem.

The first thing that tourism generally devoid cultural destinations off, authenticity Tourist's view was taken on this

TABLE 4.10

Do you Think that the Tourist Visiting a Dargah will Result in Staged Performance of Rituals.

CAN'TSAY	3
YES	3
NO	24
TOTAL	30

Source: Primary Survey

80 per cent of the tourist feel the rituals are too established to let tourism and tourist effect them 10 per cent felt that authenticity can be at stake 10 per cent of tourist were undecided and couldn't gauge and forse the effect.

Islam is generally devoid of musical instruments as discussed earlier except for Sufism Qawwalis brought in the sounds for tourist visiting the Dargah. They were asked about this also.

TABLE 4.11

Did you enjoyed the music at the Dargah

YES	12
NO	18
TOTAL	30

Source: Primary Survey

60 per cent of the visitors were not attracted by Qawwalis. Due to congestion and lingual barriers. 40 per cent of the visitors enjoyed it.

Tourist requires facilities and dargahs will not be an exception. The questions regarding facilities were an open ended one and thus, a multitude of responses were marked. The demands for guides, proper washrooms, drinking water, proper restaurants, were the most marked responds. Need for security, crowd management, proper pricing, rest rooms and special Shoe lockers for tourist were the responses that followed.

Keeping mouth to mouth publicity in mind visitors were asked whether they will recommend Dargah to fellow friends.

TABLE 4.12

Will You be Recommending the Dargahs to Your Friends and Fellow Tourists.

YES	24
NO	6
TOTAL	30

Source: Primary Survey

It was also measured whether the tourist were interested in an all Dargah circuit for their next visit. the answer was in negative being supported by 80 per cent.

TABLE 4.13

Are you Interested for an all Dargah Package for your Next Visit

YES	6
NO	24
TOTAL	30

Source: Primary Survey

The tourist saw Dargahs as an excursion point from their base again supported by 80 per cent.

TABLE 4.14

You will Consider your Visit to Dargah as

An excursion from base point	24
A place of stay	6
TOTAL	30

Source: Primary Survey.

At last tourists were asked for their recommendations. The tourist repeated their demands for facilities this time adding specific points like signage's, better communication between the caretakers and visitors.

Thus, Dargah in itself has hazy chances of becoming raison d'etre for tourist but is welcomed as a part of a package. May be the transformation may take place at a later stage where Dargahs instead of being a part of a package may become a package in itself.

Conclusion

The dargah it seems has a universal appeal as from the survey it could be seen that men and women of different age and irrespective of the fact that they are single or married visit it. On an average the dargah attracted an approval or likeness average of point six on the likert scale which is satisfactory in case a new product is formulated. There are a variety of parameters which provide attractiveness to the dargah. While designing religious significance has to be kept in mind followed by cultural attractiveness index. The tourist have been complaining of staring at places in the developing world. But in the case of dargahs the tourists found that the host population was casual which is acceptable. The tourist gets his/her space in such a scenario and has more chances to enjoy the product. Whether the tourists have to be made a part of the ritualistic practices at dargah is a decision which will vary from the perspective of every visitor. The product survive provider has to take a final call on this depending on the taste of the tourists. Already the satisfaction level with the facilities at dargah was found to be at average as tourism enters it will make way to further enhancement of comfort level with enhancement of facilities. Initially the dargah has been a serendipitous experience for the tourists and second major reason was religious. The visit to dargah may be as an add-on cultural attraction and even the primer reason for the visit in case the tourist seem religiously inclined. WOMA as a source of advertising is supported by visitors to the dargah. The travel agents to have to be targeted to promote the product. Almost all the tourist surveyed were first time traveller thus it has advantage to be marketed as a noveau product in the market. The facilities seems to be expensive and this alongwith other reasons does not put it as a preferred choice for the tourists to stay there.

Like all other spiritual and religious products dargahs will have its own set of do's and don'ts to avoid blasphemy. Various visitors have their own experiences which could be the next progression in this series of study.

References

BADLICK, J. (1998). Mystical Islam New York. NA.

BURMAN, B. R. J. J. (2012). Hindu-Muslim Syncretic Shrines and Communities. Mittal Publication. New Delhi: 125.

CARL, E. (1985). Words of Ectasy in Sufism. Albany : 117.

CHALINE,E(2002) Zen and the Art of Travel London. MQ Publications Ltd.

DECES, I.C. (2011). A Companion to the Anthropology of India. UK. John Wiley and Sons.

DOUGLAS, J. (1893). Bombay and Western India Vol 1. London : 289.

DUNN, HALBERT L. (1961): High Level Wellness. Arlington, VA: R.W. Beatty, Ltd.

DUPRE, L. (1987). Mysticism. in ELIADE, M. (Eds.) Encyclopaedia of Religion. New York. 10: 247.

HENDERSON, C.E. and WEISGRAU, M. (2007). Raj Rhapsodies. Great Britain. Antony Rowe Ltd.

JARRET, H.S. (1984). (Trans.) FAZL, A.A.A Ain-I-Akbari Persian. Calcutta. : 241.

ROSE, H.A.. (1920) A Glossary of the Tribes and Castes of Punjab Vol II 1911-1919. Lahore : 173.

SHARMA, S. (2012). Ajmer Sharif Dargah Authorities Unhappy with Filmstars. TNN July, 24. Available at http://timesofindia.indiatimes.com/entertainment/hindi/bollywood/news-interviews/Ajmer-Sharif-Dargah-authorities-unhappy-with-film-stars/articleshow/15106744.cms. Accessed on 12 May 2014.

SWEENEY, T. and WITMER, J(1991) Beyound Social Interest: Striving toward Optimal Health and Wellness. Individual Psychology. 47:527-540.

YASIN, M. (1910). Halat-i-sabiri. Moradabad.

TOURIST VIS A VIS TOUR GUIDE

Sandeep Kulshrestha

Director I/C, , Indian Institute of Tourism and Travel Management (IITTM), Ministry of Tourism, Govt. of India,

Sankul7@rediffmail.com

Saurabh Dixit

Course Chairperson- PGDM (SS) and ANO, Indian Institute of Tourism and Travel Management (IITTM), Ministry of Tourism, Govt. of India, Govindpuri,

Gwalior-474011

saurabhdixit246@gmail.com

Chandra Shekhar Barua

Indian Institute of Tourism and Travel Management (IITTM), Ministry of Tourism, Govt. of India, Govindpuri,

Gwalior-474011

csbarua003@rediffmail.com

Abstract

Tourists vis a vis tour guide is based on real time experience of authors. Paper cites meaning, role, significance of a Tour Guide. We give preference to accommodation, transport, destinations. But, we forget to enquire about tour guide. Tour guide is an important active link in any tour. It is worthful especially when you are going to have technical exposure like: people working in architecture engineering going to see a fort, temples, mosque etc.

It will give you idea about a tour guide and its role in the industry in a very basic language.

Keyword: TVP- Top Visual Priorities, Dictaphone, smart technology

Background note

Mr. Tiwari is planning to visit kashmere. He has planned his travel itinerary, accommodation and booked all segments of journey directly. He took the help of my friend working in a tourism organization. He is worried about stay and places, he is going to cover. He has been exploring places over internet and has developed good knowledge about the place. I asked my colleague (who had guiding license) – what is the worth of a guide in a tour?

Many times groups visiting Manali for Mountaineering were able to survive due to tour guides and their sense of prediction (avalanche, land slide etc.)

Contents

1. Introduction
2. Who is a tour guide?
3. What is the role of a Tour guide?
4. What is expected from a tour guide?
5. What is expected from a tour guide?
6. Do I need a Guide?
7. Tools
8. Do I need a Guide?
9. Summary

Expectations from a guide
Good attire
Good mood
Good smile
Equipped with gadgets
Ready to serve
Environment friendly
Empathetic

Tour Guide is an important person in the chain of links in tourism industry. When tourist starts from his place of living, he meets the first person who will accompany him for the whole journey. He may be a Tour escort. A tour escort may also attend him on the way. Than tourist proceed to a destination. Here, we need someone to help the tourists. The person should have knowledge about the place, specialty of language, preferably be local to that region. This person's liason with the Tour escort and expedite tour in that place. After completing, tour proceeds to other place and second person takes up the job. Things goes on in this way. The person, who is local to that each place and managing the tour at that place is a tour guide.

Who is a tour guide?

Many people ask us a very very simple question. Who is a tour guide? In other, they might have intention to ask, how could I become a tour guide? My person in my contact completed his masters in tourism and wanted to stay in the same town. He started going to travel agents with the hope to find work and became a tour guide. One gentlemen went to Delhi. He is from a tourists place. He thought of working for a reputed travel agency and one fine day visited that travel agency. But, got the chance only when there was no choice for the company except his to send him as an escort.

One gentleman left his study due to personal problem. One of his friend was a tour guide. So he found it as a good work to get money. Later, he picked up in language, and commentary. He was not able to speak in his first assignment and travel agent was annoyed.

A guide is a link between people and place

Photo: Saurabh Dixit

What is the role of a Tour guide?

I am a frequent visit to Himachal Pradesh. I find people accompanying tourists for mountaineering, trekking and they help them in tent pitching. They assist them in activity. They know local flora and fauna and knowledge of area of land slide. You must have seen Bear Gryl's prgrammes in TV. A guide is a million dollar person who saves a trekker during trouble. Many times, he is also washed away in flood (Kedarnath incidence).

Our guide at Malaysia offered us good quality key rings, mementos while transfer from Hotel to Air port. Probably, he was allowed by the travel agent and he said that these things blog to the coach driver. Let us not go to the legislative part. Here, guide is a communicator, salesman who helps us by providing mementoes in the coach itself.

Once, there was a group went to Panna from Khajuraho to see tree house and unfortunately tree house were closed. He tried to get some tea for the tourists in this forest area and ultimately arranged four logs and used these logs as Torch (Mashal) to torch for safety of the group. People reached in the mid night. But, in the feedback they mentioned that it was the best part of the tour. Guide is someone who makes your tour very interesting by using innovative ideas as in the case of Panna Tree houses.

We went to Orccha and visited palace. By the time we reached Ram Raja Mandir, it was closed and we were forced to come back after lunch in Orccha. I always feel unlucky when I thing about my Orccha tour. It was my hard luck being a devotee of Ram, I could not visit his temple even after reaching there. Guide could spoil your tour, if he is not organised. So, Guide is an organiser according to the instructions of Travel Agent or Tourists.

I went to Panna National Park. We were provided a guide to accompany us in Gypsy. He started telling about forest, trees, animals, their habits. He had one binocular and spotted animals. He gave us examples about past groups. Guide must be a subject expert. He would be able to give answer to queries raised by tourists.

A group saw a sculpture in which a lady is pointing her foot. One guide near me was explaining that she is picking thorn. My guide was telling that she is painting. It was contradictory and we raised our objection. My guide explained that see her facial expressions-she is blissful. So, she is painting. Guide must be able to justify his statements.

What is expected from a tour guide?

A tour guide must have few qualities. Tourists wear casuals during the tour or they are free to wear whatever they like and it must not be objectionable by the authority or locals living there. But, guide must have sense to wear professional attire. His dress has some meaning and helps him to get recognition as a professional.

Role of a guide
Organizer
Leader
Co-ordinator
Motivator

He must be clean and not chewing Tobacco, Paan, Gudhakhu, Supary, Gutka etc. he must know hygiene status expected in that country (tourists place). He must be clean shaved or trimmed beard. In Rajasthan you will find guides with peculiar moustache and style of suits (Jodhpuri style etc.).

Guide must wear good quality shoes. He must choose cloths suits the climate. I would not say that guide must wear tie and suit in hot summers in Khajuraho. Cloths must help him during commentary.

Guide must keep in mind culture of tourist. How to behave with them. There are many cultural differences. Something good in our culture might be wrong in some other country.

Tools

Guide also have tools to make his job successful. When you are going to forest, water fall, nature park, safari and you may come late. Carry a common torch or head mounted Torch.

Future Guides
Virtual Guide
Audio Guide
Integrated approach

Traditionally, guides were encouraging tourists to touch walls, domes in palaces to have feel of stone. But, now a days, we are environment conscious and people are requested to see from distance. A guide going to point out objects which he can not touch. Objects are at height. HE may use laser light to point the object.

Tools
Torch
Cap
Dictaphone
Pen and Paper
Mobile phone

You are going with a group and you have to leave them in lunch and again start at the same place. You may carry Dictaphone to record your commentary, questions raised by the tourists. These questions may be repeated before giving answer. Guide may play questions during lunch and answer unanswered questions after lunch. Guide may use Dictaphone as a recording device which helps them to improve guiding skills.

I was taking to my friend over telephone while on the tour. He requested to write a number. Immediately, I requested my guide to give me a pen and paper.

Once, gentlemen meet with an accident while on the tour. Guide contacted ambulance and took him to the nearest hospital. In few cities of Madhya Pradesh government started 108 service(s) for citizens and tourists. It is a multi-purpose service.

It was a nice experience when guide offered us paper napkins after a tour to palace in hot summer.

I found many guide friends keeping a smart phone with internet connectivity. They are updated with weather, public utility, important numbers related information. Even they can book a ticket using their phone and palmtop.

Do I need a Guide?

Many tourists avoid hiring a guide. Many prefer to have a person who is engaging them in story telling beside other roles as your care taker for that time, your interpreter. Guide indentifies your needs and serves you to satisfy your anxiety to the level you feel that you are again in the past (if you are at heritage site). Guide will number each and every plant if you are visiting Himalayas.

I pay good share of my expenses on transport, hotels and shopping. But, guide is the persons who create your dialogue with the monument for example Tajmahal. Why people visit a particular place again and again? I think, they find same or favourable vibrations and feel happy when they visit a particular place. Guide could help you to make you tour more blissful. Tour guide tells you about TVPs (top visual priorities) of a place. He creates interesting tales about the place and helps you make your tour memorable.

Future tour guide

When a visit a place I feel that there is good number of people working as a guide. Do I need so many people flocking around. Number does not matter. A good person having qualities and supported by supporting gadgets like: laser torch, binoculars etc. and know how to handle the situation and attract tourists by his personality (if tourists are in need of a guide) will be able to survive and work successfully in the trade.

There will be more use of smart technology in future.

Future guides will be a facilitator. There will be adoption of virtual guiding, audio guiding etc.

References

Dixit Saurabh (2012), Tourism Management- Adventure Sports, APH Publishing Corporation, New Delhi, 978-81-313-1567-5

Dixit Saurabh (2013), Introduction to Tourism, Travel and Hospitality, APH Publishing Corporation, New Delhi

Collins, B.R. (2000). Becoming a Tour Guide, Continuum International Publishing Group, Limited

TOURISM AND HOSPITALITY MARKETING

B Muniraja Sekhar

Associate Professor, K.M.M.Institute of Post Graduate Studies, Department of Management Studies, Tirupati-517502, Email:bmrajasekhar@gmail.com

K.V.S.N. Jawahar Babu

Associate Professor, Department of Tourism, Nellore, Mobile: 9440494141, Email: sudhajaahar@gmail.com

S.Ismail Basha

Assistant Professor, K.M.M.Institute of Post Graduate Studies, Department of Management Studies, Tirupati-517502, Email:sib.comp2011@gmail.com

Abstract

Tourism is travel for recreational, leisure, or business purposes, usually of a limited duration. Tourism is commonly associated with trans-national travel, but may also refer to travel to another location within the same country. The World Tourism Organization defines tourists as people "traveling to and staying in places outside their usual environment for not more than one consecutive year for leisure, business and other purposes".[1]

Hospitality Management is the study of the hospitality industry. A degree in the subject may be awarded either by a university college dedicated to the studies of hospitality management or a business school with a relevant department. Degrees in hospitality management may also be referred to as hotel management, hotel and tourism management, or hotel administration. Degrees conferred in this academic field include BA, Bachelor of Business Administration, BS, MS, MBA, and PhD. Hospitality management covers hotels, restaurants, cruise ships, amusement parks, destination marketing organizations, convention centers, and country clubs. The hospitality industry is a broad category of fields within the service industry that includes lodging, event planning, theme parks, transportation, cruise line, and additional fields within the tourism industry. The hospitality industry is a several billion dollar industry that mostly depends on the availability of leisure time and disposable income. A hospitality unit such as a restaurant, hotel, or even an amusement park consists of multiple groups such as facility maintenance, direct operations (servers, housekeepers, porters, kitchen workers, bartenders, etc.), management, marketing, and human resources. A hotel manager or hotelier is a person who holds a management position within a hotel, motel, or resort establishment. In most hotels, the title - hotel manager or hotelier, may solely be referred to the General Manager of the hotel. Hotel management titles, duties, and functions vary by hotel size, function, and company/ ownership.

Introduction

Tourism and Hospitality Management is an international, multidisciplinary, refereed (peer-reviewed) journal aiming to promote and enhance research in all fields of tourism and hospitality including travel, leisure and event management.

The journal has been published regularly since 1995, twice per year (in June and in December) by the Faculty of Tourism and Hospitality Management, Opatija, Croatia in cooperation with WIFI Institut for Economic Promotion, Austrian Economic Chamber, Vienna, Austria and T.E.I. - Alexandreion Technological Educational.

Tourism has become a popular global leisure activity. Tourism can be domestic or international, and international tourism has both incoming and outgoing implications on a country's balance of payments. Today, tourism is major source of income for many countries, and affects the economy of both the source and host countries, in some cases it is of vital importance.

Tourism suffered as a result of a strong economic slowdown of the late-2000s recession, between the second half of 2008 and the end of 2009, and the outbreak of the H1N1 influenza virus. It then slowly recovered, with international tourist arrivals surpassed the milestone 1 billion tourists globally for first time in history in 2012. International tourism receipts (the travel item of the balance of payments) grew to US$1.03 trillion (€740 billion) in 2011, corresponding to an increase in real terms of 3.8% from 2010. In 2012, China became the largest spender in international tourism globally with US$102 billion, surpassing Germany and United States. China and emerging markets significantly increase their spending over the past decade, with Russia and Brazil as noteworthy examples.

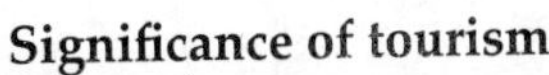

Significance of tourism

Strand orb chairs on Usedom Island, Germany. Not only the service sector grows thanks to tourism, but also local manufacturers (like those producing the strandkorb), retailers, the real estate sector and the general image of a location can benefit a lot.

Tourism is an important, even vital, source of income for many countries. Its importance was recognized in the Manila Declaration on World Tourism of 1980 as "an activity essential to the life of nations because of its direct effects on the social, cultural, educational, and economic sectors of national societies and on their international relations."

Tourism brings in large amounts of income into a local economy in the form of payment for goods and services needed by tourists, accounting for 30% of the world's trade of services, and 6% of overall exports of goods and services. It also creates opportunities for employment in the service sector of the economy associated with tourism.

The service industries which benefit from tourism include transportation services, such as airlines, cruise ships, and taxicabs; hospitality services, such as accommodations, including hotels and resorts; and entertainment venues, such as amusement parks, casinos, shopping malls, music venues, and theatres. This is in addition to goods bought by tourists, including souvenirs, clothing and other supplies.

Hospitality Marketing

Hospitality marketing is unique because it deals with the tangible product, like a bed in the hotel or food in the restaurant, but it also deals with the intangible aspects of the hospitality and tourism industry. It is about the experience in a trip and social status it brings eating in a fine-dining restaurant. Hospitality marketing is very critical in the success of any hospitality and tourism product, organization and tourist destination. Proper marketing effort promotes a product or service that fills the needs and wants of the consumers and at the same time, bring profits to the organization or country that features it.

Content of the Student Manual

There are three important aspects associated with hospitality marketing: 1) services marketing, 2) the marketing plan, and 3) electronic marketing. Specifically, this manual contains the following contents:

Services Marketing

1. The marketing concept
2. Product marketing vs. services marketing

The Marketing Plan

1. Analyzing marketing opportunities and challenges: The macro-environment

2. Analyzing your markets: Consumer vs. business markets
3. Market segmentation
4. Conducting market research
5. Marketing mix
6. The promotional mix

Electronic Marketing

1. Internet and database marketing

Services Marketing

The Marketing Concept

This topic defines what marketing is and it explains the core components of the marketing concept. Are you familiar with the word 'marketing'? How would you explain 'marketing' to your teachers or classmates? Many students think of marketing as promotion, advertising, sales, and/or making profit per se, but I can assure you that these images only partially represent what marketing is. According to the definition provided by the American Marketing Association (2008), marketing refers to "an organizational function and a set of processes for creating, communicating, and delivering value to customers and for managing customer relationships in ways that benefit the organization and its stakeholders." In essence, marketing is a consumer-oriented philosophy or way of doing business; companies that are consumer-oriented will put consumers' needs and wants on their top priority. From this perspective, the ultimate goal of marketing is therefore to create and retain profitable customers by satisfying their demands. It is worth noting that the goal of retaining profitable customers is particularly challenging in Asia including Hong Kong. This is because people in this region tend to be more group-oriented and the word-of-mouth effects are especially strong. Let's find out how much you understand the idea of satisfying customers' demands before we move on to address other core issues about the marketing concept. Take a look at the following questions:

1) If a chef intends to add two new items that he particularly likes to its existing menu, would you say he is applying the consumer-oriented marketing concept?

2) What if the two new items added to the menu are based on the preferences of the restaurant's current and targeted customers? Is he applying the consumer-oriented marketing concept? I hope your answer to the first question is NO because consumers are not given the priority in this instance. Similarly, employees who reject customers' requests or suggestions without giving them serious considerations are not exercising the marketing concept either. If we go back to the second question above, it is clearly a Hospitality Marketing

3) Customer-oriented practice because changes are made to the menu to specifically tailor to the customers' preferences instead of the chef's personal needs. Another important idea about the marketing concept is, companies do not aim to make profit per se; instead, they focus on generating profits by creating values to customers and satisfying their needs better than competitors. Marketers who apply the marketing concept trust that, if they put their customers first, profits will take care of themselves. One final point about the marketing concept - it is not a function that can be left to people working in the marketing department only. Successes in marketing require the involvement of employees from all levels and functional departments to serve their customers' interests. It is important that you bear all these in mind because inappropriate view of marketing will not allow your marketing efforts to come to fruition.

The Marketing Concept

Profitability

Customer's needs & wants

Integrated marketing

1) Customers' needs/ wants/ demands – the focus of the marketing concept is to satisfy customers' needs, wants, and demands;

2) Profitability – companies aim to generate profits by satisfying their customers' demands better than their competitors;

3) Integrated marketing – marketing is a concerted effort from all personnel within a company.

Product Marketing vs. Services Marketing

This topic introduces the fundamental differences between marketing products and marketing services. Discussion for the latter will be addressed specifically in the hospitality context. By now, you should know that the focus of the marketing concept is to satisfy customers' demands, and these demands can be in the form of physical products and/or services. It is common for people to refer to products as objects, devices or things and services as actions, performances or experiences. Marketing was initially developed in connection with the physical products, but with the growing interest in consumers for services today, selling services have become an increasingly important component of the marketing concept. Just to give you an idea to what extent services have affected our global economies: In Australia, Canada, France, Japan, Norway, and the United Kingdom, 60 percent or more of the gross domestic product (GDP) comes from services, and the service sector comprises of approximately 85 percent of the GDP in Hong Kong. It is important for you to know that although the core outputs for many hospitality organizations are primarily performances or experiences (i.e. services), it does not mean that absolutely no tangible elements are tied to the process. For instance, the food and beverages will be considered the tangible element we experience when dining out in a restaurant.

Conclusion

Security threats (crime, terrorist acts, etc.) are an inseparable component of tourism. There is a number of reasons why tourism is a favorite target to various criminal, terrorist, and other groups

- Connection to traffic and financial centers16;
- Connection to big business and corporations;
- Publicity;
- Big fluctuation of capital, merchandise, and people;
- Symbolizing of national cultural treasure and history.

The paper does not address all possible threats to hotel companies for the reason of lesser degree of risk prioritization or need for their detailed elaboration. We single out: vibrations, radar radiation, acoustic radiation, electromagnetic radiation, instability of electric energy supply, electric power strikes, radiation danger, chemical and biological hazard, air pollution, sea water pollution, big fires, and contagious disease epidemics. The appearance of acute respiratory syndrome SARS (the so called birds' flu) in 2003 had a direct and severe effect on whole geographic regions. The direct economic damage immediately reflected on business activities, tourism industry and touring Asia and Canada. Indirectly, hotel business on the whole was in danger due to a weaker flow of tourists into specific parts of the world. War, terrorism, and political unrests are not the only threats that can jeopardize economic conditions of tourist industry development, particularly the interests of the private sector and hotel companies. A list of assessed threats may encompass natural, technical-technological and other danger that, combined with the human factor, can have devastating effects. It is interesting to have a closer look at different scenarios of combining threats: a terrorist attack with the possibility of setting an explosive device on the evacuation rout; total lack of water in the town water supply system with using biological weapons on their water supply sources etc.

Reference

"UNWTO technical manual: Collection of Tourism Expenditure Statistics". World Tourism Organization. 1995. p. 10. Retrieved 26 March 2009.

"International tourism challenged by deteriorating global economy". UNWTO World Tourism Barometer (World Tourism Organization) 7 (1). January 2009. Retrieved 17 November 2011.

"UNWTO World Tourism Barometer Interim Update". UNWTO World Tourism Barometer (World Tourism Organization). August 2010. Retrieved 17 November 2011.

"UNWTO World Tourism Barometer". UNWTO World Tourism Barometer (World Tourism Organization) 11 (1). January 2013. Retrieved 2013-04-09.

"International tourism receipts surpass US$ 1 trillion in 2011" (Press release). UNWTO. 7 May 2012. Retrieved 15 June 2012.

"China - the new number one tourism source market in the world". World Tourism Organization. 2013-04-04. Retrieved 2013-04-09.

Griffiths, Ralph; Griffiths, G. E. (1772). "Pennant's Tour in Scotland in 17.69". The Monthly Review, Or, Literary Journal (London: Printed for R. Griffiths) 46: 150. Retrieved 23 December 2011.

Harper, Douglas. "tour (n.)". Online Etymology Dictionary. Retrieved 23 December 2011.

Theobald, William F. (1998). Global Tourism (2nd ed.). Oxford [England]: Butterworth–Heinemann. pp. 6–7. ISBN 0-7506-4022-7. OCLC 40330075.

Houlot, Arthur. (1961). Le Turisme et La Biblie. Revue l'Académie Internationale du Turisme. Monaco.

Leiper, Neil (1983). An Etimology of Tourism. Annals of Tourism Research (2). New York: Pergamon Press. Volume 10

Korstanje, M. 2007 The Origin and meaning of Tourism: Etymological study.E Review of Tourism Research. Vol 5 (5): 100-108. Texas A&M University, US

Korstanje, M. (2012). Examining the Norse mythology and the archetype of Odin: The inception of Grand Tour. Tourism, an international Interdisciplinary Journal. Vol. 60, issue 4, pp. 369-384

"Manila Declaration on World Tourism". World Tourism Conference. Manila, Philippines. 10 October 1980. pp. 1–4.

"2012 Tourism Highlights". UNWTO. June 2012. Retrieved 17 June 2012.

HERITAGE TOURISM: A STUDY ON JAIVILLAS PALACE

Shikha Sharma

Institute of Vocational Studies (MTA), H .P. University, Summer Hill, Shimla, Himachal Pradesh Email address: ssharma.shimla@ gmail.com

Introduction

Heritage Tourism is one of the oldest and fastest growing segments of the tourism industry. Cap stick 1985; Mooney-Melvin 1991 et.al).Heritage as the word signifies focuses on the historical aspect of the destination. The other aspects included are natural heritage, built heritage or intangible heritage. According to Boyd (2002), heritage tourism encompasses landscapes, exploring the cultural and natural heritages of the locals, and historic landmarks. Some focus on architecture such as churches, castles, government buildings, and so on while other focus on natural heritages likes national parks and wildlife sanctuaries. Some focus on archaeological significance and the history of the ethnic group, as in case of Canada. Australia and New Zealand focuses on natural environment and surroundings. In a tourism destinations, cultural attractions such as Museums, define the culture and Heritage tourism Product of the destinations.

Heritage tourism comprises of visiting a number of Heritage sites, monuments, like museums, aquarium, performing arts centres, archaeological digs, theatre, historical sites, monuments, castles, architectural relics, religious centres, and even zoos. From natural park to Heritage sites each has its own contribution in Heritage.

(Poria, Butler, Airey 2003).In the Rock and Roll Hall of Fame.and Museum in Cleveland, visitors can listen to numerous rock and roll classics by the mere touch of the screen .At the Bath Museum In Bath, England, Visitors can take an audio tour of facility by using the Headset the carries that carries the tour in Multiple language for visitors (Zeppel 1996).In IMAX, theatre they have focussed on becoming technological canters, using technology and cinematography to educate the young audiences. The Brooklyn Museum completed a $ 63 million improvement plan 2004, and Cincinnati's Taft Museum of Art reopened after spending $22.8 million in renovations. (Arts Business News, 2002).

Literature Review

The Cambridge Dictionary Online defined museums as "places of study, buildings where objects of historical, scientific or artistic interest are kept, preserved and exhibited". To The Museums Association, a museum is "an institution which collects documents, preserves, exhibits and interprets material evidence and associated information for the public benefit". Since 1998, this definition has changed. Museums now enable the public to explore collections for inspiration, learning and enjoyment. They are institutions that collect, safeguard and make accessible artefacts and specimens, which they hold in trust for society.

Museums cater to young, old, families, friends, schools and couples. Every artefact in the museum has some historical story behind it to recite. Museums offer unique environment and they are free-choice learning centres (Falk & Dierking, 2000). Museums are a way to connect to visitors by different linkages such as objects, information, and learning's, experiences. (Bradburne, 1998; Carr,2003a; Falk, 2004; Falk & Dierking, 1992, 2000; Hein, 1998; Hooper-Greenhill,2000; Silverman, 1995; Weil, 1997).

Museums are the places which are stocks of knowledge having a multiple role of inviting visitors to learn, wonder, and encounter (Schauble, Leinhardt & Martin, 1997, p.3). However in the present scenario there are many challenges faced by the Museums. Not only in India but across the world museums are finding tough competition in the marketplace as compared with other leisure, learning and educational providers (Falk & Dierking, 2000; Lynch et al., 2000; Mintz, 1994) within what has been called the "experience economy", defined as the wide Range of currently available educational leisure experiences (Pine & Gilmore, 1999). The demands of the "information age" have raised new questions for museums, particularly in the areas of access and authority (Cameron, 2003, 2006; Freedman, Kelly, L. (2000).

Museums like other destinations have always been tourist destinations. According to Bennett (1995) the earliest museums were founded on the basis of education for the uneducated masses. Weil(1995,p 257) defined museums as the cabinets of curiosities which are established to increase the level of public understanding , and to raise the spirit of its visitors in order to purify and raise the common taste .

Museums have always been linked to leisure, especially in the studies related to museums marketing's (Burton & Scott, 2003; Crang, 1996; Harkin, 1995;Lynch et al., 2000; Masberg & Silverman, 1996; Packer & Ballantyne, 2002; Prentice, Witt & Hamer, 1998; Ryan & Glendon, 1998; Scott & Burton, 2000; Tian, Crompton & Witt, 1996; Witcomb, 2003).Studying the motivations behind visiting museums the researchers such as (Moore, 1997; Packer, 2004; Packer & Kelly, L)found it to be leisure and entertainment.

Objectives

1. To study the Strengths, Weakness, Opportunities, Threats of Jai Villas Museum in relation to Heritage Tourism
2. To find the relationship between heritage tourism and Museums.

Jai villas Museum

The museum known as the Scindia Museum was built by Maharaja Jayajirao in 1874. It occupies 35 rooms of the Jai Villas Palace. Museum possesses some unique items such as hall carpet weaved by the convicts and it is the largest in Asia, the gold paint around the durbar hall weighing half a tonne ,250 light –bulbs, 3.5 tonne chandeliers being largest pair in the world. The most amazing items are the Belgian cut-glass furniture and stuffed tigers, ladies swimming pool, a boat, wine cabinet, silver train weighing 24 kg in totality.

The museum is a way to give a powerful boost to the culture of Madhya Pradesh .It reminds the tourist about the powerful Maratha lineage and gives insight into the lifestyle of the princely families. Museums depict the life of the princes, king, queens through the pictures, portraits of the family, trophies. Museums provide a way to see, feel and know about the things which we see in books, magazines or television. It inculcates the experience among the tourist which is not possible otherwise.

Methodology

In order to achieve the objectives of the study i.e. to identify the various strengths, weaknesses, opportunities and threats both – qualitative and quantitative techniques were applied. Literature study was done to provide background to study, presenting a total understanding and relationship between heritage tourism and Jai Villas Museum . Interviews and direct observations were used in the collection of data. Questions were also asked from the tourists and locals as well.

SWOT Analysis regarding the Museum and Tourism

Strengths

1. The Museum is operating under a clear concept i.e. the history of The Scindia family, making the museum a famous tourist attraction. It also help in making the museum an obvious tourist attraction. It serves as a major source of knowledge to have the first hand experience regarding the Scindia family and understanding the role of the family in developing Gwalior through ages.
2. The entire Jai Villas Palace is very attractive, beautiful and outstanding which incorporate in itself- museum and darbar hall.
3. It serves as a source of knowledge for the school students who find history interesting, young and old tourists who can view each and every artefact in detail.
4. The museum's location is easily approachable within the city

making it very easy to find and quite accessible. It is connected by road .

5. Most of the objects on display are unique, well maintained and accessible for visitors, though they are protected against damages.
6. The museum have lot of potential as being attractive and functional and being only the royal museum in the entire Gwalior .
7. The museum has a capability to attract a large number of tourists and capacity to cater to large number of tourists due to its well maintained state.
8. The organization of the museum is quite clear, the staffs are skilled and the political support towards its operation and mission is good.
9. The museum has a long history and tradition (especially linked to the building). It is recognised, as an important centre of data and the collection is immense. The existing relationship between tourist, locals and museums have been positive so far.
10. The museum plays a traditional role in generating awareness and is influential in generating tourism in the region due to its presence.
11. Guides are available for the tourists interested to know the historical background of the museum
12. It is easily approachable with vehicle dropping tourists in the vicinity of the museum.

Weaknesses

1. There are no activities for the tourists in the museums to perform.
2. There is lack of determination towards focussing on tourists.
3. Lack of marketing strategies and public relation strategies.
4. Lack of attracting more tourists towards museum.
5. There are no thrilling activities available in the museum.
6. The displays have only few artefacts which are of utmost amazement.

7. The area is quiet big but it has not been fully and properly utilized.
8. There cannot be any bookings of the ticket through internet.
9. The museum does not have large variety of souvenirs to be sold off.
10. There is no regular bus facility to the museum.

Opportunities

1. The museum already has great potential with its rich cultural history and legacy and not much has to be done to make it more tourist-oriented.
2. The museum can be made more known to the public by it effective marketing and strategic planning in order to generate more tourists to the museum.
3. It is the only massive, royal and attractive museum in the Gwalior thus having greater and more tendency to attract more number of tourists and enthralling their experience.
4. The historical background and the history of the Scindia can be presented in a more interesting manner with the help of videos, audios, short movies, documentaries etc.
5. It can be a centre of learning and exploration for the domestic and International tourist if it is placed in that way.
6. There can be greater opportunities for more employments in and around the museum.
7. The museum already is source of income for many locals. The people benefited the most are the auto riders as they are the only major means to reach to the destination in case tourist has not hired a private vehicle.
8. The locals should be made aware and their participation should be taken into consideration to make it more popular outside the region as well.
9. Large number of tourist already visit Jai Villas and it has capacity to cater to more number of tourists.
10. Belonging to the royal family of Gwalior it has the benefit of authenticity, royalness and grandeur, and no financial problems are attached to it.

Threats

1. The changes made should not be too immediate that they may have adverse effect on the museum.
2. It should not lack in strategies and proper implementation.
3. It should not merely remain a heritage place but rather different other activities should run in parallel to it.
4. It is going to face competition with other kind of thrilling activities so it should keep up with the expectations of the visitors.
5. There is risk of overcrowding of the museum on some days .proper care should be taken to increase the level of tourist but with substantial growth.
6. There should be no more construction in and around museum area.
7. Gwalior has not been able to receive as much number of tourists as it could have being a heritage city. This aspect has not been used properly because very less foreign tourist visit Gwalior city.
8. The condition of the roads is worst in Gwalior and it is becoming even worse day by day. This could be a major factor in prohibiting tourist to visit the museum.
9. The museum does not deal with live aspect of culture.
10. Other features could have been added to make the museum more popular –like dance shows, folklore, folksongs etc.
11. It should be protected against adverse climatic conditions.

Scope

There is lot of scope for further improvement as the various weaknesses can be overcome and the various opportunities can be utilized to make it a better tourist destination so that not only the national but international tourists are able to visit Gwalior. It should be marketed in extreme manner so that tourists are motivated to visit Gwalior and also the Museum. The various threats should also be overcome in order to generate better flow of the tourists and hence prove beneficial to the state as well.

Conclusion

The museums are considered as places where tourist comes to know about its culture. But with the changing time the concept of the traditional museum is changing to modern one. The museums are now considered as places which should also incorporate some fun element along with learning experiences. The museum provide the visitor respect as being a part of the same culture, choice and variety of artefacts, involvement and active and varied learning experiences, involvement and a contemporary experiences. The Jai Villas Palace also incorporates a museum in it. The museum is large, well maintained and attractive .But there are many factors which make it unique and adorable. Museums are a means of telling the stories of the past and it can be seen and felt in the present .The Jai villas Museum is also having the same storied entangled to it but here it also has some Strengths, Weaknesses, Opportunities and Threats. All these should be properly considered in order to make Jai Villas a major museum hunter's destination. Museums will always be an important part of the cultural and heritage tourism and culture and heritage cannot be separated from any place, destination, and region of India.

References

Bennett, T. (1995). The Birth of the Museum: history, theory, politics. London:Routledge

Bradburne, J. (1998). Dinosaurs and White Elephants: the Science Centre in the 21st

Century. Museum Management and Curatorship, 17(2), 119-137.

Burton, C., & Scott, C. (2003). Museums: Challenges for the 21st Century. Marketing

Management, 5(2), 56-68.

Cameron, F. (2003). Transgressing fear - engaging emotions and opinion - a case for

museums in the 21st century. Open Museum Journal, 6.

Cameron, F. (2006). Beyond Surface Representations: Museums, Edgy Topics, Civic

Responsibilities and Modes of Engagement. Open Museum Journal, 8.

Capstick, B. (1985). Museum and Tourism. International Journal of Museum Management and Curatorship, 4, 365-72.

Carr, D. (2003a). Observing Collaborations Between Libraries and Museums. Curator, 46(2),123-129.

Cash, S. (2004). New nuilding for new museum. Uk: Artworld.

Crang, M. (1996). Magic Kingdom or a Quixotic Quest for Authenticity? Annals of

Tourism Research, 23(2), 415-431.

Cook, T. (2001). Archival science and pst modernism:New formulations for old concepts. Archives and Museum Informatics, 1(1), 3-24.

Falk, J., & Dierking, L. (1992). The Museum Experience. Washington: Whalesback Books.

Falk, J., & Dierking, L. (2000). Learning from Museums: Visitor Experiences and the Making of Meaning. Walnut Creek: AltaMira Press.

Falk, J. (2004). The Director's Cut: Toward an Improved Understanding of Learning from

Museums. Science Education, 88(Supplement 1), S82-S96.

Freedman, G. (2000). The Changing Nature of Museums. Curator, 43(4), 295-306.

Harkin, M. (1995). Modernist Anthropology and Tourism of the Authentic. Annals ofTourism Research, 22(3), 650-670.

Hein, G. (1998). Learning in the Museum. London: Routledge.

Hooper-Greenhill, E. (2000). Museums and the Interpretation of Visual Culture. London:

Routledge.

Kelly, L. (2001). Developing a model of museum visiting. Paper presented at the Museums

Australia Annual Conference, Canberra.

Lynch, R., Burton, C., Scott, C., Wilson, P., & Smith, P. (2000). Leisure and Change: implications for museums in the 21st century. Sydney: Powerhouse Publishing.

Masberg, B., & Silverman, L. (1996). Visitor Experiences at Heritage Sites: A

Phenomenological Approach. Journal of Travel Research, 34(4), 20-25.

Melvin, M. (1991). Historic sites as tourist attraction harnessing the romance of the past:preservation,tourism,history. Public Historian, 2(13), 35-48.

Mintz, A. (1994). That's Edutainment! Museum News, November/ December.

Pine, B., & Gilmore, J. (1999). The Experience Economy. Museum News,March/April,45-48

Moore, K. (1997). Museums and Popular Culture. London: Cassell.

Packer, J., & Ballantyne, R. (2002). Motivational Factors and the Visitor Experience:A Comparison of Three Sites. Curator, 45(2), 183-198.

Poria, Butler, Y. R., & Airey, D. (2003). The core of heritage tourism. Annals of Tourism Research , 1(30), 238-254.

Prentice, R., Witt, S., & Hamer, C. (1998). Tourism as Experience. The Case of Heritage Parks. Annals of Tourism Research, 25(1), 1-24.

Ryan, C., & Glendon, I. (1998). Application of Leisure Motivation Scale to Tourism.Annals of Tourism Research, 25, 169-184.

Schauble, L., Leinhardt, G., & Martin, L. (1997). A Framework for Organising a Cumulative

Research Agenda in Informal Learning Contexts. Journal of Museum Education,22,3-8.

Scott, C., & Burton, C. (2000). What do we seek in our leisure? Museum National (May),26.

Silverman, L. (1995). Visitor Meaning Making in Museums for a New Age. Curator, 39(3), 161-169.

S, B. (2002, February). Cultural and heritage tourism in Canada:Opportunities , Principles and Challenges. Tourism ad Hospitality Research, 3, 211-233.

Tian, S., Crompton, J., & Witt, P. (1996). Integrating Constraints and Benefits to Identify

Responsive Target Markets for Museum Attractions. Journal of Travel Research ,Fall,34-45.

Weil, S. (1997). The Museum and The Public. Curator, 16(3), 257-271.

Weil, S. (1995). A Cabinet of Curiosities: Inquiries Into Museums and Their Prospects .

Washington: Smithsonian Institution Press.

Witcomb, A. (2003). Re-Imagining the Museum: Beyond the Mausoleum. London:Routledge

Zeppel, H. (2004). Indigenous cultural tourism :1997 Fulbright Symposium. Tourism Management, 1(19), 103-106.

COMMUNITY BASED ECO-VILLAGE TOURISM IN MANIPUR HILLS : LESSONS FROM THE STATES OF SIKKIM AND NAGALAND

R.K. Tamphasana

Associate Professor, G.P. Women's College,

Email: rktamphasana55@gmail.com

N. Lokendra Singh

Registrar, Manipur University, Email: lokendra_n@rediffmail.com

Introduction:

Tourism is currently one of the fastest growing industries in the world, having tremendous potentiality for earning foreign exchange and generation of income of backward regions through its various linkage effects. Although the Restricted area permit which is issued by the home Ministry has been presently suspended for two years, lack of basic services and facilities i.e. hotels, connectivity, law and order problems etc in the peripheral hilly areas of Manipur where most of the tourist spots are located, hinder inflow of the tourists. Community based eco-tourism therefore, would prove to be sustainable as it can create employment opportunities for a large number of people of the state with minimal investment as well as less adverse impact on the environment and culture of the local communities. It has also the potential to stimulate the overall economy of the state through its forward and backward linkages with a host of sectors like agriculture, forestry, transport, health, education, banking etc. In fact, this form of tourism is essentially targeted at promoting travelling to places of rich flora and fauna, natural lakes, caves etc. which are the original gifts of nature . Manipur hills have their own set of cultures the hill communities (tribes) have protected and nurtured for centuries. As they are very close to nature, their habits are simple and livelihood uncomplicated. Touring Manipur hills therefore gives an opportunity to the visitors to explore nature which is largely unspoiled as compared to other parts of India.

Community Development through Eco-Village-Tourism:

Tourism & nature conservation has been a synergistic one. From the perspectives of traditional branches of local economy, Nature based tourism, community based Tourism, Eco-village tourism development can represent a competing factor of socio-economic & cultural development even though there is conflict between nature & development.

The present paper attempts to analyse and assess the positive impact of Eco-Village Tourism on community development. Many well-known economists and policy makers gave due emphasis that eco-village tourism under the jurisdiction of Nature based Tourism involve more than simply establishing co-housing, co-communities in the country sides, growing one's economy. Eco-Village tourism do have the potential to provide a sustainable alternative to the to the shifting cultivators of Hill areas by accelerating the increasing demands of nature lovers as well as environmental concerns in the long run.

Eco-Village Tourism is a form of Tourism that showcases the rural/hill life, art & culture of the primitive ethnic groups at different hill/village locations thereby benefitting the local communities economically and society as well as enabling good interaction between tourist & local people for a far more enriching tourism experience (Lucy & Binota, 2012).

Community Based Eco-Village Tourism At Sindrabong, West Sikkim:

Ghose, Dipankar (2007) in his write up entitled "Community based ecotourism and sustainable livelihood: Sindrabong, Sikkim" gives a penetrating analysis of how a community of pastoral yak herders was transformed over a period of five - six years into a settled community with tourism as one of their important source livelihood. Sindrabong which constituted a cluster of six hamlets i.e Chougri, Lunmo, Dara, Sosing, Sankhola, Barseybong and Sindrabong with a total population of approximately 500 people in 48 households is located in the westSikkim district (India). The majority of population in these villages, are scheduled tribes i.e. Bhutias, Sherpas and Subhas or Limbus. Most of the villagers are pastoral yak herders. The pastoral life style had an adverse effect on the village forest as well as on the social life of the families as Yak grazing and firewood collection led to large scale deforestation in the area. The children of the yak herders did not have opportunities to attend school as they were involved in pastoral yak tending far away from where the schools are located. In 2004, an international N.G.O. the Mountain Institute, in collaboration with the Govt. of Sikkim and local communities initiated activities for sustainable livelihood and bio-diversity conservation in Sindrabong. A local community based 'Yumbong Eco-tourism committee' was formed to manage the village based tourism. Initially a sum of Rs 200000/- was invested by the Mountain Institute for supply of water, construction of toilets etc. An additional matching amount of Rs 1,50,000/- was spent by the villagers in addition to another Rs 2,00,000/ provided by the State Govt for procuring camping equipments and repairing of trekking trails. Just over two – three years of the beginning of the Project seventy percent of the village people were involved in this process. Capacity buildings of the villagers were also conducted for alternative income generation through provision of eco-tourism services and community dairying. The villagers were also attracted to settled life because of the possibility of their children's education. In fact the number of yaks had been reduced to 15% in the next two – three years of the beginning of the project. In October 2005, about 146 persons from 14 trekking groups from USA, U K, Spain, France, Italy, Switzerland and Netherlands participated. A total of Rs 5,82,030/- went to the local communities during 2005-2006 of which Rs 297,540/- was distributed among the 13 pack animal operators and the other Rs 2,84,490/- among the porters.

Gradually, domestic and foreign trekkers were begun to be provided with home stay facilities and local delicacies by the members of Yumbong Ecotourism Committee. Regular cultural programmes were also organized to welcome the visiting guests who helped conserve local culture and tradition by providing generous donations/gifts. In 2006-2007, the Ecotourism Committee strengthened the infrastructure by the development of a village campsite which consisted of a kitchen cum porters camp, toilets with running water and leveled ground for camping. Fourteen toilet facilities were also created in the village, for which Rs. 2, 500/- was contributed by the Mountain Institute and Rs 2000/- by the community. Poly house vegetable production was also introduced in the village, to help the villagers in generating additional income and thus helped the villagers in providing education to their children. The Mountain Institute also set up a community dairy which was augmented by free labourers provided by the village. Thus in a short period of time i.e. by 2007 Sindrabong villagers were begun to be transformed from nomadic pastoralist to that of a settled dairy farming community with additional economic benefits derived from ecotourism.

Communitised Tourism at Khonoma Village, Nagaland:

In the neighbouring state of Nagaland, a similar experiment was taken up by the Angami Naga inhabited Khonoma village. Chawii, Lian (2007) in a perceptive paper entitled "Community initiative in biodiversity conservation: Khonoma, Nagaland" discusses the application of a communitisation model for enhancing and upgrading the quality as well as quantity of governance in the far off villages. The Khonoma village had less than 600 households and a population of only 3000 tribal people. In 2003, the state Govt. had selected it as a Centre for Green village project with financial assistance from Ministry of Tourism, Govt. of India. The villagers were enthusiastic about the new project. The road leading to the village was neatly paved and lined with waste basket. Well maintained public toilets were also constructed at regular intervals. The residence of the village also painted their roofs green. The farmers of the village also optimized the produce from their Jhum fields, by cultivating alder trees which regenerate the soil and check erosion. Every year the state Govt. organized Hornbill festival at Kisama village to attract domestic and international tourists. In February 2013, Princess Maha Chakri Srindhorn of Thailand along with the big delegation consisting of entrepreneurs and government officials participated in the festival. Further, since most of domestic and international travelers who visit Manipur and Myanmar passed through Khonoma located on the National Highway 39 , the villager received a great deal economic opportunities as shopkeepers, rentiers , taxi drivers, porters etc. Although the main source of income is still derived from farm produce, the Khonoma Nagas, had other source of livelihood such as stone masonary or carpentry which fetches Rs 200/- to 300/- per day. Presently the Khonoma presents a fairly modernized and economically self sufficient community of people. The greatest strength for the growth of the village as generally understood was the traditional spirit of the community consciousness. In Nagaland, the strength of the traditional village community organization was successfully used by the Govt. in various sectors of administration i.e. school education, rural health etc. Communitisation involves devolution of power and authority to the traditional village community by transferring the assets earlier controlled by the government. Every village has a village development board consisting of representatives from the Government, tribal traditional authority and representatives of the N.G.O's. local academics and intellectuals etc who worked for the success of various programmes of the government. There is thus a dynamic relationship between the state apparatus and the traditional village community.

Present Status of Tourism in Manipur Hills

Indeed the Government of India had long recognized the critical role that could be played by the tribal communities in the development process of the region. As early as 1981, the Planning Commission noted: "The traditional structures like village Councils can be used to secure the participation and involvements of people in the development effort. These Councils can provide a point of contact between the state and the people. The accent has to be on what people can do to improve their prospects with some help from the state ". It is important to note that prior to the British rule the hilly areas many of the north eastern states were characterized by little hamlets with independent self governing institutions/village councils, led by a chief. Some of the chiefs in councils were born arbitrary and authoritarian as in the case of the Kukis and Mizos whereas the chiefs of many of Naga tribes are more democratic and therefore had less power. One of the above two categories of chiefship is seen in case of majority of two hundred or so tribes which inhabit in north east India.

Manipur, essentially a land-locked, and backward border state with an area of 22,327 sq. km. recorded a total population of 23,88,641 in 2001 census. While the density of population in the valley was 628 persons per sq. km, in the hills the aggregate density is 49 persons only. The central valley which covers an area of 2238 sq. km. (10% of the total area of the state) has a concentration of 65% of total population whereas the remaining 35% live in the vast hilly and mountainous tracts of the state. Another data which provides interesting insights in the land-man ratio in Manipur hills is that of the forest cover. In 1994-95 as much as 17,621 sq. kms. were covered by forests of which 1,467 sq. kms. were occupied by reserved forests while 4,171 sq. km. and 11,983 sq. kms. were under the protected and unclassified forests respectively. It must however be noted that despite such classifications made by the State Government, the hill people had long been practising their traditional customary land use system in major parts of Manipur hills.

The 34 tribes which inhabit Manipur hills can be broadly categorized under the Naga and Kuki constellations. The traditional system of community control and administration in the Naga village is by and large more democratic with the chiefs having nominal power whereas among the Kuki-Chin tribes, the chiefs used to have paramount power in the administration of the tribe including access to and control of their village land. The Kuki chiefs thus, behaved like big landlords with practically no rights of the tenants whereas in the case of the Nagas, individual Hillman could have their respective agricultural and other terrace fields with more possessory and heritable rights. These lands were also saleable but that was to be within the community itself. Among the Kukis, however, the villagers were pure tenants with no property rights.

Though some traditional institutions are still functional in some parts of Manipur, due to modern influences the traditional systems have been considerably eroded. Till 1956, the Areas of Manipur remained largely un-administered with little participation of the local people in any democratic process, except on occasions of election to the Manipur Legislative Assembly. In 1956, the Manipur Village Authorities (in hill areas) Act, 1956 was enacted thereby introducing for the first time a local body of self – governance at the local level (village). It provided a system of election to the village body which will be headed by the nominated chief (ex – officio Chairman). Under this act the chief will continue to be the nominated head of the tribal Council and the village authority will continue to administer the tribal areas where civil administration is quite ineffective. Despite the merger of Manipur with India in 1949 with an aim of establishing the de facto power still lies with the village authority with the nominated chiefs. Although, according to the Manipur Hill Areas (Acquisition of Chiefs rights act, 1967) the power and authority of the village chiefs were supposed to have been handed over to the government, but this act is not yet fully operational due to a variety of reasons and the chiefs still command in most of the Kuki villages.

The Manipur District Council Act, 1971 passed by the Parliament provided self governing Council for the hill areas. According to the act, all hill areas of Manipur were divided into six autonomous districts with a Council of its own, each having 18 elected and 2 nominated members. The Councils which started functioning in 1973 continued till 1989, but after due to interference from various pressure groups there have been no election till 2012. During this period the officials elected under the village authorities with the nominated chiefs had been practically running the administration of the hill areas with indirect support of the District authorities.

In Manipur, the Tourism Department has not been performing too well. The state government has not initiated pro active measures to open up the hill areas to the domestic and international tourists. Although the law and order problem had discouraged the inflow of both domestic and international tourists whoever had visited Manipur during the last one decade had not moved out of the Imphal city. In the given situation, the tremendous potentialities of ecotourism available in the form of verdant forest, valleys, mountain peaks, deep streams, fresh water lakes, and above all delicious ethnic cuisines, colourful festivals and hospitable people could be harnessed at the earliest. The improvement of roads, airways etc. as a fall out of India's Look East Policy (1990) had tremendously increased the domestic and international visitors during the last five years. This project on reinvention of tourism in Manipur hills, through the traditional tribal communities, thus could constitute the broad contours for formulating a viable tourism policy for Manipur hills. Considering the fact that there is a similarity of culture, values and customary practices between the ethnic communities of Manipur and those of Sikkim and Nagaland the model can be viewed as an alternative approach for developing the hill areas of the state. Indeed, reinvention of tourism through the tribal communities can be a way out to make tourism a successful venture in Manipur.

Conclusion:

Eco-Village Tourism as major part of Tourism Sector is another solution to eradicate the poverty of hill communities. In the backward states like Manipur, Nagaland, and Mizoram, Eco-Village Tourism can emerge as central pillar of the local economy. As well it is to preserve this socio-cultural & heritage conservation intake in a sustainable way out. This is the long run can become the key player for providing sustainable development in the hill areas of NE States.

By providing proper road connectivity & implementation of basic infrastructures by the Government, and initiating the Tourism ideas by the intellectuals/academics, the very concept of Tourism development would go a long way to achieve community development planning in the hill economy. It will be of utmost interest for the future researches to develop more in depth study in this particular area with field study so that eco-village tourism can become as one of the most effective socio-economic tool for combating hill areas development and opens an avenue for young/women unemployed and entrepreneurs in the near future.

References:

Bansal, S.P. & Kumar, J. (2012) Rural Tourism, Heritage and Sustainability. In Manhas, P. (ed.) Tourism Destination Management: Strategic Perspective and Policies. New Delhi: Kanishka Publishers & Distributors.

Bhattacharya, P. (2003) Ecotourism as means of Conserving Wildlife Sanctuaries and National Parks of Assam. In Baruah, P.P (eds.) Proc. Biodiversity of Eastern Himalayan Protected Areas. Guwahati: Baniprokash Mudranee.

Binota, meinam (2010) Prospects & Opportunities of Community Tourism in NE India. Research paper, International seminar on Road Map Development of Tourism in NE India, 11-12 Dec. 2010, Sibasagar, Assam.

Chawii, Lian (2007) Natural Resource-Based Income and Livelihood Improvement Initiatives in North East India, paper commissioned as an input to the study 'Development and Growth in North East India: The Natural Resources, Water, and Environment Nexus', January.

Chawii, Lian (2007) Community initiative in biodiversity conservation: Khonoma, Nagaland in North East India, paper commissioned as an input to the study 'Development and Growth in North East India: The Natural Resources, Water, and Environment Nexus'.

Das, N. (2003) Ecotourism and its impact on Bio-diversity-A Geo-Ecological Study of Sonitpur District. In Baruah, P.P. (eds.) Proc. Biodiversity of Eastern Himalayan Protected Area. Guwahati, Baniprokash Mudranee.

Devi, R.K. Tamphasana (2013) Reinventing School Education in Manipur Hills: Lessons from the Communitisation of Education Programme. In Ch. Ibohal (ed.) Youth and Good Governance. Imphal.

Ghose, Dipankar (2007) Community-based ecotourism and sustainable livelihoods: Sindrabong, Sikkim in North East India, paper commissioned as an input to the study 'Development and Growth in North East India: The Natural Resources, Water, and Environment Nexus'.

Jajo, Lucy & Binota, M (2012) Prospects and Opportunities of Community Based Tourism in North East India: A Case Study of Ukhrul District, Manipur. In Sarkar, S.S. et al (ed.) Sustainable Tourism: Issues and Challenges. New Delhi: Macmillan Publications India Ltd.

Rajkumari,Tamphasana (2012) Ethnic Process in North East India. New Delhi.

Singh, N. Lokendra (ed.) (2004) Land use system in Manipur Hills. New Delhi: Rajesh Publications.

BHIMBETKA, INDIA'S ROCK ART HERITAGE SITE: PROTECTION, PROMOTION AND MANAGEMENT

Usha Agrawal

Head- Department of History and Tourism, Govt. P.G. College, MIG II 241, Kitiyani Colony, Mandsaur (M.P.) agrawalusha1@gmail.com

Abstract

Rock heritage is term used to describe aesthatic, spiritual and social values. Art has always been the medium of expression for conveying not only unsaid but also the said in the form of visuals. Bhimbetka is the only WHS in the country that has been inscribed in cultural landscapes. The rock paintings of Bhimbetka are among the earliest manifestations of human creative expression recorded in India.

The paper throws light on the management aspects of rock art in Bhimbetka from tourism point of view. It can play the vital role in promotion of the rock art heritage site worldwide and also generate revenue for government and local people. The present study will help to understand the current problem in the study area and needs of the tourists. The main aim of the study is to measure the potential of tourism at Bhimbetka and related challenges and opportunities. Today, at the site, there is need of protection, promotion and management related steps to be taken in order of sustainable development of the site.

Keywords:- Rock art heritage; Bhimbetka; Cultural landscape; Protection; Promotion; Sustainable development.

Art has always been the medium of expression for conveying not only the unsaid but also the said in the form of visuals. It is through this form, one could communicate a lot with the society, even if the audience was not literate (Rana, 2014).

The term rock art appears in the published literature as early as the 1940s (Goodall,1946). It has also been described as "rock carvings"(Chadwick,1907), "rock drawings" (Winkler,1938), "rock engravings (Wells,1920) "rock inscriptions" (Deutsch,1874),, "rock paintings" (Ethies,1908), "rock pictures" (Man,1939), "rock records" (Moore,1861), "rock sculptures" (Tylor,1865).

Rock heritage is a term used to describe aesthetic spiritual and other social values. It includes knowledge, dance, music, language and the cultural spaces. Almost all early painting in India survives in caves, as very few buildings from Ancient India survive, and though these were probably often painted, the work has been lost. The history of cave paintings in India or rock art range from drawings and paintings from prehistoric times, beginning around 30,000 BCE in the caves of Central India, typified by those at the Bhimbetka rock shelters to elaborate frescoes at sites such as the rock cut artificial caves at Ajanta and Ellora, extending as late as the 8th - 10th century CE (Wikipedia.org).

India is known for its rich art heritage that attracts a large number of tourist and scholars from all over the world. It has third largest concentration of rock art, after Australia and Africa (ibiblio. org). India has a huge spectrum of temple, forts, caves, mosque, monument and many other things. Well in other words we can say that India has a pride possession of the cultural heritage in the form of temple, stupas, and rock shelter paintings etc.

We know that heritage means the property which is received from our ancestors and which has passed on a legacy to the next generations. It is a place where we can preserve our Cultural and Natural heritage (Shastri, 2014). The world heritage has 24 cultural and 6 natural sites from India (UNESCO, 2013).

Bhimbetka is the only WHS in the country that has been inscribed cultural landscapes. This site is known for its largest complex of painted rock shelters, continuous prehistoric cultural remains and livings cultures as legacy to the past. The rock paintings of Bhimbetka are among the earliest manifestations of human creative expression recorded in India. There are over 700 rock shelters in the region. Of these, more than 400 caves and rock shelters with paintings, distributed over five hills, have been protected by the Archaeological Survey of India (Ota, 2008). No doubt that this Cultural as well as Natural heritage site has always been a special attention of tourists.

The paper throws light on the management aspects of rock art in Bhimbetka from tourism point of view. It can play the vital role in promotion of the rock art heritage site worldwide and also generate revenue for government and local people. The present study will help to understand the current problem in the study area and needs of the tourists. The main aim of the study is to measure the potential of tourism at Bhimbetka and related challenges & opportunities. The specific objectives of the study are:-

- To highlighted the importance of site from tourism point of view.
- To understand the potential kinds of tourism at Bhimbetka
- To study tourist profile & present condition of the site.
- To improve sites as a Heritage tourist destination.
- To analyze the existing demand and supply patterns (both effective and potential) and the tourist satisfaction and dissatisfaction levels.
- To make suggestion for Heritage protection, promotion and management of tourism at Bhimbetka.

Methodology-

The methodology of the study is empirical and exploratory in nature. Data for the study have been collected both from primary and, secondary sources. To get a better insight into the present scenario of heritage tourism in Bhimbetka and understand the perception, needs and problem of the visiting tourists, it is important to view it from tourist's point of view. So far as primary data are concerned, these are collected through pre structure questionnaire, discussion and interviews with the tourists, and observations. The questionnaire was served to 70 tourists during their visit to the Bhimbetka. Out of the total sample size only 55 were returned and final analysis was done with 50 questionnaires. The secondary data have been collected from published material of various official reports, Department of Madhya Pradesh tourism, Department of Archaeology, journals, Published news items and articles in news papers, books, Gazetteer, magazines and websites.

Present Scenario of Bhimbetka-

Bhimbetka rock shelters, series of natural rock shelters in the foothills of the Vindhya Range, central India. They are situated some 28 miles (45 km) south of Bhopal, in west-central Madhya Pradesh state (Britannica.com). The paintings in the Bhimbetka Rock Shelters range in age from 9,000 years old into the Medieval era, although it is possible some are as much as 12,000 years old (McGuigan,2014).

The name of "Bhimbetka" (the place where Bhim sat down) comes from from the mythological association of the place with Bhima, one of the five Pandava princes in the Hindu epic Mahabharata (rang7.com). At one point Bhima was exiled, and is said to have spent his exile in the Bhimbetka Rock Shelters, sitting on the stones and surviving off of the bounty of the forest including water, plants and fruits (Wikipedia.org).

The area has abundant natural resources in its perennial water supplies, natural shelter, rich forest flora & fauna and bears a striking resemblance to similar rock art sites such as Kakadu National Park in Australia or Kondoa lrangi in Tanzania. The nominated area covers 1,893 ha and is surrounded by a Buffer Zone of 10,280 hectares (ICOMOS,2003).

Bhimbetka Rock Shelters are like a mirror reflecting the evolution of man through time. In particular, it is possible to glimpse into the activities of the pre-historic man, his clothing, food, tools, and daily household activities. Here one can see the Rock Shelters where ancient man lived. It is amazing and eye opener to see how human were staying in olden days. The cave also has a small inscription of the Maurya / Sunga period. Within the general area of Bhimbetka group of rock shelters, small stupas have been found. There are a large number of Shanka Lipi inscriptions in the Bhimbetka cluster of rock shelters. Of particular interest to the tourist are the rock paintings of Bhimbetka, Auditorium Rock Shelter, Zoo Rock and Boar Rock in Bhimbetka Cluster (Indiavideo.org). Excellence natural caves with amazing shapes and sculptures and rock cave painting in very nice and well kept condition.

The paintings, which display great vitality and narrative skill, are categorized into five distinct periods of time. Apart from that many nice painting deal with hunting scenes, showing animals such as tigers, deer, crocodiles, elephant, wild boar, lions, rhinoceros and bears. Other depicts body decoration, group dance; battle scenes, music etc are found on rock shelter. The oldest are dated to the late Paleolithic period (10000 +BC) like the Lascaux paintings, are very simple line paintings showing animals such as bison and tigers. Painting from Mesolithic age (5000 BC) were the first true paintings, smaller in size, with stylized figures and mostly focus on hunting , communal dances, pregnant women, and everyday activities. During mesolithic period, microliths were hafted and different types of weapons were made such as spear, bow and arrow, sword etc (Gupta,2006). In addition to more advance trading culture and development of communal style living represented in chalcolithic age (2000 BC). Still later come pictures from an early historic age, where a decorative and schematic style of painting dominated this age with religious symbols like tunic dresses and headgear making an appearance. The scenes were complex and painted in colours of bright red, white and yellow colours. Lastly are scenes from the Medieval era, which are less complex and detailed than those from the early historic age.

These paintings are geometric linear and more schematic, but they show degeneration and crudeness in their artistic style. The paintings of this age include Hindu Gods like Ganesha and Natraja. In facts, the depiction at bhimbetka provide a glimpse of the vast changes in the beliefs across time as understood form the study of rock art (Manuel,2006).

The detailed study of Bhimbetka paintings show that 34.03% of paintings are representational, 38.49% of abstract variety, and 25.07% are those of geometric variety. The remaining 2.41% comprise indeterminate category and inscriptions. Likewise, the subgroups of colour filling types show that 56.09% constitute silhouetted or shadow graphic, 27.10% are of outlined drawings, 14.40% are semi-silhouetted and partially decorated and remaining 2.41% constitute inscription and abstract figures (Ota,2008).

It comprises more than 700 rock caves of which over 400 painted caves and rock shelters are distributed over five clusters. Only 15 of the 700 odd caves and shelters are open for tourists viewing. Archaeological survey of India and Madhya Pradesh tourism has done a great job in maintaining the site with good markers and description on the site and the rock have been numbered and properly secured and protected.

They were put on the World Heritage List in 2003. This is the 22nd World Heritage Site declared by UNESCO in India (Asi.nic).

History

The earliest discovery of prehistoric rock art was in India, twelve years before the discovery of the paintings of Altamira in Spain, Archibald Carlleyle discovered paintings in the caves and rock shelters at Sohagighat in the Mirzapur district of Uttar Pradesh in 1867 (Pathak,2006). F.Faweett brought to light the first rock engravings of South India from Kupgallu in 1892 (Kantikumar,2006).

The first scientific article on Indian rock painting was published by J.Cockburn in 1883 and the first reference to Bhimbetka as a "Buddhist site" was in 1888 by W.Kincaid, published in a paper on information from local adivasis (ICOMOS,2003).

Bhimbetka's naturally formed rock shelters provided the perfect structures and environment for Stone Age people. With over hanging rock ledges to give them shelter from sun and rain and the forest full of water, plants, fruits, and animals for food. The Rock Shelters were discovered in 1957 by an Archaeologist, V.S.Wakankar, from Vikram University, in Ujjain.

The first archeological investigations in 1971 with limited excavations of rock shelter III F-13 by K.D.Bajpai and S.K.Panday of the H.S. Gour University, Sagar. In the following year a systematic survey of the wider area from Karitalai to Jaora was undertaken by Wakankar. His classification divided the groups of painted rock shelters into seven topographical areas (I-VII), subdividing each area alphabetically into clusters of groups of shelters and numbering individuals shelters in each clusters (ICOMOS,2003). This survey identified 700 shelters of which 243 are in The Bhimbekta group. It also showed the Lakha Juar group to be as rich as Bhimbetka in rock painting with 178 shelters spread over two hills (Ota,2008).

Between 1972 and 1977 excavations revealed a continuous sequence of Stone Age cultures form the late Acheulian to the late mesolithic and also some of the world's oldest stone walls and floors (travel.india.com).

Tourist Arrivals

Bhimbrtka receives of a large number of domestic and foreign tourists round the year. Incidentally much of the tourists visit this place for watching Bhimbetka's Rock Shelters and paintings. Table 1.1 gives the detail breakup of domestic and international tourists.

Table 1.1

Tourist Arrivals in Bhimbetka

Year	Domestics	Foreigners	Total	Growth in Percentage
2006	24632	390	25022	-
2007	40989	750	41739	66.08%
2008	36782	1492	38274	-8.30
2009	36744	1489	38233	-.01
2010	44896	2113	47009	22.9
2011	40307	1356	41663	-11.37
2012	44351	1576	45927	10.23

Source-Madhya Pradesh Tourism Department Corporation, Bhopal

Tourist Arrivals in Bhimbetka

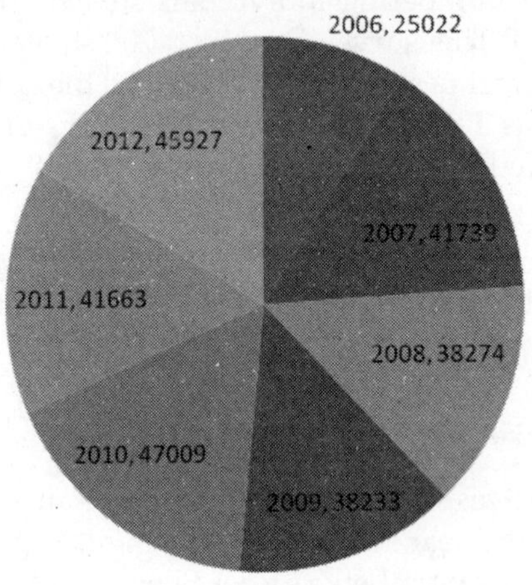

Accessibility

Bhimbetka is 45 kms south to Bhopal. Bhopal being capital city of M.P., is well connected to all important cites of India via Air, Rail & Road.

Location---------------------------------NH 69----------------------------

Bhopal---------Mandideep---------Obaidullagang-----Hoshangabad

Bhimbetka

Accommodation-

In terms of accommodation there is only one accommodation unit called "Highway Treat", which is owned by Madhya Pradesh tourism department. In this unit there are A/c rooms available for staying overnight but most of the travelers prefer to stay in Bhopal being the capital city of Madhya Pradesh.

Table 1.2

Classifications on the basis of Age

S.No	Age Group	No. of Respondents	Percentage
1	Below 25	15	30

S.No	Age Group	No. of Respondents	Percentage
2	25-40	30	60
3	Above 40	5	10
	Total	50	100.00

Source- collected Data with the help of questionnaires

Table 1.2 is evident that 60% of the total tourist visiting Bhimbetka belongs to age group of 25-40, whereas respondent below age 25 year are 30%. Only 10% of the responding is above age 40.

Hence it can be concluded from the table 1.2 that about 70% of the total tourist belongs age above 25.

Table 1.3

Gender wise classification of Respondents in Bhimbetka

S.No	Gender	No. of Respondents	Percentage
1	Male	26	52
2	Female	24	48
	Total	50	100.00

Source- collected Data with the help of questionnaires

Table 1.3 is evident that 52% of the total tourists are male, whereas 48% are female.

Hence it can be concluded from above table that male and female tourists are almost equal.

Table 1.4

Classifications of Respondents according to their Educational Level

S.No	Educational Level	No. of Respondents	Percentage
1	Below Metric	2	4
2	Matriculate	6	12
3	Graduate	30	60
4	Post-Graduate	10	20
5	Above P.G	2	4
	Total	50	100.00

Source- collected Data with the help of questionnaires

Table 1.4 shows the profile of tourists according to their educational level. It can be revealed that 4% of the tourists are below metric, 12% are matriculate, 60% are graduate, 20% are post graduate and 4% are having degree of above post-graduation.

Hence it can be concluded from above table that 84% of the total tourist are having educational level of graduation or above.

Table 1.5

Classifications of Respondents according to their Occupation

S.No	Occupation	No. of Respondents	Percentage
1	Private sector	16	32
2	Public sector	5	10
3	Businessman	14	28
4	Students	12	24
5	Any other	3	6
	Total	50	100.00

Source- collected Data with the help of questionnaires

Table 1.5 shows the profile of tourists visiting Bhimbetka according to their Profession/Occupation. It can be revealed that 32% of the total tourists are working in private sector, 28% are businessmen, 24% are students and 10% of the tourists are working in public sector. Only 6% of the tourists belong to other professions like NGO's, agriculture, house wife etc.

Hence it can be concluded that most of the tourist who visit Bhimbetka are in private sector job. It also attracts a large number of businessman and students.

Table 1.6

Classifications on the basis of Monthly Income

S.No	Income	No. of Respondents	Percentage
1	Below Rs. 5000	4	8
2	5001-10000	17	34
3	10001-20000	22	44
4	Above 20000	7	14
	Total	50	100.00

Source- collected Data with the help of questionnaires

Table 1.6 shows the classification of tourists on the basis of their monthly income. According to the table, 44% of the respondent belongs to the income category of Rs.10001-20000, 34% belongs to Rs.5001-10000 and14% above Rs.20000. Only 8% of the respondents are having monthly income below Rs.5000.

Hence it can be concluded that most of the tourist are having monthly income from 10000 to 20000.

Table 1.7

Classifications on the basis of Purpose of visit

S.No	Purpose of visit	No. of Respondents	Percentage
1	See Rock Shelters & Paintings	32	64
2	Scenic beauty	4	8
3	Visiting friend and relative	12	24
4	Business	0	0
5	Religious	0	0
6	Any other	2	4
	Total	50	100.00

Source- collected Data with the help of questionnaires

Table 1.7 shows the profile of tourists visiting Bhimbetka on the basis of their Purpose of visit. It can be revealed that 64% of the total tourists come to see Bhimbetka's rock Shelter & paintings; whereas 24% of the tourists come for visiting their friend and relatives. Only 8% of the tourists come to see Scenic beauty; whereas 4% of the tourists come for other work like NGO, researchers work etc.

Hence it can be concluded that maximum numbers of the tourists visit Bhimbetka's Rock Shelters and paintings.

Table 1.8

Classifications on the basis of Mode of Transportations

S.No	Mode of Transport used	No. of Respondents	Percentage
1	Own Vehicle	23	46
2	Hired Vehicle	12	24

S.No	Mode of Transport used	No. of Respondents	Percentage
3	Public Transports	13	26
4	Any other	2	4
	Total	50	100.00

Source- collected Data with the help of questionnaires

Table 1.8 shows the classification of tourists according to their mode of transportation. It is evident that 46% of the total tourists surveyed use their own vehicle, 26% use public transports like bus & train and 24% of use hired vehicle. Only 4% of tourist used other mode of transportation i.e. tour packages buses.

Hence it can be concluded that large numbers of the tourists use personal vehicle as mode of transportation to Bhimbetka.

Table 1.9

Classifications on the basis of number of visit to Bhimbetka

S.No	Visit to Bhimbetka	No. of Respondents	Percentage
1	1st visit	42	84
2	2nd visit	5	10
3	3rd visit	2	4
4	More	1	2
	Total	50	100.00

Source- collected Data with the help of questionnaires

Table 1.9 shows the classification of tourists according to their number of visit to Bhimbetka. The majority of respondents, i.e., 84% had visited Bhimbetka for the first time; where as 10% of respondents have visited for the second times and only 4% visited thrice.

Table 1.10

Willingness to come back to Bhimbetka

S.No	Willingness to come back	No. of Respondents	Percentage
1	Yes	37	74

S.No	Willingness to come back	No. of Respondents	Percentage
2	No	7	14
3	Can' say	6	12
	Total	50	100.00

Source- collected Data with the help of questionnaires

Table 1.10 shows the Willingness of the tourist for coming back to Bhimbetka. It is revealed that 74% of the tourists wants to come back Bhimbetka but 14% dose not and 12% are in dynamic stage.

Hence it can be concluded, most of the tourist want to visit Bhimbetka once more.

Table 1.11

Responses of the tourists regarding the Heritage tourism in Bhimbetka

S.No	Statements	SA	A	NC	D	SD
1	The Caves and paintings of Bhimbetka is in good condition.	22 (44%)	18 (36%)	1 (2%)	6 (12%)	3 (6%)
2	There is lack of adequate infrastructure facilities like accommodation, foods, water, electricity etc.	4 (8%)	7 (14%)	2 (4%)	7 (14%)	30 (60%)
3	Government is doing efforts for the promotion and the development of tourism	28 (56%)	18 (36%)	1 (2%)	2 (4%)	1 (2%)
4	By increasing level of advertisement we can promote Heritage tourism	20 (40%)	26 (52%)	1 (2%)	2 (4%)	1 (2%)
5	Celebration of local fair & festivals in a grand way may attract more tourist	30 (60%)	14 (28%)	2 (4%)	3 (6%)	1 (2%)

Source- collected Data with the help of questionnaires

SA- Strongly agree, A-Agree, NC-No Comment, D-Disagree, SD-Strongly Disagree

Fifty tourists have reflected their opinions regarding the tourism phenomenon on the site which are shown in the table 1.11. The first question asked was about the caves and paintings in Bhimbetka, in response to this question 80% of the tourist agreed with the statement that the condition of caves and paintings are good, while asking about the second statement on infrastructure facilities in Bhimbetka. Only 22% of respondent agree that infrastructure facilities are good. A large number that is 74% of the respondent said it poor. More than 92% of the respondent agreeing with the statement that Government is doing efforts to promote and develop tourism. Similarly 92% of the respondents are agreeing with the statement that by increasing level of advertisement can promote Heritage tourism. 88% of the respondents are agreeing with the statement that the celebration of fairs & festivals in a grand way may attract more tourists.

Table 1.12

Opinion of tourist regarding the following attributes at Bhimbetka

S.No	Attributes	SA	A	NC	D	SD
1	Transport facilities is good	12 (24%)	18 (36%)	3 (6%)	10 (20%)	7 (14%)
2	Accommodation facilities is good	3 (6%)	8 (16%)	2 (4%)	25 (50%)	12 (24%)
3	Food & beverage is good	2 (4%)	12 (24%)	1 (2%)	30 (60%)	5 (10%)
4	Entertainments facilities is good	1 (2%)	4 (8%)	3 (6%)	32 (64%)	10 (20%)
5	Condition of road is good	4 (8%)	22 (44%)	1 (2%)	15 (30%)	8 (16%)
6	Other Facilities like- Banking, Medical, Shopping etc.	2 (4%)	5 (10%)	2 (4%)	23 (46%)	18 (36%)

Source- collected Data with the help of questionnaires

SA- Strongly agree, A-Agree, NC-No Comment, D-Disagree, SD-Strongly Disagree

Fifty tourists have reflected their views regarding the facilities available in Bhimbetka are shown in the table 1.12. The first question tourists reflect their view regarding the transport facility for Bhimbetka. 60% of the respondent said that the transport facility for Bhimbetka is good, whereas 24% of the respondent said it as poor. The second statement about the Accommodations facilities in Bhimbetka, only 22% of respondent agree that Accommodation facilities are good; a large number 74% of the respondent said it as poor. Similarly while asked about the Food & beverage only 28% said it good but 70% of the respondent said it as poor. The forth question tourists reflect their view regarding the entertainment facilities in Bhimbetka. Only 10% of the respondent rated as good but 74% of the respondent rated it as poor. In statement about the Condition of road from Bhimbetka 52% of respondent said it good and 46% of respondent said it as poor. In other statement about the other facilities like banking, medical, shopping etc, 14% of respondent said it good and 82% of respondent said it as poor.

Table 1.13 Opinion of the tourist regarding the problem faced by them

S.No	Problem	Very much	Some what	Not at all	No comments
1	Cleanliness & hygiene	2 (4%)	3 (6%)	38 (76%)	7 (14%)
2	Language Problem	5 (10%)	8 (16%)	32 (64%)	5 (10%)
3	Water and Sanitation	6 (12%)	26 (52%)	12 (24%)	6 (12%)
4	Crime & Cheating	3 (6%)	3 (6%)	40 (80%)	4 (8%)
5	Traffic Problem in local	1 (2%)	2 (4%)	42 (84%)	5 (10%)

Source-collected Data with the help of questionnaires

Fifty tourists have reflected their opinions regarding the problems faced by them during their visit to Bhimbetka are shown in the table 1.13. In response to the statement about the cleanliness and hygiene condition in Bhimbetka only10 % of the respondents faced such type of problem, whereas more than 64% of the respondents faced no problem with language. About 64% of the respondents faced the water and sanitation problem a lot. While asked about the crime and cheating in Bhimbetka only 12% of the respondents said they have to face such problem. Most of the tourist said that there is very less crime & cheating in Bhimbetka. 84% of the respondents said that they have no face traffic problem in Bhimbetka.

Findings

- The image of Bhimbetka is that of a tourism destination with rich cultural and architectural heritage.
- Out of the total respondent visiting Bhimbetka about 70% are of the age above 25.
- 78% of the total respondents are having education above graduation, while 6% of the tourists are educated above post graduation.
- Most of the tourists who visit Bhimbetka are private sector employee and businessman.
- Most of the tourists are having monthly income from 10000 to 20000.
- Maximum number of tourist visit Bhimbetka for seeing Rock Shelters.
- The majority (84%) of respondents were visiting Bhimbetka for first time.
- More than 74% of the total tourists who are visiting Bhimbetka are willing to come back.
- Most of the tourist did not face any problem related to language.
- Tourists feel that we can attract more tourists by increasing level of advertisement.
- There is very less crime and cheating. It has been seen as a safe and peaceful destination by tourists.
- 86% of the respondents feel that tourism is creating employment opportunity in Bhimbetka.
- 68% of the respondents are agreeing with the statement that MPSTDC and ASI are play important role in preserving monument and the development of Heritage tourism in Bhimbetka.

- Bhimbetka is very small and not well developed. Accommodation facilities are not very proper. Most of tourists prefer to stay in Bhopal because there is absence of budget class hotels.
- There is absence of adequate facilities at Bhimbetka especially food and beverage, recreation facilities, entertainment facilities etc.
- There are no travel agents/tour operators in Bhimbetka. They are available only in Bhopal.
- Most of the tourist faced problem relating to water and sanitation in Bhimbetka.
- Due to rock dwellings, Bhimbetka becomes extremely hot during day time and in summers and there is no sufficient sitting facility also.
- There is a lack of adequate facilities at monuments especially the information brochures and publicity material on the monument.
- There is not even a single handicraft/souvenir shop at Bhimbetka.
- There is no electricity supply in Bhimbetka. Only few solar lamps is installed at the office of security guard.
- The condition of monument is in good condition but there is a need to improve the condition of other monuments also.
- Transport facilities from beyond the entry point (T- junction) to main caves is really poor because no mode of public transport (Auto or taxi). Tourist need to walk 3kms (6 km return). Most of the tourists come with private vehicle or taxi.

Suggestions

Many suggestions have been pictured out while taking the survey about tourist visits to Bhimbetka, it manly deals with protection, promotion and management system for the tourism development.

1. Protection

The A.S.I. is primarily responsible for the preservation, restoration and conservation of antiquities and Heritage of

India. But it is also the duty of people of India, the society; Local Government, Community, Government Agencies, NGOs, INGOs and international agencies like UNESCO to adopt and practice the measures of conservation, preservation and environmental development in order to save our monuments, sites.

For development of a sustainable and self-reliant system for preservation of Heritage, following steps is suggested;

- Popularizations of cultural heritage is an important set of activities, which largely influences the understanding and awareness of the society about the preservation, protection and use of ancient buildings, monuments, art and other items. Public awareness is usually raised by means of radio, TV, internet, press, lectures, conferences, etc.
- Promote heritage protection for tourism development at college and school level.
- More awareness programs to be organized for the public and tourists to preserve and protect the Rock Shelters, caves and paintings in Bhimbetka.
- All site staff should be aware of the heritage value and well trained in management of rock arts.
- We can help by creating an awareness of the importance of preserving these invaluable sites by sharing news and links through social networking sites such as Face book and Twitter.

2. Promotion

Promotion of the site plays a crucial role in attracting the tourists and promoting tourism. A well-planned publicity program is found efficacious in this very context.

- The site should be focused in movies as well as high TRP daily soaps.
- The high profile and authorized tour operators should visit the site so that they could include this particular site in their tour packages
- All India Photographic Exhibitions can be organized to bring this site into lime light.
- Government should promote various departmental seminars and workshops here.

3. Management

Management is one of the most important parts in increasing tourism at Bhimbetka. In management we deal with development of the site like Accommodation, Hygiene and cleanness, Policy & Program, Interpretation Centre, Well trained guide etc. A brief explanation of these activities is given below.

- Provision for decent quality accommodation at reasonable prices should be made for domestic as well as foreign tourists of all segments. Encourage private investors. This could be done by way of offering special inducements such as subsidies, tax concessions, and preferential rates of interest credits.
- Cafeterias/refreshments centers should be opened at Bhimbetka.
- Provide visitor information and interpretations services covering particularly (i) what to see (ii) how to see, and (iii) how to behave. It can be by way of brochures, specialized guide and magazines etc.
- Focus on water scarcity especially in summer needs immediate attention from the tourism planners and developers.
- Maintenance of cleanliness around tourist sites also needs to be taken care of by the local authorities concerned.
- Training for guides should include good behavior with tourists.
- Proper landscaping of the Bhimbetka should be done to give it a face-lift and make it soothing and interesting for visitors.
- Maintain visitor feedback register for development point of view.
- Prepare tourism policies and programs for the speedy and sustainable developments.
- The approach road to Bhimbetka (a patch of 3 kms) should be constructed and public transportation facility should be improved.

Thus, if all the above suggestions are seen into practice then this would generate the sustainable development of the Bhimbetka Rock Shelters.

References

Chadwick H. M (1907), The rock-carvings at Tegneby, Origin Eng. Nation., 306

Chatterjee Gautam,www.ibiblio.org.

Deutsch, Rem. (1874) The long rock-inscription of Hamamât.,177

Ethics I (1908). The rock-paintings are either stenciled or painted in outline, 822/2,

Goodall E. (1946) Domestic Animals in rock art, Proceedings and Transactions of the Rhodesian Scientific Association , 57-62

Gupta Kumar Rajesh (2006) The depiction of weapons in the Bhimbetka rock paintings Bhopal, 61

ICOMOS (2003). Bhimbetka (India) No. 925, 43-46

Kantikumar A.Power (2006) Rock paintings from vidrbha region-A culture study, Bhopal, 45

Man No.119. (1939) On one of the stalactite pillars was found a big round stone with traces of red paint on its surface, as used in the rock-pictures, 178/2

Manuel J (2006) Rituals and beliefs in rock-art at bhimbetka Bhopal, 44

McGuigan Brendan (2014) www.wisegeek.com/what-are-the-bhimbetka-rock-shelters.htm

Moore G. (1861), with translations of Rock-Records in India. The Lost Tribes and the Saxons of the East.

Ota,S.B. (2008) Bhimbetka World Heritage Site, New Delhi, 5

Pathak Meenakshi (2006) Indian rock art- prehistoric painting of the Pachmarhi Hills, Bradshaw Foundation, 1

Rohilla Rana Jyoti (2014), Buddhist living art traditions of Bodhgaya, Sir Alexander Cunningham and the Art Heritage of India, BHU-Varanasi, 72

Shastri Andrey (2014), Preservation of Heritage Monuments and Sites, Sir Alexander Cunningham and the Art Heritage of India, BHU-Varanasi, 83

Tylor, (1865), and bush art or bushmen art. Early Hist. Man, 88

UNESCO (2013). New Biosphere Reserves

Wells H. G. (1920): From rock engravings we may deduce the theory that the desert was crossed from oasis to oasis, 126/1

wikipedia.org/wiki/Cave_paintings_in_India

Winkler H. A. (1938), The discovery of rock-drawings showing boats of a type foreign to Egypt, 26

www.Asi.nic.in>monument

www.britannica.com/EBchecked/topic/.../Bhimbetka-rock-shelters

www.indiavideo.org/text/rock-shelters-bhimbetka-bhopal-1540.php

www.rang7.com/bhimbetka-rock-shelters

www.travel.India.com/destinations/bhimbetka.

www.wikipedia.org/wiki/Bhimbetka_rock_shelters.

TOURISM IN INDIA: A 360 DEGREE BOON

P.K.Yadav

Head and Dean, Department of Business Administration,MJP Rohilkhand University, Bareilly - 243006

Sanjay Mishra

Sr. Faculty Member, Department of Business Administration, MJP Rohilkhand University, Bareilly – 243006

Abhishek Sharma

Associate Professor, LBSIMT, Bareilly

Charu Yadav

Assistant Professor, Jaipuria Institue of Management, Ghaziabad

Abstract

Tourism from being regarded as a pastime activity for the leisured few in society has grown into a multi-billion industry and a multi faceted activity. Tourism is one of those economic activity that is considered by many as an individual industry in itself that lends its support and encompasses benefits not only for the industry itself but trickles them down to related sectors as well. Our present research is in the area of tourism in general and Indian tourism, in particular. The objective of the present paper is to understand the prospects of tourism industry in India and its further implications on the other related industries such as Retail, Infra structure, Rural economy, Medicine & Hospitality industries, hence economy in general. Indian tourism industry today is on the threshold of a big change for large economic gains. By making use of appropriate secondary data, the authors try to understand the interactivity between economics of tourism industry and complementary industries with various stakeholders. The quest for alternative tourism or newer forms of tourism like health tourism, rural tourism is also examined, briefly.

Keywords : Inbound Tourism, Foreign Exchange, Rural Tourism, Medical Tourism, Retail

Introduction:

The Indian tourism and hospitality industry has emerged as one of the key drivers of growth among the services sectors in India. Tourism in India has not only led to employment generation but also has enhanced & encouraged entrepreneurship. Tourism in India is a also proving to be a significant source of foreign exchange for the country. In 2013, the travel and tourism industry contributed Rs 2.17 trillion (US$ 36 billion) or 2 per cent to the country's gross domestic product (GDP). This is expected to rise to Rs 4.35 trillion (US$ 72.17 billion) in 2024. Before we go any further the economic activity of tourism can be divided in to three parts: a) Inbound tourism b) Outbound tourism c) Domestic tourism. The Inbound tourism is where the foreigners visit India. The outbound tourism is when the Indian tourists go abroad & then there is domestic tourism in which citizens of India visit tourist sites located within the domestic territory of India itself. Amongst the three the most vibrant tourism economic activity is the inbound tourism.

The tourism industry in India is thriving due to an increase in foreign tourist arrivals (FTA) and a greater number of Indians travelling to domestic destinations than before. The revenue from domestic tourism is likely to grow by 8.2 per cent in 2014 as compared to 5.1 per cent a year ago, according to the World Travel and Tourism Council (WTTC). Hotels are also an extremely important component of tourism industry.

The Indian hospitality sector has been growing at a cumulative annual growth rate of 14 per cent every year adding significant amount of foreign exchange to the economy.

Prospects In Tourism Industry:

The Indian tourism and hospitality industry has emerged as one of the key drivers of growth among the services sectors in India apart from being an economic activity that helps not only the people directly involved in the activity but also the local communities.

The foreign direct investment (FDI) inflows in hotel and tourism sector during April 2000 to January 2014 stood at US$ 7,013.29 million, as per the data released by Department of Industrial Policy and Promotion (DIPP).

The following are some of the major investments and developments in the Indian tourism and hospitality sector:

- Hilton Worldwide has signed a management agreement with Palm Grove Beach Hotels Pvt Ltd, hospitality arm of K Raheja Constructions Group, to open the first Conrad hotel in India. Conrad – the luxury brand of Hilton Worldwide – will be launched in Pune, Maharashtra next year.
- Indian hotel chain Lemon Tree Hotels is planning to enter the luxury segment. The company is in talks with two luxury brands in the US and Asia. Lemon Tree is keen on acquisitions to expedite its growth.
- Thomas Cook (India) announced a part-cash part-equity merger deal with Sterling Holidays to create India's largest holiday company. "The merger aims at building a holiday behemoth which will take holidays to a larger population," as per Mr Ramesh Ramanathan, Managing Director (MD), Sterling Holidays.
- Marriott International plans to open a dozen hotels in India by 2015, adding to its existing count of 23 properties. "Currently we have about six to eight definite openings in 2014 and 2015 is going to be a very strong year for us," as per Mr Rajeev Menon, Area Vice President – South Asia and Australia, Marriott Hotels.
- Muthoot Leisure and Hospitality Services, the hospitality division of the Muthoot Group, has announced the acquisition of Costa Rica's high-end property – Xandari Resort & Spa. This is the first acquisition by an Indian hospitality company in Central America.

The 360 Degree Economic Development As a Result of Tourism:

Infrastructure, Small Scale & Middle Scale Development: A Case of Goa

Tourism in its most basic and intrinsic concept cannot stand alone. It has to be supported by & in return supports many other Industries & economic activities that make it a viable offer for the tourists. Although Africa is a much sought after tourist destination yet Somalia inspite of its beautiful beaches is never a choice for obvious reasons. Let us discuss a union territory of India to understand the role and importance that tourism can play in enhancing the overall economy of a state. Goa was liberated much after the rest of India and yet has proceeded to grow at a much faster rate than most of the states with in the republic of India.

At the time of Liberation in 1961, there were hardly any industrial activities in Goa with the exception of mining. Contributing to this was that the State had lost out on two Five Year Plans that had provided the rest of the Country a valuable lead in economic growth.

Goa today has over 6700 Small Scale Industrial units, 147 Large and Medium Scale Industries employing over 50,000 people. The State has developed/ established 20 industrial estates; some of them are among the best in the country. The industrial activities encompass about 50 sub sectors which include tourism, pharmaceuticals, electrical and automobile accessories etc. The Government is now gearing up for accelerated industrial development and overall economic growth. While drafting this policy, proper environmental concern, social infrastructure, well being of its people and needs of existing industries have been taken into consideration.

Goa has done fairly well in last two decades on the Industrial front in spite of various handicaps. The explanation for this lays not so much in any planned development strategy that the State adopted - indeed there was a pointed lack of any such strategy but in Goa's natural advantages and inherent strengths. The breath-taking natural beauty of Goa attracts tourists from all over the world creating a flourishing tourism industry that is a significant source of revenue and employment generation.

Goa is strategically located in terms of tourism & transport hence the major focus was to develop good infrastructure facilities such as centrally located airport, a seaport, connectivity by excellent road network as also other essential infrastructure like Container Freight Station etc . Today the State boasts of one of the country's highest telecom densities. Fibre optic connectivity too has spread its network across the State, bringing state of art telecommunication to the people. Every village in the State is electrified. As regards power for the industry, there is sufficient power reserve and the tariff has been pegged at very reasonable rates. All these efforts are primarily made for & by the revenue generation through enhancing tourism experiences of the travelers who visit this amazing destination with astonishing & breathtaking natural beauty.

Goa is the only State in the country which possesses the distinction of achieving high level of both economic and social development. Average economic growth of 10% per annum, the highest per capita income (Rs.61,301 per annum) and high level of Social Infrastructure Indicators are the testimony for the same. Thus, the State has extremely favourable climate to aim to become a "Model State".

Tourism & Retail:

The first thought of any lady who is packing for a travel is whether the site has good shopping prospects or not. It is the thrill & pleasure of bringing back something for the house and the loved ones that make an integral part of an overall travel experience. The first question that is asked by the family and friends of the people who have just made it back from a travel is " What did you get for Us?" Hence retailing and tourism have shared a long and successful journey, often it is known only by all those who have been out for travel. Discussing one such tourist destination that displays a direct relation of tourism & retail Maria Fok , in her essay "Beyond our imagination – the retailing and tourism relationship" (Woolsworth, NSW), up to 81% of visitors to Australia consider shopping as one of their primary leisure activities. Tourism generated $77 billion in consumption in one year in Australia out of which $17.7 billion (23%) was retailing expenditure by the tourists.

We know of countries like Hong Kong, Singapore and Dubai, which have successfully leveraged retailing to develop tourism. Fifth largest shopping destination globally, India is packed with beautiful things to buy and when one feels to shop for traditional & ethnic handicrafts, each state of India has something to offer the tourists.

Incredible India' has been established as a brand by government initiative, which can be used as a marketing tool to promote the Indian authenticity of their products. At the same time, India tops A T Kearney's list of emerging markets for global retailers for the last two years.

This relationship is playing a major role in generation of revenue stream for both sectors. This economic relationship in turn can be beneficial for hotel industry, travel and tours business, shopping mall developers, corporate chains focused on themed retailing, airport retailing, highway retailing etc. Further the development of "Themed Market Places" as a viable format of retail has only been possible with the focus on tourists as shoppers. Dilli-Haat in New Delhi is a prime example of the same. It showcases ethnic Indian clothes and artifacts for selling to tourists.

Rural Development Through Rural Tourism:

India is known as "Land of Farmers". Farmers have always played an important role in the economy of India where they have been a part of the Green & White revolution the two most vibrant economic revolutions in economic history of India. But today more than 77 crore farmers living in 5.5 lakhs of village (2001) are facing tough times. Today the Indian Agriculture has to face tremendous competition because of the driven global trends. To add to this the agriculture crop growth is also weakened due to the uncertain climatic conditions. There is no minimum support price guarantee also. Agriculture contributed about 18.5% of the national income (2006-07) as compared to a high 50% in 1950. 85% of population of India still depends on Agriculture hence Agriculture is not mere business, but is still the "True Culture of India".

These changes have altered the form and practices of farming operation and forced farmers to look beyond traditional farming to generate income via various forms of direct on farm marketing and farm based non-agriculture business.

Global economic restructuring has created a climate in which many local economies have to adjust, in order to maintain or enhance their socio-economic viability. As Butler et al. (1998) note economic and social forces operating at the global level are determining both the nature and form of the rural landscape and how we value and use it. These changes, coupled with new ideas and approaches to leisure and recreation time are encouraging tourism development in rural areas at an ever increasing pace (Williams 1998: Reid et al. 2000).

Rural tourism development would not only be beneficial for the tourism industry in itself but would rather provide the farmers with a viable economic option to agriculture. They will have an additional source of income along with their agricultural income. Employment creation, increase in the price of land, improvement in public services, modernization of agriculture and development of local businesses are other important incremental benefits that the Hinterland can certainly do with.

Promotion to Medicine & Hospitality Industry:

India is perceived as one of the fastest growing medical tourism destinations. According to a recent RNCOS report 'Booming Medical Tourism in India', Indian medical tourism industry is anticipated to register a compound annual growth rate (CAGR) of more than 20 per cent during 2013–15, therefore creating a huge scope for investments.

Hotels are also an extremely important component of tourism industry. The Indian hospitality sector has been growing at a cumulative annual growth rate of 14 per cent every year adding significant amount of foreign exchange to the economy.

Conclusion:

Over the decades, tourism has experienced continued growth and deepening diversification to become one of the fastest growing economic sectors in the world. Tourism has become a thriving global industry with the power to shape developing countries in ways never imagined. No doubt it has become the fourth largest industry in the global economy.

Similarly, in developing countries like India tourism has become one of the major sectors of the economy, contributing to a large proportion of the National Income and generating huge employment opportunities. It has become the fastest growing service industry in the country with great potentials for its further expansion and diversification. And India for its own sake will have to find ways of generating and keeping the tourism traffic while preserving its own culture & economy that are in fact the cause of the traffic.

References:

Haldar Piali "Rural Tourism – Challenges and Opportunities."

Kunal and Asif Zameer "Significance of Relation between Retailing and Tourism in Designing Credit Derivative Products for Financing Tourism and Retailing Infrastructure."

http://www.goaditc.gov.in/industry.html

www. tourisminindia.com

http://www.ibef.org/industry/tourism-hospitality-india.aspx

www.medicaltourismassociation.com/

ISSUES IN TOURISM DEVELOPMENT

ISSUES IN TOURISM DEVELOPMENT

"Artists are not cheerleaders, and we're not the heads of tourism boards. We expose and discuss what is problematic, what is contradictory, what is hurtful and what is silenced in the culture we're in."

—Junot Diaz

The above quote truly depicts the spirit of this section of the book. This section of the book is an attempt to present readers an overview of the inherent issues related with the development of tourism. The chapters contributed by the researchers are focused on various aspects of the very diverse tourism industry. The first chapter 'A Study of Work Life Balance in the Hotel Industry of Punjab- a Case Study of Jalandhar & Ludhiana' by Anjali Khanna has taken a study of hotel industry and the chapter has put forward the issues related with the work life balance in hospitality industry. Chapter says that it is difficult for the hotel employee to make balance between their personal and professional life because of long working hours that may extend to more than 15 hours. Employees do not find enough time to meet their social needs for e.g. Time to spend with family and friends, community activities, enjoy and organizing the parties etc. Editors have deliberately chosen this chapter as the inaugural chapter of this section, since human resource is much more fragile resource and needs proper care and nurturing.

The chapter 'Impact of Globalization on Hotel and Catering Industry in India: HR perspective' by S.Meera and P.Premkanna attempts to analyse 3 aspects first, the radical changes in hospitality industry, with focus on hotel and catering sector as a result of globalization. Second, high employee turnover increase due to globalization, problems faced by various employees serving the hotel industry which could be the contributing factor to the high rate of attrition in this sector. Finally, employee retention strategies exclusively appropriate for the hospitality sector has been suggested.

Chapter 'Cooperative Tourism: a driving force of local and State development' by R.P.Nainta concluded that the important role of participatory and community based organizations like cooperatives in promoting tourism has yet to be recognized. As a result, the concepts like "sustainable tourism", "poverty reduction through tourism", 'community tourism', etc. which can be best implemented through participatory institutions have yet to be popularized in a big way.

N N Sharma in the chapter 'Impact of Tourism Industry in India' has attempted to study the scenario of tourism Industry and to analyze impact of Foreign tourist Arrival on growth of foreign exchange earnings in India. Chapter 'Good Governance: Sine Qua Non Of Tourism Industry in Manipur' by Oinam Momoton Singh and RajendraKshetri tries to conceive good governance as an important component of tourism industry from a sociological perspective.

Charu Sheela Yadav and Pawan Gupta in their chapter 'Role of Celebrity in Tourist Destination Marketing in India' tried to bring out the role and importance of celebrity marketing in tourism industry in India with special reference to "Khoshboo Gujarat Ki" campaign by Amitabh Bachchan. Chapter 'Perception, Attitude and Satisfaction of Packaged Tourism Users of Tamil Nadu' by P.Premkanna and G.B.Karthikeyan concluded that the business of tour operators is booming at a fast pace in spite of several limitations. There has been a growth in the tourism industry which has come up as one of the fastest booming industries in many countries across the globe.

'Emerging Tourist Preferences and Attractions in HP: A Survey' the chapter by S L Kaushal and Balbir Singh concluded that most of the tourists prefer HP for natural beauty and pleasant weather. It is noted that majority tourists decide destination on the issues of climate and personal safety. The tourists identified major irritants in tourism industry of HP like transportation facilities, road conditions and hotels availability.

Chapter 'Comparative Analysis of Marketing Practices of Hotels of Chandigarh and Delhi Managerial Prospective' by Tanvi has provided an insight about two different cities that how the marketing practices vary among them. The findings of a survey on hotels of these two cities suggest that practices like association with tour operator, travel agencies and airlines, loyalty and reward programs are given equal importance but there is a little variation in certain marketing practices like integrated marketing with front office, identifying profitable customers, green marketing with eco- friendly products etc. The main of chapter 'Tourism for Community Development: Issues, Lessons and Ideas' by Yashwant Gupta and Shakti Singh is to highlight this modern concept of "tourism for community development" and bring forward the aspects associated with it.

With the passage of time, a paradigm shift has been noticed from traditional to non-traditional resources resulting in diversification of the tourism product. During the past decade, particularly in the new millennium, a number of dimensions have been added to the tourism product. Some of the dimensions are

1. Diversification in travel pattern: There is evident change in old and modern travel pattern. Earlier there was flow of tourists from east to west, now it is North-South flow. People now taking trips to within their region, which lead to end in the Atlantic dominance. This paradigm shift suggests the Asia-Pacific dominance. There is also a shift in duration of tour from long tour to short journeys, reasons may be lack of time and development in transportation facilities. Now travel is considered as a free trade.
2. Diversification in destinations: The travel has now changed from established tourism destinations to unexplored travel destinations. Emergence of China, African countries and India in global tourism map is the best example of this shift in destination choice.
3. Diversification in industry attitude: The attitude of tourism industry has changed a lot. Earlier countries were concerned with number of visitors but now they are thinking of economic and social benefits of tourism. Earlier there was a lot of competition among countries but now they are opting for intelligent cooperation. Product was the major dominating

factor in old tourism, which now has been changed to customer orientation.

4. Diversification in products: Earlier travel was limited to natural environment and people were interested in single activity and biggest constraint on tourism was seasonality. Now the product has changed to artificial environment and people are opting for multiple activity based tours. Present tourism is now has taken shape of all weather tourism.
5. Diversification in developer control: The developers control over tourism has also changed with time. There was the time of political lobbying, which now changed to approvals via referendum. These days' developers are giving more importance to jobs and small businesses rather than just going for more and more economic impacts of tourism. We have changed our focus from environment protection to environment improvement. Earlier tourist arrival was considered as cultural intrusion, where as these days this is considered as a major force for heritage protection.
6. Diversification in financial attitude: Present concern is now on developing franchise opportunities, meeting investors' needs through economic simulation. Tourism is now on top priority list of states' budget.
7. Diversification in consumer attitude: Tourist has also changed a lot. He is now a value conscious traveller, who is traveling for self improvement through vivid experiences.
8. Diversification in observing technologies: The observing technologies have also changed from simple print media to interactive media and maps has been replaced by GIS and GPS technology.
9. Diversification in marketing style: This is one of the best thing happened to tourism. Now targeted customers are considered as data base rather than socio-economic groups. The place of one way communication has been taken by relationships through customer management techniques (Bansal Et. Al 2011).

A STUDY OF WORK LIFE BALANCE IN THE HOTEL INDUSTRY OF PUNJAB- A CASE STUDY OF JALANDHAR & LUDHIANA

Anjali Khanna

Associate Dean, School of Hotel Management and Tourism, Lovely Professional University Phagwara, Punjab.

anjali.khanna@lpu.co.in

Abstract

Work-life balance has always been a concern of those interested in the quality of working life and its relation to broader quality of life. Work-life balance is about effectively managing the responsibilities at work, at home, and in other aspects of life. The study examines the key issues associated with Work-Life balance, team work, personal needs, compensation & benefits, time management of employees in hospitality sector particularly in hotels in Punjab. The research focused on Luxury Hotels located in Ludhiana, Jalandhar, Phagwara and a sample of 50 respondents was taken randomly. The data was collected from the people working in different luxury properties in select cities. The study also identified implications on factors like effects on social needs, time management, and personal needs.

Keywords: Work life balance, Hotel industry, Punjab, personal needs, issues

Introduction

Work-life balance

WLB has been defined as a state of equilibrium in which the demands of both people's Job and personal life are equal (Work Life balance, 2002, the word spy). Greenblatt (2002) described work life balance as acceptable levels of conflict between work and non-work demands. This according to her usually involves managing competing demands for the resources. She suggested that achieving work life balance is dependent on attaining and managing sufficient resources to make possible the achievements that people regard as the most important. The team Work life balance was coined in 1986, although its usage in everyday language was sporadic for a number of years. Interestingly, work/life programs existed as early as 1930's. beforeWW2, the W.K Kellogg Company created for six hour shifts to replace the traditional three daily eight hour shifted and the new shifts resulted in increased employee morale and efficiency (lackwood, 2003). Work Life balance, in its broadest sense, is defined as a satisfactory level of involvement or fit between the multiple roles in a person's life. Although definitions and explanations vary, work life balance is generally associated with equilibrium or maintaining an overall sense of harmony in life. The study of work life balance involves the examination of people's ability to manage simultaneously the multi-faceted demands of life. Although work life balance has traditionally been assumed to involve the devotion of equal amount of time given to paid work and non-work roles, involvement balance i.e the level of psychological involvement in, or commitment to, work and non-work roles, satisfied balance i.e. the level of satisfaction with work and non-work roles.

The types of roles, as well as the characteristics of those roles, are important to consider in understanding the balancing of work and family. There is mixed evidence of the effects of combinations of roles on well-being. Although more roles often protect mental health, certain combinations also can contribute to strain (Barnett, 1997).

The concept of work-life balance is based on the notion that paid work and Personal life should be seen less as competing priorities than as complementary elements of a full life. The way to achieve this is to adopt an approach that is —conceptualized as a two way process involving a consideration of the needs of employees as well as those of employer (Lewis, 2000). In order to engage employers in this process it is important to demonstrate the benefits that can be derived from employment policies and practices that support work-life balance, and the scope that exists for mitigating their negative effects on the management of the business.

Hospitality industry

Hospitality industry is the fastest growing industry in the world. One of the most exciting aspect of this industry is that it is made up of so many different professions. As diverse as the hospitality industry is, there are some powerful and common dynamics, which include the delivery of services and products and the guest's impressions of them. Whether an employee is in direct contact with the guest or performing duties behind the scenes, the profound and most challenging reality of working in this industry is that hospitality employees have the ability to affect the human experience by creating powerful impression- even brief moments of truth- that may last a lifetime.(John R. Walker,2012). Hospitality industry is the field that specializes in delivering services to direct customers. The hospitality industry ensures that the recipients are well treated to ensure that they enjoy their leisure time to the maximum The hospitality industry is, in general, a labour-intensive industry that depends on the abilities and motivations of its employees (King, 2010).

The Indian tourism and hospitality industry has emerged as one of the key industries driving growth of the services sector in India. Hospitality and Tourism in India has registered significant growth in the recent years and the country has tremendous potential to become a major global tourist destination.

Work-life balance and hospitality industry

The hospitality industry is a highly guest service-oriented business which means that encounters between employees and guest determine the success of the business. Consequently hospitality researchers and business leaders have acknowledged the significance of hiring and retaining competent employees and have arguably considered the company's employee as the most valuable asset to hospitality firms. Therefore, Training and qualification is an important avenue to explore. This is especially true in the hospitality industry where longer work hours is considered the accepted norm-Where other industries have 35-40 hrs.' a week, hospitality is approximately is 50hrs with the expectation of a further time commitment whenever necessary. One of the biggest challenges in the service industry is managing manpower. Company controlled flexibility to maintain competitiveness may be forcing a number of workers into an irregular time schedule. The labour force has always included workers who have had to adjust to irregular social hours. Police staff, hospital and airport staff, maintenance workers in electricity, telephone and Water services together with employees in the hospitality industry. Today citizens who have to work irregular hours are not restricted to such categories of workers (Saviour Rizzo). The recent study by Pocock et al (2007) is consistently associated with worse work – life outcomes on all our work life measures'. Such findings suggest that there is an unhealthy acceptance of long working hours, especially in the service industries of hospitality and tourism. What is equally important, particularly for younger workers, is the fact that these hours are unsocial and often mean that there is little flexibility in the way that such workers conduct their social / family lives. Ultimately, this lack of flexibility often leads to employees leaving the industry, not just the organization, further exacerbating the labour shortages being experienced in a range of industries.

Literature review

Swamy,(2007) defined Work-Life balance as a practice that is concerned with providing scope for employees to balance their work with the responsibilities and interests they have outside their work. It enables them to reconcile the competing claims of work and home by meeting their own needs as well as those of their employees. Work life balance and personal life are interconnected and interdependent. Spending more time in office, dealing with clients and pressure of job can be interfere and affect the personal life, sometimes making it impossible to even complete the household chores(Hudson,1998).on the other hand personal life can be demanding if you have a kid or aging parents, financial problems or even problems in the life of dear relative. It can lead to absenteeism from work, creating stress and lack of concentration at work. Work personal life conflict occurs when the burden, obligations and responsibilities of work and family roles become incompatible. (Duxbury & Higgins, 2001). Brought et al(2008) examined that there was increasing evidence that work life imbalance had a direct impact on societal issues, such as delayed parenting, declining fertility rates, ageing population, and decreasing labor supply. It was documented that work life balance policies were beneficial for individuals, their families, organizations and society. However, other evidence demonstrated that the associated benefits were not always realized and work life balance policies result in reinforced gender inequities and increased levels of work life conflict. This paper reviewed the ability of work life balance policies to actually influence some key social and organizational issues. Current developments, such as increased casual workforce and the impact of changes in newly industrialized nations, were discussed. Recommendations for work life balance to be addressed via comprehensive multilevel approach are made. Margaret Deery(2008) said that the long, unsocial hours within the industry, the levels of stress associated with job insecurity, role ambiguity, job autonomy and time pressures, together with home-life pressures and psychosomatic symptoms, are variables that impact negatively on WLB.

Objectives

- To understand the meaning of Work-Life balance for employees in the hotels of Jalandhar & Ludhiana
- To understand the various factors affecting the Work-Life balance of employees in the Hotels of Punjab.
- To study the relationship between Work-Life balance and, Social Needs, Personal Needs, Compensation &Benefits, Time Management, and Team Work.

Research methodology

The sample frame of the study was luxury hotels located in Ludhiana, Jalandhar, Phagwara. Viz. Radisson Windsor, Ramada,

Cabana, Park Plaza, Hyatt etc. Structured questionnaire were used to obtain response from the 50 employees of the selected hotels using random sampling. Secondary data was collected through research articles, journals, websites and magazines.

Findings and Discussion

It is difficult for the hotel employee to make balance between their personal and professional life because of long working hours that may extend to more than 15 hours. Employees do not find enough time to meet their social needs for e.g. Time to spend with family and friends, community activities, enjoy and organizing the parties etc. Most of the employees work for extra hours to get their work done, so it is not easy for them to manage time and not able to adjust their working schedule to attend their life priorities. Employees are not able to meet there personal needs, sometime they get stuck in meeting etc. the response is more than average in meeting the personal needs. They meet the expectations of their colleagues, they enjoy and want to work in team to complete the assigned work on time and correctly. Employees like the kind of work they do, they don't have any difficulty in meetings the expectations. Overall result of the analysis is that the work life is not completely balanced because the scale result 53.78 out of 100. An overview of the statements and their interpretations are as follows:

40% of the employees said that they do not find it difficult to take leave at the time of social emergencies, 30% of the employees neither agreed nor disagreed with the statement, 20% of the employees disagreed with the statement that they do not find it difficult to take leave at the time of social emergencies, 8% strongly agreed and 2% strongly disagreed with the statement. Majority of the respondents agreed with the statement that they do exercise and take care of their health. 52% people agreed with the statement that they work for extra hours to get their work done. Most of the respondents agreed that they meet the expectations of their colleagues and workmates. Also most of the employees agreed with the statement that they feel pressure while working when a given a deadline.

50% employees agree with the statement that they do not find enough time to spend with family and friends, 14% people strongly agreed, 26% people gave a neutral response, 6% disagree and 4% people are strongly disagree with the statement. It was also found that employees do not experience work pressure while doing a group task. Another important finding of the study is that many respondents are not able to help their children/siblings for their exams. Further 36% of the employees disagreed with the statement that they do not get the time for their sick parents/child/partner, 28% gave neutral response, 26% agreed with the statement, 8% strongly disagreed, 2% strongly agreed. Study also revealed that employees do not get time to invite their friends for a party at home and most of the employees found the traveling time to organization uncomfortable. Yet the positive findings say maximum employee enjoy doing their job, however many time employees have to do overtime to complete their work.

Recommendations

The recommendations are the important part of any type of study because through this one comes to know about the shortcomings of their study and helps in further improvements. The following recommendations were made after the study:

- The employees should not give excess work so that they feel over burden with work
- They employees should be given annual leaves so that it can be used by the hotel employee time to time for different purpose.
- The management should pay for the overtime work done by the employees.
- Fringe benefits apart from the basic salary in terms of festive season bonus, increments in salaries etc. should be given to the employees at all the levels so that they feel motivated because a motivated employee always contribute maximum towards his/her place.
- Festival must be celebrated, so that even if the employees are not able to attend with family they won't feel.
- There should be healthy relationship among the employees
- Organizations should acknowledge that individuals at all stages of their lives work best when they are able to achieve balance between work and all other aspects of their lives.

- Organization should highlight the employers and employees joint responsibility to discuss workable solutions and encourage partnership between individuals and mangers.
- Flexible working hours should be given to the employees so that they would be able to balance their personal life and professional life.
- Organizations should recognize effective practices to promote work life balance will benefit the organization and its employee.
- If the proper work life balance policies are provided than employees would feel more motivated towards work and will be stress free and work with their full potential.

References

Barnett, R. C. (1997). Gender, employment, and psychological well-being: Historical and life course perspectives. In M. E. Lachman& J. B. James (Eds.), Multiple paths of midlife development. Chicago: University of Chicago Press.

Baum, T. (2002), "Skills Training In The Hospitality Sector: A Review Of Issues", Journal Of Vocational Education & Training, 54 (3), 343-63.

Brough, P. et al. (2008) The Ability Of Work Life Balance Policies To Influence Key Social/Organizational Issues, Asia Pacific Journal Of Human Resources,46(3),261-273.

Deery, M. (2008), Talent management, work-life balance and retention strategies, Emerald Group Publishing Limited, International Journal of Contemporary Hospitality Management 20 (7), 792-806.

Eva H. Chittenden, M.D.1 and Christine S. Ritchie M.D. (2011), —Work-Life Balancing: Challenges and Strategies. Journal of Palliative Medicine, 14(7).

Evans (2001) Greater flexibility in deploying staff such as an ability to offer extended hours of Business to customers. Human Resources Development Canada.

Igbinomwanhia, O. I., Festus I. (2012). Employee Work-Life Balance as an HR Imperative. 6 (3), 109-126.

King C (2010) One Size Doesn't Fit All—Tourism and Hospitality Employees 'Response to Internal Brand Management. International Journal of Contemporary Hospitality Management, 22(4): 517–534.

Lewis, S. (2000) Workplace Programmes and Policies In The United Kingdom, In Haas L., Hwang P. And Russell G. (Eds.) Organisational Change and Gender Equity, London: Sage.

Naithani. P. (2010), Overview of Work-Life Balance Discourse and Its Relevance in Current Economic Scenario. Vol. 6, No. 6.

Nancy R. L. (2003), Work/Life Balance Challenges and Solutions, Society for Human Resource Management.

Rabia U., &Rehman, M. Z. U. (2013),—Impact Of Work-Life Balance And Work-Life Conflict On The Life Satisfaction Of Working Women: A Case Study Of Higher Education Sector Of Twin Cities Of Pakistan Academic Research International.

SaviourRizzo. Work-Life Balance With Focus On Family Life, Malta Employers' Association.

Swamy,(2007). Work-Life Balance Organizational Strategies for Sustainable Growth, Hrm Review.

Walker, J. R. (2010). Introduction to Hospitality Management. Pearson.

IMPACT OF GLOBALIZATION ON HOTEL AND CATERING INDUSTRY IN INDIA: HR PERSPECTIVE

S. Meera

Assistant Professor (International Business), Indian Institute Of Tourism and Travel Management (Under Ministry Of Tourism), Government of India, Nellore, Andra Pradesh

P. Premkanna

Associate Professor & Head, Department of Catering & Hotel Management, Hindusthan College of Arts & Science, Coimbatore. Tamilnadu.

premkannap@gmail.com

Abstract

Hotel, Catering and the Hospitality Industry has assumed a lot of significance with the growth of tourism and related activities. Globalization has engulfed all the emerging economies and has cast its shadow on all industries; hospitality not being an exception.

This paper attempts to analyse 3 aspects first, the radical changes in hospitality industry, with focus on hotel and catering sector as a result of globalization. Second, high employee turnover increase due to globalization, problems faced by various employees serving the hotel industry which could be the contributing factor to the high rate of attrition in this sector. Finally, employee retention strategies exclusively appropriate for the hospitality sector has been suggested.

Keywords: Globalization, Employee turnover, Human Resource Management.

Hospitality industry includes Hotels, Restaurants, Casinos, Resorts, Clubs and any other service position that deal with tourists. (Percy, 2008). Hotel and catering Industry has been a part of the hospitality sector. Hotel and catering industry in Indian context refers to all the hotels ranging from 5 star to the uncategorized hotels. There is lot of documented work on the human resource requirements, HR problems faced in hotel industry etc in comparison to other sectors associated with tourism. However, not much work is done on uncategorized hotels, as their contribution to tourism is not significant. Now with the growth of domestic tourism, uncategorized hotels have a prominent role to play, as they are affordable in terms of cost to the middle class population.

Impact of globalization in Hospitality Industry

Globalization, as a process and as a phenomenon has influenced all the economies especially the emerging economies. The hotel and catering industry is not an exception. It is evident through:

1. Growth in tourism Sector has resulted in expansion of hospitality sector: Tourism sector as a whole has witnessed growth since 2000-2001. As of May 2011, contribution to the hospitality industry which comprises of hotels, restaurants and allied services to Indian gross domestic product was a significant 2.2%.Hospitality sector handled 5.58mn international tourist arrivals (8.1%) y-o-y growth and 740.21 mn domestic tourists in 2010(10.7%) y-o-y growth. The robust growth in tourism would not have been possible without the expansion in hospitality sector. Hospitality industry is expected to grow US $36 billion by 2018 and this means a significant growth is expected in hotel and catering sector.
2. Increase in domestic tourist arrivals: Domestic tourist arrivals have increased in all destinations due to the growing prosperity of middle class, which is a result of globalization.
3. Growth in hotel management education: Hotel management Education has increased in number and also in terms of quality, to cater to the requirements of tourists.

4. Tough Competition: Competition has tightened in all the sectors especially among hoteliers as a result of globalization because the hospitality industry is linked to other sectors like tourism, which is expected to grow in near future. Maintenance of skilled human resources has become a must for enhancing the quality of services.
5. Employee attrition: Hospitality Industry has witnessed high employee turnover. The attrition rates are high as employees switch over to either other lucrative professions like BPO's etc which have mushroomed due to globalization or employees move to hotels with favourable working conditions, salary etc. According to Hemdi and Nasurdin(2006),hotels all over the world have experienced high turnover rates, which is estimated to range from 60% to 300%.
6. Mismatch between demand and supply requirements in hotel and catering industry: There is a mismatch between the demand and supply of skilled labour force in hotel industry. The demand has increased due to growth and expansion in this sector while the supply is less.
7. Free movement of skilled labour force across borders has become possible due to international agreements like GATS, which has led to movement of human resources in hospitality sector move abroad in search of lucrative jobs.

Background of study

An attempt has been made to understand the radical changes in hospitality industry in the backdrop of globalization due to high rate of employee attrition on one hand and the growing demand for skilled manpower in hospitality industry on the other. In such a situation, it becomes necessary to study the existing conditions in hotel and catering industry to understand the possibility of voluntary turnovers as result of job dissatisfaction. According to O'Connell(2007),Turnover is high when employees are dissatisfied. According to Mobley Model, due to job dissatisfaction an employee thinks in terms of quitting the present job. The problems faced by the employees of this sector as highlighted below indicates the areas of dissatisfaction, which when neglected in long run might result in high voluntary employee Turnover which can affect the industry as a whole. Better human resource management is the only solution to reduce the turnover.

Objectives

1. Analyse the impact of globalization on hospitality industry.
2. Problems faced by employees across different levels, serving hospitality industry are analyzed.
3. Recommend employee retention strategies appropriate for hospitality industry.

Methodology

Primary data through schedules has been collected from uncategorized hotels, around 10 hotels in Thirupati, Andhra Pradesh. On the basis of convenience sampling, 15 employees of each hotel were considered from various categories: waiters, receptionists, room service for the purpose of study. The questionnaire had open ended questions with the purpose of identifying the prominent problems.

Limitations

1. Only uncategorized sized hotels have been considered for the study.
2. Sample size is small.
3. Certain categories of employees in the hospitality sector have only been included for the study.

HR Problems

On the basis of the primary data collected, following problems were identified:

1. Low salary: The salaries offered by the hotels were extremely low. It was ranging from Rs 3000 to Rs 5000 in the lower management and from Rs 8000 to 12000 in the middle level management. As the salaries were not attractive, nearly 95.3 %(143 employees) of the employees were planning to quit, if they got better opportunities.
2. Work environment: Congenial work environment is required

to increase productivity of labourers as well as to increase their job satisfaction. In the case of nearly 75.3 %(113 employees) of the employees work environment was a deterring factor.

3. Working hours: Very long working hours without break was yet another discouraging factor. 82% of employees (123 Nos) were dissatisfied with the long working hours, especially women.

4. Perks and other benefits: Overtime duties were not paid. If at all it was paid it was very paltry. Accommodation was not provided or it was not very comfortable in most of the cases. Other perks like medical allowances, bonus, and travel allowances were given in accordance to whims and fancies of owners without much regard to seniority etc. Out of 150 employees, 141 had expressed dissatisfaction. (94%)

5. Career Advancement: Performance based promotions were not there. Around 66.7 %(100 employees) had expressed concern. However the People in the lower management like laundry service, sweepers etc were not much aware of career advancement.

6. Training opportunities and enhancement of skills: Training opportunities to enhance skills are not provided by employers. Even if other organizations are providing the same, employees are not allowed to participate. Training is imparted in some hotels at induction level. However this has not been construed as a problem by those in lower levels.56.6% has identified this as a major issue.

7. Employee-Employer relations: Most of the employees, 90% (135 out of 150) opined that the employers are hostile and prejudice prone. Decision making was purely centralized.

8. Job security: Job security was not there among 94.66% of employees. Most of them were enrolled on contract basis and long term employment was not assured. Most of them were threatened on the basis of this and more work was extracted.

9. HR practices were not standardized: Policies pertaining to recruitment, promotion, retrenchment etc are not standardized. Lack of transparency is evident.98.66% were of this opinion. Probably if the HR practices are standardized most of the problems cited above can be resolved.

10. Threat of closure of hotels: Competition among hoteliers poses a threat to the employees. Nearly 20% of the employees were of this opinion.

Retention Strategies

Standardised Human resource management practices are mandatory for capitalizing on the human resources. Professional ethics with respect to recruitments, promotions, and work culture is a must for sustaining HR gains in long run.

Supply of competent and skilled human resource is the biggest challenge before Indian Industry especially at managerial level. (CII, Seminar on HR, October 2007)

Hotel and catering sector must offer services which are personalized in nature in order to attract customers.

Persistent attempts to build teams across categories and efforts to increase employee motivation must be a part of HR department. HR departments must follow modern HR methods of recruitment, training, performance appraisal etc.

Apart from clearly defined performance expectations of hotel employees, accurate job descriptions, and career opportunities human resource managers in hotels, as their counter parts in other industries, need to become increasingly aware of other elements of integrated human resource management strategy designed to meet corporate objectives and increasingly raise productivity and thence profitability levels. These practices include job rotation, training and development, performance management, effective employee communication, rewards system, turnover and wastage analysis.(Percy,2008).

The hotel and catering industry has a very important role to play in terms of generating employment. However, despite its potential to provide employment, it has often been known for employee churn out and employee switch over which is a disturbing trend. It is high time for hoteliers to rise to the occasion and attempt to cater to the needs of the employees, identify the gaps in Human resource management to prevents further attrition.

Bibliography

K.Singh, Percy. HRM in Hotel and Tourism Industry ,Existing Trends and Practices. New Delhi: Kanishka Publishers, 2008.

Laws, Eric. Improving Tourism and hospitality services. UK: CABI PUBLISHING, 2004.

Mukesh R, Ashish Chandra. Tourism and hospitality in 21st century. New Delhi: Discovery publishing house, 2003.

CO-OPERATIVE TOURISM: A DRIVING FORCE OF LOCAL AND STATE DEVELOPMENT

R.P.Nainta

Principal, Agriculture Cooperative Staff Training Institute, Sangti, Summerhill, Shimla

rpnainta@gmail.com

1. Backdrop

The economic liberalization in India has given a big push to Indian tourism especially in rural areas through cooperatives. Cooperative tourism is today projected as an engine of economic growth and an instrument for eliminating poverty, curbing unemployment problems, opening up new fields of activity and the upliftment of downtrodden sections of society. New opportunities are being tapped in rural areas through cooperatives to promote eco, adventure, rural, postage, wildlife and health and herbal including medical tourism. With the increasing number of foreign tourists coming to India every year and domestic tourism is gaining popularity. Tourism has long been identified as one of the sunrise sectors for India which can serve the dual purpose of not only earning foreign exchange as well as the disposable domestic income but also boosting inclusion. With its backward and forward linkages and local connect, tourism becomes an important driver of equitable growth and prosperity offering an alternative source of livelihood, development and growth in remote locations, preservation of local skills, enterprise development at the micro level, and sustainable environment management. In India, while tourism is one of the largest employers, it remains grossly underutilized as a means of creating sustainable financial inclusion. The concept of Cooperative Tourism aims to deliver sustainable economic development by building the capacity of local communities to realize the potential value of their natural and cultural heritage to create tourism enterprise opportunities through a co-operative destination management model, which not only supplement incomes, but act as an incentive (or motivational factor) to preserve local art and culture, and maintain traditional practices like architecture, cuisine, clothing etc. This is where the cooperative model can help bridge the divide. Rather than individual efforts being driven single-handedly, the cooperative model brings all the aspects of a tourism product under the ambit of a cooperative structure, which not only controls the structure and volume of tourist activity, but ensures that the entire destination is promoted rather than fragmented independent entities.

2. Role of Cooperative Tourism in the Development of State

Cooperation means living, thinking and working together. It is working together to learn to live in our society peacefully and harmoniously. A cooperative is an autonomous association of persons united voluntarily to meet their common, economic, social and cultural needs and aspirations through a jointly owned and democratically controlled enterprise. Cooperatives are based on the values of self-help, self-responsibility, democracy, equality, equity and solidarity. Cooperative members believe in the ethical values of honesty, openness, social responsibility and caring for others.

Cooperative institution(s) in India has worked wonders and legitimately the country has proud to be the leader. Starting in 1904, the cooperative movement has made rapid strides in all areas of socio-economic activities. Today, there are more than 5.5 lakh cooperative societies in the country with a membership of 25 crores and working capital of Rs. 200.00 million. IFFCO and KRIBHCO are two cooperative fertilizer giants which have matched global standards of performance. The cooperative credit institutions are disbursing 46.15% of agricultural credit and cooperatives are distributing 36.22% of total fertilizers in the country. Dairy cooperatives in India with their strong and extensive network have excelled in their areas of operations. They have ushered in milk revolution in the country. India is the largest producer of milk in the world. The housing cooperatives in India have not only reaped economic reforms, but have also contributed to peace through promoting social harmony and community living.

In India the cooperatives have played an important role in employment generation. About 15.47 million individuals are employed in the cooperative sector and the numbers of persons who are self-employed in the cooperatives are more than 14.39 million. The cooperatives have shown their strength in social sector too. For example, the sugar cooperatives in Maharashtra have come up in the field of education, health and tourism. In the field of environment, the cooperatives have played an important role in environment preservation. IFFCO has played a laudable role in protecting environment through pollution control measures through its plants and farm forestry cooperatives.

3. Community-Based Initiatives through Cooperatives

At a time when cooperative tourism initiatives have gained momentum in India, the situation is ripe for popularizing the concept of "Peace through Tourism" in a big way through strong advocacy and practical action. Cooperative Tourism as a strategy to promote peace by solving the problems of poverty, unemployment, etc. can succeed if effective inter-linkages are established between "cooperative tourism initiatives" and "peace", and appropriate action plans are devised accordingly. Community-based initiatives through cooperatives based on people's participation have been quite effective in India in solving the socio-economic problems of the people. They have also been successful in building up strong collaborations based on people's efforts which have led to creation of a peaceful and cordial atmosphere. In fact, the peaceful under-currents of Indian democracy are evident in the working of cooperative community-based ventures.

No doubt, in this scenario the value-based organizations have an important role to play in peace-building. The cooperatives have a strategic advantage over other organizations in this respect. The principles and values of cooperatives are the best guidelines to create a sustainable and peaceful world. They are intended to safeguard the human rights and enable the members to practice democracy and enjoy freedom of action. Cooperatives are the organizations which have strong community roots. They are embedded within the communities in which they exist. They work for sustainable development of communities through emphasis on values which create a peaceful atmosphere within the community. 800 million people around the world are members of cooperatives. Worldwide the cooperative movement has contributed to peace by helping eliminate poverty, sustain environment, provide employment, and enrich social standards of the people. The value-based orientation of the cooperative movement has played a crucial role in checking the capitalist tendencies in the society by creating an equalitarian society through which chances of conflict are minimized.

The institutions like cooperatives can play an important role in peace building if they are involved in tourism. In India tourism policy shift towards promoting decentralized form of tourism in which there is participation of all sections of the society is clearly visible. Though instances of cooperatives involved in tourism are negligible, the Indian cooperatives have strong potentialities to emerge as a lead player in the field of tourism.

4. Rural Tourism Development through Rural Cooperatives

The important role of participatory and community based organizations like cooperatives in promoting tourism has yet to be recognized. As a result, the concepts like "sustainable tourism", "poverty reduction through tourism", 'community tourism', etc. which can be best implemented through participatory institutions have yet to be popularized in a big way. Rural tourism development has become a top priority of the economic agenda of all the countries. The government has identified rural tourism as one of the thrust areas. The strength of rural tourism lies in the villages, and the cooperatives field 100% of the villages.

There are a variety of terms used to describe tourism in rural areas, including farm tourism, agritourism, soft tourism and even ecotourism. Any form of tourism that showcases the rural life, art, culture and heritage at rural locations, thereby benefiting the local community economically and socially as well as enabling interaction between the tourists and the locals for a more enriching tourism experience can be termed as rural tourism. The cooperatives in the rural areas in India have strong cultural affiliations. The cooperatives can not only acquaint the foreign tourists with rich culture of the region, but they can also understand their urge to participate in and experience the local culture closely. The cooperatives can play a big role in strengthening international bonds of cultural heritage by making the tourists feel that they are a part of cooperative culture which is built on peace.

Rural tourism is essentially an activity which takes place in the countryside. It is multi-faceted and may entail farm/agricultural tourism, cultural tourism, nature tourism, adventure tourism, and eco-tourism. As against conventional tourism, rural tourism has certain typical characteristics like; it is an experience oriented, the locations are sparsely populated, it is predominantly in the natural environment, it meshes with seasonality and local events and is based on preservation of culture, heritage and traditions. Rural tourism has many potential benefits for rural areas.

In the present environment, rural tourism can be an important source of jobs for local communities and state development can only be witnessed through cooperatives. Formation of tourism cooperatives for guiding, escorting, maintain local handicrafts, etc., can generate jobs, and end their poverty. Tourism can be an important force for developing disadvantaged rural areas. In particular, rural communities with few other options for development may perceive that tourism represents a panacea for growth.

However, like other tourism activities, rural tourism results in a full range of environmental impacts. Rural tourism in India doesn't have a long history because of insufficient infrastructure and preparation. India definitely has the great potential for tourism especially rural and ecotourism. The only problem and difficulty are in attracting the tourists. However, there are some other steps that should be taken, such as rural infrastructure, accessibility (roads, transportation) and Building rural capacity for tourism development.

Rural tourism has some advantages in rural are in India, for example, it provides employment for local residents and prevents their immigration to cities. Currently young people leave country-sides and go to big cities to study or work. Usually they never come back to their homelands. Some of the reasons for failure of these efforts are that the role of the rural cooperatives is not defined vis-à-vis socio- cultural and political barriers also exist in the system, and furthermore lack of human and economic resources at local and state level.

5. Challenges before Cooperative Tourism

Infrastructure is the biggest stumbling factor in development of tourism. The cooperatives which have stronghold over the rural areas in the recent years have taken initiatives to promote infrastructure development. For example, cooperatives in many states have built up the roads, and have come up with schools. The areas in which cooperatives are strong in infrastructure can be developed for formulating effective tourism strategies. The Government is willing to support the cooperatives who desire to come up in the field of tourism by providing them assistance in infrastructural development.

6. Barriers of Cooperative Tourism

Understanding barriers of rural cooperative tourism is important when a community is getting organized for involvement in tourism activates. This understanding can help individuals, community and organizations more effectively impact the tourism policy-making process. Further, it is important for the government to understand that rural also face barriers that can hinder its progress in responding and recognizing the priorities of local communities in India. Overcoming the barriers to tourism development presents a challenge to both local communities and state government, and will serve to facilitate the policy making process. Rural cooperative tourism in India has several barriers that cannot develop. Roads and accommodation infrastructures were cited as the two main barriers for growing rural cooperative tourism in India. In the long-term, developing accommodation, sealing the road, and providing other services like cafes and shops are essential to fulfil the tourism potential of India. Following are the main barriers:

i) Inability to analyze the changing socio- economic dimensions of rural cooperative tourism in India, and demarcate the areas in which rural cooperatives have a strategic advantage over other forms of organizations.

ii) Lack of policy research in this field which can provide definite indicators for future.

iii) Inability to strategically link the rural cooperatives with the rural tourism in those cities in which tourism is in a boom. But, the rural cooperatives have not yet to come up in this field.

iv) Inability of the cooperatives to extend their areas of operations or activities in the field of rural tourism.

v) Weak advocacy for rural cooperative tourism development is also a big hindrance. Holding of Advocacy conferences by the cooperatives in the area of cooperative tourism can set the ball rolling in a big way and create a conducive atmosphere for rural tourism development also states tourism as a phenomenon of affluent contemporary societies is a particularly difficult concept in local communities in developing countries to grasp. In this sense tourism development may be more difficult than other activities. Shortcomings are similar to those local communities, but a few factors tend to be more pronounced among local area:

vi) Lack of formal education and appropriate managerial training

vii) Lack of foreign language skills

viii) Different ways of dealing with hygiene, litter, maintenance of infrastructure

ix) Limited knowledge of food preparation for foreigners, including catering to dietary, nutritional and culinary tastes

x) Lack of decision making and planning skills concerning the possible consequences of tourism, coupled with limited ability to control tourism, unpredictable political climates, and long-term funding uncertainty. As consequence, rural tourism facilities and services may be unacceptable for international tourists. Hence building capacity through rural cooperatives is necessary for stakeholders involved in tourism in local communities. However, due to lack of awareness, this is not being done at present.

Similarly, lack of development of cooperatives in the field of cooperative tourism is also a sign of weak advocacy. There is also lack of documentation of few successful models of cooperative tourism in the Region.

7. Successful Models of Cooperative Tourism in India: A Case Study

A review of the cooperative trends in the recent times indicates that cooperatives are aware to diversity in new areas like tourism. There are numerous cooperative institution(s) in the country, which are involved in the promotion of rural tourism with an objective to change the life of rural people so that they may also contribute for the development of state. The following are some of the successful models of cooperative institution(s), which are engaged in the activities of promoting the rural tourism in India:

7.1 Cooptour, a cooperative organization is involved in mainly ticketing and outgoing tourism. Besides the business and support from cooperative organizations, its professional services have led to increasing business with non-cooperative organizations. Cooptour feels that it has tremendous opportunities of growth in the areas of international cooperative tour packages, transport, rural tourism, etc. if there is full support from national and international cooperative organization.

7.2 TRIFED is the national level organization of tribal cooperatives in the country. It has already identified certain regions for promoting tourism. The organization stands for holistic development of the tribal sector in all aspects and in this regard tourism is considered an important component. Tribal Cooperative Marketing Development Federation of India is planning to start Tribes shops in all the major international airports so that all the traditional and ethnic tribal products are showcased for foreign tourists.

The example of TRIFED clearly indicates that cooperative sector is aware of the need for marketing its products from a tourism point of view. UHP milk powder is already distributed in all the pilgrimage tourist sites. The cooperative products have developed strong brands which clearly indicate that cooperative principles and values can be used for effective business. For example "Amul", brand of Gujarat Cooperative Milk Marketing Federation is a household name in India signifying milk revolution. The natural beauty of Himachal Pradesh has made Himachal Pradesh Tourism really popular for a long time now. Tourists in Himachal Pradesh can indulge in a plethora of activities while they are on vacation. In Himachal Pradesh, tourists can go trekking and camping, indulge in adventure tourism, eco-tourism, religious tourism, visit wildlife sanctuaries, tour lakes, and attend fairs and festivals.

7.3 HRG took initiative for household based tourism enterprise in tribal Sangla Valley of District Kinnaur in Himachal Pradesh. Beautiful wood carved houses, costumes, food/beverages, handloom, handicraft, jewelry forms major components of the tribal area household based tourism enterprise. HP Tourism Department facilitates the registration and more than 50 households registered in Sangla Valley under 'Home Stay Scheme' Tribal women were trained in hospitality and hygiene technique provided in preparation of menu and serving of food items in addition to housekeeping. Annual Household Tourism Festival was celebrated with participation of Home Stay households, artisan, weaver, cultural groups, dry fruit traders and farmers in last week of May every year. Tourists were attracted through scientific validation and serving of traditional food of Fagopyrum esculentum (Oghla), F. tataricum (Phaphra) & Prunus armeniaca (Chuli). Rich supply of flavonoids, rutin, protects against diseases by acting as antioxidant. Fagopyrum lipid lowering activity is largely due to rutin. Maintain blood flow and high ratio of good cholesterol (HDL) to total cholesterol. Oghla lower blood sugar up to 12-15%, prevent post menstrual breast cancer. Cozy wood houses are less energy consuming and provide required ambience. Model provides opportunities to local artists to showcase their tribal art through cultural presentations and exhibitions of traditional dress and jewelry. Highland tracking provide knowledge of important biodiversity of the valley. Traditional food and craft have made a comeback with this tourism model. Tribal were successful in doing brisk sale of handicraft, handloom, dry fruits, pulses, buckwheat, apricot oil, honey etc.

7.4 Medially Fishermen's Cooperative Society (MFCS) in Calcutta is a successful fishery cooperative which has successful utilized waste water to produce fish. The genesis of the cooperative can be traced when fishermen in Anta village of Howah had to migrate to wastelands near Kolkatta Dock in search of jobs due to drying up of Damodar River. By using the urban refuge and polluted water of the city, the society now undertakes various activities such as improving waste water quality, using waste water to produce fish, marketing fish, etc, providing credit facilities to fishermen, engaged in poultry, piggery, dairy and cottage industries. The society has now ventured into developing a Nature Park which has now emerged as a hot tourist spot in the city where pollution is a big problem. The Park has attractive boating facilities and an ecosystem has been created that attracts many birds. The animal Park is another attraction having deer, rabbits, tortoise different kinds of ducks; etc. The society has adopted professional norms in functioning by indulging in multifarious activities. The production of fish by the society has been soaring high. The example of this society indicates that cooperatives involved in preserving environment can venture into tourism activities by diversifying their operations. Commercialization of tourism may lead to neglect of ecology as economic considerations for developing a tourist site may lead to neglect of social aspects, like environment. In this scenario forming a cooperative to promote eco tourism can be highly successful.

7.5 Tour fed is an apex body of Tourism Co-operative Societies in the state of Kerala and is providing tourism related services like Tour, travel operations, sightseeing trips and also tourism product promotions, destinations marketing, marketing for tourism investments and ventures. It is a federation of Co-operative societies in Tourism under Government of Kerala, Department of Co-operation to plan, manage and facilitate the cooperative tourism societies in the state of Kerala affiliated or owned by the Federation. Tour fed will also assist in promotion/organising of new tourism societies/ventures either of its own or at the instance of its affiliated societies/ ventures, will also engage in tourism projects developments.

7.6 ATDC - Alleppey Tourism Development Co-operative Society Ltd., is the premier body in the district of Alleppey, Kerala for the promotion of tourism. It was the first Co-operative movement in Kerala for promoting tourism. ATDC has gained a unique position in Kerala's tourism arena as the organizers of India's first elephant rally and the first motor boat rally. ATDC has also initiated many festivities and functions which later served as precedents for the State Government to make those a regular feature of Kerala's tourism calendar. ATDC also arranges cultural performances (Kathakali), Snake boatraces, Elephant march etc. for the tourist groups. The infrastructure backbone of ATDC such as the Houseboats, Luxury Cruisers are owned and maintained by Kerala Backwaters Pvt. Ltd. Kerala Backwaters has a fleet of 15 boats stationed at Alleppey. The fleet includes, Sanchari luxury cruiser with a seating capacity of 40 persons on top, shuttling between Alleppey and Quilon every day during season time. ATDC owns a new luxury cruiser named "Safari", which is also having a capacity of 40 persons on top.

7.7 Uttarey Eco-tourism Development and Service Co-operative Society Limited

Sikkim is one of the most beautiful states of the Indian Union and Uttarey Eco-tourism Development and Service Co-operative Society is playing an important role in promoting the tourism in the state. Sikkim prides the third highest Mt. Khangchendzonga in the world, which is also worshiped as the Guardian Deity of Sikkim. It is adorned with snowy mountains, luxuriant forests with exotic flora and fauna, pristine waterfalls, sacred lakes, holy caves, medicinal hot springs, cascading rivers and gentle streams. Gangtokis the capital of Sikkim with a population of approximately 50,000 has emerged into the mainstream of the Tourism Industry, with more and more tourists visiting this little Himalayan state every year.

8. Concluding Remarks

As per the above discussion, we can conclude that cooperatives serve several purposes. First, they allow for local human, economic, and natural resources to be maximized with a great deal of local control. Second, while immediate economic opportunities may arise from cooperatives, they also allow for longer-term sustainable economic development in areas that traditionally have had little opportunity to engage in such processes. By providing a local job base, public input, and clear linkages to local development, cooperative members take a much more active role in local development than they do in projects designed by extra-local organizations or interests. Equally important, cooperatives can serve to enhance essential social structures and identities, establish lines of communication and interaction, and support cultural components, which are seen as being vital to the development of community.

The important role of participatory and community based organizations like cooperatives in promoting tourism has yet to be recognized. As a result, the concepts like "sustainable tourism", "poverty reduction through tourism", 'community tourism', etc. which can be best implemented through participatory institutions have yet to be popularized in a big way. Rural tourism development has become a top priority of the economic agenda of all the countries.

The tourism scenario in India is ideal for formulating effective tourism strategies for promoting local and state development. Amongst the tourism strategies for promoting peace, the cooperative strategy merits consideration. The Indian cooperative movement which is the largest movement in the world is best suited for promoting cooperative tourism.

9. References

Ashish Nag, A Study of Tourism Industry of Himachal Pradesh with Reference to Eco Tourism, Vol.2 (4), April (2013)

Fariborz Aref & Sarjit Gill, Rural Tourism Development through Rural Cooperatives, Nature and Science, 2009 7 (10)

Entrepreneurship Development of Rural Tourism: Exploring a

Cooperatives Business Model, World Applied Science Journal, 31(4):573-582(2014)

Babu P George, Alleppey Tourism Development Cooperatives, The Case of Network Advantage, The public Sector innovation Journal, Volume 12(2) 2007, Article 9

Nor Haniza Mohamad, Tourism Cooperative for scaling up community-based tourism Vol.5 No.4, 2013

Bushell, R., & Eagles, P. (Eds.). (2007). Tourism and Protected Areas: Benefits beyond Boundaries. London CAB International, UK.

Sanjay Kumar Verma, Promoting Peace through Tourism: Role of Cooperatives, http:// www.ncui.net

http://www.sciencepub.net/nature

www.himachaltourism.gov.in.

IMPACT OF TOURISM INDUSTRY IN INDIA

N N Sharma
Associate Professor, Department of Commerce and Management, Govt. P.G. College Dharmshala, Himachal Pradesh (India)
nnsharma585@gmail.com

Abstract

Tourism is recognised as a major global industry today. It is a sizable but complex service industry. In the last 40-45 years, tourism has seen rapid and continuous growth. This industry although doing a wonderful work and had come up with number of attractive tourist destinations in India and is widely accepted by the different governments due to profit motive but due to some negative social and environmental impacts of tourism have voiced their concern against it. Hence tourism development strategy must get defined in different regional context. The significance of tourism has been recognized in both developed and developing countries. This can be seen in the establishment of government departments of tourism, widespread encouragement and sponsorship of tourist's developments, and the proliferation of small businesses and multinational corporations contributing to and deriving benefits from the tourism industry. There is widespread optimism that tourism might be a powerful and beneficial agent of both economic and social change. Today tourism is the largest service industry in India, with a contribution of 6.23% to the national GDP and providing 8.78% of the total employment. India witnesses' more than 5 million annual foreign tourist arrivals and 562 million domestic tourism visits. The tourism industry in India generated about US$100 billion in 2008 and that is expected to increase to US$275.5 billion by 2018 at a 9.4% annual growth rate. The Ministry of Tourism is the nodal agency for the development and promotion of tourism in India and maintains the "Incredible India" campaign. According to World Travel and Tourism Council, India will be a tourism hotspot from 2009-2018, having the highest 10-year growth potential. As per the Travel and Tourism Competitiveness Report 2009 by the World Economic Forum, India is ranked 11th in the Asia Pacific region and 62nd overall, moving up three places on the list of the world's attractive destinations. It is ranked the 14th best tourist destination for its natural resources and 24th for its cultural resources, with many World Heritage Sites, both natural and cultural, rich fauna, and strong creative industries in the country. India also bagged 37th rank for its air transport network. The India travel and tourism industry ranked 5th in the long-term (10-year) growth and is expected to be the second largest employer in the world by 2019. The present paper is an attempt to study the scenario of tourism Industry and to analyse impact of Foreign tourist Arrival on growth of foreign exchange earnings in India.

Keywords: GDP –Gross Domestic Products, Incredible India.

Introduction:

The tourism industry of India is economically important and grows rapidly. The World Travel & Tourism Council calculated that tourism generated INR6.4 trillion or 6.6% of the nation's GDP in 2012. It supported 39.5 million jobs, 7.7% of its total employment. The sector is predicted to grow at an average annual rate of 7.9% from 2013 to 2023. This gives India the third rank among countries with the fastest growing tourism industries over the next decade. India has a large medical tourism sector which is expected to grow at an estimated rate of 30% annually to reach about 95 billion by 2015.According to provisional statistics 6.29 million foreign tourists arrived in India in 2011, an increase of 8.9% from 5.78 million in 2010.

This ranks India as the 38th country in the world in terms of foreign tourist arrivals. Domestic tourist visits to all states and Union Territories numbered 1,036.35 million in 2012, an increase of 16.5% from 2011. The most represented countries are the United States (16%) and the United Kingdom (12.6%). In 2011 Maharashtra, Tamil Nadu and Delhi were the most popular states for foreign tourists. Domestic tourists visited the states UttarPradesh, AndhraPradesh and TamilNadu mostfrequently. Chennai, Delhi, Mumbai and Agra have been the four most visited cities of India by foreign tourists during the year 2011.

Worldwide, Chennai is ranked 41 by the number of foreign tourists, while Delhi is ranked at 50, Mumbai at 57 and Agra at 65 and Kolkata at 99. The Travel & Tourism Competitiveness Report 2013 ranks India 65th out of 144 countries overall. The report ranks the price competitiveness of India's tourism sector 20th out of 144 countries. It mentions that India has quite good air transport (ranked 39th), particularly given the country's stage of development, and reasonable ground transport infrastructure (ranked 42nd). Some other aspects of its tourism infrastructure remain somewhat underdeveloped however. The nation has very few hotel rooms per capita by international comparison and low ATM penetration. As per the UNWTO World Tourism Barometer, December 2013, India's rank in the World Tourism Receipts during 2012 was 16th and rank in international tourist arrivals was 41. The rank of India was 7th among Asia and the Pacific Region in terms of tourism receipts during 2012. The Ministry of Tourism designs national policies for the development and promotion of tourism. In the process, the Ministry consults and collaborates with other stakeholders in the sector including various Central Ministries/agencies, state governments, Union Territories and the representatives of the private sector. Concerted efforts are being made to promote new forms of tourism such as rural, cruise, medical and eco-tourism. The Ministry also maintains the Incredible India campaign.

India's rich history and its cultural and geographical diversity make its international tourism appeal large and diverse. It presents heritage and cultural tourism along with medical, business, educational and sports tourism.

Role of Government

The role of the Government in tourism development has been redefined from that of a regulator to that of a catalyst. Apart from marketing and promotion, the focus of tourism development plans is now on integrated development of enabling infrastructure through effective partnership with various stakeholders.Tourism development in India has passed through many phases. The development of tourist facilities was taken up in a planned manner in 1956 coinciding with the Second Five Year Plan. The approach has evolved from isolated planning of single unit facilities in the Second and Third Five Year Plans. The Sixth Plan marked the beginning of a new era when tourism began to be considered a major instrument for social integration and economic development.

However, it was only after the 80's that tourism activity gained momentum. A National Policy on Tourism was announced in 1982.In 1992, a National Action Plan was prepared and in 1996 the National Strategy for Promotion of Tourism was drafted. In 1997, a draft New Tourism Policy in tune with the economic policies of the Government and the trends in tourism development was published for public debate. The draft policy is now under revision. The proposed policy recognizes the roles of Central and State Governments, Public Sector Undertakings and the Private Sector in the development of tourism. The need for involvement of Panchayati Raj institutions, local bodies, non-governmental organizations and the local youth in the creation of tourism facilities has also been recognized.

Objectives of study:

a) To study and overview the Tourism industry in India.

b) To study and analysis the relationship between foreign tourist arrival and Foreign Exchange Earnings

c) To study the impact of tourism industry on India's economic growth.

Hypothesis:

Null Hypothesis: There is no relationship between Foreign Tourist arrival and generation of Foreign Exchange in India.

Alternative Hypothesis: There is perfect relationship between Foreign Tourist arrival and generation of Foreign Exchange in India.

Research Methodlogy

The present study is of analytical nature and makes use of secondary data. The relevant secondary data are collected from various publications of Ministry of Tourism Government of India;, websites, annual reports, World Bank reports, DIPP, research reports, already conducted survey analysis Published by UNCTAD etc. The reference period is restricted from 2001 to 2012. The present study considers 12 years data starting from 2000 to 2012.

Analytical Tools & Technique

In order to analyze the collected data the statistical tool(SPSS) such as correlation model is used. Correlation coefficient is a statistical measure that determines the degree to which two variable's movements are associated. Correlation coefficient value ranges from -1 to 1. Negative value of correlation indicates: if one variable increases in its values, the other variable decreases in its value and positive value indicates: if one variable increases in its values the other variable also increases in its value. In the current study to study the linear relationship between variables such as Foreign Tourist Arrival and Foreign Exchnage . The multiple regression analysis is a statistical technique used to evaluate the effects of two or more independent variables on a single dependent variable.

Tourism industry in India

Tourism is an important catalyst in the socio-economic development in the modern times, contributing in multiple ways and strengthen the inter-connected processes. While often portrayed as panacea for many evils such as underdevelopment, unemployment, poverty eradication, social discrimination and so on; its contribution in creating a global and regional socio-political environment for peaceful co-existence of the cultures and societies has been equally established at various levels. Perhaps, this realization took many advocators to position tourism as one of the biggest 'peace industries', a means to strike equilibrium of global peace process though development. Because, tourism practiced in responsible and sustainable manner bring about the peace and prosperity of the people and that its stakeholders share benefits in fair manner, which is a necessary condition for the equilibrium of sharing to sustain.

Tourism in India is broadly classified by its regions - North, East, West and South Indian tourism. Each part of India offers identifiable differences from the rest of the nation. The creation of niche tourism products like medical tourism, wellness tourism, religious circuits, adventure tourism, cruise tourism, and caravan tourism has served to widen the net of this sector. Inbound tourism is booming and the country is going all out to lure more travelers from around the world. Contrary to perceptions across the world that tourism in India is still confined to traditions, the country is opening up with trendy tour packages and affordable air travel deals to woo inbound visitors from every segment

Present Scenario of Tourism in India

The Indian Tourism sector is one of the largest service industries in the country in terms of its contribution to the Gross Domestic Product (GDP) and Foreign Exchange Earnings, as well as for providing employment to millions. The sector in fact is expected to generate around US$ 42.8 billion (INR 1,897.7 billion) by 2017, according to an industry research. The amount of foreign direct investments (FDI) inflow into the hotel and tourism sector during April 2000 to April 2013 was worth US$ 6,664.20 million. Foreign tourist arrivals (FTA) during the Month of June 2013 stood at 0.44 million as compared to FTAs of 0.43 million during June 2012, registering a growth of 2.5 per cent and the domestic tourism is expected to increase by 15 per cent to 20 per cent over the next five years. Tourism in India is witnessing widespread growth on the back of increasing inbound tourism by the burgeoning Indian middle class, rising inflow of foreign tourists and successful government campaigns for promoting 'Incredible India'. Infrastructure development holds the key to India's sustained growth in the Tourism sector.

Types of Tourism in India:

All types of tourism in India have registered phenomenal growth in the last decade ever since the Indian government decided to boost revenues from the tourism sector by projecting India as the ultimate tourist spot.

- Adventure tourism :As a kind of tourism in India, adventure tourism has recently grown in India. This involves exploration of remote areas and exotic locales and engaging in various activities. For adventure tourism in India, tourists prefer to go for trekking to places like Ladakh, Sikkim, and Himalaya. Himachal Pradesh and Jammu and Kashmir are popular for the skiing facilities they offer.
- Wildlife tourism : India has a rich forest cover which has some beautiful and exotic species of wildlife – some of which that are even endangered and very rare. This has boosted wildlife tourism in India. The places where a foreign tourist can go for wildlife tourism in India are the Sariska Wildlife Sanctuary, Keoladeo Ghana National Park, and Corbett National Park.
- Medical tourism :Tourists from all over the world have been thronging India to avail themselves of cost-effective but superior quality healthcare in terms of surgical procedures and general medical attention. There are several medical institutes in the country that cater to foreign patients and impart top-quality healthcare at a fraction of what it would have cost in developed nations such as USA and UK.
- Pilgrimage tourism :India is famous for its temples and that is the reason that among the different kinds of tourism in India, pilgrimage tourism is increasing most rapidly. The various places for tourists to visit in India for pilgrimage are Vaishno Devi, Golden temple, Char Dham, and Mathura Vrindavan.
- Eco tourism :Among the types of tourism in India, ecotourism have grown recently. Ecotourism entails the sustainable preservation of a naturally endowed area or region. This is becoming more and more significant for the ecological development of all regions that have tourist value. For ecotourism in India, tourists can go to places such as Kaziranga National Park, Gir National Park, and Kanha National Park.
- Cultural tourism:India is known for its rich cultural heritage and an element of mysticism, which is why tourists come to India to experience it for themselves. The various fairs and festivals that tourists can visit in India are the Pushkar fair, Taj Mahotsav, and Suraj Kund mela.

◈ Eco-Tourism: Eco-tourism means making as little environmental impact as possible and helping to sustain the indigenous populace, thereby encouraging the preservation of wildlife and habitats when visiting a place. This is responsible form of tourism and tourism development, which encourages going back to natural products in every aspect of life. It is also the key to sustainable ecological development.

.The details of year – wise financial achievement under Scheme "Eco-Tourism" are:

Plan Period	**Year**	**Expenditure (Rs. in lakhs)**
Tenth Plan (2002-07)	2002-03	7.41
	2003-04	14.36
	2004-05	15.12
	2005-06	35.43
	2006-07	31.68
Total		**104.00**
Eleventh Plan (2007-12)	2007-08	47.79
	2008-09	49.79
	2009-10	62.54
	2010-11	12.97
Total		**173.00**

Table no -1

Source: Answer to Lok Sabha Question no.4653 dated 8.12.2010

Foreign Tourist Arrivals (FTAs)

During 2011 FTAs in India were 6.31 million with a growth of 9.2% over 2010. FTAs during 2012 were 6.65 (provisional) million with a growth of 5.4%, as compared to the FTAs of 6.31 million during 2011.

Foreign Exchange Earnings (FEE) from Tourism

Tourism is an important sector of Indian economy and contributes substantially in the country's Foreign Exchange Earnings. FEEs from tourism, in rupee terms, during 2011 was Rs.77,591 crore (provisional), with a growth of 19.6%, as compared to the FEEs of Rs.64,889 crore (provisional) during 2010.

During 2012, the Foreign Exchange Earnings (FEEs) from tourism registered a growth of 21.8% from Rs.77,591 to Rs.94,487 crore (provisional) when compared to FEEs during 2011. A statement giving FTAs in India and FEEs from tourism fro the years 2000 to 2012 is given below:

Foreign Tourist Arrivals and Foreign Exchange Earnings During the years 2000-2012

Year	Foreign Tourist Arrivals (in nos.)	Percentage Change Over Previous Year	Foreign Exchange Earnings in Crore	Percentage Change Over Previous Year	Foreign Exchange Earnings (Million US$)	Percentage Change Over Previous Year
2000	26,49,378	6.7	15,626,	20.6	3,460	15.0
2001	25,37,282	-4.2	15,083	-3.5	3,198	(-)7.6
2002	23,84,364	-6.0	15,064	-0.1	3,103	3.0
2003	27,26,214	14.3	20,729,	37.6	4,463	43.8
2004	34,57,477	26.8	27,944	34.8	6,170	38.2
2005	39,18,610	13.3	33,123,	18.5	7,493	21.4
2006	44,47,167	13.5	39,025	17.8	8,634	15.2
2007	50,81,504	14.3	44,360	13.7	10,729	24.3
2008	52,82,603	4.0	51,294	15.6	11,832	10.3
2009	51,67,699	-2.2	53,700*	4.7	11,136*	(-)5.9
2010	57,75,692	11.8	64,889#	20.8	14,193#	27.5
2011	63,09,222	9.2	77,591#	19.6	16,564#	16.7
2012	66,48,318	5.4	94,487#	21.8	17,737#	7.1

#Advance Estimates *Revised Estimates

Source: Ministry of Tourism, Annual Report 2012-13

Table no: 2

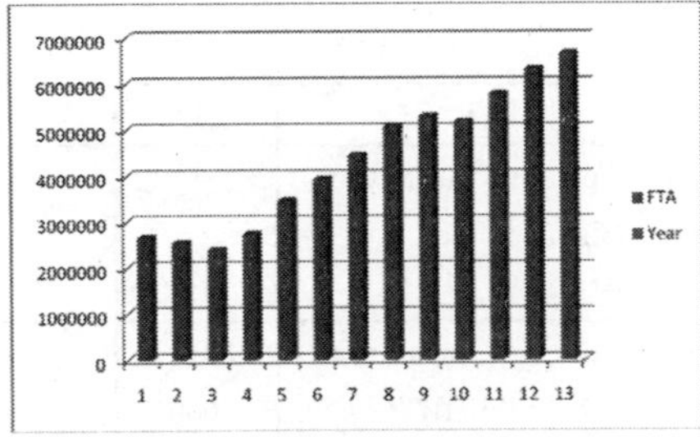

Fig no 1: Foreign Tourist Arrival

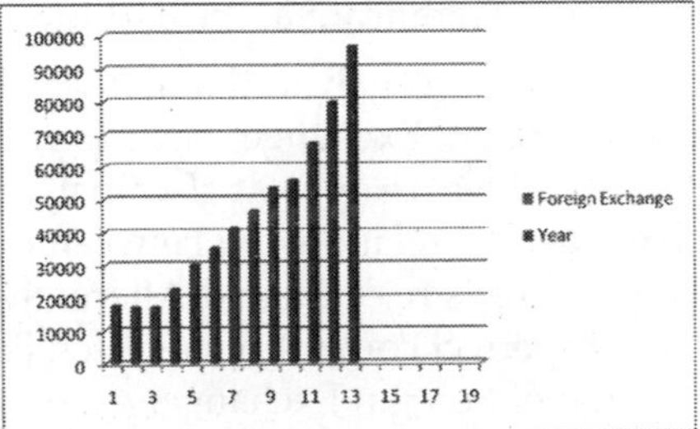

Fig no 2: Foreign Exchange Earnings

4.3 Relationship between Foreign tourist arrival and Foreign Exchange Earnings

	FTA	Foreign Exchange
2000	2649378.00	15626
2001	2537282.00	15083
2002	2384364.00	15064.00
2003	2726214.00	20729.00
2004	3457477.00	27944.00
2005	3918610.00	33123.00
2006	4447167.00	39025.00
2007	5081504.00	44360.00
2008	5282603.00	51294.00
2009	5167699.00	53700.00
2010	5775692.00	64889.00
2011	6309222.00	77591.00
2012	6648318.00	94487.00

Table no-3

Correlations

		FTA	Foreign Exchange
FTA	Pearson Correlation	1	.970(**)
	Sig. (2-tailed)		.000
	N	13	13
Foreign Exchange	Pearson Correlation	.970(**)	1
	Sig. (2-tailed)	.000	
	N	13	13

** Fig no 3 Correlation is significant at the 0.01 level (2-tailed).

Interpretation: Above Figure analysis that Foreign Tourist arrival and generation of Foreign Exchange have perfect correlation between these two variables (r= .970). It also analyses that both of these variables have perfect relationship between them. So under this case Null Hypothesis is rejected and Alternative Hypothesis is accepted i.e there is perfect correlation between Foreign Tourist arrival and generation of Foreign Exchange.

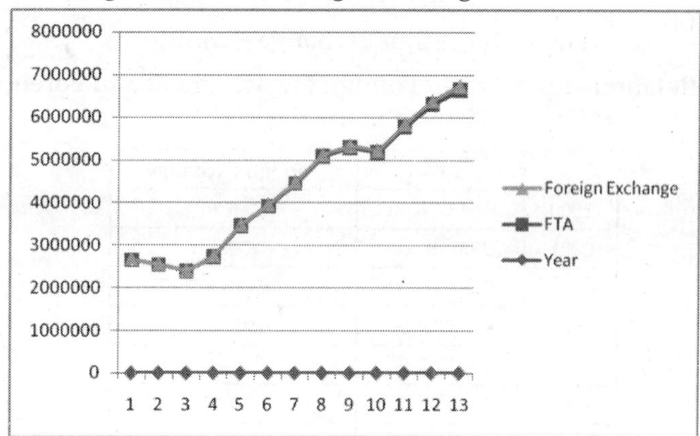

Fig no-5

Impact of India's Economic Growth on Tourism

The impact of India's economic growth on tourism in the country, one need to study this feature as part of the larger picture of the developing world's contribution to this fiscal boost. While some economists may attribute the success of Indian economy to the profits generated by the tourism sector, which in turn were boosted by innovative marketing, brand-building and strategic planning of tour packages, other thinkers may credit the rise in number of MNC's and diversifications of the Indian open industries norm as being the chief cause. There has been a tremendous growth in tourism in India because of the policies of the government and support from all levels.

Percentage share of Tourism in Indian GDP:

Year	Value	% change
2003	8.8	-
2004	8.7	-1.14%
2005	7	-19.54%
2006	7.1	1.43%
2007	7.2	1.41%
2008	7.2	0.00%
2009	6.7	-6.94%
2010	6.5	-2.99%
2011	6.6	1.54%
2012	6.5	-1.52%

Table no-4

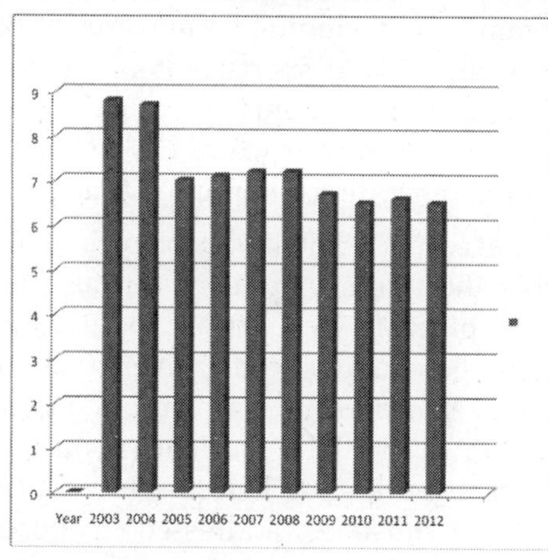

Fig no-6

Source: Ministry of Tourism

Positive Impacts

- Generating Income and Employment: Tourism in India has emerged as an instrument of income and employment generation, poverty alleviation and sustainable human development. It contributes 6.23% to the national GDP and 8.78% of the total employment in India.
- Source of Foreign Exchange Earnings: Tourism is an important source of foreign exchange earnings in India. This has favourable impact on the balance of payment of the country. The tourism industry in India generated about US$100 billion in 2008 and that is expected to increase to US$275.5 billion by 2018 at a 9.4% annual growth rate.
- Preservation of National Heritage and Environment: Tourism helps preserve several places which are of historical importance by declaring them as heritage sites. For instance, the Taj Mahal, the Qutab Minar, Ajanta and Ellora temples, etc, would have been decayed and destroyed had it not been for the efforts taken by Tourism Department to preserve them. Likewise, tourism also helps in conserving the natural habitats of many endangered species
- Developing Infrastructure: Tourism tends to encourage the development of multiple-use infrastructure that benefits the host community, including various means of transports, health care facilities, and sports centers, in addition to the hotels and high-end restaurants that cater to foreign visitors. The development of infrastructure has in turn induced the development of other directly productive activities.
- Promoting Peace and Stability: Honey and Gilpin (2009) suggests that the tourism industry can also help promote peace and stability in developing country like India by providing jobs, generating income, diversifying the economy, protecting the environment, and promoting cross-cultural awareness. However, key challenges like adoption of regulatory frameworks, mechanisms to reduce crime and corruption, etc, must be addressed if peace-enhancing benefits from this industry are to be realized.

Negative Impacts:

- Undesirable Social and Cultural Change: Tourism sometimes led to the destruction of the social fabric of a community. The more tourists coming into a place, the more the perceived risk of that place losing its identity. A good example is Goa. From the late 60's to the early 80's when the Hippy culture was at its height, Goa was a haven for such hippies.
- Increase Tension and Hostility: Tourism can increase tension, hostility, and suspicion between the tourists and the local communities when there is no respect and understanding for each other's culture and way of life. This may further lead to violence and other crimes committed against the tourists. The recent crime committed against Russian tourist in Goa is a case in point.
- Creating a Sense of Antipathy: Tourism brought little benefit to the local community. In most all-inclusive package tours more than 80% of travelers' fees go to the airlines, hotels and other international companies, not to local businessmen and workers. Moreover, large hotel chain restaurants often import food to satisfy foreign visitors and rarely employ local staff for senior management positions, preventing local farmers and workers from reaping the benefit of their presence. This has often created a sense of antipathy towards the tourists and the government.
- Adverse Environment and Ecology: One of the most important adverse effects of tourism on the environment is increased pressure on the carrying capacity of the ecosystem in each tourist locality. Increased transport and construction activities led to large scale deforestation and destabilization of natural landforms, while increased tourist flow led to increase in solid waste dumping as well as depletion of water and fuel resources..

Conclusion

The tourism industry of India is economically important and grows rapidly. The World Travel & Tourism Council calculated that tourism generated INR6.4 trillion or 6.6% of the nation's GDP in 2012. It supported 39.5 million jobs, 7.7% of its total employment. The sector is predicted to grow at an average annual rate of 7.9% from 2013 to 2023. This gives India the third rank among countries with the fastest growing tourism industries over the next decade. India has a large medical tourism sector which is expected to grow at an estimated rate of 30% annually to reach about 95 billion by 2015.According to provisional statistics 6.29 million foreign tourists arrived in India in 2011, an increase of 8.9% from 5.78 million in 2010. This ranks India as the 38th country in the world in terms of foreign tourist arrivals. Domestic tourist visits to all states and Union Territories numbered 1,036.35 million in 2012, an increase of 16.5% from 2011. The most represented countries are the United States (16%) and the United Kingdom (12.6%). In 2011 Maharashtra, Tamil Nadu and Delhi were the most popular states for foreign tourists. While analysing the foreign tourist arrivals and foreign earnings in India during last twelve years perfect correlation was observed and so far as its positive impact is concerned it was noticed on Generating Income and Employment, Source of Foreign Exchange Earnings which generated about US$100 billion in 2008 and that is expected to increase to US$275.5 billion by 2018 at a 9.4% annual growth rate. While tourism also protects and Preserve National Heritage and Environment, developing Infrastructure which tends to encourage the development of multiple-use infrastructure that benefits the host community, including various means of transports, health care facilities, and sports centers activities in addition it is also promoting peace and stability.

References

Batra G.S., Tourism in the 21st century, (1996) Anmol publications Pvt. Ltd.,.245 Pgs

Dirk William velde and Swapna Niar, (2005), Foreign Direct Investment, service trade negotiations and development - The case of tourism in Caribbean, Overseas Development Institute.

Federation of Hotels & Restaurants Association of India ltd, www.fhrai.com.

Govt. to review FDI in Tourism Sector, News and Features, New Delhi, February 2007

GOI, (2005) „Mid term Appraisal of the Tenth five year Plan (2002-2007) Planning Commission, New Delhi.

http://planningcommission.nic.in/plans/mta/midterm/english-pdf/chapter-13.pdf accessed in January 2009 Kundu, S.K. and F.J. Contractor (1999) "Country location choices of service multinationals – an empirical study of the international hotel sector," Journal of International Management 5(4): 299-317.

Investment opportunities in Tourism Sector, Government of India portal Investment Commission (http://www.investmentcommission.in/tourism.htm#v)

Manpower recruitment in Hotel industry, A market plus report of Ministry of tourism, Government of India. (http://tourismindia.com)

Sanford, D.M. and H. Dong (2000) "Investment in familiar territory: tourism and new foreign direct investment," Tourism Economics 6(3): 205-19.

Schwarz, G. (1978). "Estimating the dimension of a model," Annals of Statistics 8: 461- 464.

Tisdell, C. and J. Wen, (1991) "Investment in China◎s tourism industry: its scale, nature, and policy issues," China Economic Review 2(2) pp175-93.

Toda, H.Y. and P.C.B. Phillips (1993) "Vector autoregressions and causality," Econometrica, 61(11):1367-1393.

Meyer, D, Foreign Direct Investment in Tourism - The Development Dimension – Expert Advisory Committee (2005- 2006). Funded by United Nations Conference on Trade and Development, Geneva, Switzerland.

Sinha P. C.,Tourism Impact Assemement ,Anmol Publications, New Delhi

Negi JagMohan,Travel agency and Tour operation,Kaniska Publicatios New delhi

Dutt Gourav,Mahajan Ashwani Indian Economy ,S Chand & Co. New Delhi http://dipp.nic.in

India Tourism Statistics 2012,Government of India

http://business.mapsofindia.com/tourism-industry/types/#sthash.N9DYJReu.dpuf

GOOD GOVERNANCE: SINE QUA NON OF TOURISM INDUSTRY IN MANIPUR

Oinam Momoton Singh

Assistant Professor, Department of Sociology D.M. College of Arts, Imphal, Manipur,

momotonoinam@gmail.com

RajendraKshetri

Professor of Sociology, Nagaland (Central) University Lumami, Nagaland,

aardhikshetri@gmail.com

Abstract:

Manipur, the easternmost state of India, is endowed with natural beauty, ethnological diversity and rich cultural and traditional heritage that it can have high degree of economic and social development through tourism industry. Tourism industry is referred to as smokeless industry and it generates economic surplus without causing irreparable damage to environment and conflict to individual and social ethos. Development of tourism industry for inclusive development of Manipur strongly requires good governance in the state. The present paper tries to conceive good governance as an important component of tourism industry from a sociological perspective.

Keywords: Sine qua non, smokeless industry, governance, inclusive development, transparency, accountability

Methodology:

The present paper used both primary and secondary data. For the purpose of collecting primary data which are collected afresh, personal interview method has been employed and takes interview of some political leaders of the state. The present work also does not leave observation method unutilized so that informations related to the political behaviour of the political leaders are gathered first hand.

Introduction:

Manipur, literally meaning a 'jeweled land', lies in a lush green corner of North East India. It is bordered by Nagaland on the north, Cachar of Assam in the west, by Mizoram in the south-west and by Burma (now Myanmar) on the south and east. It is one of the smallest states of India with an area of 22, 327 sq. km and lies between 230 501 and 250 421 latitudes north and between 920 591 and 940 451 longitudes east. According to 2011 census, Manipur has a total population of 27, 21, 756 persons (13, 69, 764 males and 13, 51, 992 females). The sex-ratio is found to be 987 and is higher than the national average of 947. The literacy rate is 79.85% (86.49% male and 73.17% female) and it is higher than the national average of 74.04%. Manipur is inhabited by various ethnic communities having their own distinctive cultural affinity. Only 30.21% of the total population lives in towns (51 in number as per 2011 census) while the remaining 69.79% live in 2,588 villages. It also represents diversity in religious persuasions, faith and belief system from tribal forms of religion to Hinduism, Christianity, Islam, Sikh, Buddhism, Jainism and others.

For administrative purpose, Manipur is divided into nine districts, four in the valley and five in the hill areas of the state. The districts are sub-divided into 38 sub-divisions.

The state has two-tier Panchayati Raj system (Gram Panchayat at the village level and Zila Parishad at the district level). There are also altogether nine municipalities being headed by the Municipality Commissioners. However, in the hill areas of the state, there are district councils of elected representatives of the people to take care for the development work in each hill district.

Manipur is represented by two members in the Lower House (Lok Sabha) and by one member in the Upper House (Rajya Sabha). It also has a strong and impartial judiciary (Manipur High Court) which is part and parcel of a democratic system.

Tourism Potentials in Manipur:

Manipur has various resources which can act as pull factors in tourism industry. It is endowed with rich cultural and traditional heritage, religious spots, abundant natural gifts, temperate climate, moderate rainfall and above all the hospitality and generosity of its people. Added to these are the newly flourishing medical tourism and sports/adventure tourism.

The important elements of Manipur art and culture include, among other things, Raas Lila, Nupa Pala, PungCholom, Maibi Dance, KhambaThoibi Dance, LuiNgai Ni, GaanNgai, Kut etc. The state is also considered as the power house of Indian sports as sports persons from the state have represented the nation in various international events and have brought laurels to the nation and the state. Manipur is believed to be the birth place of the game of Polo and the traditional forms of sports like Mukna (wrestling), Kang, HiyangTanaba (boat race) and YubiLakpi (Rugby type of game played with oiled coconut) would be wonders to the rest of the world. A variety of adventure tourism facilities like training in Spider-net, Burma-bridge, Parasailing, Rock climbing, Hill trekking, rafting and parasailing are available in the state. In medical sector also, Manipur is having two major government hospitals, Jawaharlal Nehru Institute of Medical Science (JNIMS) and Regional Institute of Medical Sciences (RIMS) which provide medical service to the public. There are many private health care institutions among which Shija Hospital and Research Institute is an ISO 9001:2008 certified institute. Many patients from neighbouring states and country like Myanmar come to Manipur to avail medical treatment of their ailments.

All the nine districts of Manipur are characterized by attractive tourist spots. Some of the attractive tourist's destinations of each district in Manipur can be seen in the following table.

Tourist Destinations in Different Districts of Manipur

District	Tourist Destinations
Imphal West	Kangla fort, Manipur state museum, Saheedminar, Ima market, Zoological garden, Khonghampat orchid centre, Langthabal old palace, NupiLal complex, RKCS Art gallery etc.
Imphal East	Govindaji temple, RamjeePrabhu temple, Hanuman Thakur temple, World War II cemetery, Indian Army war cemetery, Khumanlampak sports complex, Manipur Mountaineering and Trekking Association etc.
Bishnupur	Loktak lake, Keibullamjao National park, Sendra, INA memorial complex, Loktak project, Vishnu temple, Phubala, Loukoi pat, Red Hill etc.
Thoubal	Kongjom War memorial, Thongam Mondum Mahadev temple, Waithou, Serou etc.
Ukhrul	Ukhrul town, Khangkhui cave, Shirui Hill etc.
Chandel	Chandel town, Moreh (town at Indo-Myanmar border), Tenoupal etc.
Churchandpur	New Churchandpur, Tonglon cave, Cheklaphai, Behiang, Tepaimuk, Kaihlam Hill range, Manipur Mountaineering Institute (MMI) etc.
Tamenglong	Zaliad lake, Tharon cave, Barak waterfalls, Deep gorges, splendid waterfalls, exotic orchids etc.
Senapati	Senapati main town, Makhel cave, SaduChiru waterfalls, Mao (the oldest hill station), Dzuko valley, Mount Iso (the highest peak of Manipur) etc.

Source: Department of Tourism, Government of Manipur

The Kangla Fort is a centre of pilgrimage for the Manipuris residing in Manipur, Assam, Bengal, Uttar Pradesh, Bangladesh, Myanmar etc. It is believed that there are 360 sacred places in Kangla. Kangla is also the seat of political power. It was from this Centre that the 'Ningthouja' clan gradually wielded enough political and military power and grew up as the most dominant clan in Manipur. The first Anglo-Manipur war occurred in 1891, in which the British forces attacked kangla, the Manipur Fort, in the early hours of 24th March, 1891. The British conquered kanglaFort on 27th April, 1891. World War II cemetery at Imphal, another tourist spot, is being maintained by War Graves Commission commemorating the memories of the British and Indian soldiers who died during the war. It memorizes those soldiers who sacrificed their lives when Imphal was invaded in 1944 by the Japanese force in collaboration with Subash Chandra Bose's Azad Hind Fauz (Indian National Army). The 'Battle of Imphal and Kohima' – the 'Greatest Battle' that Britain had ever fought in her military history came to end when Japanese force along with the Azad Hind Fauz after remaining in possession of nearly 1500 sq. miles of Manipur for about 6 months finally began to retreat.Choosing of a tourist destination by the tourists is guided by many factors such as availability of suitable accommodation, cost of accommodation and transportation, security or law and order situation at the destination, drinking water, basic nature of the place, enough publicity about the tourist destinations in Manipur to enrich the knowledge and awareness about them etc. All these guiding factors can be developed in the state through proper planning of tourism industry which intensely requires, as pre-requisite, good governance in the state.

Good Governance - A Sine qua non of Tourism Industry for Socio-economic Development:

Human society is dynamic, not static and it has progressed and developed by passing through various stages. Historically, progress has ethical connotation and is taken to mean advance towards the ultimate moral values which human kind had been striving all down the ages to attain. One important component in the realm of socio-economic development is tourism industry. Socio-economic development through tourism industry needs to bring better adjustment between human needs and aspiration on one hand and tourism policy and programme on the other. Developing tourism industry in the state must have the objective of eradicating poverty, ignorance, inequality, irrationality, oppression prevalent in the society and improving the quality of life of all citizens. It also need to see and evaluate the need of the people and introduce some structural changes in society – discarding some old outdated institutions and creating new institutions or changing some existing institutions. It should also mean more wealth, more employment, more amenities and more education with a proper and systematic arrangement of things into proper place and in the right time. It requires the effective intervention of the political leaders who are solely responsible for policy making and planning.

Manipur urgently needs effective good governance so that there is development of tourism industry for inclusive growth/ development where the benefits of growth reach all cross sections of the society. Good governance is a prerequisite for development of tourism industry to promote societal well being. Kofi Anan, the former Secretary General of United Nations stated that good governance is perhaps the single most important factor in eradication of poverty and promoting development.1Good governance is the process whereby public institutions conduct public affairs, manage public resources and guarantee the realization of human right in a manner essentially free of abuse and corruption and with due regard for the rule of law. The meaning of governance becomes meaningful only in the context of the question: governance for whom and for what? Governance which is considered good for the privileged few may actually be bad for the common man and vice-versa. Our focus here is to see if governance is good or bad only in relation to the masses. The philosophy of good governance is to provide a government that is responsive and participatory. Indeed, the six main principles of good governance are (i) Legitimacy and Voice (ii) Direction (Strategic vision) (iii) Performance (iv) Accountability (v) Fairness and (vi) Transparency.

Given the dismal scenario of tourism industry as means to socio-economic development in the state, it is not surprising to come across several explanations of it, be it – centre's neglect of the state, sickening condition of communication, law and order problem, insurgency problem, lack of fund etc. These factors altogether have something to do with the dismal scenario but the most important causal factor is lack of good governance in the state. Governance in the state has failed to bring development in the state. It has failed to improve the quality of life of the common people. A political leader2 said that now in Manipur, there is neither good governance nor bad governance. Rather, there is no governance in the state. Another political leader3 said that there is no good governance in Manipur and people are responsible for it. People will get the government they deserve. Sharing the same opinion, another political leader4 opined that good governance is yet to come in Manipur. A Sitting MLA5, however, claimed that there is good governance in the state. It is very essential to have very effective governance in the state. It is not that the state cannot have good governance in the state. What is needed is pro-people governance. That the government is trying at its best level to have it in the state is an old story.

The welfare of people is the first and foremost condition of governance and its legitimacy. It is unfortunate that the governance system in Manipur have failed in several fronts, the major one being vision and mission, corruption, education, values and integrity and nationalist spirit Etc. Winning elections and forming governments seem to have defined the goals of all political parties in the state. Manipur is not governable but it is made ungovernable by those who stand to gain by it. The state is now characterized by load-shedding – not even three of hours of electricity, dusty roads including national highways, dying and dysfunctional schools and colleges, large population of unemployed youths, drug addiction and problem of insurgency and HIV/AIDS. Corruption has become obsessive concern of the public life. But it has never been an issue of significance in any crucial exercise of public decision making. By and large, those who can spend a big amount will have the upper hand. Corruption today is generally treated as a service perk than moral erosion.

To say that corruption is widespread in the state is to state the obvious. Bribery - or what is delicately called 'grease money' – is ubiquitous for almost anything that required administrative sanction. It takes days together (even months together) for a file to travel from one table to another. More often than not, it does not travel at all unless an acceptable bribe helps to propel it. Instances are galore where files were/are processed/cleared not on the basis of merit but on the basis of individual names. It is not possible to accurately measure the extent of corruption in the state. But then, measuring the extent is not as important as the belief widely held by the people that corruption is rampant and it is increasing. Political institutions can support an almost limitless weight of corruption as successive state governments have displayed since its statehood in 1972. This has resulted into an increasing wave of cynicism among the people and a common withdrawal of trust.

The successive Chief Ministers of the state reigned but did not rule. They commanded but did not conduct. They lorded but did not govern. They arbitrated where they should have resolved. Their cabinet consisted mainly of courtiers and sycophants chosen for their personal loyalty or influence or money and muscle power; in short for everything but their policies. They failed not because they antagonized too much but because they were afraid to antagonize enough. They retained Ministers whom they should have dismissed for corruption or incompetence and they dismissed Ministers whom they should have retained for their ideas and principles. This is the legacy that 42 long years of the state governance have produced. Such governance have accelerated the pace not of socio-economic development but that of corruption, nepotism, favoritism, sectarianism and all the vices associated with corruption.

The infrastructure of the state is such that the common people are deprived of any decent means of livelihood. On the other hand, a handful enjoys rapid increase in financial capacity without a known source and such persons are able to lure voters at the time of election and some of them come out as representatives of the people in such a way that the latter are not conscious of ideology of a political party or another. Those in power formulate policies but not to solve the problem with a holistic approach, rather to be manipulated for their vested interests. The policy so far made in the state failed to capacitate the state producers and could not provide those facilities to enable them compete with the producers of other states. Compelling the producers to live and work without availing them the essential infrastructure is an unfavorablestate of affairs in the state. In such a dismal scenario, one cannot but wonders whether tourism industry in Manipur can be promoted and developed successfully.

Suggestive Note:

Good governance is a prerequisite for socio-economic development via tourism industry in Manipur. It may be mentioned here that it is only because of good governance that the state of Gujarat is successfully projected as the model of development including tourism industry in the country. It is therefore essential that political leaders responsible for the art of governing need to be reputed for integrity, straight forwardness, discipline, work ethic and decisiveness in governance so that tourism industry for inclusive development is developed in the state. They must be darling of the common people and take decision at the right moment. They must be truly patriotic and interact with people from all works of life and be guardian of the people. It is mostly common people who actually need the true service of the political leaders who need to prove a point to the people that they can provide clean and efficient administration. Initiative may also be taken up to give more emphasis to private sector and foreign direct investment on tourism sector of the state rather than emphasizing on public sector and central aid. Drawing the attention of foreign and domestic private investment requires good culture of entrepreneurship in the state through social and academic institutions. Begging Bowl System of governance should be removed. Transparency, responsibility, accountability, participation and response to the needs of the people are the need of the hour.

End Notes:

Quoted in John Graham, Bruce Amos and Tim Plumpter, Principles of Good Governance in the 21st Century –Policy Brief No. 15, Institute of Governance, Ottawa, Canada, 2003.

Personal interview with RadhabinodeKoijam (Ex-Chief Minister, Manipur).

Personal interview with H. Bhubon (Ex-MLA, Manipur).

Personal interview with RishangKeishing (Ex- Chief Minister/ MP).

Personal interview with Gaikhangam (Deputy Chief Minister, Manipur).

References:

Aiyer, Shankkar (2009),'India's Best and Worst States'India Today, Vol. XXXIV,

No. 39, September 22-28, New Delhi.

Andrew, K., Nada K. and Davies, Linda Lee (2008), 'Leading for Success: Seven

Sides to Great Leaders',Polgram Macmillan, New York.

Census (Manipur), 2011, Directorate of Census Operation, Imphal, Manipur

Govt. of India, '20 Years Perspective Plan for Manipur', Ministry of Tourism, New Delhi, 2003.

Govt. of Manipur, 'Draft Tourism Policy of Manipur -2011', Department of

Tourism, Imphal, 2011

Graham, John., Amos, Bruce and Plumptre Tim(2003), 'Principles of Good

Governance in the 21st Century – Policy Brief No. 15', Institute of Governance, Ottawa, Canada.

Jenkins, K. (2002), 'The Emergence of Governance Agenda: Sovereignty, Neoliberal Bias and the Politics of International Development' in V.

Desai and K.Potter (eds.), The Champion to Development Studies, London : Edward Arnold, 2002.

Kshetri, Rajendra (2013), 'Governance and Development in Nagaland: Musings of a Sociologist', in KedilezoKikhi (ed.), The Dynamics of Development in North East India, Bookwell, Delhi (2006), 'District Councils in Manipur: Formation and

Functioning', Akansha Publications, New Delhi.

Lord, Carnes, 'The Modern Prince: What Leaders Need to Know Now', Yale

University Press, London, 2003.

M. Binota, et. al., (eds.), 'Strategic Interventions in Tourism Development:

Regional Perspective', Bharti Publications, Delhi.

Roy, Jotirmoy, 'History of Manipur' East Light Book House, Calcutta, 1973.

Singh, OinamMomoton and RajendraKshetri (2014), 'Planning Tourism in

Manipur: Some Sociological Insights' in M. Binota, et. al., (eds.),

Strategic Interventions in Tourism Development: Regional Perspective, BhartiPublications, Delhi.

Singh, Oinam Momoton (2012), 'A Sociological Study of Political Elite in

Manipur', Ph.D. Dissertation (unpublished), Nagaland University (Sociology).

ROLE OF CELEBRITY IN TOURIST DESTINATION MARKETING IN INDIA

Charu Sheela Yadav

Indian Institute of Tourism and Travel Management, NOIDA

charupg@rediffmail.com

Pawan Gupta

Indian Institute of Tourism and Travel Management, NOIDA

drpawan.gupta@yahoo.com

Abstract

Tourism industry is economically beneficial to the destinations as it brings foreign exchange, jobs, investment etc. This very economic importance of tourism creates a challenge for the destinations to be able to fetch tourists to their place and also overcome competition faced by their competitive destinations. Marketers always look for unique strategies for promoting tourist destinations. Celebrity marketing is one such strategy. This paper tries to bring out the role and importance of celebrity marketing in tourism industry in India with special reference to "Khoshboo Gujarat Ki" campaign by Amitabh Bachchan.

Keywords: Celebrity, celebrity marketing, destination, tourism industry.

Tourism is a hugely complex industry and to deliver a complete tourism experience it involves a broad range of businesses, organisations and government agencies working together at various levels. Each component in the chain is important as it contributes to the overall holiday experience of the customer - from initial destination marketing through to the ground level experience. Tourism plays an important role in the growth and wellbeing of a destination. It provides valuable foreign currency exchange and government revenues through taxation and can be a major source of employment as well as a vehicle of economic and social progress.

Marketing is very essential for tourist destinations. For marketing of tourist destinations the marketers have to understand the structure, nature and characteristics of tourism industry.

Figure 1: Structure of Tourism Industry

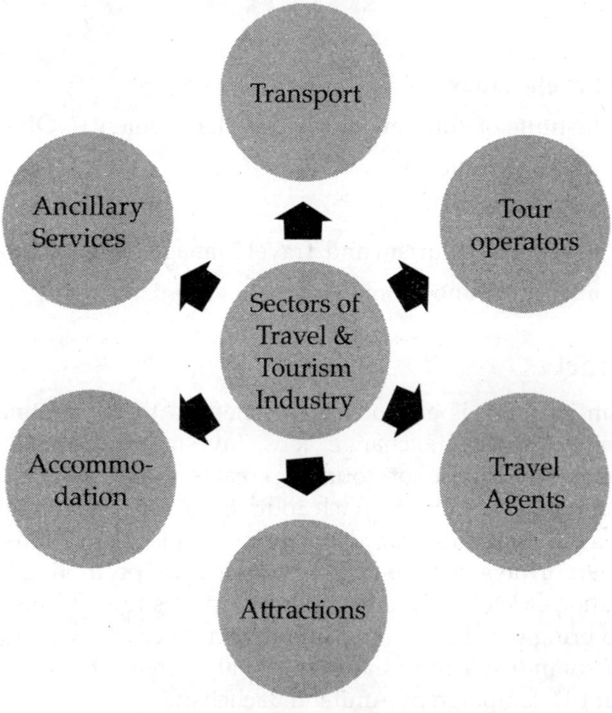

Source: http://www.pearsonschoolsandfecolleges.co.uk/feandvocational/travelandtourism/alevel/asgcetravelandtourism/samples/sampleunit/asttdoubleedexcelunit1.pdf

Each component of tourism industry is integral part of tourist experience at the destination. It comprises of transport to and from the home country of tourist to the destination and within the destination. Accommodation is required at the destination which is as per the requirement and budget of the tourist. Attractions natural or cultural are pulling factors which keep the tourist engage. Ancillary services like banking, ATMs etc are add-ons and must haves at the destination. Travel Agents and Tour Operators are intermediaries which facilitate the whole process of travel, stay and sightseeing arrangements of the tourists.

Characteristics of tourism industry:

Fragmentation of supply

The tourist product is a combination of attractions, transport, accommodation, entertainment and other services. In most countries, there are many separate suppliers of these various components – airlines, hotel companies, tour operators etc. This fragmented nature of tourism products on supply side is a challenge as there is demand for combined set of these products. This calls for coordination and integration of all components across all sub-sectors of the tourism industry - that is, of supply.

Interdependence and complementarily of tourist services

It follows from the fact that tourism demand is for a composite product that the various tourist products and services are interdependent and complementary. The supply of one (for example international air transport to/from a destination) depends on the supply of another (such as hotel accommodation) and they complement each other. A destination's reputation can be set by the weakest link in the tourist product chain. This leads to the marketing policies and actions of one enterprise directly influencing other enterprises. A country with a liberal charter policy and/or an airline with an aggressive pricing policy may result in the attraction of low budget tourists, something that could damage the high quality image central to the marketing of a five-star hotel chain in the destination. There is again then the need for coordination and cooperation in order to enhance the effectiveness of individual marketing and promotional efforts of the various tourism suppliers.

Rigidity of supply

Much tourism demand cannot be easily and quickly be adjusted in the short term to variation in demand. A hotel, for example, cannot add or remove rooms in line with demand. This relative lack of flexibility has obvious operational and economic implications. When demand falls below capacity, waste of resources occurs; when it exceeds capacity, the tourism industry fails to maximize its revenue. This "short term" can extend to years if the rigidity is caused by lack of airport or hotel capacity, given the extensive lead-time to construct a new airport or hotel.

Fixed in time and space

The composite tourism product cannot be stored – it is perishable – so a hotel room on a particular night or a seat on a given flight is available only once, and if not utilised, the sales opportunity is lost. Similarly, it cannot be transported. The need is to bring the consumer to the tourist product. The importance of ensuring, through marketing, as high a level of utilisation as possible is particularly marked because of the high fixed costs of many tourist operations. A hotel has to meet its fixed costs whether it has 5 guests or 200. The non-transportability of tourism products means there is no physical distribution in the strict sense in tourism marketing. Similarly, there are limited opportunities for merchandising activities, in consequence of the fact that the tourist product, unlike consumer goods, cannot be displayed at points of sale other than via proxy representations.

Intangible

Tourist products, except items like souvenirs, are services rather than goods. They are intangible that is it involves perception based on feelings and experience without any physical sensation. For example a good aircraft can be physically felt but the pleasure of good service can only be experienced.

The tourism product cannot be test driven or known about with certainty in advance of being consumed. The tourist therefore builds mental images of the destination and of the facilities and other components of the tourism product of that destination. He/she has a set of expectations about the place to be visited.

Experiences because the intangibility of tourism products means that the tourist engages in a series of activities – typically, for example, riding on transport, visiting attractions, staying in some form of accommodation, eating, drinking, recreating, interacting with other people – none of which produce a final physical product to take home. Each tourist trip, therefore, is a combination of various experiences.

At the end of the trip the tourist is left with nothing more than memories – the derivation of the word souvenirs - and proxies of the trip – such as photos or videos.

Price elasticity of demand

Most forms of tourism demand involve the use of personal discretionary disposable income and free time. Holidaymakers or vacation travellers need both money and time to engage in tourism. They have freedom of choice as to how to use their money and time for tourism purposes, affecting decisions such as how much to spend, how long to go for, where to go, when to go etc. As a result, tourists are highly sensitive to price, and generally their demand for tourist services exhibits a significant degree of price elasticity.

Seasonality

It is a characteristic of most tourism markets that demand fluctuates over the course of the year. The principal determinant is climatic – either in the destination or the tourist generating markets. Tourists from South India shall travel to hill states during summer months like April, May and June. So these summer months for service providers in hills are peak season. Winter months are lean season as the number of tourists travelling to hills is decreased. Thus demand fluctuates greatly between seasons of the year. As a result, the occupancies in many tourism businesses increase to 90 to 100 per cent in the high season but drops to 30 per cent or less in the lean season.

These demand variations are all the more acute because of the fact that any tourism product cannot be stored – the perishability factor – and the concern of marketers is to generate as much demand in the trough periods as possible since the fixed cost element of any tourism operation do not change between seasons. The marketing response to seasonality can range from the reduction of prices in order to induce people to travel in periods other than would be their normal preference to targeting geographic markets with different seasonal patterns of travel so that the demand for the destination from one group complements that of the other group.

Inseparability

The production and consumption of tourism products and services are simultaneous – and that they cannot be made in advance and stored. It also does not take place in the consumer's home environment.

The nature and characteristics of tourism industry poses various challenges to the DMOs and service providers in marketing the destination and tourism products. The marketing strategies are adopted by them includes advertisements, road shows, FAM trips, participating in travel trade shows etc. But apart from these some unique marketing strategies need to be adopted. Celebrity marketing is one such strategy which is being implemented by the DMOs and service providers in marketing the destination and tourism products.

Celebrity Marketing

Celebrity endorsements are widely used by marketers in India and across the world. Celebrity marketing started in 1980s but emerged as a phenomenon in 1990s with companies extensively using celebrities to communicate their brands to consumers. This was due to media as there was an increase in the number of brands advertised on TV from around 3,000 in 1990s to almost 11,500 in early 2000. (India Today – December 2004). It is said that for the same period, the number of commercials being aired is up by over 3,000 per cent (India Today – December 2004). Research conducted by leading Indian research agency IMRB indicated that 86 % of the respondents say the most prominent advertisement that they remember has a celebrity in it (The Economic Times - 28 March, 2008). According to an estimate, the celebrity endorsement market is considered to be worth more than Rs. 10000 million ($ 200 million) business (The Economic Times – 3 February, 2010).

Celebrity marketing is a major business. Artists, musicians, CEO's, physicians, high-profile lawyers and financers and other professionals all get help from celebrity marketers (Rein et al 2006). Messages delivered by attractive or popular sources can achieve higher attention and recall, which is why advertisers often use celebrities as spokespeople (Kotler et al, 2009). Spokesperson's credibility is important. Three most important factors underlie spokesperson's credibility. They are expertise, trustworthiness and likability (Kelman & Hovland). Expertise is the specialized knowledge the communicator possesses to back the claim. Trustworthiness is related to how objective and honest the source is perceived to be. Friends are trusted more than strangers or salespeople, and people who are not paid to endorse a product are viewed as more trustworthy than people who are paid (Moore and Mowen). Likability describes the source's attractiveness. Qualities such as candor, humour, and naturalness make a source more likeable. The most highly credible source would score high on all three dimensions-expertise, trustworthiness and likability.

Effectiveness of celebrity advertising is dependent upon the appeal of the celebrity endorser, mostly those celebrities who are famous in the host countries are preferred. However, international celebrities whose appeal goes beyond the borders have also been effective endorsers for a host of products. For example, cricketers like Steve Waugh (MRF Tyres), stars like Pierce Brosnan (Reid & Taylor men's suiting) etc have been utilized by business houses to promote national and international brands in South Asia.

Defining a 'Celebrity'

According to Collins Dictionary celebrity means 'a famous person'. As per Oxford dictionary celebrity means 'A famous person, especially in entertainment or sport'. A celebrity is a person who has a prominent profile and commands some degree of public fascination and influence in day-to-day media. The term is often synonymous with wealth (commonly denoted as a person with fame and fortune), implied with great popular appeal, prominence in a particular field, and is easily recognized by the general public. Various careers within the fields of sports and entertainment are commonly associated with celebrity status. People become celebrities due to media attention for their extravagant lifestyle or wealth (as in the case of a socialite); for their connection to a famous person (as in the case of a relative of a famous person); or even for their misdeeds (as in the case of a well-known criminal). Celebrities may be known around the world (e.g., pop stars and film actors), within a specific country (e.g., a top Australian rugby player); or within a region (e.g., a local television news anchor). (http://en.wikipedia.org/wiki/Celebrity)

Celebrities are people that exert significant influence in several facets of society, ranging from arts, music, movies and television, sports, culture, politics and even religion. The term Celebrity refers to an individual who is known to the public (actor, sports figure, entertainer, etc.) for his or her achievements in areas other than that of the product class endorsed (Uche Okonkwo).

The term celebrity refers to an individual who is known to the public (actor, sports figure, entertainer, etc.) for his or her achievements in areas other than that of the product class endorsed (Friedman and Friedman, 1979). "The celebrities are the names that need no further identification. Those who know them so far exceed those of whom they know as to require no exact computation. Wherever they go, they are recognized, and moreover, recognized with some excitement and awe. Whatever they do has publicity value. More or less continuously, over a period of time, they are the material for the media of communication and entertainment. And, when that time ends – as it must – and the celebrity still lives – as he may – from time to time it may be asked 'Remember him?' That is what celebrity means." (C. Wright Mills ,1956, pp. 71–72).

According to McCracken (1989), celebrity may be any individual who enjoys public recognition and who uses this recognition on behalf of a consumer good by appearing with it in an advertisement. According to Christina Schlecht, celebrities are people who enjoy public recognition by a large share of certain group of people having attributes like attractiveness and extraordinary lifestyle. One of the latest definitions says that celebrity is an individual "whose name has attention-getting, interest-riveting and profit generating value that stems from the high level of public attention and interest" (Gupta, 2009).

The term celebrity is normally associated with individuals who are frequently in the public eye and typically have a high profile in, among others, the sports and entertainment industries. Such individuals are used to endorse consumer services, products, ideas or organization (Canning & West 2006). Fleck et al. (2012) concluded that once a celebrity becomes famous and popular, he/she immediately appears in an advertisement and sometimes several at the same time. When speaking about characteristics that ideal celebrity needs to have, Keller (2008) mentions credibility in terms of expertise, trustworthiness, likability, attractiveness and specific associations that carry potential product relevance.

'Celebrity Endorsement'

According to BusinessDictionary.com celebrity endorsement is 'Using a famous person's image to sell products or services by focusing on the person's money, popularity, or fame to promote the products or services. If the famous person agrees to allow his or her image to be used, it is termed a celebrity endorsement. The promotion might be through formal advertisements in the media, or it might occur through the famous person displaying the products by using them or wearing them. The implication is that the famous person uses the product or service that he or she endorses; for example, a supermodel with beautiful hair might be contracted to promote a certain brand of shampoo, giving the impression that her beautiful hair results from using the shampoo. However, the person might not even use the product or service he or she endorses; in which case, he or she is often said to be "selling out."

Endorsement is a channel of brand communication in which a celebrity acts as the brand's spokesperson and certifies the brand's claim and position by extending his/her personality, popularity, stature in the society or expertise in the field to the brand. In a market with a very high proliferation of local, regional and international brands, celebrity endorsement was thought to provide a distinct differentiation. Celebrities in India are on such high pedestal that over 60% of brands in India use celebrities to push products, compared to 25% in the US, revealed a study by IIM- Ahmedabad titled 'Role of culture in celebrity endorsement: Brand endorsement by celebrities in Indian context'.

Celebrity endorsement is phenomenon that has developed over years. Good definition of this term is provided by Khatri (2006) who stated that in endorsement celebrities usually lend their names to advertisements for product or services for which they may or may not be the experts". However, celebrity endorsement could be defined as one of the most popular forms of marketing used to promote a range of consumer products and services (Halonen-Knight & Hurmerinta 2010). According to Byrne et al. (2003), celebrity endorsement has become one of the communication strategies employed by marketers trying to build a congruent image between the brand and the consumer. According to Friedman and Friedman (1979) a "celebrity endorser is an individual who is known by the public for his or her achievements in areas other than that of the product class endorsed".

Celebrities score high on the characteristic 'familiarity' (a component of the characteristic 'attractiveness'), and mostly they are well known for achievements in an area other than the advertised product. There are various celebrities types such are such as pop, film and TV stars, sportsmen/-women, politicians, artists, writers and scientists (Meijer, 2010).

Celebrity marketing helps in the following ways:

Quick connect	Quick Brand Differentiation	Quick Recall	Quick Brand Values
Celebrity connects with masses	In a category where no brand is using a celebrity, the first that picks one up could use it to differentiate itself in the market	star power ensures that the brand stays on top of the consumers mind.	Brand Message comunicated fast without elaborate story telling
Ranbir Kapur connects with youth in Pepsi	Boost did it in the malted beverage category by using Sachin Tendulkar.	Amitabh Bachchan in promoting Gujarat Tourism	Roger Federer and Rolex are inseparable to the consumer since both radiates class

Promoting tourist destinations through celebrity in India

Many DMOs are using celebrities to promote their destinations both in domestic and international market. The pop singer Rihanna is in a new "interactive" campaign promoting holidays to Barbados. She has been described as the "pride of Barbados" and will share what the island means to her during the campaign. She is the latest in a long line of celebrities who have been called on to inspire tourists. Jamaican Tourist Board in 2010 cashed on to the Olympic success of Usain Bolt by launching campaign "Once you Go, you Know". Rupert Grint, of Harry Potter fame was to promote England as the place for a "staycation". In times of need, Japan was able to call on Lady Gaga to boost tourist numbers. The eccentric singer became an ambassador for the country while touring after earthquake. Canada Tourism Commission in 2010 have taken Bollywood King Akshay Kumar as a Canadian tourism ambassador to India. "California Calling" (Pamela Anderson) – Visit California 2009, "You Gotta Be Here" (Kim Cattrall, Steve Nash, Sarah McLachlan and Michael J. Fox) – British Columbia/ Canada 2010, "Come and say G'day" (or else Paul Hogan's famous "Shrimp on the barbie" quote – Australia Tourism Commission 1984 etc are some other popular destination promotion campaigns by celebrities.

The celebrity endorsement in tourism is also picking up in India. For tourism promotion in the states following states are endorsed by celebrities:

Amitabh Bachchan- Gujarat

Shah Rukh Khan: West Bengal

Aamir Khan: Incredible India

Preity Zinta: Himachal Pradesh

Prachi Desai: Goa

Saina Nehwal: Andhra Pradesh

Hema Malini: Sparsh Ganga campaign (Uttarakhand)

Mahendra Singh Dhoni : Corbett National Park that turned 75 in 2013 (Uttarakhand)

Amitabh Bachchan may also endorse Amritsar, Jaipur, Tirupati and Khajuraho. Rajasthan tourism department is also looking forward to associate an international celebrity to give boost to the state's tourism. Judi Dench is being considered for promoting Rajasthan Tourism. Bollywood celebrities are using social media to promote their brands they endorse and around 27 percent conversation of Bollywood celebrities are about their work or films.

Research Methodology

Objectives: The present paper tries to bring out the role and importance of celebrity endorsement in destination marketing in India with special reference to "Khushboo Gujarat Ki" Campaign by Amitabh Bachchan.

Data Collection: The present research study is based on both primary sources and secondary sources of information. Primary source includes information collected through questionnaire survey method. The secondary information is based on website of Gujarat Tourism and other internet sources, books, journals, newspapers.

In the present research study, every person having ever travelled to the state of Gujarat, or seen the ads of "Khushboo Gujarat Ki" campaign comprise the universe of the study. Samples from various categories have been selected using "Random Sampling" method. Sample size is restricted to 55. 55 sample units have been stratified into respondents having actually travelled to Gujarat and respondents having seen the advertisements of the campaign. A multiple-choice and close ended questionnaire has been prepared, in which a set of eight close ended questions have been prepared to get a clear view for the success of the promotional campaign started by the Gujarat government.

Interviews of travel and tourism professionals was conducted. A separate set of questions were administered on them. Fifteen travel professionals were interviewed.

Limitation of the study: The sample size of both respondents i.e. tourists and industry professionals is very less. They sample is restricted to Delhi NCR so the universe of data collection is very limited.

The "Khushboo Gujarat Ki" campaign to promote tourism in Gujarat with Amitabh Bachchan as the Brand ambassador

The "Khushboo Gujarat Ki" campaign started off in 2010-11 and is ongoing. This was done in order to boost tourism in Gujarat and attract tourists from all over the world. Amitabh Bachchan is the brand ambassador. He is a popular superstar across the globe. His credibility as brand ambassador is very strong. The other reasons for choosing him were ensured attention, PR coverage and a higher degree of recall. In India the campaign features on TV, radio, print and outdoor. Internationally the campaign features in in-flight and reputed travel magazines. The campaign has run on channels like CNN, Sky News etc.

The campaign features various destinations of Gujarat and showcasing their unique features and never seen before images. The Gujarat State has a variety of destinations to meet the tastes of all types of travellers – beaches, forests and natural ecosystems, gardens and lakes, heritage monuments, archaeological sites, museums, religious sites etc.

Besides the tourist destinations, the colourful festivals of Gujarat also attract travellers. The Monsoon festival, Tarnetar fair, Navratri festival, the Rann Utsav and the international kite festival are some of the events, which have been attracting tourists from across the globe to Gujarat.

The industry has recognized the growing popularity of Gujarat among the tourists and Gujarat Tourism has won many notable awards. The "Khushboo Gujarat Ki", featuring megastar Amitabh Bachchan, received the prestigious National Tourism Award 2011-12 in the category of Best Tourism Film. Gujarat was adjudged the third best state in the category of Comprehensive Development of Tourism. Tourism Corporation of Gujarat Limited (TCGL) received the award for most innovative use of IT.

"Khushboo Gujarat Ki" has been by far the most successful campaigns amongst all the celebrity campaigns promoting various states. The promotional campaign has spurred tourist influx to Gujarat with an increase of 54 lakh visitors in the last two years. It has also helped in promoting the previously lesser known locations of Gujarat. The campaign has also helped in promoting the non conventional forms of tourism in Gujarat like event tourism, health tourism, medical tourism, business tourism etc.

Clearly, domestic tourist arrivals in Gujarat have increased considerably, with an almost 33 % rise in the numbers from within the state, a 50% rise from other parts of India and from NRIs, and an almost 100% increase from foreign tourists as can be seen from the figures below.

Origin	2009-10		2010-11		2011-12		2012-13	
	No	%	No	%	No	%	No	%
Within Gujarat	130.77	77	150.62	76	171.76	77	195.36	77
Other Indian States	36.24	21	43.55	22	47.28	21	53.56	21
NRI	2.03	1	2.57	1	2.85	1	3.16	1
Foreigner	1.07	1	1.39	1	1.75	1	2.01	1
Total	170.11	100	198.12	100	223.64	100	254.09	100

There has been a 44% increase in tourism since the campaign was launched and Sasan Gir has seen the greatest impact.

Gujarat Tourism has adopted a multi-pronged strategy to promote some of the world class tourist destinations in the state. It has created infrastructure facilities like excellent connectivity by roads and trains, security apparatus in place, information centres, sanitation and other amenities to ensure safety and comfort of the tourists. Leveraging the PPP mode, it has roped in the private sector to set up commercial ventures like hotels and resorts.

Data Analysis

Figure 2

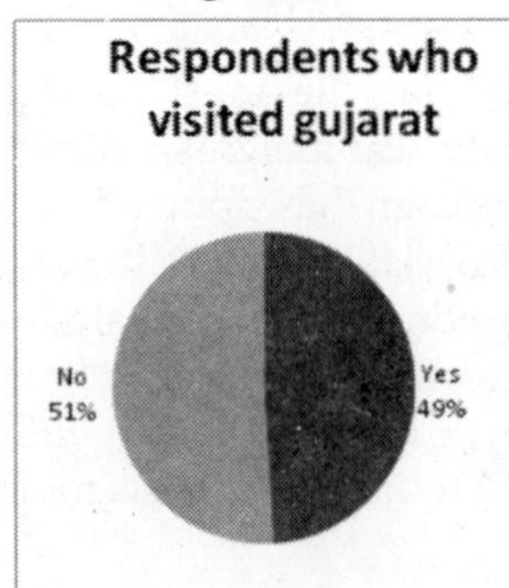

Figure 3

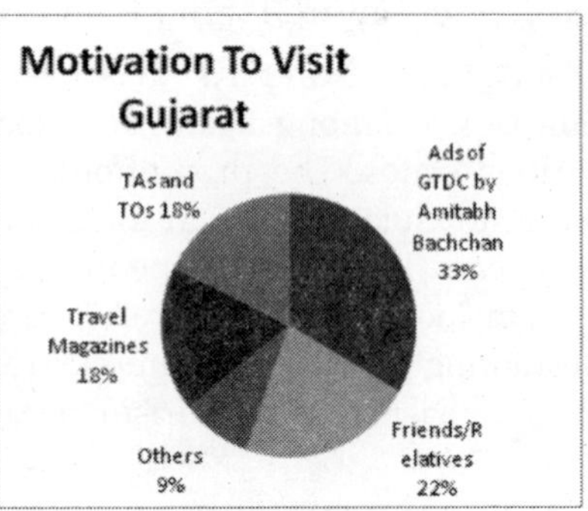

49 % respondents agreed to having travelled to Gujarat and 51 % respondents disagreed on having travelled to Gujarat .

Out of the respondents who had travelled to Gujarat, 33% agreed to have become aware of Gujarat tourism because of GTDC Campaign Ads "Khushboo Gujrat Ki" by Amitabh Bachchan, next 22% agreed to have gone on recommendations by friends /relatives, 18% through travel agents and tour operators, 18% through travel magazines and 5% people agreed to have become aware of Gujarat because of other sources like participating in trade fairs/shows, internet, posters in metro train.

Figure 4

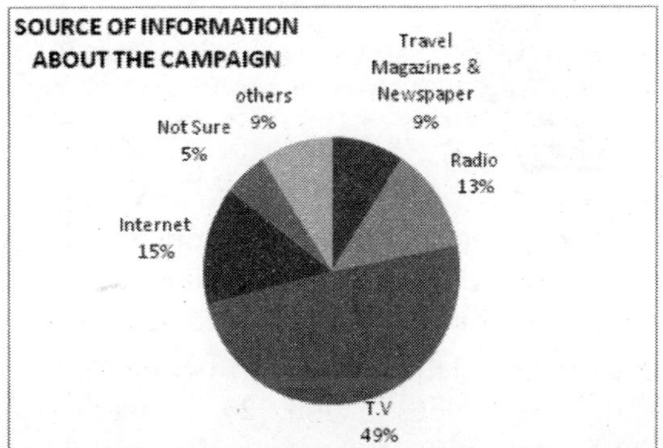

The source of information about the campaign for 49% was television, 13 % radio, 15% internet, 9% travel magazines and newspapers, 9% other sources like posters on Delhi Metro etc. 5 % are not sure about the campaign's source of information.

Figure 5

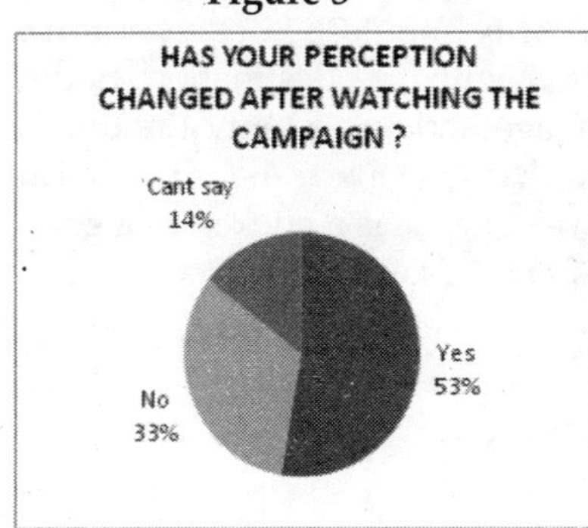

Figure 6

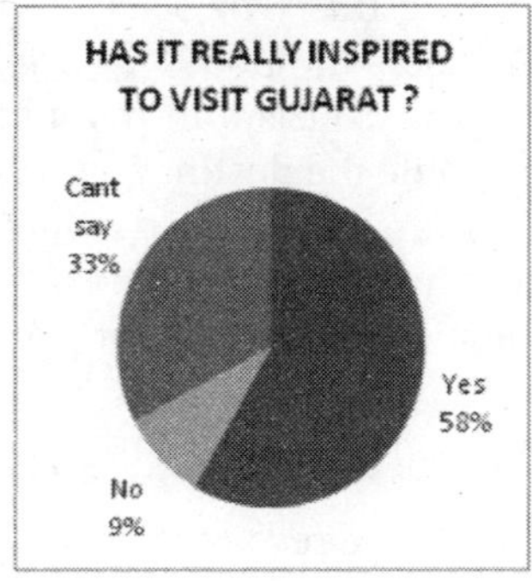

53 % of the respondents agreed to having a change in their perception about Gujarat after seeing the Khushboo Gujrat Ki campaign, 33 % disagreed and 14% were not sure.

58 % of the respondents agreed to have been inspired to visit Gujarat, 33% were not sure of visiting Gujarat after seeing the advertisement, 9 % are not inspired to visit Gujarat.

Figure 7

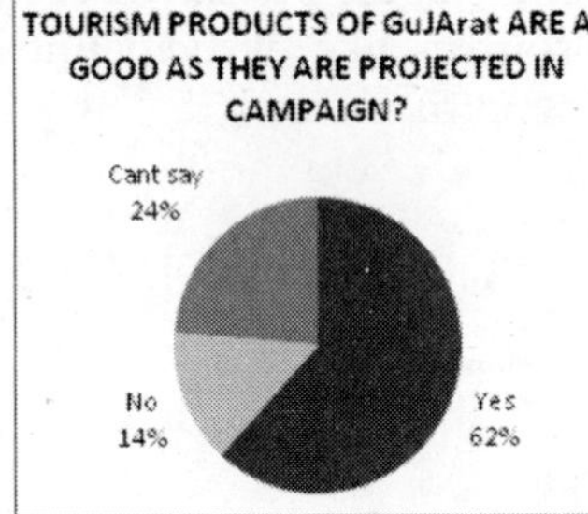

Figure 8

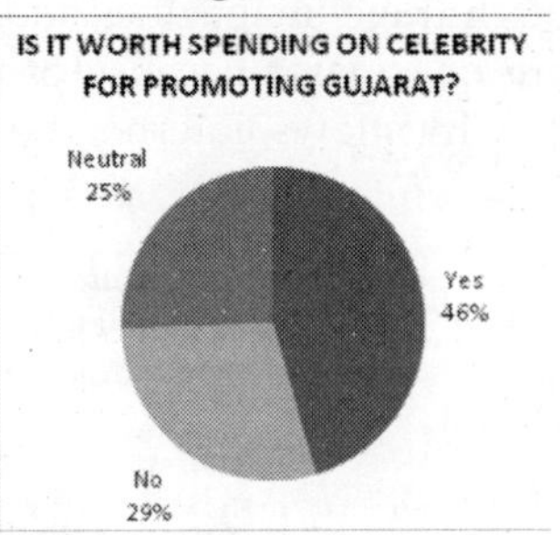

62% respondents agreed that tourism products of Gujarat are as good as projected in the campaign, 24% respondents are not sure and 14% disagreed to the fact.

46 % respondents agreed that it was worth spending on celebrities for promoting tourist destination, 25 % were neutral and remaining 29 % were against it.

The industry views that celebrity endorsing a destination is not useful. Having a celebrity endorsing a tourist destination is not cost effective. The DMOs should have good strategy for tourism promotion then only a celebrity can be helpful. Apart from using them for quick publicity they should be used for long term results. The selection of celebrity should be done carefully. The person should be well-versed with the destination. South African Tourism in India has engaged cricketer Jonty Rhodes to promote the destination among Indian travellers. As he is a South African, knows the destination well and he is a cricketer - a good combination to spread the message. Usain Bolt always paints Jamaica in a good light.

Conclusion and Suggestions

The above results show that "Khushboo Gujarat Ki" campaign of

Amitabh Bachchan started by TGCL in 2010 to promote tourism in Gujarat has been successful in making people aware of the varied tourism products of Gujarat. The campaign has helped in portraying Gujarat in an extremely positive light. Majority of the respondents were aware of Gujarat, and the awareness was mostly due to the "Khushboo Gujarat Ki" campaign of Amitabh Bachchan broadcasted on television, as well as via radio and internet. Majority of the respondents agreed it is worth spending money on celebrity driven campaigns to promote a destination like in case of Amitabh Bachchan a superstar of international stature has been able to bring out the real essence of Gujarat. Majority of the respondents agreed to have had a change in their perception towards Gujarat and were inspired to visit it, after having seen the campaign. Majority of respondents who had travelled to Gujarat agreed to its tourism products being as good as being projected in the campaign.

In 2012 Gujarat got over 22 million tourists and witnessed a tourism growth rate of over 16%, which is double of the national tourism growth rate (http://www.narendramodi.in/those-who-know-the-tourism-sector-know-what-potential-there-is-gujarat-cm-at-gujarat-travel-mart/). This can be attributed to the success of the marketing campaign of Gujarat involving Amitabh Bachchan by TGCL, as well as the overall development in the infrastructure and the business opportunities as well as investment opportunities in Gujarat.

Other states have started using the concept of celebrity endorsements with West Bengal using Shahrukh Khan for endorsing it, so destinations which need to gain recognition on the tourism platform should definitely use celebrities in order to capture audience attention. Though as per the industry people it is expensive to have a celebrity. The selection of celebrity and what the destination want to achieve in long term perspective should be clear.

Celebrity endorsement has been established as one of the most popular tools of advertising in recent time. The celebrity selection criteria should be chalked out in such a way that he/she is able to connect with national and international market. Though celebrity endorsing a tourist destination is expensive option but if right choice of celebrity is made and there is good tourism development strategy then it is one of the best choices. Thus it can be concluded that "messages delivered by attractive or popular sources can achieve higher attention and recall, which is why advertisers often use celebrities as spokespeople (Kotler et al, 2009)".

References

1. Irving J. Rein, Philip Kotler, Michael Hamlin and Martin Stoller, High visibility, 3rd ed. (New York: Mc Graw hill, 2006)
2. Herbert C Kelman and Carl I. Hovland, "Reinstatement of the communication in Delayed measurement of Opinion Change," Journal of Abnormal and social Psychology 48 (July 1953): 327-35
3. David J. Moore, John C. Mowen and Richard Reardon, "Multiple Sources in Advertising Appeals: When Product Endorsers are paid by the Advertising Sponsor," Journal of the Academy of Marketing Science (Summer 1994): 234-43
4. Abhishek & Arvind Sahay , "Role of culture in celebrity endorsement: Brand endorsement by celebrities in Indian context". W.P. No. 2013-07-01 , July 2013
5. http://www.iimahd.ernet.in/assets/snippets/working paperpdf/12087729752013-07-01.pdf
6. Uche Okonkwo, Luxury Brands & Celebrities: An Enduring Branding Romance, http://www.brandchannel.com/papers_review.asp?sp_id=1234
7. http://www.collinsdictionary.com/dictionary/english/celebrity
8. http://www.oxforddictionaries.com/definition/english/celebrity
9. http://en.wikipedia.org/wiki/Celebrity
10. http://www.businessdictionary.com/definition/celebrity-endorsement.html
11. Ahmet Salih Kansu & Agim Mamuti, The Use of Celebrity Endorsement as Marketing Communication Strategy by Turkish Airlines, International Journal of Academic Research in Business and Social Sciences, December 2013, Vol. 3, No. 12, ISSN: 2222-6990 ,

12. http://hrmars.com/hrmars_papers/The_Use_of_Celebrity_Endorsement_as_Marketing_Communication_Strategy_by_Turkish_Airlines.pdf
13. https://usdr.us/usdrinc/downloads/Celebrity-Endorsements.pdf
14. http://www.isrj.net/uploadeddata/390.pdf
15. http://www.iimahd.ernet.in/assets/snippets/workingpaperpdf/12087729752013-07-01.pdf
16. http://www.linkedin.com/groups/Many-tourism-boards-companies-take-74800.S.250390254
17. http://hrmars.com/hrmars_papers/The_Use_of_Celebrity_Endorsement_as_Marketing_Communication_Strategy_by_Turkish_Airlines.pdf
18. http://www.slideshare.net/roopanroyjohn/celebrity-endorsements-report
19. http://www.proparco.fr/webdav/site/proparco/shared/ELEMENTS_COMMUNS/PROPARCO/Revue%20SPD%20vraie/PDF/SPD7/SPD7_UK.pdf
20. http://www.business-standard.com/article/management/iim-a-to-study-gujarat-tourism-s-branding-campaign-114013001120_1.html
21. https://in.lifestyle.yahoo.com/celebrities-promoting-different-indian-states-120558193.html
22. Judi Dench as Rajasthan's brand ambassador? Richa Shukla,TNN | Mar 6, 2014, 12.00 AM IST, http://timesofindia.indiatimes.com/entertainment/english/hollywood/news-interviews/Judi-Dench-as-Rajasthans-brand-ambassador/articleshow/31482442.cms
23. Bollywood celebs using Twitter to promote brands, PTI | Dec 16, 2013, 07.28 PM IST, http://timesofindia.indiatimes.com/tech/social/Bollywood-celebs-using-Twitter-to-promote-brands/articleshow/27482659.cms
24. Brand India, Shalini Singh, Hindustan Times, June 25, 2011 , http://www.hindustantimes.com/news-feed/travelold/brand-india/article1-713809.aspx
25. http://deshgujarat.com/2014/01/30/iima-to-study-gujarat-

tourisms-branding-campaign-in-pictures-amitabh-bachchan-at-iima/

26. http://www.telegraph.co.uk/travel/celebritytravel/9655474/Celebrity-backed-tourism-campaigns.html?frame=2388868
27. http://aboutourism.wordpress.com/2010/08/01/using-celebrities-for-destination-marketing-91-celebrity-tourism-campaigns/
28. http://www.iimahd.ernet.in/assets/upload/media/630729686IIMAPR30012014.pdf
29. http://www.ffymag.com/admin/issuepdf/Tourism%20in%20Gujarat_FFY%20March-13.pdf
30. Ajeet kumar Singh, Marketing of Tourism and Hospitality Products: Study of the impact of Celebrity Endorsed Advertisements on Hospitality Products and Services , http://www.ibmrdjournal.com/index.php/ibmrd/article/view/47380/39307
31. National Tourism Award 2011-12, Ministry of Tourism, Govt. of India, http://www.tourism.gov.in/writereaddata/CMSPagePicture/file/Primary%20Content/Awards/tourism%202011-12%20new.pdf

PERCEPTION, ATTITUDE AND SATISFACTION OF PACKAGED TOURISM USERS OF TAMIL NADU

P. Premkanna

Associate Professor & Head, Department Of Catering & Hotel Management, Hindusthan College Of Arts & Science, Coimbatore. Email: Premkannap@Gmail.Com.

G.B.Karthikeyan

Assistant Professor & Head, Department of International Business, Chikkanna Government Arts College, Tirupur.

Introduction

Tourism plays a vital role in the economic development of a country. Tourism is the second largest foreign exchange earner in India. The tourism industry employs a large number of people, both skilled and unskilled. It promotes national integration and international brotherhood. Tourism is the second largest foreign exchange earner in India. Hotels, travel agencies, transport including airlines benefit a lot from this industry.

Hassle-free traveling is what every tourist wants. A country like India can provide so many wonderful vacation and tour options, but the lack of proper information and facts can ruin any holiday plans. Many people save money throughout their lives in order to have a dream vacation in an exotic land like India but unorganized and ill-planned tours steal the fun out of the holidays. It is always wise to take the help of a travel agent while planning a tour to India or any Country in order to make the most out of a tour.

Need for the study

A package combines two or more products so the customer and market segment being targeted gain an advantage compared with buying the items separately. Core holiday components, such as transport, accommodation, meals, attractions and entertainment, can be carefully combined into a complete packaged experience. Packages provide the customer with either greater convenience or a more competitive price.

Traditional objections to packaging, such as it is down market or only useful to inexperienced travelers, large groups or older holidaymakers, are changing. With the introduction of more flexible packaging methods that represent good value for money, packages can be attractive to other markets, such as the growing free and independent traveler (known as FITs) market. Flexible packages can be tailored to meet the needs of FITs, for example, by presenting components that appeal to their travel values. The benefits include 1. Customer convenience 2. Savings 3. Ease of payment and planning 4. Low stress.

Statement of the problem

The types of packages available in today's market are vast and varied. This ensures all consumers' needs and desires are met. Package tours can be further broken down into specific tour types. Tours available range from Special-interest tours, Adventure tours, City or Regional tours, Group tours and Fully Escorted tours. Special-interest tours are designed around a particular interest area which could include arts, food and wine, sport, cultural or agricultural. Specialist tours may include an expert or celebrity guide who relates to the theme of a tour (e.g. a gardening expert accompanying a garden tour, or an art expert accompanying an art tour). Adventure tours are designed to allow the consumer to participate in their area of interest for the length of the tour and more experience based.

They generally are physical and require a certain level of fitness, however, can sometimes be modified to meet your needs depending on the other travelers. Some examples of this tour type include diving, rock or mountain climbing, horse riding, skiing or cycling. Fully escorted tours are often a good idea for solo travelers and especially women travelling alone. This type of tour offers a sense of security or overcomes language and cultural barriers. Also, these types of tours are often somewhat educational, the escort providing local, historical and cultural knowledge or insight gives the consumer are more worthwhile experience and understanding of the country (place) visited.

In order to find out the attitude and perception of the packaged tourism a 600 sample respondents were selected over the various tourism spots of Tamil nadu.

Review of literature

Susanna Curtin* and Graham Busby (1999)1 Tourism has had a profound and irreversible effect on many destination areas. As the demand for new destinations increases, there is an unrelenting pressure for development in order to satisfy the growth of this complex, pervasive industry. This article presents the results of research undertaken into business attitudes towards sustainable tourism development by the British Federation of Tour Operators and Association of Independent Tour Operators members. The price-cutting competition' of undifferentiated mass market operators continues to be a threat to sustainable destination development. Moulana and Smith (2000)2 pointed out that the Central government have the pivotal role in the international tourism infrastructure by framing appropriate tourism policy. Systematic approach to the study of travel and tourism was pioneered by Gunn who has referred to the functioning of tourist system by involving five components like marketing, attractions, service/facilities, transportation and information promotion.

Graburn and Jafari1 (2001)3 state that no single discipline alone can accommodate, treat or understand tourism; it can be studied only if disciplinary boundaries are crossed and if multi-disciplinary perspectives are sought and formed. For example, Churchill2 adopted scientific method of tourism marketing. Gunn, Clare found out that simulation and modelling have useful approaches in out-door-recreation demand study.

Statistical tools used:

The analysis was carried out with1. Percentage analysis 2. KMO 3. Factor analysis.

Table – 1 Demographic factors of the packaged tourists .

Age	**Frequency**	**Percent**
Less 25 years	49	8.2
26-30 years	139	23.2
31-35 years	108	18.0
36-40 years	107	17.8
41-45 years	80	13.3
More than 45 years	117	19.5
Total	600	100.0
Gender	**Frequency**	**Percent**
Male	336	56.0
Female	264	44.0
Total	600	100.0
Marital status	Frequency	Percent
Married	321	53.5
unmarried	279	46.5
Total	600	100.0
Educational qualification	**Frequency**	**Percent**
school level	118	19.7
under graduate	210	35.0
post graduate	127	21.2
Others	145	24.2
Total	600	100.0
Occupation	**Frequency**	**Percent**
Govt Employee	25	4.2
Private Employee	89	14.8
Professionals	86	14.3
Retired Persons	99	16.5
Student	133	22.2
Business People	93	15.5

Others	75	12.5
Total	600	100.0
Monthly Income	Frequency	Percent
less than Rs.10,000	43	7.2
Rs10,000 to Rs20,000	145	24.2
Rs20,000 to Rs30,000	188	31.3
Rs 30,000 to Rs 40,000	133	22.2
above Rs 40,000	91	15.2
Total	600	100.0

Table 1 explains the Demographic information of the respondents who were using the packaged tourists services. When considering the age group of the respondents who have utilized the packaged tour operators service. It was understood that 23.2 percent of the respondents were in the age group of 26 – 30 years, 19.5 percent of them were in the age group of more than 45 years, 18 percent of them were in the age group of 31- 35 years, 17.8 percent of them were in the age group of 36 – 40 years, and the remaining 8.2 percent of them were in the age group of less than 25 years. While considering the Gender group of the respondents, it was understood that 56 percent of the respondents were male and the remaining 44 percent were female . When taking in to account the details of the educational qualification of the respondents, 35 percent of the respondents have completed under graduation, 24.2 percent of them have completed other forms of education like diploma, and other certificate courses, 21.2 percent of them have completed post graduation and other remaining 19.7 percent of them have completed school education. While accounting the occupation of the respondents, 22.2 percent of the respondents were Student, 15.5 percent of them were Business people, 16.5 percent of the respondents were retired persons, 14.8 percent of them were private employees, 14.3 percent of them were professionals, 12.5 percent of them were of other category people, and a remaining 4.2 percent of them were government employees. When analyzing the monthly income , 22.2 percent of the employees have a monthly income of Rs. 30,000 – 40,000, 31.3 percent of the respondents have a monthly income of Rs 20,000 – 30,000, 24.2 percent of them were drawing a monthly income of Rs. 10,000 – 20,000 and a remaining 7.2 percent of them were drawing a monthly income of less than Rs. 10,000.

Table 2- Reasons for preferring the Packaged Tour

Reasons for preferring the Packaged Tour	**Mean Rank**	**Mean Rank**
Confirmed travel ticket	5.39	XV
Conveyance/transport	5.38	XVI
Accommodation	5.46	XIII
Toll, parking fees, entrance fees	5.45	XIV
Catering services	5.39	XIV
Services of tour guides	5.36	XVII
To visit large number of tourist spots in a given period	10.87	IX
For safe travel	11.04	II
Economic pricing	10.98	V
Friends/relatives/family members	10.87	IX
Tour operator/agents	10.84	XII
Advertisements	10.90	VII
To enjoy trips	10.90	VII
Convenience planning and departure dates	11.15	I
To overcome hygiene problems	10.98	V
For better accommodation	11.01	IV
For better conveyance	11.02	III

Table 2 presents the reasons for selecting the packaged tourism. Out of the various factors selected for analyzing the reasons for preferring the packaged tourists, the Ist , II nd , III rd ranks were secured by the factors of Convenience planning and departure dates, For safe travel and For better conveyance. The IV, V, VII th ranks were secured by the factors of For better accommodation, To overcome hygiene problems and Economic pricing, the VII th rank was shared by two factors viz., Advertisements and To enjoy trips. The IX th rank was secured by the influence of Friends/relatives/family members, and To visit large number of tourist spots in a given period. The XII th rank was secured by the factor of influence of Tour operator/agents. The other factors include Toll, parking fees, entrance fees , Confirmed travel ticket and Services of tour guides .

Hence it could be understood that the maximum factors of influence towards the selection of packaged tours include Convenience planning and departure dates, For safe travel and For better conveyance.

Respondents agreeability towards the aspect of relationship with bank were identified through a five point scaling technique ranked from 5 – 1 (5 – Highly Agree, 4 – Agree, 3 – Neutral, 2 – Disagree, 1 – Highly Disagree). The factor analysis was carried out by using SPSS package for 13 factors. The analysis was done on various stages such as the extraction method, i.e., Principal component analysis with Varimax rotation and is depicted in Table No. 3

Table –4 KMO And Bartlett's Test

Kaiser-Meyer-Olkin Measure of Sampling Adequacy.		.897
Bartlett's Test of Sphericity	Approx. Chi-Square	11951.580
	Df	210
	Sig.	.000

The Significance value and the KMO test justifies the sampling adequacy and proceed for further analysis of factor analysis .

Table 3 – Perception of Tourists towards packaged tourism – Communalities

	Initial	Extraction
The distribution of the interior favored confidentiality and privacy	1.000	.664
The establishment was neat and well organized	1.000	.352

The installations were spacious, modern and clean	1.000	.864
The establishment was well located	1.000	.925
They were good professionals and they are up to date about new items and trends	1.000	.926
They knew their job well	1.000	.875
Their advice was valuable	1.000	.962
The knew the tourism packages	1.000	.775
The tourism package purchase was well organized	1.000	.885
The quality of tourism package was maintained throughout	1.000	.868
Relative to other tourism packages purchased, it had an acceptable level of quality	1.000	.954
The result was as expected	1.000	.852
It was good purchase for the price paid	1.000	.772
The tourism package purchased was reasonably priced	1.000	.778
Relative to other tourism package purchased it had an acceptable level of quality	1.000	.988
The result was expected	1.000	.794
I am comfortable with the tourism package purchased	1.000	.822
The personnel were always willing to satisfy my wishes as a customer, whatever product i wanted to buy	1.000	.996
The personnel gave me a positive feeling	1.000	.988
I felt relaxed in the travel agency	1.000	.976
The personnel dint hassle me to decide quickly	1.000	.963

Using the services of the travel agency has improved the way with other people perceive me	1.000	.929
The tour operators packages are taken by many people i know	1.000	.739
Taking the tourism packages improved the way iam perceived by others	1.000	.730
People who take the trip of package tourism obtain social approval	1.000	.988
I have always felt satisfied	1.000	.962
My expectations are been met at all times	1.000	.900
The level of satisfaction attained was high when compared to that of all the other travel agency	1.000	.971
Iam satisfied	1.000	.880
My expectations are fulfilled	1.000	.817
The comparative satisfaction was high	1.000	.313

Extraction Method: Principal Component Analysis.

Table – 5 Total Variance Explained

Component	Initial Eigenvalues			Extraction Sums of Squared Loadings		
	Total	% of Variance	Cumulative %	Total	% of Variance	Cumulative %
1	23.426	75.567	75.567	23.426	75.567	75.567
2	1.486	4.795	80.362	1.486	4.795	80.362
3	1.295	4.177	84.539	1.295	4.177	84.539
4	.904	2.918	87.456			
5	.806	2.600	90.056			
6	.668	2.153	92.209			
7	.463	1.494	93.703			
8	.426	1.373	95.075			
9	.348	1.122	96.197			
10	.257	.828	97.025			

11	.231	.744	97.769			
12	.199	.641	98.410			
13	.159	.512	98.922			
14	.092	.295	99.218			
15	.062	.201	99.419			
16	.051	.165	99.584			
17	.042	.134	99.718			
18	.024	.079	99.797			
19	.018	.059	99.856			
20	.015	.049	99.906			
21	.014	.046	99.951			
22	.009	.028	99.980			
23	.004	.014	99.994			
24	.002	.006	100.000			
25	.000	.000	100.000			
26	.000	.000	100.000			
27	.000	.000	100.000			
28	.000	.000	100.000			
29	.000	.000	100.000			
30	.000	.000	100.000			
31	.000	.000	100.000			

Extraction Method: Principal Component Analysis.

Table – 6 Component Matrix(a)

	Component		
	1	**2**	**3**
The distribution of the interior favored confidentiality and privacy	.757	-.139	-.868
The establishment was neat and well organized	.574	-.102	.106
The installations were spacious, modern and clean	.880	.202	-.222
The establishment was well located	.941	.142	-.143
They were good professionals and they are up to date about new items and trends	.803	.103	.819
They knew their job well	.896	-.113	.242
Their advice was valuable	.974	-.116	-.002

The knew the tourism packages	.795	.356	.125
The tourism package purchase was well organized	.934	-.026	-.113
The quality of tourism package was maintained throughout	.906	-.164	.139
Relative to other tourism packages purchased, it had an acceptable level of quality	.453	.997	.090
The result was as expected	.915	-.100	.963
It was good purchase for the price paid	.686	.442	.326
The tourism package purchased was reasonably priced	.566	.650	-.190
Relative to other tourism package purchased it had an acceptable level of quality	.690	-.025	.888
The result was not satisfactory and expected	.673	.307	.897
I am comfortable with the tourism package purchased	.877	-.231	.004
The personnel were always willing to satisfy my wishes as a customer, whatever product i wanted to buy	.990	-.127	-.008
The personnel gave me a positive feeling	.990	-.025	-.088
I felt relaxed in the travel agency	.962	-.212	.070
The personnel dint hassle me to decide quickly	.961	.102	-.169
Using the services of the travel agency has improved the way with other people perceive me	.960	-.076	-.047
The tour operators packages are taken by many people i know	.740	.400	-.175
Taking the tourism packages improved the way iam perceived by others	.678	.098	-.511
People who take the trip of package tourism obtain social approval	.990	-.025	-.088
I have always felt satisfied	.960	-.199	.024
My expectations are been met at all times	.907	-.276	.041
The level of satisfaction attained was high when compared to that of all the other travel agency	.977	-.130	-.011
Iam satisfied	.935	.010	-.076
My expectations are fulfilled	.902	.005	.859
The comparative satisfaction was high	.550	.092	-.944

Extraction Method: Principal Component Analysis.

a 3 components extracted.

Table 7 – Grouping of factors.

S.No	Factors	Factor loadings
I. Establishment and Job performance	The establishment was well located	.941
	Their advice was valuable	.974
	They were good professionals and they are up to date about new items and trends	.803
	They knew their job well	.896
II. Perfect Information and Quality service	Their advice was valuable	.974
	The tourism package purchase was well organized	.934
	The quality of tourism package was maintained throughout	.906
	The result was as expected	.915
III. Service quality and Caring employees	The personnel were always willing to satisfy my wishes as a customer, whatever product i wanted to buy	.990
	The personnel gave me a positive feeling	.990
	I felt relaxed in the travel agency	.962
	The personnel dint hassle me to decide quickly	.961
	Using the services of the travel agency has improved the way with other people perceive me	.960
IV. Satisfaction	People who take the trip of package tourism obtain social approval	.990
	I have always felt satisfied	.960
	My expectations are been met at all times	.907
	The level of satisfaction attained was high when compared to that of all the other travel agency	.977
	Iam satisfied	.935
	My expectations are fulfilled	.902

Conclusion:

Travel and tourism is the largest service industry globally in terms of gross revenue and foreign exchange earnings. It is also one of the largest employment generators in the world. It has been a major social phenomenon and is driven by social, religious, recreational, knowledge seeking and business interests and motivated by the human urge for new experience, adventure, education, and entertainment. Tourism is both cause and consequence of economic development. It has the potential to stimulate other sectors in the economy owing to cross-synergistic benefits and its backward and forward linkages. The tour operators business encompasses a large range of offerings. In the said business, you can include tour planning and organizing services related to tour travel, leisure travel, subject travel, sports travel, education travel, etc. It can also include tour related services for inspection, exhibition, training, conference, etc. for business clients. Destinations from the whole world can be included in your packages. Packaged tour operators cater to inbound or outbound tour services like travel booking, hotel bookings, arrange travel schedules, VISA arrangements, etc. The scope of tour operators business is vast; however operators must do a cost benefit analysis before actually deciding what to offer in a tour operators business. The various limitation includes 1. High competition levels 2. Element of Uncertainty 3. Stringent regulatory laws 4. Language constraint 5. Relations between countries 6. Different interests of travelers 7. Fluctuations in demand.

The business of tour operators is booming at a fast pace in spite of several limitations. There has been a growth in the tourism industry which has come up as one of the fastest booming industries in many countries across the globe.

Reference

Sustainable destination development: the tour operator perspective - International Journal of Tourism Research, Volume 1, Issue 2, pages 135–147, March/April 1999

Churchill,Gilbert, A, Jr., Marketing Research: Methodological foundations, 5th Edn, Hindsale,IL, Dryden Press, 2001.

Graburn, Nelson, H.H. and Jafar Jafari (Eds.), "Tourism Social Science", Special Issue, Annals of Tourism Research, 18(1), 2001

EMERGING TOURIST PREFERENCES AND ATTRACTIONS IN HP: A SURVEY

S L Kaushal
HP University Business School, Shimla
Balbir Singh
Research Scholar, HPUBS, Shimla

Abstract

Tourism is the fastest growing industry and it has traditionally acted as a major source of income world over. The governments are investing huge amounts in tourism and also encouraging public-private partnership in this sector including India. The Himachal Pradesh is also making policies and taking various initiatives to promote tourism and attracting tourists. But there exists a gap between plans and tourists turnover. So the tourism management attracts attention of the policy makers, academics and researchers in view of the strong competition and changing outlook of tourists. The present research paper is an effort to explore the match mismatch between the facilities, services and the expectations of the tourists in HP. Opinion survey on the attractions and irritants of HP Tourism has been conducted on a random sample of 100 tourists in Himachal Pradesh through a questionnaire having 26 items on various aspects of tourism. Thus, the collected data have been analysed with the help of weighted mean.

From the results and findings it is concluded that most of the tourists prefer HP for natural beauty and pleasant weather. It is noted that majority tourists decide destination on the issues of climate and personal safety. The tourists identified major irritants in tourism industry of HP like transportation facilities, road conditions and hotels availability. Therefore, it is strongly suggested in order to attract more tourists HP needs to get better connectivity and accessibility especially by air and improve roads and developing hotels and basic amenities particularly in tribal areas. However, tourists indicated satisfaction on the gains out of money spent and the education and learning during their visit to Himachal Pradesh. Thus, indicate the immense tourism potential of Himachal that require to be tapped and need to be served professionally to holiday makers.

Keywords: tourist preferences, destination image, tourist satisfaction.

Prelude

Tourism is the fastest growing industry and it has traditionally acted as a major source of income world over. The governments are investing huge amounts in tourism and also encouraging public-private partnership in this sector including India. Among states Himachal Pradesh is a hilly and cool climate conferring destination making policies and taking various initiatives to promote tourism and attracting tourists. But there exists a gap between plans and tourists turnover. Hui1 emphasized that developing tourism industry is very vital for a place as it make grow retail, transportation and construction along. Therefore, tourism development and management attracts attention of the policy makers, academics and researchers in view of the strong competition and changing outlook of tourists.

Tourist Arrivals in Himachal Pradesh (2006-2012)

Year	Domestic (Crores)	Foreigner (Lacs)	Total (Crores)
2006	0.77	2.8	0.80
2007	0.85	3.4	0.88
2008	0.94	3.8	0.97

Year	Domestic (Crores)	Foreigner (Lacs)	Total (Crores)
2009	1.10	4.0	1.14
2010	1.28	4.5	1.32
2011	1.46	4.8	1.50
2012	1.56	5.0	1.61

Source: Compiled from Tourism & Civil Aviation Department, Shimla

Himachal Pradesh has immense tourism potential. It has got the natural beauty, the cold & calm climate, etc. But this potential has not been tapped efficiently. In order to improve HPTDC has divided state into four tourism circuits like Satluj, Beas, Dhauladhar and Tribal circuits. Though absence of infrastructural facilities, lack of well coordinated and properly directed efforts in marketing is also a reason behind the inability of the Himachal tourism industry to mobilize a good number of tourists from within and outside India. The data reveals growth of tourist arrivals has declined by 7% during last three years in the state. So the study is an effort to find out problems in tourism and suggesting measures to improve tourist inflow in Himachal Pradesh. Xia felt that destination image has direct relationship with tourists' expectations, behavior and consequent their satisfaction. So image building in tourism industry is of paramount importance. In Himachal, the home stay, har gaon ki kahani initiatives of the government is doing well and tourism promotion has been given more teeth and adventure tourism is in focus. Another the tourism department has identified new adventure and eco tourism circuit Kullu, Manali & Katrain that indicates Government's intentions and seriousness about this sector. It has been observed that tourism getting impetus in view of rising income level, improved infrastructure, persistent promotion and emergence of tour operators and attractive packages. The view is further strengthened as Baken & Bhagwatula reported that though tourism in India has been a largely unplanned exercise but Kerala, Goa J&K, and Himachal Pradesh Governments have been more consistent to incorporate tourism into State's five year plans. But question remains to answer that whether tourists are attracted, served and returned happy or not. Sadeh, Asgari & Mousavi identified that destination image, tourist expectations and perceived value as major influential factors of satisfaction. So promotion activities play major role in tourism. Ritchie, Tung & Robin stressed that essence of tourism has been the development and delivery of travel and visitation experiences but found to be more management specific. Thus, present study gains more importance in view of the improved facilities, growing competition, expanding number of tourists, escalating aspirations, inflating earnings and changing spending habits.

Objective of the Study

- To examine the emerging attractions of tourists in HP and suggesting measures to improve tourism management.

Research Methodology

The study is exploratory in nature which attempts to analyze various factors affecting tourism in the state of Himachal Pradesh.

Sources of data

The study uses both primary and secondary data.

Sample

The survey has been carried out on a random sample of 100 tourists selected on the convenience basis. The target respondents were tourists who had been to Himachal Pradesh. The sample distribution is as follows;

Table 1: Sample Distribution

Gender		Age			Occupation			Native Place		
Male	Female	20-35	35-50	50-65	Job	Business	Student	North	South	Foreign
65	35	45	40	15	30	45	25	55	35	10

Instrument

The opinion of tourists have been gathered through a well drafted questionnaire containing 26 questions with a good mix of likert scale, closed and open ended type.

Statistical techniques used

The collected data have been analysed with the help of mean and higher mean indicates higher tendency.

Results and Findings:

The collected data have been tabulated as follows.

Table 2: Native place wise Mean Difference Analysis of Tourism Attractions in HP

Attraction	North India (Mean)	South India (Mean)	Foreign (Mean)
Natural Beauty	43.8	30.4	8.4
Pleasant weather	43.6	29.6	7.2
Clean environment	45	28	7.2
Visiting un crowded destination	44.8	28.5	8.6
Experiencing remote and unspoiled nature	42.8	26	28.5
Mountains	40.6	43.8	8.6
Forest	43.2	39.8	8.6
To see unusual plants and animals	36	27.8	23.2
Increasing confidence through challenging activities	32.8	29.6	5.2
Supporting economic benefits to local communities	30.6	26.4	9.2
Interacting with local people	19.8	24.2	7.2

Note: multiple & no response choice permitted.

The table shows native place wise analysis of tourists that North Indians liked natural beauty and pleasant weather the most, whereas mountains and forests are preferred most by south Indians and foreigners liked remote, tribal and unexplored areas and flora and fauna.

Table 3: Native place wise Mean Difference Analysis of Destination Choice Consideration in HP

Destination Choice Consideration	Northen India (Mean)	Southern India (Mean)	Foreign (Mean)
Personal safety and security	45.2	24.4	6.4
The destination can be easily reached	39	27.4	3.8
Overall cleanness of destination	41.6	27.4	5.6
Unspoiled nature	42.8	28.4	8.4
Climate consideration	37.4	29.6	6.2
Diversity of cultural/historical attractions (Architecture, tradition & customs)	38.6	28	7.8
The quality of the accomodation on hotel, motel and apartments	40.2	25.8	5.6
Friendliness of the local people	44.8	28.6	8
Organisation of the local transpotation services	32.4	14.2	5.4
Offer of the local cuisine	23.2	21.6	7.4
Possibilities of shopping	41.4	24.2	7
Nightlife and entertainment	18	14.6	5.8
Opportunities for rest	35.6	26.6	9
Availability of sport facilities and recreational activities	24	27.6	4.4
Offer of culture and other events	21.6	27.4	6.2

Note: multiple & no response choice permitted.

The table shows native place wise analysis of considerations in selecting a tourist destination. It has been noted that north Indian tourists considered safety & security and friendly people as most important whereas south Indian pointed out cold climate and friendly people and the foreigners indicated their preference for rest opportunities and unspoiled nature.

Table 4: Native place wise Mean Difference Analysis of Tourists' Irritants in HP

Irritants	Northern India (Mean)	Southern India (Mean)	Foreign (Mean)
Transportation	27.2	20	7
Hotel & basic facilities	29.8	23.2	7
Roads	23.4	33.8	6.4
Railways	25.2	26	7.8
Coolie age	31.4	28.6	6.8
Problem on tours	25.2	24	8.6
Language and communication	21	20.8	9.6
Cheating	27	23.4	4.2
Poor information			

Note: multiple & no response choice permitted.

The native place wise analysis presents that north Indian felt coolieage whereas south Indian believed roads and foreigners opined communication as key problems in Himachal tourism.

Table 5: Native place wise Mean Difference Analysis of Tourists' Satisfaction in HP

Satisfaction	Northern India (Mean)	Southern India (Mean)	Foreign (Mean)
Overall, staying in this tourist destination has been very valuable	28.8	29.6	9.2
Gaining new knowledge and experience in the destination	42.2	27.8	8.4
Visit has been worth every rupee paid	38.4	28.6	7.6

Note: multiple & no response choice permitted.

Native place wise analysis pointed out that south Indian tourists have been more satisfied whereas North Indian tourists found visiting Himachal more educative, learning and worth spending experience.

Conclusion and Suggestions

From the results and findings it is concluded that most of the tourists prefer HP for natural beauty and cold weather. These are found to visit the state especially for greenery, cultural heritage and pollution free environment. It is noted that majority tourists decide destination on the issues of climate and personal safety. The tourists identified major irritants in tourism industry of HP like transportation facilities, road conditions and hotels availability. Therefore, it is strongly suggested in order to attract more tourists HP needs to get better connectivity and accessibility especially by air and improve roads and developing hotels and basic amenities particularly in tribal areas. However, tourists indicated satisfaction on the gains out of money spent and the education and learning during their visit to Himachal Pradesh. Most of the tourists were satisfied and found their visit worth for expenditures. But the south Indian tourists have been more satisfied whereas North Indian tourists found visiting Himachal more educative, learning and worth spending experience. However, tourists especially from north India felt that they would choose this tourist destination again for holiday and also would recommend it to friends and relatives for having friendly and peaceful atmosphere. Thus, indicate the immense tourism potential of Himachal that require to be tapped and need to be served professionally to holiday makers.

References:

Hui T. D. Wan, & A. Ho. (2007); 'Tourists' Satisfaction, Recommendation and Revisiting Singapore', Tourism Management, Vol. 28, pp 965-975.

Lohumi R. (2013); 'Tourist Arrivals Declines for 3rd Year'. The Tribune, January 23.

Xia W., Z. Jie, G. Chaolin & Z. Feng (2009); 'Examining Antecedents and Consequences of Tourist's Satisfaction: A Structural Modeling Approach', TSINGHUA SCIENCE & TECHNOLOGY, Vol. 14, No. 3, pp 396-406.

Tourism & Civil Aviation Departmen, Shimla

http://www.ttfotm.com/ttf/award.html

Ministry of Tourism, Annual Report, 2010-11

Baken J. R. & S. Bhagwatula (2010); 'Some Reflections on Tourism & Tourism Policy in India', p. 3. www.iimb.ernet.in/research/... papers.

Sadeh E., F. Asgari & Mousavi L. S. Sina (2012); 'Factors Affecting Tourist Satisfaction and Its Consequences', Journal of Basic & Applied Scientific Research, Vol. 2, No. 2, pp 1557-1560.

Ritchie J. R. B., V. W. S. Tung & J. B. R. Robin (2011); 'Tourism Management Experience Research: Emergence, Evolution and Future Directions', International

Journal of Contemporary Hospitality Management, Vol. 23, No. 4, pp 419-438.

COMPARATIVE ANALYSIS OF MARKETING PRACTICES OF HOTELS OF CHANDIGARH AND DELHI MANAGERIAL PROSPECTIVE

Tanvi

Assistant Professor University Institute of Hotel Management & Tourism, Panjab University, Chandigarh,

tanubeniwal@yahoo.com

Abstract

The increasing competition environments have put pressure on hospitality Industry to pay attention on gaining competitive advantage by adopting marketing practices that will help in attracting customer and improving Business performance. This paper provides an insight about two different cities that how the marketing practices vary among them. The findings of a survey on hotels of these two cities suggest that practices like association with tour operator, travel agencies and airlines, loyalty and reward programs are given equal importance but there is a little variation in certain marketing practices like integrated marketing with front office, identifying profitable customers, green marketing with eco- friendly products etc. Being variation in adopting the marketing practices amongst the cities these practices all together help in improving the business performance.

Introduction

Marketing is a restless, changing, and dynamic business activity. Marketing pay regular attention only on selling and advertising of products services this is a common perception. Marketing consists of many other functions that can be seen far more important than just the exchange of goods (Kotler & Armstrong 2004). Marketing, we can say then, is concerned with what has varyingly been called 'demand creation' (A.W. Shaw in Usui, 2008; Doubman, 1924), 'demand activation' (Copeland, 1958) or 'demand generation' (Shaw and Jones, 2005), with one scholar going so far as to associate marketing with propaganda and 'the conditioning of buyers or sellers to a favorable attitude' (Shaw and Jones, 2005: 247). 'Marketing students', Converse (1951: 3) attested, 'are interested in increasing or stimulating human wants, in general and for the good of individual sellers.

Marketing roles were traditionally found in commercial firms, but increasingly all kinds of organizations feel the need to employ marketers or to commission services from marketing consultants. The role of marketing itself has changed dramatically due to various crises—material and energy shortages, inflation, economic recessions, high unemployment, dying industries, dying companies, terrorism and war, and effects due to rapid technological changes in certain industries. Such changes, including the Internet, have forced today's marketing executive to become more market driven in their strategic decision-making. There is a requirement of a formalized means of acquiring accurate and timely information about customers, products and the marketplace and the overall environment. The winning edge is the marketing practices and often marketing practices becomes the crucial differentiation factor. As clear from the reference of marketing practices suggested by (Kotler (1997) that reflections on marketing practices as the marketing strategy can be thought of as a game plan that outlines, often in a list form factors such as the target market, positioning, distribution channels, price, advertising and possible research and development.

As the superlative marketing practice today in marketing environment as (Bowie and Buttle (2004) identified a hotel can use different websites to advertise their products and services and also use brand identification to their advantage. It has been realized that Hospitality marketing is unique because it deals with the tangible product, like a bed in the hotel or food in the restaurant, but it also deals with the intangible aspects of the hospitality industry. So, the combine effect of tangible and intangible service is encouraging the hospitality industry to focus more on marketing concept and practices.

No two universes are similar and the clients would differ from a city to another city and also from one property to another. Yet the competitiveness remains between different properties. The current study tries to compare the marketing practices of hotels of Chandigarh and Delhi to understand the concept of how marketing practices differentiate properties and also contribute to a property's success.

Review of Literature

Marketing practice

An extensive review of this research will rectify that research on marketing practices in context of hotel industry. Sigala (2005) carried out a research on integrated customer relationship management from Greek hotel industry. His research is suggest to value for external marketing which including, understanding guest needs and requirements, products development and innovation, personalizing promotion and communication strategies, personalizing staff-guest encounters, enhance customer services, personalizing reservation process, personalizing pricing and yield management strategies, identifying and handling guest complaints, developing affiliated marketing strategies with other partners were major marketing practices. Currently a research study conducted by Yoo and Bai (2013) on customer loyalty marketing with the purpose of this study was to review published research on customer loyalty to better understand its evolution and development in the hospitality industry. The researcher argued that customer loyalty is a topic that has received much attention since the 1990s as relationship marketing has become a popular marketing scheme.

Increasing role of internet in marketing is becoming first choice for today customer Doolin et al (2002) believed that the Internet has become an innovative marketing tool in offering travel information and online transactions. As the website component of internet Lituchy & Rail, (2000) argued that websites are well-designed and easy to navigate provide independent hotels with an inexpensive and effective platform for marketing and advertising, which potentially increase their competitiveness in the marketplace. Hashim et al (2010) examined the rapid adoption of Internet marketing by hotels. Shuai and Wu (2011) examined from Taiwan hotel industry most important marketing practices are guest room facilities, price information; email for requesting information, promotion information, online dining reservation, online room reservation and this research express that Internet marketing can affect the operating performance of tourist hotels. Hoteliers should adopt a more strategic Internet approach to increase business success.

Green marketing is new concept for hotel marketing. Chan (2013) conducted a research study on green marketing with main aim of this study is to investigate Hong Kong hotel manager perceptions of the relative importance of different green marketing strategies. This research is suggested that "Hotel green marketing should begin with green product and service design". Internet is an effective channel to market a hotel's green initiatives to customers directly" as the top green marketing ploys. Thus study is more focusing on especially marketers to better understand the implementation and importance of different green marketing strategies.

Business performance

Research is over one decade focusing on business performance through marketing Pan (2005) mentioned in his research the impact of market structure and location on profitability of Taiwanese hotels. Moving ahead Sin et al (2006) analyzed the effects of relationship marketing orientation on business performance in Hong Kong hotels. Similarly Wang et al (2011) also observe the relationships among total quality management, market orientation and the exploration of the use of new performance measurement techniques in an international hotel chain. Claver-Cortés et al. (2007) also studied the hotel performance in Chinese hotels and the impact of strategy on hotel performance in Spain.

All be above mention research are highlighting that there is always been seen the effect of marketing practices on business performance of various hotels of different countries.

In continuation Sainaghi (2010) provides a literature review of 20 years of research relating to hotel performance using the balanced scorecard as a model to summaries the main research areas of customer perspective, strategy and process perspective and according to the main functional areas of strategy, production, marketing and organization. Pan (2005) also found positive relationships between hotel performance and external macroeconomic factors of market concentration particularly relevant to this study; market orientation has been found to have a strong positive relationship with hotel performance.

Sin et al (2005) carried out a research study on relationship between market orientation and business performance in Hong Kong hotel industry with objective an investigation into the link between market orientation and business performance in the hotel industry. Researcher suggested the market orientation is positively associated with financial performance, return on investment, return on sales, sales growth, and market share and marketing performance, customer retention, customer satisfaction, and trust in the hotel industry. Wu and Lu (2012) conducted study on customer relationship management and its effect on relationship marketing and business performance. Results of this research showed that implementing CRM has a significant and positive influence on the RM effect, positively affecting business performance for both hotels and Bed and breakfast.

Review of this study is revealed that extensive marketing practices are most important for hotel industry and for its best performance these are the keys to open up an organization into market.

Objectives

1. To analysis Marketing Practices which are adopted by Hotels of Chandigarh and Delhi.
2. To analysis business performance through marketing practices of hotel of Delhi and Chandigarh.

Research Methodology

Research methodology for this study Delhi and Chandigarh hotel industry were selected for universe of data collection and convenience sampling was used for collecting data from marketing department of hotels and two sample T test was used for analyzing the comparison between Delhi and Chandigarh city through the 18 version of SPSS.

Table1: Mean, SD and t value between Delhi and Chandigarh for marketing practices needed

	Delhi		Chandigarh		t value	df	p value
	Mean	SD	Mean	SD			
Integrated marketing with front office	4.85	0.36	4.54	0.98	1.84	73	0.07
Integrated marketing with F&B service	4.65	0.48	4.57	0.78	0.53	73	0.60
Association with tour operator, travel agencies and airlines	4.75	0.44	4.71	0.46	0.34	73	0.73
Selling Banquet	4.60	0.81	4.03	1.29	2.32	73	0.02*
Selling spa,bath and health facilities	4.25	0.78	4.26	0.78	-0.04	73	0.97
Extensive selection of marketing partners	4.65	0.48	4.51	0.78	0.92	73	0.36
Joint marketing with other hotels	3.75	1.15	3.80	1.13	-0.19	73	0.85
Interact with individual customer	4.85	0.36	4.83	0.38	0.25	73	0.80
Determine customer demographics	4.60	0.74	4.20	1.02	1.95	73	0.05
Identifying profitable customers	4.75	0.44	4.40	0.77	2.45	73	0.02*
Customization and community building	4.55	0.68	4.43	0.74	0.74	.73	0.46
The images of business partners and stakeholders	4.55	0.68	4.66	0.64	-0.70	73	0.49
Extensive products market studies	4.70	0.46	4.40	0.69	2.22	73	0.03*
Green marketing with eco-friendly products	4.00	0.91	3.97	1.07	0.13	73	0.90
sales promotion programs	4.65	0.48	4.46	0.66	1.46	73	0.15
E-marketing	4.55	0.68	4.43	0.74	0.74	73	0.46

	Delhi		Chandigarh		t value	df	p value
	Mean	SD	Mean	SD			
Customer orientation marketing	4.80	0.41	4.51	0.51	2.71	73	0.01**
Cross & Up selling	4.15	0.80	4.14	0.77	0.04	73	0.97
Loyalty and reward programs	4.65	0.48	4.60	0.50	0.44	73	0.66
Offering best product at lowest price	4.30	0.79	3.86	1.12	2.00	73	0.05
Giving discount at competitive product	4.15	0.74	3.94	0.91	1.09	73	0.28
Giving souvenirs and gift	4.15	0.86	3.91	0.98	1.11	73	0.27
Sharing of revenue, wet, lease and franchising with reputed property	4.00	0.91	3.89	1.02	0.51	73	0.61
Management contracts marketing	4.40	0.67	4.06	0.94	1.84	73	0.07

**p<0.01 and *p<0.05

Table1 revealed the significance difference among marketing practices needed between Delhi and Chandigarh. Significant mean difference were found for Selling Banquet (t=2.32, p<0.05), Determine customer demographics(t=2.45, p<0.05), Extensive products market studies(t=2.22, p<0.05), Customer orientation marketing(t=2.71, p<0.01), where on other non significant mean difference were found at 0.05 level of significance. Higher value of mean predicted that Delhi showed more significant mean difference than Chandigarh for marketing practices items. Mean difference for marketing practices needed items between Delhi and Chandigarh is shown in Figure1.

Fig 1: Mean difference for marketing practices needed

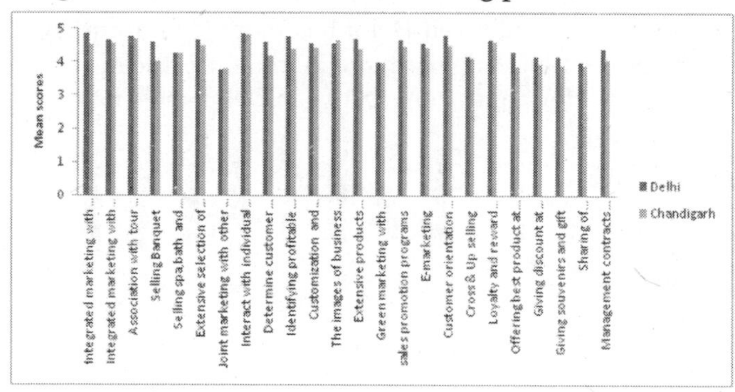

Table2: Mean, SD and t value between male and female for Business Performance

	Delhi		Chandigarh		t value	df	p value
	Mean	SD	Mean	SD			
Achieve organizational goals	4.80	0.41	4.54	0.74	1.90	73	0.06
Increase sale growth	4.85	0.36	4.51	0.66	2.78	73	0.01**
Increasing of market share	4.55	0.60	4.14	1.12	2.01	73	0.05*
New product development & internal growth	4.60	0.59	4.46	0.56	1.07	73	0.29
Growth in revenue	4.90	0.30	4.63	0.88	1.84	73	0.07
Maintain customer relationship	4.95	0.22	4.66	0.48	3.46	73	0.00**
Improve marketing performance	4.80	0.41	4.31	0.87	3.17	73	0.00**
Growth in potential customer	4.85	0.36	4.51	0.66	2.78	73	0.01**

Table2 revealed the significance difference among business performance between Delhi and Chandigarh. Significant mean difference were found for Increase sale growth ($t=2.78$, $p<0.01$), Increasing of market share ($t=2.01, p<0.05$), Maintain customer relationship ($t=3.46$, $p<0.01$),Improve marketing performance($t=3.17, p<0.01$), Growth in potential customer($t=2.78, p<0.01$) where no significant mean difference was found at 0.05 level of significance. Higher mean value showed Delhi has more significant effect on business performance items than Chandigarh. Mean difference for business performance items between Delhi and Chandigarh is shown in Figure2.

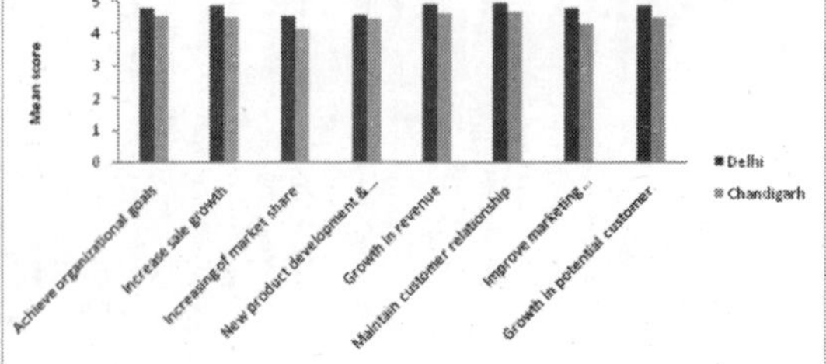

Figure2: Mean difference for business performance items

Conclusion

This research is identifying some of the most adopted marketing practices such as; Selling banquet, determine customer demographics, extensive product market studies, customer orientation marketing but these are more in Delhi than Chandigarh. Findings of this study express to these marketing practices to managers and policy makers marketing department of Chandigarh hotel industry should most focused on these marketing practices than Delhi. Findings from business performance demonstrate through adoption of these marketing practices by hotels such as; increase sale growth, increasing of market share, maintain customer relationship, improve marketing performance, growth in potential customer can be significant for hotel industry in both cities.

References

Alderson, W. and Cox, R. (1948) 'Towards a theory of marketing', Journal of Marketing, 13(2): 137–52.

Doubman, J.R. (1924) 'The modern sales manager and his developing technique', The Annals of the American Academy of Political and Social Science, 115: 174–82.

Doolin, B., Burgess, L., & Cooper, J. (2002). Evaluating the use of the Web for tourism marketing: A case study from New Zealand. Tourism Management, 23, 557–561.

Chan, E.S.W (2013). Managing green marketing: Hong Kong hotel managers'perpective. International Journal of Hospitality Management. 34, 442 – 461.

Claver-Cortés, E., Molina-Azorín, J.F., Pereira-Moliner, J., 2007. Competitiveness in mass tourism. Annals of Tourism Research 34, 727–745.

Copeland, M.T. (1958) And Mark an Era: The Story of the Harvard Business School. Boston: Little, Brown and Company.

Hashim, N. H., Murphy, J., Purchase, S., & O'Connor, P. (2010). Website and email adoption by Malaysian hotels. International Journal of Hospitality Management, 29(1), 194–196

Lituchy, T. R., & Rail, A. (2000). Bed and breakfasts, small inns, and the Internet: The impact of technology on the globalization of small businesses. Journal of International Marketing, 8(2), 86–98.

Pan, C.M., (2005). Market structure and profitability in the international tourist hotel industry. Tourism Management 26, 845–850.

Shuai, J.J. Wu, W.W (2011). Evaluating the influence of E- marketing on hotel performance by DEA Grey entropy. Expert System with Application. 38 (2011) 8763–8769)

Shaw, E.H. and Jones, D.G.B. (2005) 'A history of schools of marketing thought', Marketing Theory, 5(3): 239–81.

Sainaghi, R., (2010). Hotel performance: state of the art. International Journal of Contemporary Hospitality Management 22, 920–952.

Sin, L.Y.M., Tse, A.C.B., Heung, V.C.S., Yim, F.H.K., (2005). An analysis of the relationship between market orientation and business performance in the hotel industry. International Journal of Hospitality Management 24, 555–577.

Sin, L.Y.M., Tse, A.C.B., Chan, H., Heung, V.C.S., Yim, F.H.K., (2006). The effects of relationship marketing orientation on business performance in the hotel industry. Journal of Hospitality and Tourism Research 30, 407–421.

Sigala, M (2005). Integrating customer relationship management in hotel operations: managerial and operational implications. Hospitality Management 24, 391-413.

Wang, C.H., Chen, K.Y., Chen, S.C., (2011). Total quality management, market orientation and hotel performance: the moderating effects of external environmental factors. International Journal of Hospitality Management 31, 119–129.

Wu, Shwu-Ing. Lu, Chien-Lung. (2012). The relationship between CRM, RM nad business performance: A study of the hotel industry in Taiwan. International Journal of Hospitality Management 31 (2012) 276–285.

Yoo, M. Bai, B., (2013).Customer loyalty marketing research: A comparative approach between hospitality and business journals. International Journal of Hospitality Management 33 (2013) 166–177.

TOURISM FOR COMMUNITY DEVELOPMENT: ISSUES, LESSONS AND IDEAS

Yashwant Gupta

Professor, Himachal Pradesh University Business School (HPUBS), Shimla (HP)

Shakti Singh

Junior Research Fellow, Himachal Pradesh University Business School (HPUBS) Shimla (HP)

Abstract

Despite this potential of tourism it is a sad fact that in the 50 years since the worldwide emergence of the tourism industry communities have received few, if any, benefits from tourism. Instead, they have suffered a spectrum of negative impacts that have damaged their natural resources and changed their society and culture in multiple ways. In truth, communities have benefited very little from tourism. So the need of the hour is to make the use of tourism as an instrument for community development. The concept of community development is explored in terms of participation, empowerment and community capacity as they related to tourism development. Community development is viewed as the best way to build the capacity of community residents to engage with each other and find solutions to issues that affect their community. Helping a community to build its capacity for development is a primary goal of community development. Hence, the process of tourism development in local communities is the process of community development. Community development builds peoples' skills for community issue. Hence it is vital to the survival of local communities. The objective of this paper is to highlight this modern concept of "tourism for community development" and bring forward the aspects associated with it.

Keywords: Tourism, Community Development, Empowerment, Community based tourism.

Introduction

Amidst the social changes brought on by globalization, local communities cannot live in isolation. Communities around the world have passed the time of absolute self-reliance and are increasingly dependent upon the outside 'urban' world. Interacting with the outside world will not be easy for local communities without sufficient and strong social, cultural, and economic resources. Unfortunately, across the world, the influence of Mass-Consumerism is precipitating the degradation and destruction of natural resources crucial to local communities' livelihoods. Simultaneously, materialism and consumerism are influencing and destabilizing the value systems of established social systems and cultures. Meanwhile, on the national level, a standardized education system and a local administration controlled and directed by the central government are forcing remote, rural communities to become increasingly depend on the state. Fortunately, there are countervailing social trends in many countries that open up alternative directions for the future of local communities. An increasing number of people are becoming aware of the importance of natural resources conservation and of protecting the environment.

The democratization of societies is opening ever-greater opportunities for members of the public to use their voice, express their opinions and play a role in the direction of social development. At the same time the importance and profile of the issues of human rights and equal treatment under the law are growing in the public conscience. These trends are supported by developments in the United Nations and international institutions and by academics and conservationists who understand sustainable development. The understanding of people in urban society that have connection to rural communities is an essential base for designing and implementing successful development strategies. Tourism is one way to bring people of different backgrounds together. Ideally, tourism seems to offer hosts and visitors a unique opportunity to share their different cultures and points-of-view. Members of different societies are able to share first-hand experiences together and to develop personal relationships which can grow into powerful alliance contributing towards the sustainable development of society.

Community Development

The concept of community development is explored in terms of participation, empowerment and community capacity as they related to tourism development. Community development can be seen as building social capital for collective benefits. It uses skill and knowledge and strategy in their practice. It aims to increase citizens' participation in their community. In community development, emphasis is placed on community as a social system, bounded by geographical location or common interest. Community development is linked to community capacity building through a shared focus of building capacity to a collective participatory force. Community development is viewed as the best way to build the capacity of community residents to engage with each other and find solutions to issues that affect their community. Helping a community to build its capacity for development is a primary goal of community development. Hence, the process of tourism development in local communities is the process of community development. Community development builds peoples' skills for community issue. Hence it is vital to the survival of local communities.

Tourism and Community Development

Before delving further into the issue lets define this vague concept of "community". Community is a term that is used by politicians, social commentators, religious leaders, academics and media reporters rather invariably. However it is rarely defined – seems to be a given that we all know what is meant by the term. To understand the current widespread use of the term 'communities' one need to understand what makes a 'community'. Most modern day literature views the 'community' as a small spatial unit, homogenous social structure with shared norms and common interest. This socio- geographical definition of community is essential to understand how community development is linked to tourism.

Tourism is increasingly seen as a key community tool, with the recognition of its economic contribution in bolstering stagnating economies and its ability to unify local community residents. At community levels, tourism offers opportunities for direct, indirect, and induced employment and income, spurring regional and local economic development. Tourism development is an ongoing process. It is no economic panacea, and is best suited as a supplement to a local community for achieving development Tourism plays a role in facilitating community development through business mentoring and educational opportunities that contribute to local communities in increasing skill and knowledge in local communities and local residents as well as improving the community's economic level. The process of tourism development is important as an important tool in community development. Hence many local communities have turned to tourism development to provide economic, social, cultural and overall development of the community. However, while there is appreciation of tourism as a development tool, there is little understanding of tourism development in the literature. In recent years as local communities have realized the developmental promise of tourism, there has been also a growth in research on tourism and its contribution to community development. Tourism has grown as a topic of research in the field of community development and community development researchers have increasingly investigated tourism and it's potential.

As tourism relies on visiting places and people, it cannot exist outside a community. So, both tourism and communities it is in must be viewed simultaneously – any change to one will affect the other. Consequently, tourism is one of the most significant community development tools, particularly in marginal and peripheral communities such as indigenous, remote and rural communities. There is an increasing recognition of the intrinsic role that the host community (or destination community) plays in the creation and delivery of tourism experiences, so many have combined these terms into the term 'community-tourism'. It has been variously described as:

- Tourism in which local residents (often rural, often poor and marginalized) are active participants as land-managers /users, entrepreneurs, employees, decision makers and conservators
- An industry which uses the community as a resource, sells it as a product and, in the process, affects the lives of everyone.
- Community tourism shifts the focus away from the tourist and their experiences to the host community and THEIR experiences.

Community based tourism

Community based tourism or simply CBT does not seek to address the question: "How can communities benefit more from tourism?" It seeks instead to address a different, developmental question: "How can tourism contribute to the process of community development?" Community Based Tourism (CBT) is a unique type of tourism with characteristics quite different from mass tourism. Those who intend to put CBT into practice need to fully understand the underlying ideas, principles and components behind CBT. CBT is different from traditional top-down tourism planning approaches in that it emphasizes local input and control over the type, scale, and intensity of tourism development. By retaining or proactively obtaining control over tourism decision making, communities can direct development according to their values and interests. A defining characteristic of CBT is that it is a process generated from bottom-up community engagement to develop tourism products and services or to craft and implement a tourism strategy. CBT looks to support community-appropriate types of tourism and equitable distribution and retention of benefits within a local area, presenting an alternate response to traditional forms of tourism development driven by a focus on profit maximization.

The principles listed below present the concept of CBT, and the way the host community can use tourism as a tool for community development. CBT should:

1. Recognize, support and promote community ownership of tourism;

2. Involve community members from the start in every aspect;
3. Promote community pride;
4. Improve the quality of life;
5. Ensure environmental sustainability;
6. Preserve the unique character and culture of the local area;
7. Foster cross-cultural learning;
8. Respect cultural differences and human dignity;
9. Distribute benefits fairly among community members;
10. Contribute a fixed percentage of income to community projects;

Community wellbeing

As with so many of the terms used in the community development field, community wellbeing is intrinsically understood by many. However, for our purposes it is worthwhile to provide some sort of definition or explanation of its meaning. Simply expressed, community wellbeing refers to the quality of life and level of sustainability as seen by the members of that community. In effect, 'it is shaped by a range of social, psychological, cultural, economic and environmental factors that shape the way that people think and act in their daily lives as well as how they relate to others in their community'. What works for one community may be seen as a negative aspect in another – for instance, more people may create a lively, vibrant environment in the eyes of one community, but the same level may simply be perceived as adding to crowding and carrying capacity issues for another. As well as being important in terms of community development, wellbeing is also a tourism asset that can be used to further enhance community outcomes and wellbeing, if managed. Community members who are happy to be there create a positive environment that tourists sense and respond to. While this may not be a tangible asset, visitors soon sense if a place is one where they are welcome and one they wish to spend time in or not. If they do not feel comfortable, they will move on to the next community where they do feel welcome.

Social impact of tourism on communities

A multitude of impacts that tourism has on community development has been identified and is well documented by researchers. Table below outlines the range of these impacts in terms of the development, interactions and cultural impacts. The list does not judge whether the impacts are positive or negative or better or worse than each other, as they will often be both, for different people, or in different circumstances. In addition, the magnitude of the impacts will vary, depending on the rate of change in a community and its capacity (willingness) to embrace such change, as well as the actual community being considered.

One of the issues with the negative elements of tourism development is that it is often not until after some time that the negative impacts become evident. It may well be too late to correct some of these impacts, particularly when they affect local community attitudes and beliefs, which are difficult to consciously alter. This hidden and irreversible nature of some of the negative effects is the greatest danger of any blind acceptance of tourism as a sole development tool. Yet, when it works, tourism is an outstanding community development tool.

Table: Reported social impacts of tourism on communities.

Tourism development	Modifies the internal structure of the community.
	Divides the community into those who have/ have not relationships with tourists.
	Has a colonialist characteristic.
	Employment in tourism offers more opportunities for women.
	Instigates social change.
	Improves quality of life through infrastructure development.
	Increased pressure on existing infrastructure.
Tourist–host interactions	The nature of contact influences attitudes/ behavior/ values relating to tourism.
	Young locals are most susceptible to the demonstration effect.

	Cultural exchange/increased understanding and tolerance.
	Increased social interaction increases communication skills.
	Hosts adopt foreign languages through necessity.
	Hosts develop coping behavior and avoid unnecessary contact.
Cultural impacts	Arts, crafts and local culture revitalized.
	Acculturation process likely to occur.
	Assumed negative effects of commodification of culture.
	Meaning/authenticity not necessarily lost.

Promoting communities through tourism

In this section, the term 'promotion' signifies more than simply its marketing role. Promoting communities is really about using tourism to develop communities to meet their goals. According to Kotler et al. (1993), destination marketing is more than simply getting tourists to an area – it is also about attracting new residents (who often start as visitors) and businesses as well as to increase their exports. Tourism can be a significant contributor but should not be seen as the only option. How promotion is approached depends on the vision the community has for its future. If the intention is to have more people living in the town, then one of the aims of tourism would be to create an environment that would encourage visitors or others to desire to live there. The promotion could start by encouraging the purchase of second homes, or 'weekenders'. However, such a move may not ultimately result in the goal of more full-time residents. If the locals envisage a community where their young people remain to live and work, then employment opportunities and training in tourism skills and management may be what they require. Consequently, it is crucial to understand where (and what) the community wishes to be in not only five years, but also in 10, 20 and 50 years.

Tourism itself is a powerful promotional tool, simply by increasing outsiders' knowledge of your community, where it is, what it does and who belongs to it. Tourism promotion is approached from a positive perspective, highlighting the (usually pleasant) elements of a community to attract visitors. This often includes aspects of friendliness and welcome, relaxation and stress release, the opportunity to do something different in a safe environment and enjoying nature. For an urban environment it may include excitement, sophistication, shopping, entertainment and cosmopolitan food experiences. Consequently, tourism can positively promote a community to potential investors and residents as well as visitors. However, not all tourist images attract the desired type of resident or even reflect the community's self-image. If the marketing organization is focused solely on attracting visitors, they may simply end up promulgating outdated images and perceptions of that community. Once again, this comes back to having a community based development strategy with tourism as one possible tool that can achieve certain things, but is not the answer to everything. When looking at developing communities through tourism, one of the most important elements is that of the image of the community in its target markets. This image can create certain expectations in visitors' minds and is the lens through which they will view and interpret what they see and experience in a community. This is a complex notion, but it is important to acknowledge that if there is a conflict between the tourist's image and what they experience, they will most likely be dissatisfied. Such dissatisfaction will not lead to realizing the community's vision and goals, unless it is to discourage visitors. However, there are more constructive approaches that can be adopted. Some of the issues noted above relate to how those who market the destination respond to the community's wants and needs as described by their vision.

Promoting tourism in communities

If we decide that tourism is a positive force for our community, then we need to promote/market the concept of tourism to all of the community members. This is not unlike 'internal marketing' in an organisation, with Dann and Dann explaining that: "Employees or community members within the firm or community should be respected and treated as a client group in their own right and second, that unless employees fully support and understand the reasons behind a marketing strategy decision, implementation will be at best flawed." They stress that this is particularly true in the services marketing aspect of community based tourism, where the community members are part of the actual product by interacting with visitors. Even if it is simply passing a tourist in the street, this is part of their entire experience, which can be ruined if they are sensitive to resentment from the general community. While this may not be openly articulated by a visitor, the number of times people actually comment on the welcoming nature or friendliness of a community they have visited denotes that it is not always present.

Promoting an annual event to a community is relatively easy in that while it requires a concerted effort, it is contained. Promoting tourism throughout the year has longer-term challenges and opportunities. In many communities, one of the main challenges is convincing everyone that they are all involved in tourism in some way. A great example is that of a local bank manager who actually said that he did not gain from tourism in his community (that attracted hundreds of visitors each weekend). The tourism businesses (restaurants, motels, bed and breakfasts) stamped all their cheques and banking forms with 'paid for with tourism dollars' – the bank manager soon realized how much he gained from tourism, as did many others who felt the same (trades people in particular). An important point here is that these issues do not go away after a once-off program to promote tourism to your community – it requires ongoing communication as new people come into the community. Also, tourism can change a community, so different messages may need to be presented over time.

Conclusion

As tourists from the highly urbanized developed countries (the main source of domestic and international tourists worldwide) have become more experienced as travelers, they are looking for a different type of holiday than the mass, resort-based holidays of the past. Today's travelers are increasingly interested in new experiences and learning about other cultures while on their holidays. Visitors want to meet local people and feel that they are taking things home with them that is 'authentic', especially in relation to indigenous and rural based cultures.

So, if a community, or members of that community, resent the tourists that come to their town or region, if they feel that they are being exploited by outside commercial interests and that their privacy is being unfairly invaded, dramatic negative issues could become manifest. Unwelcoming hosts will turn visitors away, as will increases in crime and aggression towards tourists. Even if visitors get the impression that the experience is not fully supported by the local people, they may lose any sense of that important aspect of tourism – 'authenticity'. Consequently, even if community members are not directly involved in tourism, they have the power to destroy it by making visitors feel unwelcome and unsafe. It is crucial that communities are included in tourism planning and operations. It is crucial that local communities are part of any tourism venture, whether it is as consultants for a commercial venture, or as community run enterprises. Without the enthusiastic support of the local hosts, tourists will go elsewhere. Community development by its very nature is community focused, committing to employing locals, purchasing local supplies, contributing to community and environmental projects and so on. Local opportunities can start on a small scale, particularly regarding tour guiding, and build as tourism interest builds. Communities must be given the right and opportunity to choose the level and type of tourism they want. Remember, saying 'no' to tourism is also an option.

References

Allen, A., Hafer, A., Long, T., & Perdue, A. (1993). Rural residents' attitudes toward recreation and tourism development. Journal of Travel Research, 31, 27-35.

Anna Ivolga, Vasily Erokhin (2013). Tourism as an approach to sustainable rural development: case of southern Russia Economics of Agriculture 4/2013

Aref, F. (2010). Residents' Attitudes towards Tourism Impacts: A Case Study of Shiraz, Iran. Tourism Analysis, 15(2), 253-261.

Beeton, S. (2006). "Community development through tourism". In: Landlink Press, Australia.

Blackstock, K. (2005). A critical look at community based tourism. Community Development Journal, 40(1), 39–49.

Bradshaw, T. (2008). The Post-Place Community: Contributions to the Debate about the Definition of Community. Journal of the Community Development Society, 39(1), 5-16.

Bushell, R., & Eagles, P. (Eds.). (2007). Tourism and Protected Areas: Benefits Beyond Boundaries. London CAB International, UK.

Coccossis, H. (2004). Sustainable tourism and carrying capacity: U.K: Ashgate Publishing.

Dann, S. & Dann, S. (2004). Introduction to marketing. (John Wiley and Sons, Milton.)

Dredge, D. (2003). Tourism community well-being and local government. Australian Regional Tourism Convention, 3–6 September 2003.

Flora, L., Green, P., Gale, A., Schmidt, E., & Flora, B. (1992). Self development: A viable rural development option? Policy Studies Journal, 20, 276-288.

Gilchrist, A. (2004). The well-connected community: a networking approach to community development: Community Development Foundation (Great Britain), The Policy Press, UK.

Gill, A. M., & Reed, M. G. (1997). The reimaging of a Canadian resource town: Postproductivism in a North American context. Applied Geographic Studies, 1(2), 129–147

Godfrey, K., & Clarke, J. (2000). The tourism development handbook: a practical approach to planning and marketing. London: Continuum.

Hall, C. M. (2000). Tourism planning: Policies, processes and relationships. Harlow, England: Prentice Hall.

Hatton, M. J. (1999). Community-based tourism in the Asia-Pacific. Toronto: Asia-Pacific Economic Cooperation.

Ife, J. (2002). Community development: Community- based alternatives in an age of globalisation. Sydney: Longman Press.

Kotler, P., Haider, D.H. & Rein, I. (1993). Marketing places. (The Free Press, New York.)

Mowforth, M., & Munt, I. (2003). Tourism and sustainability: Development and new tourism in the Third World (2nd ed.). London: Routledge.

Murphy, P. E. (1985). Tourism: A community approach. New York: Methuen.

Singh, S., Timothy, D. J., & Dowling, R. K. (Eds.). (2003). Tourism in destination communities. Cambridge, USA: CABI publishing.

Smailes, B. (1999). Mixed reception for $150m ATC campaign. TravelWeek January 20, 3.

Smith V., Eadington W., (1992), Tourism alternatives, potentials and problems in the development of tourism, Wiley, Chichester.

Talbot, L., & Verrinder, G. (2005). Promoting Health: The Primary Health Care Approach (3 ed.): Elsevier, Churchill Livingstone, Australia.

Williams, C. C. (2004). Community Capacity Building: A Critical Evaluation of the Third Sector sApproach. Review of Policy Research, 21(5), 729-733.

CHALLENGES FOR TOURISM DEVELOPMENT

CHALLENGES FOR TOURISM DEVELOPMENT

People have always travelled, but in the first few thousand years of human history only a select few could do so. Most people were concerned with the daily task of living; their idea of a trip was to their neighbour's farm, or to the local town market. The transition from a rural society to an industrial one brought with it the tourism phenomenon. In fact, one characteristic of industrial and post-industrial society is the onset of leisure time associated with travel. The first major change in modern history came with the Industrial Revolution. Modern machines and techniques brought people into the cities. As we moved to an urban society, changes in religious organizations and in rural kinship system led to the formation of recreational groups. Leisure pursuits became a new aspect of our society. There was a change from the concept that "the idle mind is the devil's workshop" to the realization that leisure is a human right if not a God-given one. Still, old habits die hard, and whether conscious or unconscious, many people still think of idleness as wrong. The use of computers in recent years has resulted in what we may call a second industrial revolution. Computers have not only increased our ability to work quickly and produce more, they have given us even more leisure time and better incomes with which to pursue other interests. Although attitudes towards our work ethic and our free time are changing, most people still feel that they must work hard and play hard; that their leisure pursuits, which may be healthy and restful, should also keep them busy.

This section of the book is an attempt to identifying the challenges for the future development of tourism industry. The first chapter of this section 'Public Utility Services For Tourists and Travellers: an Empirical Analysis' by S.S. Narta and Devinder Sharma emphasizes upon analysis of the Public Utility Services for tourists on the basis of the empirical examination conducted in Himachal Pradesh which is a tourist region of the Country, to determine what kind of such facilities are available in the states for tourists in India. Chapter 'Promoting North East States as Tourist Destination - Problems & Issues' by Neelima Gaur and Mohit Chandra concluded that the development of tourism industry in North-East Indian states largely depend upon the formulation of a proper tourism development policy and people's co-operation and consciousness. The High·Powered Shukla Commission has recommended for establishing a North-East Tourist Development Corporation to develop tourism in the region.

R.Nithiyanandam in the chapter 'Developing brand for niche tourism segments in Pollachi' has focused primarily on four significant niche tourism products in Pollachi: Rural Tourism, Adventure and Wildlife Tourism, Tribal Tourism and Photographic Tourism. The benefits of this work to the academic community are the presentation of insights into niche tourism consumers, and an understanding of the challenges destinations face along the niche tourism life cycle. In the chapter 'Ecotourism: Conservation of Nature and Development of Locals Through Participation' by Pramendra Singh, Ravindra Singh and Sandeep Dubey has advocated the concept of ecotourism. Authors have concluded that ecotourism has been doing well for the benefit of the local community by providing job opportunities, bolstering their economy and also conserving the nature through tourism. Chapter 'Entrepreneurship in Tourism and Hospitality Industry: Previews, Views and Reviews' by Prashant Kumar Gautam reaches on the conclusions that the recent emphasis on entrepreneurship has been coupled with developments in education and teaching. The growth and diversity of the hospitality, leisure, tourism and sports industries along with increases in consumer expectations of their leisure time and experiences has placed greater demands on providers.

Sandeep Paatlan and Promila Raita in the chapter 'Role of Tour Guides towards the Promotion of Sustainable Tourism- A Study With Special Reference to Protected Areas' tried to identify the crucial role of tour guides and their contribution towards sustainability of natural resource in protected areas. Next chapter of the section 'Innovative Capabilities and Entrepreneurial Orientation of Professionally Qualified and Non Professionally Qualified Travel Agents: A Comparative Analysis' by Sandeva Khajuria and Nidhi Pathania is about the comparative analysis of innovations and entrepreneurial orientations of travel agents with tourism professional and non-tourism professional background. The study has included various aspects of these tourism entrepreneurs such as knowledge of trends in business environment, understanding of technologies and regulations which are conducive for the company, knowledge about costumers, workplace culture, organization structure etc.

Chapter 'Application of Public Private Partnership Model for Tourism Growth' by U.N Shukla and Ambar Vishal is an effort to study the meaning and concept of PPP model, process, significance in tourism, Key benefits, its role in destination development and promotion, conservation of historic sites, sustainable tourism development and challenges faced in applicability of this model with the help of primary and secondary data. Suneel Kumar in the chapter' Exploration of Buddhist Tourism Potential in Himachal Pradesh (India)' reached on the conclusion that very low proportion of tourists visited the state due to monks and monasteries and around fifty percent of total respondents opined that they don't have any idea about the Buddhist tourism. More than sixty percent tourists have not visited the Tabo monastery, did not have any knowledge about other places which were famous for Buddhism, and opined that the Buddhist circuits are remain hidden and concealed.

In the chapter 'Role of Rural Tourism in Sustainable Development: A Case Study on Rural Tourist Destination Rajgarh, Dist. Sirmour, Himachal Pradesh' by P.K. Yadav, Vivek Mittal, Anurag Agarwal, Divya Khanna and Gireesh Kumar, authors have tried to find out the role of rural tourism in increasing the level of income of rural India. Prateek Agrawal in the chapter 'New Age Tourism: Issues & Challenges' has made an attempt by critically reviewing the various aspects of the concept of new age tourism by looking at the motivations of the alternative tourists, the common characteristics of the practitioners of alternative tourism, the destinations visited, the types of accommodation used, the travel organizers specializing in this field, and the manner of implementation into the host community. In the chapter 'Community Participation in Cultural Festivals and its role in Destination Development' by Ravinder Dogra and Neelika Arora concluded that people of Mansar destination took Baisakhi festival as one of the main occasion of their destination. This festival adds happiness and energy in the life of local residents and provides them a stage where they can celebrate this festival with natives as well as with the tourists. The remarkable finding came out from the study is the awareness of the local residents about their destination and the festival's importance in attracting tourists towards the destination. The festival holds special place in the hearts of local residents of Mansar and the residents from both Hindu and Muslim religions participated in it with full enthusiasm.

PUBLIC UTILITY SERVICES FOR TOURISTS AND TRAVELLERS: AN EMPIRICAL ANALYSIS

S.S. Narta

Professor, Deptt. Of Commerce and Director, UCBS, HPU, Shimla.

nartasshpu@rediffmail.com

Devinder Sharma

Associate Professor (Commerce), Himachal Pradesh University Centre for Evening Studies, Shimla.

Abstract

Development of tourism is looked upon as the cost effective growing socio-economic source for the development of the community and region. Government of India has taken steps to boost- up tourism infrastructure and facilities for the tourists. The states have also tried to explore the possibilities to tap tourism potential. Practically, satisfaction of the tourist in not confined to the tourism potential and the facilities and infrastructure developed in the tourist locations. Rather, reaching to the tourist location without facing inconveniences is more important. In this regard, Public Utility Services during travel and transit from one place to the other including potable drinking water facility, public toilets for men and women, stay and halt places, parking facilities in the places etc. are much important for the travelers and tourists. This study emphasizes upon analysis of the Public Utility Services for tourists on the basis of the empirical examination conducted in Himachal Pradesh which is a tourist region of the Country, to determine what kind of such facilities are available in the states for tourists in India.

Keywords: Public Utility Services, Tourism Potential, Transit towards tourism locations.

Backdrop and Rationale:

Tourism, no doubt, has emerged as the most effective source of economy in terms of least cost incurred, use of resources without their destruction, growth in economic sources due to increased flow of tourists, facilitation of infrastructure and development of the communities due to development of infrastructure for the tourists, employment generation in the tourism locations for the community and many others. India has of course, abundance of resources for development of tourism which are different in the different regions based upon the geographical, social, cultural, economical and other features of the regions. Mountainous regions like Himachal Pradesh, have ever enriched with the socio-cultural inheritance and natural resources which have since ages, attracted tourists to travel in these places for different purposes including earning, sports, health, entertainment etc. Obviously, the exchange of services and facilities availed by the tourists have contributed to the economy of these regions. Himachal Pradesh itself, has registered growth in all sectors in the past four decades due to the growth in its domestic product which is the outcome of few sectors who have contributed substantially in the economy of the State.

One of these sources is the development of tourism in the State. Consequently, the sectors like industries, infrastructure and services could boost- up with the possibility of economic sources of the State particularly due to the development of tourism.

It is in this juncture, necessary for the Government and the related institutional network to emphasize upon implementing innovative ideas for the growth of tourism for which, it is essential to focus upon the set- up of facilities and services to the tourists and the travelers.

Tourism is not simply a concept of developing locations and destinations for the tourists and providing them facilities in these destinations. A traveler or tourist prefers to come to a location keeping in view, the objectives of coming to that location. In a country like India where despite of diversification of the resources, there is substantial option of availability of the similar kinds of the services and facilities in different places and in such a situation, the traveler and tourist prefers to come to the location or destination where all such facilities, services and the comfort is maximized in order to achieve the motives or objectives by coming to such locations. In fact, it is the moral responsibility of the concerned region, state government, concerned institutions of the tourism locations to facilitate good services for the tourists and travelers and to ensure comfort of the travelers. India is a country of religious and spiritual enrichment. The value system of the Country is to pay regards to the guests by placing them as the shadow of Almighty and welcoming guests as God. 'ATITHI DEVO BHAVA'. Entry of the guest who is considered as the reflection of God in the place of the selected location is not the only place where he or she is welcomed. Of course, the happiness of the guest depends upon the process of welcoming through the complete mechanism of considering comfort of these guests while traveling. Public Utility Services are the services meant and made for the general public for their use. These services include potable drinking water, facilities of toilets for public separately for men and women, rain sheds or stay houses etc. These services are most essential for a tourist or traveler who has to travel through different modes of transportation for long distances. In this paper an attempt has been made to empirically examine the public utility services for the tourists and travelers in Himachal Pradesh.

Scope of the Study

The study is purely empirical based upon the personal experiences of the researchers after traveling in different locations and destinations of nine districts; Shimla, Solan, Sirmaur, Una, Kangra, Hamirpur, Bilaspur, Kullu and Mandi districts and also consulting people traveling along with during transition to these districts of Himachal Pradesh. The survey period is April and May 2014.

Objectives of the Study

The major objective of the research is to know about the public utility services being provided to the touristsans travelers which are also useful for the communities ans different locations. However, the stipulated objectives of this research are depicted as under:

- To study the impact of public utility services on satisfaction and retention of tourists as the customers of tourism industry.
- To analyze Public Utility Services for tourists and travelers.

Methodology:

The research is empirical. During traveling, 85 persons were consulted by the researchers and based upon own observations as well as the response of these 85 persons, the identification and position of the public utility services in the study area have been determined and analyzed. The major locations studied during traveling in the nine districts of the State include: Sainj, Kingal, Narkanda, Theog, Chhaila, Kotkhai, KharaPatthar, Jubbal, Nerwa, Chopal, Rajgarh, Noradhar, Sharampur, Kumarhatti, Batoli, Chaled, Mubarakpur, Amb, Daulatpur, Chintpurni, Dhaliara, Dehra, Nainital, Mataud, Nadaun, Gummar, Morsu, Bhota,Dangar, Dadhol, Seo, Ghagas, Jukhala, Brahampukhar, Bhrarighat, Chamakripul, Darlaghat, Ghanahatti, Padha, Gumma, Nagar, Oat, Baijnath, Banjar, Alampur, Rajpura, Maranda, Thural, Sujanpur and Nerchowk. Simple tools of research analysis including percentage and correlation have been applied to analyze the research problem. Based upon the analysis of the research, conclusions have been drawn and the researchers could come to the concrete findings which are the basis for measuring suggestions in this research.

Analysis and Discussion:

The findings of the research are analyzed and discussed as under:

Public Utility Services and Customer Retension

The requirements of the tourists and the travelers during travel from one place to the other include all such services which are related to rest, halt, and other services. Some of the major requirements are Potable Drinking Water, Public Toilets, Shops for Refreshments:, Parks:, Parking Places:, Taxi Services:,

Security Arrangements for Self and Luggage: and Stay and Halt. A key principle of marketing is the retention of customers through varying means and practices to ensure repeated trade from preexisting customers by satisfying requirements above those of competing companies. This technique is now used as a means of counterbalancing new customers and opportunities with current and existing customers as a means of maximizing profit and counteracting the "leaky bucket theory of business" in which new customers gained in older direct marketing oriented businesses were at the expense of or coincided with the loss of older customers.

Retention cost is the amount of money a company has to spend in a given period to retain its existing customers. Examples of retention costs include billing, customer support, and promotional programs aimed at brand loyalty. In context to the tourism industry, customer retention simply means stay of the tourists in the tourism destination. However, in context to the present research, the motive behind customer retention in case of tourists and travelers is to identify the flow of motivation that influences the existing tourists and travelers to encourage the incumbent or potential tourists and travelers to come to the tourism destinations and to know how much tourists and travelers consider public utility services for their comfort during traveling to convince others. Customer lifetime value is a multi-period calculation, normally 3–7 years into the future depending on the lifespan of the product and the nature of the industry. In reality, evaluation beyond this point is generally viewed as too speculative to be reliable due to changes in the product lifecycle and the market. In context to the tourism industry, customer lifeline can be seen in terms of the impression being carried by

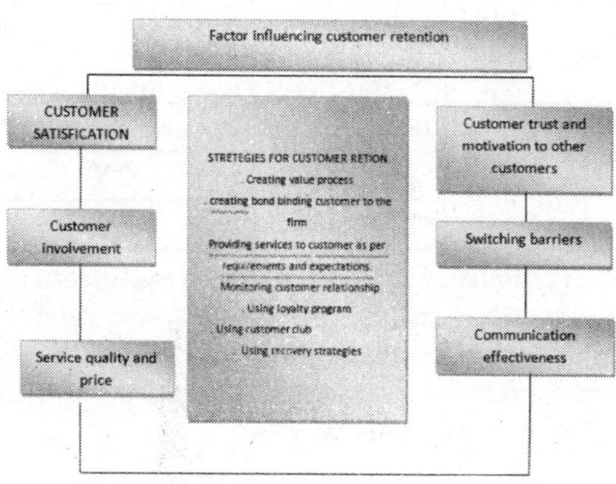

the existing structure of tourists and travelers to the potential structure.

The theories and key elements on factors influencing customer retention are:

Key elements of factors effecting CR	Concerned Author
Customer satisfaction	Fonel (1992) Renaweera and Prabu (2003)
Customer trust	Renewere and Prabu, Sharma 2003
Level of involvement	Richards 1996
Attractiveness of alternative and switching barriers	Richards 1996 Sharma (2000)
service quality	Renawera and Neelly (2003)
Communication effectiveness	Sharma and Patterson (1999)

The relationship between public utility services and satisfaction as well as retention of the tourists as well as travelers has been analyzed on the basis of the responses of the selected respondents as under:

Correlation Analysis

		Customer satisfaction	Customer retention
Customer satisfaction	Pearson Correlation	1	.688**
	Sig. (2-tailed)		000
	N	180	180
Customer retention	Pearson Correlation	.688**	1
	Sig. (2-tailed)	.000	
	N	180	180

The results indicate that there is a significant relationship between customer Satisfaction and the customer retention. This means that the independent variables of the public utility services result to explain 67.8% of customer satisfaction and thereby, retention of the tourists and travelers

Public Utility Services for Tourists and Travelers

The responses reveal that public utility services have not been paid much attention in Himachal Pradesh as a great majority of the transit locations (the places travelled by the tourists and travelers during visit) are not providing such services and facilities and causing inconvenience. The responses in terms of the selected public utility services are analyzed as under:

S.No	Public Utility Services Not available	No. of Respondents	%age
1.	Public Toilets	85	100
2.	Potable Drinking Water	64	75.2
3.	Shops for Refreshments	47	55.3
4.	Parking Places	81	95.3
5.	Taxi Services	83	97.6
6.	Parks	79	92.9
7.	Security Arrangements for Self and Luggage	85	100
8.	Halt and Stay	80	94.1

Amongst all the public utility services, facilitation of the public toilets is a must for the tourists and travelers in places of road and other transit. In Himachal Pradesh, road transportation is the only and major mode of traveling. Surprisingly, the tourists and travelers stated that in all the places through they traveled, the facility of toilets is not available for common travelers. In very few places where public toilets are constructed along the road sides, these are not worth to be used. It has been stated that tourists and travelers have to go to toilet on the road side which is a crucial problem particularly for women. Further, three- fourth of the respondents revealed that during travel it is essential to carry water for drinking as in places sometimes water is not available to drink. The natural sources of water are scarce on the road sides and shops are not frequently available where from mineral water can be purchased. It is worth to mention that exceeding one half percentage (55.3%) of the respondents are of the view that shops and restaurants are not easily available in the places during travel. Himachal Pradesh itself is a hill region having beautiful and picturesque places. But, in order to attract tourists particularly when people travel through different places, for refreshments and halt, attention has not been paid for the development of the public parks as 92.9 percent respondents agree with it. Similarly, 95.3 percent argued that to park their own vehicle and to use public transport system, the problem being faced generally is the unavailability of the parking places for the vehicles. It is also necessary to mention that in case of fault in the vehicle used for traveling or to park own vehicle and to use public taxi facility, according to 97.6 percent respondents taxi services are not frequently available. The respondents are not happy with the security arrangements for self and luggage as according to them, such arrangements are not provided. It is only the person who has to take special precautions and special care. Moreover, 94.1 percent advocated that during transit, there is not proper public facility system of stay and halt due to which, the travelers and tourists feel exploited by the few private agencies providing such services.

Findings and Suggestions:

It has been found that in Himachal Pradesh special attention has been paid for the development of the tourism destinations. The tourism infrastructure, services and facilities are the priorities which have been taken care of in these locations and destinations for which, the government, tourism corporation and private tourism system have taken measures for the convenience of the tourists. Tourism system including the government and the private tourism industry have vehicle services for the tourists. In Himachal Pradesh, people in a great majority travel through the Corporation and private transport system. In the places between the place of travel and the place of tourism destination when the traveler or tourist passes through different locations and places of the State, a series of problems and challenges are being faced by the traveler due to unavailability of the public utility services during travel and halt. It has been found that such challenges are influencing the level of satisfaction and retention of the tourists in terms of their stay in the tourism destinations as well as to motivate others to come to the places of tourism as the message is passed that the travelers and tourists have to face problems in the absence of public utility services during travel in the State.

Based upon the findings of the study, it is recommended that the Block Development Offices must be directed to take on first priority and ensure provision of the public utility services through Local Self Government and local bodies. The financial assistance being provided to this organization for philanthropic purposes and for the development of the local areas and communities must be with the consideration of providing these facilities to both; the local communities and also for the tourists and travelers. In order to maintain and procure the public utility services infrastructure, it is necessary for the local self government and the local bodies to employ services for these purposes.

The tourism development corporation and the other development agencies like Public Works Department and other organizations must assist financially and by constructing and providing public utility services in the transit locations. The government must ensure that the facilities are provided and stringent actions must be taken against the Block development office, local body or the organization concerned for any kind of lapse as public services are meant for public and due to these services, not only the community is being served but the interest of specific classes like women is taken care of and the tourists are contributing to the state economy and it is the moral duty of the Government to keep the interest of all in its first agenda of development.

References:

Hunt, S. D. & Morgan, R. M. (1995), The Comparative Advantage Theory of Competition, Journal of Marketing, 59(2), pp. 1–14.

Janz, B. D., and Prasarnphanich P. (2003), Understanding the Antecedents of Effective Knowledge Management: The Importance of a Knowledge-Centered Culture, Decision Sciences, 34 (2), 352–384.

Ndubisi, N.O. (2003). Service quality: understanding customer perception and reaction, and its impact on business. International Journal of Business, Vol. 5 No. 2, pp. 190-207.

Pathak, P., Modi, P. (2004), Quality of Services: Issues and Challenges, An Indian Perspective, Synergy Journal of Management, Vol. 6 (1), 2004, pp. 75-80.

Reed, Richard, and Robert J. DeFillippi (1990), Causal Ambiguity, Barriers to Imitation, and Sustainable Competitive Advantage, Academy of Management Review, 15 (1), 88–117.

Schneider, B. and Bowen, David E. (1999), Understanding customer delight and outrage', Sloan Management Review, 41:1, 35-45.

Srivastava, Rajendra K., Tasadduq A. Shervanie, and Liam Fahey (1999), Marketing, Business Processes, and Shareholder Value: An Organizationally Embedded View of Marketing Activities and the Discipline of Marketing, Journal of Marketing, (Special Issue), 168–179.

Stefanou, C., Sarmaniotis, C. and Stafyla, A. (2003), CRM and Customer-centric Knowledge Management: an Empirical Research, Business Process Management Journal, Vol. 9 No. 5, pp. 617-34.

Stringfellow, A. Winter N. and Bowen, D. (2004), CRM: Profiting From Understanding Customer Needs, Business Horizons, Vol. 47 , No. 5, pp. 45 – 52

Thompson, E.(2005), Beyond CRM: The scenario for customer-centric strategies'. In Gartner Symposium/ITXPO (2005), 1-3 August, Cape Town, Gartner Group.

Vandermerwe, S. (2004), Achieving deep customer focus, MIT Sloan Management Review, Vol. 45 No. 3, pp. 26-34.

Vijayadurai, (2008) Service Quality, Customer Satisfaction and Behavioral Intention in Hotel Industry, Journal of Marketing and Communication, Vol. 3 (3), pp. 14-26

PROMOTING NORTH EAST STATES AS TOURIST DESTINATION - PROBLEMS & ISSUES

Neelima Gaur
Vivek Khand 4/381, Gomti Nagar
neelimagaur@gmail.com
Mohit Chandra
Director , Amity School of Hospitality, Amity University Lucknow
Malhaur, Gomti Nagar Lucknow
hittsindia@gmail.com

Abstract

Today tourism is the largest service industry in India, with a contribution of 6.23% to the national GDP and providing 8.78% of the total employment. India has witnessed more than 5 million annual foreign tourist arrivals and 562 million domestic tourism visits. Main reason of this achievement is promotion of tourism products successfully that allows to tourists to appreciate what India has to offer to visitors. That context is the overall image, or brand, of India. The brand value or name is one of the significant instruments which create the activity of entities in the modern competitive market. India's North East, called the land of the eight sisters (Assam, Meghalaya, Arunachal Pradesh, Nagaland, Manipur, Mizoram, Tripura and Sikkim), and is a region which can be best described as virgin, wild and untouched from the modernizations taking else where in the world. North-East of India is the land of Blue Mountains, Green Valleys and Red Rivers. Nestled in the Eastern Himalayas this region is abundant in Natural Beauty, Wild life, Bird watching Destinations, Important scenic spots, snow clad mountains, cultural heritage places, popular religious institutions, traditional dance performance, international fairs & festivals, ancient temples, trekking routes, tea farms, Floricultures, Handicraft Shops, Flora & Fauna and its Colorful people. A blend of all these makes it the most beautiful Eco-Tourism destination in South Asia. In North East the districts in Assam like Goalpara district, Nagaon district, Kamrup district has been identified under the UNESCO declared "World Heritage Sites". North East India is receiving very less percentage of the total Tourist Arrivals in India. The arrivals are not even 1% of the total tourist arrivals in the country. The positive thing about the arrivals is the states like Assam, Meghalaya, Tripura and Sikkim have the considerable share of the total tourist arrival. Some of the important issues to be concerned as a developing strategies to make North –East India as a brand include, safety & security of tourists, connectivity between all the states, sufficient funds by state and central Govt., most importantly the good marketing strategy in national as well as international fronts for recognition as a brand. Recognition of the brand directly creates consumers' loyalty and makes competitive advantage over other brands on the market. Recognition and value of the brand comes from its market power only. When all is said and done, truly there will be a tourism brand for North-East that will be marketable to bring additional tourists to the region.

Keywords: Tourism, India, North East India, Assam, Word Heritage

Introduction

Tourism is the industry that helps a country to get economical stability.

Tourist generates business in a country and plays a key role in achieving the socio-economic goals of development plans of the nation. Tourism is one of the most exciting and progressive industries in India. Part of the visitor economy, tourism is also big business and it impacts on almost every other industry.Tourism is travelling for recreational, leisure, or business purposes. The idea of travelling for pleasure or exploration soon emerged as a therapeutic and recreational concept. Tourism is a temporary movement of people to destinations outside their normal places of work and residence, the activities undertaken during their stay in those destinations, and the facilities created to cater to their needs. Tourism businesses such as hotels, restaurants, airlines and tour operators represent only a small proportion of the people employed in the tourism industry or who benefit from it (1-4).

In the words of Union Tourism Minister Sh. Chiranjeevi, there is a provision of complimentary space to the North Eastern states in India Pavilions set up at major International Travel Fairs and Exhibitions. Relaxation in Leave Travel Concession (LTC) norms for Central Government employees. 10% of the annual plan allocation of the Ministry of Tourism mandatorily earmarked for releasing central financial assistance (CFA) to the North Eastern States. 100% central financial assistance for organizing fairs & festivals allowed only to the North Eastern States & the State of Jammu & Kashmir. In a written reply in Lok Sabha today the Minister further said that his Ministry has undertaken many measures to focus on the tourism potential of (including religious spots) in the North Eastern region such as releasing television campaigns on various TV Channels, a separate section on the North Eastern region included on the promotional website of the Ministry of Tourism www.incredibleindia.org. The North Eastern region has been the theme of the India Pavilion at the South Asian Travel & Tourism Exchange (SATTE) organized annually in New Delhi for the past few years. Publicity material produced and distributed widely through India tourism offices in India and overseas including South East Asia and China. Development & promotion of tourist places, including religious/ Buddhism tourist places, are undertaken primarily by the State Governments/Union Territory Administrations. The Ministry of Tourism, Government of India, however, extends central financial assistance for tourism related projects identified in consultation with them under various tourism schemes of the Ministry and subject to availability of funds.

The Tourism System

Before developing a tourism place or product, it is necessary to understand how this system operates. The given diagram show the component involved in this industry.

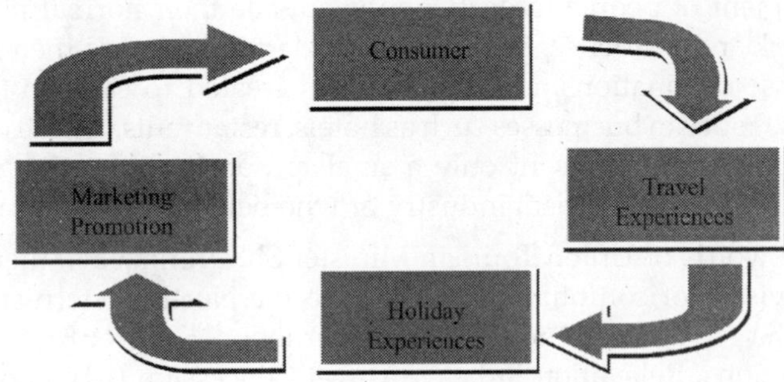

Figure 1. The system of tourism

The Consumer

The consumer is the most important part of the tourism system because the all the industries depends on consumer. Everyone working in tourism must ensure that the consumer is considered first and foremost in all business and planning decisions. Consumers spend their money and time in many ways. If consumers wish to spend their money on a holiday, they generally decided about their budget, time period, mode of travel, type of destination they would like to visit and decide make reservation according to their schedule through a hospitality company, over the internet or directly.

The Travel Experience

The travel experience relates to the mode of travels to the destination and the experiences they have during the journey in the way. Travel choices include air, train, buses, car, boat, motorbike or any other as they like. The mode of travel affects the type of consumer experience. If the transport facility and services are minimum or low standards, that tourist place often neglect by the tourists. Tourist never decide to visit or spend their holidays at such places where availability of mode of transport services is not adequate. Many issues affect the quality of the travel experience, including the variety of attractions, facilities and accommodation available, many routes, the road quality and signage; and the frequency of transport services.

The Holiday Experience

When tourists decide to spend their holiday, they have many expectations of the experience they will have. This could relate to the quality of hotels, service and food, range and cost of activities available, variety of shopping, cafe and restaurant opening hours. Their satisfaction will be based on how well the holiday met their initial expectations or exceeded them.

Marketing a Business

Marketing refers to the multi-faceted process that any successful business perpetually works through. It includes activities such as researching the market, consumers and products; developing the business and products; developing the skills of personnel; and promoting, advertising or working with the media to raise awareness of the product to generate sales. Promotion is the means by which consumers are made aware about the places, products or services, to help them choose the places for spend their holidays. Promotion can be made by many elements such as brand ambassador, media, including internet, websites, print (magazines, newspapers, brochures, direct-mail), television and radio.

Scenario of Tourism in North-East India:

North East India, the amalgam of eight sisters is a known for its mountain ranges, lush green valleys with its traditional tribal culture. It is situated in the lap of Eastern Himalayas, this region is abundant in natural beauty, wildlife, exotic flora and fauna, a amalgam of these unique features makes it the most beautiful Eco-Tourism destination. Its thick lush forests give a breathtaking view of the flora and fauna. Besides the animals and the birds of various kinds roaming singing and playing in the vast green forest, the region has many ornamental fishes, rare plants, medicinal herbs and exotic orchids. It has many tranquil lagoons and reverie locations like Bhalukpung, Loktok, etc. that will attract the tourists for angling and boating. The location of the region is strategically important as it has international borders with

Bangladesh, Bhutan, China and Myanmar. The amalgam of eight states the gorgeous states of North East India comprises of Assam, Arunachal Pradesh, Nagaland, Manipur, Mizoram, Tripura, Sikkim and Meghalaya. These places are heavenly beautiful and the only route that connects them to India is the Siliguri Corridor. North East India is receiving a poor percentage of the total Tourist Arrivals in India. The arrivals in North East India are not even 1% of the total tourist arrivals in the country. States like Assam, Meghalaya, Tripura and Sikkim are the main states and they have considerable share of the total tourist arrival in North East India.

Table 1. North East India Tourist Trends

State	2004-05		2005-06		2006-07		Share in India Arrival % (06)	
	IND	FOR	IND	FOR	IND	FOR	IND	FOR
ASSAM	2288093	7285	2467652	10782	2768824	10374	0.60	0.09
A.P.	39767	321	50560	313	80137	607	0.02	0.01
MAN	93476	249	94299	316	116984	295	0.03	0.00
MEG	443495	12407	375901	5099	401529	4287	0.09	0.04
MIZO	38598	326	44715	273	50987	436	0.01	0.00
NAGA	10056	1084	17470	883	15850	426	0.00	0.00
SIKKIM	230719	14646	251744	16523	292486	18026	0.06	0.15
TRIPUR	260907	3171	216330	2677	2306456	3245	0.05	0.03

(**Source:** Dept. of Tourism Govt. of India Tourism Statistics)

Table 2. Hotels in North East India

State	5 Star Hotels	4 Star Hotels	3 Star Hotels	2 Star Hotels	1 Star Hotels
Arunachal Pradesh	-	-	1	1	-
Assam	-	3	13	4	-
Manipur	-	-	1	1	-
Meghalaya	-	1	-	-	-
Mizoram	-	-	-	-	-
Nagaland	-	-	-	-	-
Sikkim	1	1	2	5	-
Tripura	-	-	-	-	-

(**Source:** Ministry of Tourism Govt. of India)

Table 3. Hotels in India

5 Star	4 Star	3 Star	2 Star	1 Star
Hotels	Hotels	Hotels	Hotels	Hotel
82	113	611	120	73

(**Source:** Ministry of Tourism Govt. of India)

http://tourismpmis.nic.in/Scripts/InterfaceReport/Hotel/HotelSubCatlist.aspx

Prospects of Tourism in North-East India

The Kaleidoscope of eight states that makes up the North Eastern part of Indian can best be described as 'Asia in Miniature'. The North East lies in the lush green corner of Eastern India. There is an ample scope for tourism to grow as an industry in with it diverse endowments of tourist interests. The following are the existing and potential variety of tourism:

Nature Tourism

Eight Sister States of the North-East are known for their geographical diversity, which resulted in varieties of nature tourism. With its dense forests, uneven topography, flora and fauna, the majestic Brahmaputra and its tributaries, wild life sanctuaries and many rare species of animals, North East India offers basically nature-centric tourism. From one end to the other, the states offers to the tourists so many places of natural beauty with wide variety of wildlife that very few places in the world can compete with it. Nature tourism is understood in terms of wildlife sanctuaries constitutes the core of tourism in North East India. The tourists, both domestic and foreign, are likely to find these places attracting, nature alluring, provided a well-definite itinerary is planned.

Tea Tourism

Tea was first discovered in Assam in 1823 by two intrepid British adventurers, Robert and Charles Bruce and since then tea has become an integral part of Assam's economy. Tea tourism is also known as ecotourism. It is a attraction of tourists to travel to natural areas, which conserves the environment and improves the welfare of local people. Tea tourism in India is fast catching on popularity with more and more tourists making their way to the lush green tea estates of India. Tea tours to north east India will not only take tourists around luxuriant plantations around the country but will also give you the perfect opportunity to know all about its history and its commercial importance i.e. Tea, Timber, Trading and Tourism is the backbone of the present financial status of this region. Stay at luxurious tea bungalows, enjoy the best of comforts, enjoy interacting with tea workers, and try your hand at plucking tea leaves, visit tea factories - all as part of tea tourism.

Eco-tourism

Eco-tourism is a new concept, developed around the idea of travelling to places of natural beauty, moving around and staying with the places of nature for a couple of days. It has the twin objectives of conserving environment and improving the welfare of the local people. Many countries have already successfully promoted eco-tourism. Kerala presents a unique success story of eco-tourism in India. On this similar line, Northeast India is one of India's secrets, a remote unexplored land rich in biodiversity and indigenous cultures. Filled with rain-forests, Himalayan mountains and hills, tourism in the region is a delicate affair which revolves around environment and cultures, creating a mutually benefiting relationship of sorts. North East India has many scopes for eco-tourism, as its natural scenario and climatic condition. The states are virtually free from industrial pollution. Its green forests, blue hills, enchanting rivers are the basis on which an eco-friendly tourism can be developed. It may be noted that eco-tourism is yet to come to the take-off stage ..

Cultural Tourism

North East India festivals highlight the region's rich indigenous culture with folk songs, tribal dances, food and crafts. The North East of India constitutes the states of Arunachal Pradesh, Assam, Manipur, Meghalaya, Mizoram, Nagaland, Sikkim and Tripura.

These states are the conglomeration of various ethnic tribes and group each having a distinct language, culture, way-of-life, festivals, songs and dances. Most of these people have their spring festivals. Songs and dances, display of colourful dresses, tasting of innumerable varieties of both vegetarian and non-vegetarian dishes mark these festivals. Some of the most popular festivals in these states are Hornbill Festival, Nagaland, Bihu Festival, Assam, Brahmaputra Beach Festival, Assam, Dehing Patkai Festival, Assam, Torgya Monastery Festival, Arunachal Pradesh, Shillong Autumn Festival, Meghalaya, Nongkrem Dance Festival, Meghalaya, Wangala Festival, Meghalaya, Chapchar Kut, Mizoram, Kang Chingba, Manipur, Kharchi Puja, Tripura. These festivals are the attraction for the domestic tourists as well as foreigner tourists.

Pilgrim Tourism

India is a land of often bewildering diversity. People of every faith and religion, living together here to create a unique and colourful mosaic of culture and community. The glorious past of ancient India has gifted North India with many splendid temples that have found a place in World Heritage list. North India pilgrimage places are the centre of attraction for their amazing architecture, so one may try a tour to north east india temples. The age old customs and traditions of India speak loudly through these temples. The tour to these North Indian temples are must while your North India tour. North India pilgrimage Tour Packages includes visit to the temples and ghats in Varanasi, the Khajuraho Temples in Madhya Pradesh are some of the example of North India Temples, speaking the past culture and tradition of North India. Assam has many ancient temples and shrines, some of which like Kamakhya date back to pre-historic time. As stated already Kamakhya is one of the most revered religious places in the country .

Adventure Tourism

The enchanting blue hills and speedy rivers of North East India provide an enormous scope for the development of adventure tourism like rock-climbing, trekking, para-sailing, water sports, river rafting and angling are promoted by the Department of Tourism. Some other areas of adventure tourism like hang gliding are yet to grow. Assam has a number of ideal places like Nilachal hills (where the Kamakhya temple situated) in the city of Guwahati and the hills around Kaziranga. Since most of the tourists come to the state through Guwahati and visit Kaziranga, there is an enormous scope for hang gliding. Tourists are also attracted to living root bridges of Meghalaya, which are marvel examples of sustainable and Eco-friendly architecture. Also The Bailey Trail trek in the high eastern Himalayas of western Arunachal Pradesh offers an experience through some breathtaking landscapes of virgin pine, oak and rhododendron forests. At an average of 4000 meters, the panoramic views of the Kangto and Gorichen peaks, two of northeastern India's highest, is a sight to remember .

Golf Tourism

Golf has been enjoyed by many for a long time. Earlier it was enjoyed as a sport but in recent times it has developed into a hot tourism product. There are many golf courses located mostly within the compact areas of tea gardens. The Oil India maintains a very good golf course in the industrial town of Duliajan. These offer a unique opportunity to develop golf tourism in the state. Most of the courses are located near to air-strips and helipads maintained by the tea garden management. In recent years, domestic and foreign tourists are coming to play golf in different golf courses, and a good number of them use these air-strips and helipads. Golf tourism can be integrated with eco and tea tourism. One has to recognize that some tourists may show more than one interest and may like to combine various aspects of tourism described above. These tourists take exclusive golfing holidays wherein their accommodation is also arranged near the course and they return after serious golf playing .

The number of tourism projects and amount sanctioned to the North Eastern states under the scheme "Product/Infrastructure Development for Destinations and Circuits (PIDDC)" during the 11th Five Year Plan and for the current financial year (upto 30th September, 2012) are as follows:-

Table 4. Tourism projects and amount sanctioned to the North Eastern states (Rs. in crore)

Sl. No	Name of the State	Amount Sanctioned											
		2007-08		2008-09		2009-10		2010-11		2011-12		2012-13 (as on 30th September, 2012)	
		No.	Amt.	No.	Amt.	No.	Amt.	No.	Amt.	No.	Amt.	No.	Amt.
1.	Arunachal Pradesh	11	43.30	13	31.47	14	36.54	13	32.26	11	30.68	07	21.11
2.	Assam	06	17.47	04	21.08	07	22.76	04	23.55	05	11.08	00	00
3.	Manipur	05	11.11	09	29.44	09	27.14	08	39.40	05	30.73	01	0.50
4.	Meghalaya	02	6.74	07	17.14	07	14.73	09	22.53	03	0.50	02	0.68
5.	Mizoram	06	26.93	04	3.18	07	24.06	09	11.51	07	13.91	03	1.02
6.	Nagaland	22	32.41	11	25.40	13	24.60	10	29.10	19	65.45	06	19.47
7.	Sikkim	25	55.91	20	66.78	19	42.36	14	23.48	08	25.15	03	20.35
8.	Tripura	11	11.11	06	3.61	13	20.67	12	40.73	06	15.44	00	00

Source: Press Information Bureau, Govt. of India.

Tourism Package For The North East

Tourism in North East India cannot be viewed in isolation. Assam is the gateway to North-East; itself is a reservoir of natural beauty with great variety. Many tourists would like to visit Shillong, Cherapunji in Meghalaya and a number of places in Arunachal Pradesh like Tawang, Bomdila, Tezu and Meo. There may be an integrated approach to promote tourism in the region with an attractive package of nature, eco, tea, adventure tourism. The Union Tourism Ministry has given 'special attention' to develop an integrated approach to eco and adventure tourism. The North-Eastern Council should come up to play an integrated role in this regard. It will be easy to have coordination with Meghalaya, but it will be a difficult task to have coordination with Arunachal Pradesh where the inner line system is in operation.

Challanges of Tourism Promotion in North-East India

A tourist should ensure all possible facilities; tourists are to be treated as honoured guests. Apart from infrastructure, tourist information, travel services and trained guides are needed for attraction of tourists. Some of the given problems are occurred for the attraction of the tourists in North East India.

Absence of a Tourism Policy

The Government of India has a policy to develop tourism into an industry and a target to achieve in respect of attracting foreign tourists, who constitute an important source of hard foreign currency. As a result, process tourism has become the second largest foreign exchange earner. It has taken steps to revise the National Tourism Policy, 1982 and to redraft the draft policy of 1993 to envision global tourism based on four S – Swagat (welcome), Suvidha (facilities), Soochna (information) and Suraksha (security). It is said that Assam has a policy on tourism prepared in November 1987. Unfortunately, it is not available in any of the offices connected with tourism. It appears that there was an attempt in November 1987 to formulate a tourism policy and then in December 1992 an exercise was done to frame certain rules on tourism. It appears that these steps did not bring forth any concrete result. The media, in the recent time has been giving adequate publicity highlighting the importance of tourism in the economic development of the state. Most of the newspapers in both English and Assamese have been publishing good number articles in frequent intervals highlighting various aspects of tourism and its potentiality in the sustainable development of Assam. Ideas on this matter are generated through media, but these are yet to be crystallized and institutionalized, as result tourism remains in the domain of ad hocism.

Restricted Area Permit (RAP)

The RAP to the North-Eastern region was enforced in 1955 in the backdrop of alleged missionary involvement in the Naga rebellion. Under this a foreigner intending to visit North-East including Assam had to undergo a long arduous procedure of obtaining permission from the Home Ministry. With RAP in force till May 18, 1999 it was an uphill task for any foreign tourist to visit Assam and other places in the North-East. Unfortunately, the ghost of RAP still continues to loom large and the efforts to disabuse the false apprehension in the mind of the foreign tourists are minimal.

Insurgency

Assam, and for that matter almost whole of North-East, has been experiencing violent movements, some of which are secessionists in nature, since 1953 when A Z Phizo fired the first salvo of armed struggle against Indian Union. The foreign and the domestic tourists consider it risky to visit this part of the country, in view of the prevailing law and order situation. The general impression has been that any foreign or domestic tourist could be a soft target of the insurgents. Therefore, they are reluctant to undertake an adventurous journey to Assam and North-East. Contrary to this general impression, however, there is not a single instance of harassment, not to speak of threat to life to any domestic or foreign tourists visiting the region since the outbreak of the Naga movement. But the general impression about the deteriorating law and order situation is enough to ward off any tourist. On the top of this, Manas sanctuary, undoubtedly one of the most beautiful natural parks in the country has been virtually under the control of the Bodo militants for which it is still not considered to safe to visit the place. Recently, Manas has been opened for the tourists, but it will take time to ward off the long-standing impression of the tourists about the sanctuary.

Lack of Infrastructure

To attract tourists, there must be dissemination of information, infrastructural facilities like good hotels and tourist lodges, affordable and reliable communication network, food stuff, restaurants, knowledgeable and skilled guides and accommodation, drinking water sports equipment, and the like. Most of the places of tourist attraction are not by the side of the national highways, and road networks in bad condition. This is a strong discouraging factor, which works against a good inflow of the tourist. It appears that the potentialities for developing tourism to a stable source of revenue are not matched by proper policy and strategy .

Lack of Coordinated Efforts

There is a palpable lack of coordination among several agencies like Department of Tourism and Department of Archaeology in handling the demands of the tourists in places of both historic and religious importance. There is virtually no coordination between various public industries and private sectors like tea industry, oil and coal on one hand, and the Department of Tourism or Assam Tourist Development Corporation (ATDC), on the other, in the efforts towards developing eco and tea tourism. Similarly, there is no tangible and effective coordination between the twin bodies of Assam tourism, that is, the Directorate of Tourism and ATDC on one hand, and road and river transport system run by both Government and private sectors on the other. Therefore, stagnation has been the striking mark of the status of tourism in Assam.

Absence of Tourist Guides

Assam virtually does not have any trained guides placed in important places of tourist attraction. Consequently, as the tourists arrive at such a place there is hardly anyone to satisfy the inquisitiveness of the tourists. The Department of Tourism initiated a programme to train tourist guides. The effort did not yield good result as most of the trainees left the job. Some of them found other means of livelihood while others found it to be less paying because of the poor inflow of the tourists to the state. It is a chicken-and-egg syndrome which can be resolved by the state government by adopting a two-front strategy – (i) tourist guide training programme for a very limited number of youths, and (ii) setting a target of inflow of the tourists.

Conclusion

The development of tourism industry in North-East Indian states largely depend upon the formulation of a proper tourism development policy and people's co-operation and consciousness. The High Powered Shukla Commission has recommended for establishing a North-East Tourist Development Corporation to develop tourism in the region. It has also recommended to issue Inner-Line Permits relax the Restricted Area Permits as well as to introduce Charter Flights for NE Package tours etc. Moreover, an honest and strong will of the government coupled with people's hearty co-operation will definitely boost up tourism industry in North-East Indian states in near future.

Reference

Annonymous. Customer Service in Tourism Industry. 2012 [cited 2012 29 th November]; Available from: http://www.vivocha.com/2012/11/customer-service-in-tourism-industry/.

Bandyopadhyay R, Morais DB, Chick G. Religion and identity in India's heritage tourism. Annals of Tourism Research. 2008;35(3):790-808.

Hannam K, Butler G, Paris CM. Developments and key issues in tourism mobilities. Annals of Tourism Research. 2014;44(0):171-85.

Patil V. Narrating political history about contested space: Tourism Websites of India's Northeast. Annals of Tourism Research. 2011;38(3):989-1008.

Annonymous. A Guide to Understanding The Tourism Industry. [cited 1].GOI. Annual Report 2011-12. In: Tourism Mo, editor. New Delhi: Ministry of Tourism, Government of India; 2012.

Kumaran VS. New Tourism Products Development in Northeast India. In: Indian Tourism, editor. Guwahati, Assam: Govt. of India.

Tourism in India. Wikipedia, the free encyclopedia [Internet]. 2012 November 2012. Available from: http://en.wikipedia.org/wiki/Tourism_in_India#Nature_tourism.

Annonymous. INDIAN TEA TOURISM. Available from: http://www.httipl.com/www/heat-flexi holidays/ himalayanpromotion/teatourism/teatourism1.html.

Pasture G. Greener Pasture, Eco-tourism in North-East India - 3 Responsible Destinations. Available from: http://greenerpasturesind.wordpress.com/2012/11/15/eco-tourism-in-north-east-india-3-responsible-destinations/.

Cook S. North East India Festivals Guide.

Pilgrimage NI. North India Pilgrimage.

India TCSN. Travel Conserve Sustain Northeast India.

Khan MA. ETHNIC TOURISM IN INDIA: ACASE STUDY OF PUNJAB.

Hussain MM. Role of Tourism in the Socio-Economic Development of Assam, Dialogue July-September2012; 14(1). Available from: http://www.asthabharati.org/Dia_Jul%20012/moon.htm.

DEVELOPING BRAND FOR NICHE TOURISM SEGMENTS IN POLLACHI

R. Nithiyanandam

Director, Sree Ramu College of Arts and Science, Pollachi, Coimbatore DT.Tamilnadu

directorsrc@yahoo.in

Abstract

Niche tourism refers to how a specific tourism product can be customized to meet the needs of a particular tourist or market segment. There are locations in Pollachi area which have specific niche products and this can be established niche tourism destinations. Niche tourism, through image creation, helps destinations to differentiate their tourism products and compete in an increasingly competitive and jumbled tourism environment. Through the use of the niche tourism life cycle it is clear that niche products in the Pollachi region will have different impacts, marketing challenges and contributions to destination development as they progress through it.

Authors contribution to academic knowledge and understanding within this area is summarized within the four key themes of niche tourism product development, niche tourist profiling, destination development and region building frame work in the Pollachi area through niche tourism.

To illustrate this, the paper has focused primarily on four significant niche tourism products in Pollachi: Rural Tourism, Adventure and Wildlife Tourism, Tribal Tourism and Photographic Tourism. The benefits of this work to the academic community are the presentation of insights into niche tourism consumers, and an understanding of the challenges destinations face along the niche tourism life cycle.

Finally, the practical benefits of this work to industry include a greater understanding of niche tourist behavior in Pollachi area to better aid them in positioning and targeting their products. It concludes with an identification of the limitations of this body of work and proposes areas for future research.

Keywords: Niche Tourism, Pollachi Area, Rural Tourism

Introduction

'Niche Tourism' is largely borrowed from the term 'Niche Marketing' which refers to how a specific product can be tailored to meet the needs of a particular audience or market segment. This is then extended into the idea of 'niche tourism products' and 'niche tourism markets'. In addition to the focus on tourist activities and what tourists engage with at a destination there is also a dimension by which locations with specific niche products are able to establish and position themselves as niche destinations. destination development often begins with new ideas and initiatives; it is as much to do with attractions and services as it is about marketing and promotion.

Thus, the development of specific tailored products at a destination level is seen to be a way of attracting high-end, high-yield tourists through an extremely personalized 'niche' service.

Niche tourism is, therefore, seen to be a response to an increasing number of more sophisticated tourists demanding specialist tourism products. It is a means by which destinations can focus their offerings to differentiate their tourism products and compete in an increasingly competitive and cluttered tourism environment (Sharpley and Telfer, 2002). This critical appraisal presents an exploration of various forms of niche tourism. How destinations develop themselves to create unique products and images, which appeal to the tourism market, is a critical component of the research. It is this product-led approach, shaped by a more discerning and experience seeking tourist consumer, which will provide the context for the publications presented and examined further in this critical appraisal.

Literature Review

Hutchinson (1957) is largely attributed with introducing the idea of 'niche' referring to an optimum location that an organism can exploit against its competitors. A later definition is given by Keegan et al. (1992), describing a niche as a smaller market not served by competing products. The term 'niche' was subsequently adopted by the business literature inventing the phrase 'niche marketing'. As Tofton and Hammervoll (2010) state, there appears to be no widely accepted definition of niche marketing. However, a number of similarities have emerged. Existing definitions include, a method to meet customer needs through the tailoring of goods and service to small markets (Stanton et al. 1991); 'small, profitable, homogeneous market segments which have been ignored or neglected by others' (Dalgic and Leeuw, 1994, p.42) and a 'process of concentrating marketing resources and efforts on one particular market segment' (Huh and Singh, 2007, p.213). Kotler (2003) also characterises niche marketing as focusing on customers, with a distinct set of needs, who will offer a premium to the company who best fulfils these. Thus markets can be reached and served and products and services matched to people's specific needs and wants. Dalgic and Leeuw (1994) review by stating that niche firms generally focus their marketing activities to a limited part of the market, with relatively few customers and competitors, through the application of company specialisation, product differentiation, relationship marketing and customer focus.

Objectives of the Study

In order to achieve this aim of Developing Brand for Niche tourism segments in Pollachi., several objectives need to be fulfilled. These include:

- An evaluation of the critical role of niche products, such as adventure, Wildlife Tourism, Tribal Tourism and Photographic tourism destinations.

- To identify the positioning level of tourism products and to explore it. To exaggerate different novel ideas to improve niche tourism.

Research Methodology

It is constructive to analyse our research methodology against the development of current research in tourism.

The use of a case study is highly relevant and illuminating when exploring key issues and seeking to introduce new research areas and explain or determine research findings. The research voyage initiated with a focus on existing data accessed through industry and governmental publications, policy documents and academic journals.

Niche Tourism – Opportunities for India

Travel is evolving rapidly the world over. There is a visible shift from mass tourism to niche tourism. It is a challenge before destinations and destination managers to prepare themselves to attract tourists around the niche in the coming time. Despite having diverse destinations and products, India's tourism industry is not yet able to rise to the level of being called a niche destination.

Travel is a new religion for people around the world. A recent survey revealed that people the world over spend almost 40 per cent of their spare income or savings on exploring new places for leisure. The trend is growing year-on-year irrespective of the changes on the global stage. With this growth come the challenges. Today's traveller does not want to spread his vacation too thin on too many things. Thanks to the communication revolution, he picks a destination after a lot of research, and comes to a destination with a definite bend of mind. He is very selective when it comes to choosing destinations and products. Traditional travel products no longer fascinate the evolved world traveller. What he is looking for, is niche or special interest tourism products. Today, there are a lot of niche travel segments, known by a whole lot of fancy names. Popular ones are Eco, Rural, Cruise, Sports, Adventure and Wildlife Tourism. But there are a lot of lesser-known niche segments gaining ground in the list. These include Ancestral Tourism, Tribal Tourism, Volunteer

Tourism, Student Travel, Lesbian Gay Bisexual & Transgender travel (GLBT), Photographic Tourism, Gastronomic Tourism, etc. For niche travel, the sky is literally the limit. There is even a new concept called 'Space Tourism'.

The Ministry of Tourism has identified some 'niche' tourism segments in India and wants to create and promote them as tourist attractions, both in the domestic and international circuits.

Top 10 Indian States visited by foreigners for tourism and the number of people who visited each state

1. Maharashtra – 51,20,287
2. Tamil Nadu – 35,61,740
3. Delhi – 23,45,980
4. Uttar Pradesh – 19,94,495
5. Rajasthan – 14,51,370
6. West Bengal – 12,19,610
7. Bihar – 10,96,933
8. Kerala – 7,93,696
9. Karnataka – 5,95,359
10. Himachal Pradesh – 5,00,284

Source: 'India tourism statistics at a glance' Incredible India 2013 (Ministry of Tourism report). From the same report, we also have the Top 5 countries whose citizens have visited India (for the year – 2010). They are: 1. USA, 2. UK, 3. Bangladesh, 4. Canada, 5. Germany.

As you can see, considerable number of people from abroad visit India every year and they come from far off places like North America and Europe. In addition to the traditional pull, it's also important to have modern tourist amenities so that tourists can have a memorable experience.

The Ministry of Tourism, India is doing its bit to promote some 'niche' tourist segments in India.

The Working Group on Tourism (WGT)

Constituted by the Planning Commission for the 12th Five Year Plan has proposed wide-ranging strategies. As per these strategies, there will be increased emphasis on skill development and capacity building for bridging the huge gap in demand and supply in skilled manpower in the hospitality sector. For developing tourism infrastructure based on carrying capacity and sustainability principles, professional agencies will be employed. Infrastructure gap in tourism destinations and circuits will be systematically covered. Greater emphasis on creating rural tourism clusters and tourism parks by adopting strategies based on convergences of resources will be specially emphasized upon. For promoting the brand of "Incredible India" publicity and promotional programmes of the Ministry will be made product specific, country specific and destination specific.

Appointment of India Tourism

Representative Offices will contribute in a big way in attracting larger number of foreign tourists. There will be focused emphasis on promoting tourism which is sustainable by adopting carrying capacity studies specially in environmentally sensitive areas. There will be more attention on promoting niche tourism products, attempting greater convergence amongst different stakeholders, and in rationalization of taxes in tourism sector.

Positioning of Niche Tourism Products

Academic literature has paid little attention to the positioning of niche tourism products. The development of niche tourism products has been a response by the tourism industry to diversify their product base to capture new, emergent tourist markets and build a more diverse customer base. Therefore, establishing very defined and individualised niches has allowed smaller independent tourism operators to compete in the highly price sensitive and competitive tourism marketplace.

The Ministry of Tourism has taken the initiative of identifying, diversifying, developing and promoting the nascent/upcoming niche products of the tourism industry. This is done in order to overcome the aspect of 'seasonality' to promote India as a 365 days destination, attract tourists with specific interests and to ensure repeat visits for the products in which India has comparative advantage.

The following Niche Products to be identified by the Ministry of Tourism for development and Promotion:

1. Rural Tourism,
2. Adventure and Wildlife Tourism,
3. Tribal Tourism
4. Photographic Tourism Tourism

Pollachi

Pollachi is a town and a taluk headquarters in Coimbatore district, Tamil Nadu state, India. Located about 40 km to the south of Coimbatore, it is the second largest town in the district after Coimbatore. Pollachi is a very popular Marketplace, with supposedly large markets for jaggery, vegetables and cattle

Pollachi was known as "Pozhil Vaichi" roughly meaning "land of prosperity". The name Pozhil Vaichi changed to Pollachi over time. It was also known as Mudi Konda Chola Nallur during the period of Cholas.

Popular Tourist Attractions in Pollachi

Azhiyar Dam

This dam is located on the foothills of Anamalai in Western Ghats. Monkey falls deriving its name due to the abundance of monkeys found in the region is located close to the dam. Vethathiri Maharishi Yoga and Kaya Kalpa Research Foundation founded by Vethathiri Maharishi is located near Azhiyar.

Valparai

Valparai is about 65 km from Pollachi and is situated at an altitude of 3500 feet above the sea level. Valparai can be reached via Azhiyar through a hilly road with 40 hair pin bends.Solaiyar Dam is 15 km from Valparai town after Mudis and is one of the largest rock dams in India. The length of the reservoir it impounds is about 20 km.

Anamalai Wildlife Sanctuary

Anamalai Wildlife Sanctuary is situated at an average altitude of 1,400 meters in the Western Ghats near Pollachi. The area of the sanctuary is 958 km². An ecological paradise, this sanctuary encompasses a National Park and was recently been renamed as Indira Gandhi Wildlife Sanctuary and National Park.

TopSlip and Chinnakallar

TopSlip is a point located at an altitude of about 800 feet in the Anamalai mountain range. It is about 37 km from Pollachi and this small town serves as an ideal picnic spot with its wooden log houses and safaris. Chinnakallar is renowned for receiving the highest rainfall in Tamil Nadu.

Parambikulam Dam and National Park

Parambikulam Wildlife Sanctuary is situated in the valley between the Anaimalai Hills of Tamil Nadu and the Nelliampathi range of Kerala. The areas hilly and rocky, drained by several rivers, including Parambikulam, Sholayar and Thekkady. It is thickly forested with stands of bamboo, sandalwood, rosewood and teak, the sanctuary has some marshy land and scattered patches of grassland. Kannimara, one of the oldest and largest teak trees is another attraction in the sanctuary. It has a girth of 6.52 metres, height of 48.25 metres when the measurement was taken in 2003. [12][13] Parambikulam Aliya multipurpose project involves a series of dams interconnected by tunnels and canals at various elevations to harness the Parambikulam, Aliyar, Nirar, Sholiyar, Thunkadavu, Thenkkadi and Palar rivers, laid for irrigation and power generation.

Niche Tourism Products

Academic literature has paid little attention to the positioning of niche tourism products. Novelli considers 'the notion of an increasingly experienced group of tourists demanding specialist holidays to meet their specific desires' and how this has provided the conditions necessary to facilitate the growth of niche tourism. Sharpley and Telfer (2002) reflect on how tourist behavior has produced a more segmented and sophisticated consumer market, and how niche tourism is a response to these specialized consumer needs and preferences. The development of niche tourism products has been a response by the tourism industry to diversify their product base to capture new, emergent tourist markets and build a more diverse customer base. Therefore, establishing very defined and individualized niches has allowed smaller independent tourism operators to compete in the highly price sensitive and competitive tourism marketplace. Niche tourism product development is often associated with high levels of entrepreneurship at the destination and an individual desire to carve out specific market niches (Novelli, 2005). Little work has been published however, examining the relationship between niche tourism development and entrepreneurship. In trying to portray the range and diversity of niche tourism products a comprehensive theoretical framework begins to emerge and niche tourism can be seen as an important subset of tourism activities.

Adventure Tourism

Adventure travel involves exploration or travel to remote ,exotic areas. Adventure tourism is rapidly growing in popularity as a tourist seeks different kinds of vacations. Any constructive activity which tests the endurance of both a person and his equipment to its extreme limit is termed as Adventure.

Initiatives of Ministry of Tourism to Promote Adventure Tourism

As per the policy for the diversification of tourism products of India, special attention is being given for the development of Adventure Tourism in the country. The Ministry of Tourism has also introduced a voluntary scheme for Approval of Adventure Tour Operators, which is open to all bonafide adventure tour operators. The Ministry of Tourism has formulated a set of guidelines on Safety and Quality Norms on Adventure Tourism as Basic minimum standards for adventure tourism activities.

These guidelines cover Land, Air and Water based activities, which include mountaineering, trekking, hand gliding, paragliding, bungee jumping and river rafting. Central Financial Assistance is extended to various State Governments / Union Territory

Administrations for development of Tourism Infrastructure in Adventure Tourism destinations. The assistance covers facilities for trekking, rock climbing, mountaineering, aero- sports , winter/water related sports, trekker huts, wildlife viewing facilities, etc. Financial assistance for purchase of water sports equipment consisting of kayaks, canoes, paddle boats, fibre glass boats, hovercrafts, water scooters, etc. is also provided to State Governments.

Special efforts are made by the Ministry of Tourism to promote Inland Water Tourism by providing necessary infrastructure facilities. Financial assistance has been extended for construction of Double Hull Boats, construction of Jetties, Cruise Vessels, Boats, etc.

The Indian Institute of Skiing & Mountaineering (IIS&M) has been made fully operational in Gulmarg from January 2009. This institute now has its own building and all modern equipment and training facilities for adventure sports. Various adventure courses have been started and are being successfully run by this institute.

Rural and tribal Tourism

The scheme of Rural Tourism was started by the Ministry in 2002-03 with the objective of showcasing rural life, art, culture and heritage at rural locations and in villages, which have core competence in art & craft, handloom, and textiles as also an asset base in the natural environment. The intention is to benefit the local community economically and socially as well as enable interaction between tourists and local population for a mutually enriching experience. The promotion of village tourism is also aimed at generating revenue for the rural communities through tourist visitations, thereby checking migration from rural to urban areas.

Rural Tourism- A niche tourism segment in Indian tourism scene

Rural Tourism in India is now one of the niche tourism products which hold good potential to attract up market clients who would like to run away from hustle bustle of concrete city life and be in rural environment seeking mental peace. Rural home stays are designed to attract tourists who desire to learn more about the varied life styles and crafts of our many villages. This also creates jobs in villages and thus it brings a halt on the exodus from villages to major cities. This facilitates local talents service in tourism sector as stake holders. Rural Tourism thus fulfils Govt's. objective of diversification of tourism products & create local employment in distant villages. It works out very well for our country and especially boost tourism industry.

In this respect the initiative of the Ministry of Tourism, Govt. of India holds lot of merit. Purely on its merit Indian Travel Industry too have supported the project in a big way.

However the success of Rural tourism will depend on projects if they are located not more than two to three hours drive from airport or railheads. They should not also be closer to main cities then charm of Rural environment will be lost.

For success of rural tourism, there should be regular capacity building progammes so that local people can be real stake holders. Local be trained for creating local flavour. They should be trained to create souvenirs, promoting local dance, costumes and food which are based on local agricultural products. Locals interest be given prime consideration & not commercialization of the rural tourism product.

The objective should be to create a sustainable level of visitor numbers and revenue without sacrificing traditional community assets. Essentially whole efforts should be to promote a form of tourism that meets four essential criteria namely.

- Environment conservation including waste management.
- Community participation.
- Sustainable operation
- Visitor satisfaction.

India's geographical spread and cultural diversity provide multiple interest all season visitor experiences. This creates a major tourism opportunity to position the Indian rural tourism product as a unique visitor experience in low impact settings. The visitors come nearer to India 's rural heritage as they vibe with the present. Rural tourism connects the visitor from the frenetic present with traditional assets of communities whose domain lies off the beaten track. It gives due weight age to women in civil society, the primacy of human developments & preservation of heritage. Rural Tourism puts special packages in art & craft imparted by skilled local/ artisans, village entertainment group unveil local history & culture, natural and oral treasurers. Thus it ensures government's developmental plan for economic & social development on environmental sustainability through rural tourism projects.

Ministry of Tourism has added another 103 new rural tourism centers for development in its gamut of product development due to its sustainable prospects & environment. Rural tourism is going to be India 's niche special interest demand segments that holds resilient power. Join India 's Rural Tourism experience.

Tourism Product Development

Product development improves the profitability of tourism businesses by increasing the number of products and services available for tourists – as well as the number of visits, length of stay and spending by individual visitors.

The Product Development focuses on development and provision of experiences, services and infrastructure that exceeds customer expectations. With particular emphasis on the following:

- Protecting our natural environment and culture.
- Strengthening and building on tourism demand influencers.
- A focus on shoulder and winter season.
- Strengthening and building on destination areas.
- Strengthening touring corridors and community hubs.
- Filling gaps.
- Generally upgrading and enhancing the market readiness of tourism products and services.
- Improving traveller services and transportation infrastructure, most particularly ferry services and highway signage.
- Strengthening the industry and government organizations.

Product development, whether it be the development of new products or refreshment of existing products is the cornerstone for the success of a tourism business. Without appropriate products or services that are relevant to visitor demand a business cannot survive. Product development should be based on the findings of the 'Planning' process of business development, in particular the situation analysis and strategic planning phases. The planning process identifies the market potential and goals for business development and growth, while the product development phase is the implementation of specific actions for the business.

A product development plan can be developed as a guide for the successful management of the product development and implementation process. A product development plan looks at the marketing mix including product, price, place, promotion and packaging. The type of product development will depend on the stage of development of the business. The Passages to Innovation Program developed by the Canadian Tourism Commission identifies the four quadrants of product development:

- **Q1 – Existing Customers / Existing Products:** a low risk strategy that aims to refresh existing products for the current market segments;
- **Q2 – New Customers / Existing Products:** a medium risk strategy that looks at repositioning existing products with a new market segment;
- **Q3 – New Customers / New Products:** a very high risk category that all new businesses start in. Extensive research and a unique selling point is required;
- **Q4 – Existing Customers / New Product:** a high risk strategy that presents new products to existing customers that are stilled aligned with the markets needs.

Niche Tourism Life cycle:

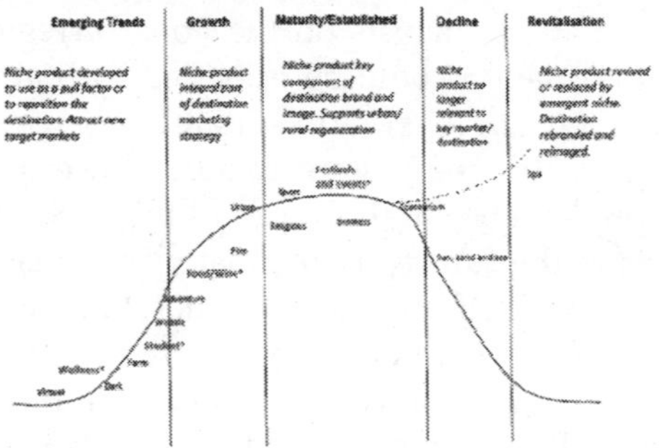

Applying the model

Leadership/Organizational Board

The development of a regional brand is an ongoing process rather than a mere, short term image campaign. For this reason, an action research approach is suggested as a methodology as it allows an ongoing (spiral like) process of analysis, implementation and control with the objective of continuous improvement of quality levels. Considerable funds and resources should be recruited for the brand development. Leadership should also assess its level of experience and expertise in terms of brand development. In case of lacking experience and expertise, the co-operation with academic institutions and/or consultancies is suggested.

Members of the Organizational Board should be aware that, due to the variety of stakeholders involved, regional brand development is a complex undertaking and requires an integrating, charismatic, visionary and value orientated leader (i.e. coming from municipality and/or Destination Marketing Organization) being able to align all stakeholders behind the region's brand. Tour operators are not recommended as leading change agents due to a perceived lack of sociological know how.

As a kick off, leadership should provide a sense of urgency by highlighting the contribution of niche tourism and its related entrepreneurial activities to economic prosperity and sustainability of the region. The convincingly communicated benefits relate to harmonizing competition for resources, investment and tourism and for addressing urgent social issues like social exclusion and cultural diversity.

A thorough situation analysis on the Pollachi region should be conducted. Information could be provided by both, quantitative (direct consumer surveys) and qualitative research (expert views). Research topics of interest could concern, for example, the tourists' provenience in the past and the desired provenience of the tourists in the future, a potential mix of macro and micro niches, de-seasonalization opportunities, the niche tourists' current region brand's associations, current media recognition of the Pollachi region, perceptions and attitudes towards the region's brand of residents, desired identity factors of tourists and potential residents, or measuring the actual brand utilization score (potential assets versus actual strength).

As part of the initial analysis, leadership also should assess the current level of development of the Pollachi area based on Butler's TALC model (2006). Related to this stage, the required competitive factors should be assessed. Related to competitiveness factors, Ritchie's and Crouch's (1993 in Wilde and Cox, 2008) Calgary Model could be used as reflective tools. Competitiveness competences gaps should be elicited to be bridged by education, training or strategic alliances. A current coherent model interlinking the development stages of the tourism area with respective competitive factors, however, is still missing (Wilde and Cox, 2008).

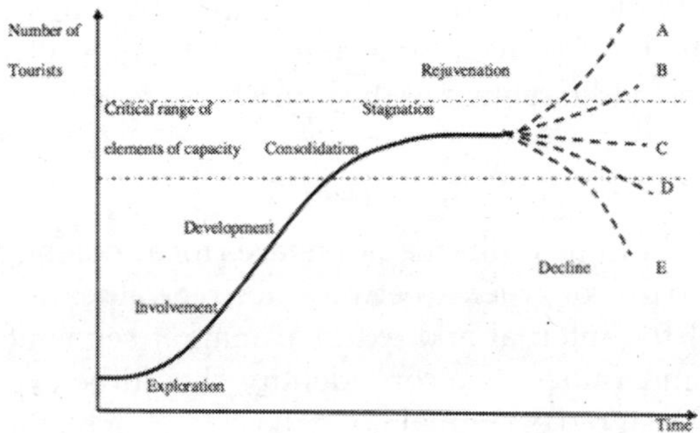

Butler's TALC model

Conceptual model of destination competitiveness

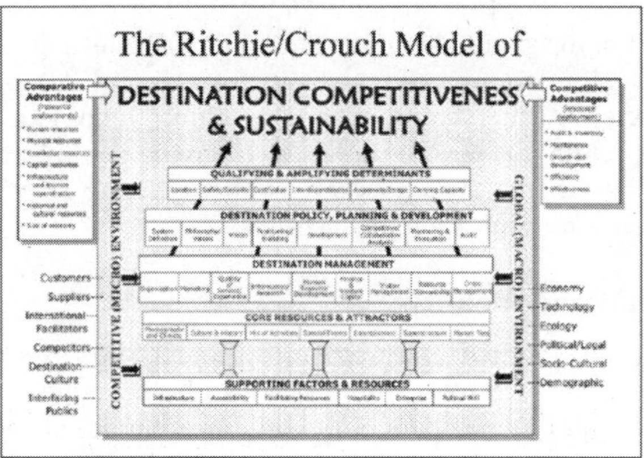

Based on the research a vision and mission statement for the Pollachi Region Brand emerges, which has to be desired by the stakeholders.

The challenge in providing cross-niche packages is seen to avoid tapping into the trap of over-standardization. Promising new niche tourism fields for Southern India as, for example, the enogastronomic, minor cultural itineraries, sport tourism, naturalist tourism ones, link between agritourism and rural tourism, cultural heritage (Rural Tourism, Adventure and Wildlife Tourism, Tribal Tourism and Photographic Tourism) should be considered as well.

Markets and Market segments

Research should lead to a clear quantitative assessment of market potential followed by a precise definition of the niches, prioritization and targeting of the tourists.

Core Identity of the Region Brand

Congruence of values is the magic panacea for attracting resources. This refers to the congruence between desired values (i.e. character identity) of the internal and external market segments and the region's brand values. The core identity should be expressed by Corporate Design (i.e. symbol, logo, flag) to which other existing corporate brands of involved stakeholders should be aligned to.

Positioning of core Region brand identity

The positioning should be communicated in a believable, durable, relevant, simple, appealing, distinctive, communicable, and deliverable way and should be of salient importance to the target segment (Quin, 2008). The target is to create positive pictorial associations in the stakeholders' as the 'guiding stars' for all integrated communication mix activities.

Internal Brand Identity

Creating an internal place identity refers, for example, to increasing the level of identification with the region's brand. First of all, all the members of the organization board should be dedicated to the vision and mission of the City brand. It is strongly suggested to directly and continuously involve the population and all stakeholders in the branding project to assure continuous support and later authentic delivery of the brand and to design the tourism services for them as well. A number of public training and communication sessions will have to take place to achieve this.

External brand identity

When choosing alliances and partnerships care should be taken that compatibility as to objectives and values exists. Strategic Alliances could refer to towns, such as Salerno, or destination clusters integrating the offers of the Pollachi region as an added service value or international twin cities.

Promotion strategies have to be based on scientifically conducted consumer research to enhance customer knowledge (i.e. identity). A place image has to be created triggering favourable place associations. This, in turn, contributes to building powerful brand origins benefiting local products and services.

Creative, imaginative and inspiring promotional strategies based on uniqueness and typicality, conveyed in appropriate media, are suggested to be developed by advertising experts. Especially advertising image strategies are proposed in this context, but also tourism exhibitions and PR activities. The various promotion techniques are suggested to be 'down to earth', reflecting depth, values and emotions.

Although TV advertising (due to its reach and ability to create intimacy) is regarded as the 'queen' of the 'above the line' promotion, intensive CRM related 'below the line' promotion should forge close customer relationships, i.e. via loyalty schemes, marketing information systems, special events or city cards integrating multiple visits to trigger visit returns and the increase of the average duration of stay. In this case, branding and CRM, often seen as mutually exclusive, are perceived as twins.

Due to the high level of sophistication and individualism of the niche tourism segment, modern IT should be used to directly approach those applying modern social media.

Diffusion of Region identity

The diffusion of the City Brand identity requires continuous close co-ordination as well as efficient collective and individual communications and training. The Leadership/Organization Board is suggested to employ a 'caretaker' for the coherent diffusion of the region's identity.

An increase in the penetration rate of the distribution system is seen as vital for Southern India. Important seems to initiate a mediating role of large tour operators mass and/or small scale specialist tour operators and a decision has to be made if co-operation is sought with large scale or specialist tourist operators. Taking entrepreneurial, specialist knowledge as well as local economic aspects into account, the latter ones seem to be preferable.

Past research points to a potential difficulty to align SMEs to the region brand objectives due to the diversity of corporate objectives inherent in entrepreneurialism. However, to build an efficient network of small firms is indispensable, for example to create a local hospitality and retailing system.

Authentic delivery of region brand's positioning

Authenticity requires the core identity of the region brand not only to be consistently communicated, but to be consistently 'lived and done' by all stakeholders. In this way, the positioning statement and core values are authentically and credibly experienced by the segments. A special emphasis is suggested to be put on training SMEs as they represent the lion share of companies which actually deliver the brand values in the various experiential service touch points.

Control of Region branding success

Quantitative and qualitative measures (i.e. increase of tourist figures, retention rates, aided and unaided recalls of core values and pictorial associations, improved perceptions, increased international media coverage) are put in place checking the overall success of the region's brand strategy in general and the authenticity of the region's brand identity in particular. Successful criteria for destination brand development might be derived from Anholt's index (2007) as well as Saffron's European City Brand

Barometer (http://saffron-consultants.com).The ultimate region's branding success is achieved when the quality of life and the relationships have improved. Various TQM related assessment tools for the tourism service providers can be regarded as control mechanism as well.

Conclusion

The paper concisely suggests the steps to develop an Pollachi regional brand based on a synthesis of relevant models and criteria. It reflects the importance of leadership, creativity, identity and co-operation to create and authentically live the region brand both internally and externally. It also creates awareness that the region brand building process is not always ' a bed of roses'.

References:

Marina novelli 2005, niche tourism contemporary issues, trends and cases

kevin hannam, anya diekmann 2010 tourism and india: a critical introduction, 139-142.

Ad aesthetics overseas pvt. Ltd., new delhi 2005 welcome to india Richard buck, agritours north america inc.

Rural tourism and agri-tourism a practical approach to niche tourism.

N.prabakaran & n.panchanatham niche tourism products of india abasyn journal of social sciences vol. 6 no. 1

J. M. Ali-knight 2011 phd by published worksthe role of niche tourism products in destination development

India tourism statisticsat a glance 2012 ministry of tourism

Web sites:

http://www.failteireland.ie/Develop-Your-Business/Work-With-Local-Partners/Destination-Lifecycle-Table.aspx

http://www.tourism.gov.in/AboutUs/DivisionDetails.aspx?DID=262144

http://shyamchat.hubpages.com/hub/niche_tourism_1

http://safariplus.co.in/KanjilalArticle.aspx?GId=15

http://www.travelbizmonitor.com/niche-tourism--opportunities-for-india-14794

ECOTOURISM: CONSERVATION OF NATURE AND DEVELOPMENT OF LOCALS THROUGH PARTICIPATION

Pramendra Singh, pramendra58@gmail.com

Ravindra Singh, singhravindra007@gmail.com

Sandeep Dubey, sandeep.kanyakubj@gmail.com

Abstract

Tourism is a multifaceted and multidimensional industry having diverse implications. Tourism is an activity which is prompted to visit and see different places around the world. These visits to the different destinations are made by the visitors for different purposes or to witness the different things. These visits may be motivated to see the culture, heritage, flora, fauna and other things of a particular destination. And they are subsequently known as different types of tourism based on their name and character. Ecotourism is one the types of tourism where visitors are intended to see the nature, flora, fauna and environment of a particular place without hampering or adversely affecting its ecology. Ecotourism is not only the engagement of the visitors with the local people and the environment but also meant to safeguard it by creating awareness amongst the society and contributing in the upliftment of local people through the conservation of nature in the form of treasure. Ecotourism has been doing well for the benefit of the local community by providing job opportunities, bolstering their economy and also conserving the nature through tourism.

Keywords: Tourism, Ecotourism, Environment, Wildlife, Conservation of Nature, Community Development.

Introduction

United Nations World Tourism Organization (UNWTO) defined Ecotourism as 'The Tourism that involves traveling to relatively undisturbed or uncontaminated areas with the specific objective of studying, admiring and enjoying the scenery and its wild plants and animals as well as any existing cultural manifestations (both past and present) found in these areas' (Ceballos-Lascurain, 1980s).

The International Eco-Tourism Society (TIES, 1990) defines 'Ecotourism as Responsible travel to natural areas that conserves the environment and improves the well-being of local people'.

World Conservation Union (formerly known as International Union for Conservation of Nature) defined Ecotourism as 'Environmentally responsible travel to natural areas in order to enjoy and appreciate nature (and accompanying cultural features, both past and present) that promote conservation, have a low visitor impact and provide for beneficially active socio-economic involvement of local people. (Ceballos-Lascurain,1996)

'Ecotourism is travel to fragile, pristine and usually protected areas that strive to be low impact and (usually) small scale. It helps educate the traveler; provides funds for the conservation; directly benefits the local environment and political empowerment of local communities; and political empowerment of local communities and fosters respect for different cultures and for human rights' (Martha Honey).

Ecotourism is a nature based activity where visitors travel to a place and make as little environmental impact as possible. This activity is motivated towards the sustainability and conservation of the nature, wildlife, flora, fauna and their habitats. Ecotourism not only confined to visiting the nature based areas or wildlife but it is also directed towards contributing in the development of local community environmentally, culturally and economically. It is also directed towards imparting sustainable knowledge to the other member of the society. This type of tourism is gaining momentum with every passing day because of the concern of depleting environment, nature and wildlife in this modern world. People are now encouraged and motivated to visit the nature based fragile and sensitive areas and make as much contributions as possible for wellbeingness of all.

Objectives of The Study

The study focuses and envisages achieving the following objectives:-

- To emphasize the role of Ecotourism in conservation of nature.
- To highlight the contribution of Ecotourism in the wellbeingness of local community through tourism.
- To bring to fore the laws and acts made by government of India and other organizations for the conservation of nature and the promotion of tourism together.
- To give suggestions how ecotourism could be more conducive in the conservation of nature and the development of local people through participation.
- To lay emphasis for working on more ecotourism projects and destinations.

Methodology

The paper is depending upon conceptual study. There have been so many scholars contributed as far as the ecotourism and its concepts are concerned. They had tried to disseminate the knowledge regarding the Ecotourism and its different aspects. Not only the scholars but also the Indian government and its different agencies made historic decisions by enacting stringent laws and acts to safeguard the nature, wildlife and their inhabitants. The study has been motivated to bring to fore all those contributions made by different stakeholders and their implications

Literature Review

The declaration of international year of ecotourism by UN and UNWTO in 2002 propagated the principles and philosophies of ecotourism for preservation of the environment and ecology. The objective is to enlighten the visitors to enjoy nature and get inspired for the conservation of nature. As a result, wildlife sanctuaries, national parks, lakes, backwaters, coral reefs and islands are identified as the ideal site for the implementation of ecotourism projects in a sustainable manner. It is the objective of all ecotourism projects to ensure the conservation of natural scenic beauty for prosperity. The concept of ecotourism is certainly the panacea for nature conservation in the protected areas and it draws attention of visitors, planners, policy-makers, promoters and tour operators for their invaluable contributions for sustainable tourism development. Above all, community participation and nature conservation is the prime objective of all ecotourism projects.

Ecotourism has achieved a great deal of popularity in the last eight years by increasing interest in visiting natural areas, experiencing authentic local living and observing wildlife have continued to grow among the nature and wildlife lovers. The ecotourism community, therefore continues to face significant challenges in generating awareness and education for actively working against green washing within the tourism industry. Hence, the ecotourism community is expected to be more inclusive of innovative and socially equitable approaches. The innovative approach must include active mobilization of indigenous communities, women, local professionals and designers as the leaders for sustainable development. (S K Swain & J M Mishra, 2012)

Ecotourism is nature based tourism and is primarily concerned with the direct enjoyment of some relatively undisturbed phenomenon of nature. For such tourism to be ecologically responsible, it must be appropriate for the specific location and should produce no permanent degradation of natural environment. When developing responsible tourism, maintaining the quality of the environment is not only desirable but necessary for maintaining visitor satisfaction. If the tourism product declines in quality, it will result ultimately, in a decline of the tourism economy. (IGNOU, 2008)

There are four main links between tourism and environment: components of natural environment as the basis for a marketable tourism attraction or product; management of tourism operations so as to minimize or reduce their environmental impacts; economic or material contribution of tourism to conservation, either directly or indirectly; and attitude of tourists towards the environment and environmental education of clients by tourist operators. Therefore there are environmental aspects to every major component of tourism business; products and markets, management, money and people. (Ralf Buckley,1994)

Ecotourism is still a relatively small segment of the overall tourism sector. At the same time, it is one of the fastest growing tourism segments and further rapid growth is expected in the future. Its main features include:

- All forms of nature tourism aimed at the appreciation of both the natural world and the traditional cultures located in natural areas;
- Deliberate efforts to minimize the harmful human impact on the natural and socio-cultural environment; and
- Support for the protection of natural and cultural assets and the well being of host communities.

The Quebec declaration (Canada, 2002)stresses that, if carried out responsibly, ecotourism can be a valuable means for promoting the socio-economic development of host communities while generating resources for the preservation of natural and cultural assets. In this way, ecologically fragile areas can be protected with the financial returns of ecotourism activities. (Frederico Neto, 2003)

Godde (1999) explains community participation and sustainable development. He says there are three types of community participations: functional, interactive and self-mobilizating. The functional participation refers to community involvement to facilitate the successful resolution of the project. This type of involvement may include decision making, when it is necessary to achieve project goals. The interactive participation refers to involvement for intrinsic reasons, wide involvement of stakeholders and openness in the system. There is a need for appropriate institutions and operational structures to make more interactive participation. Self-mobilization is another form of participation where expert advice is contracted for support and informed decisions are taken by the community.

Williams (1998) discussed that tourism-environmental relationships are not just fundamental, but also highly complex. There is as mutual dependence between the two that is often described as symbiotic.

Middleton and Hawkins (1998) explained that, on one hand, in terms of the environment, the quality of natural resources such as landscape, air, sea, water, fresh water and flora and fauna need to be preserved, while on the other hand, the magnificence of cultural resources are judged to have intrinsic value and are worthy of conservation.

Ecological sustainability is the maximum capacity of an ecosystem to ensure the functioning of the biotic and abiotic species depending directly and indirectly on the natural resources of the area. It is the process of maintaining the rich biodiversity for the long term. It consists of human actions that maintain the capacity of ecosystems to produce the range of goods and services upon which all life depends. Ecologically sustainable tourism is viewed as the development of tourism that contributes to the maintenance of the ecosystem without damaging the core elements for the promotion of nature-based tourism. At the same time, the intense demand from tourists is extracted from the ecosystem and natural areas. As a result, it may degrade or even threaten the very existence of species in the ecosystem. (S K Swain & J M Mishra, 2012).

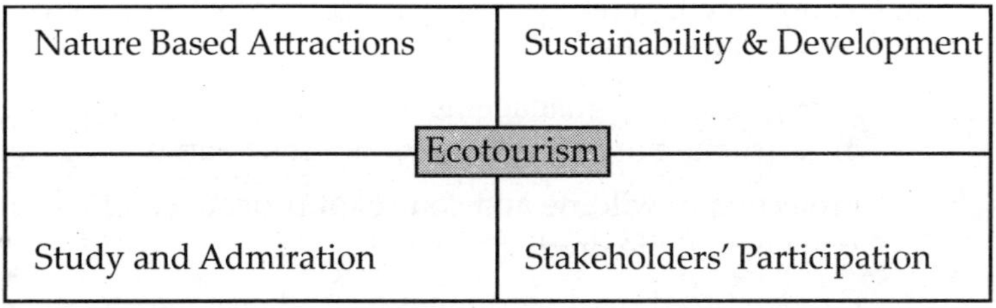

Nature Based Attractions	Sustainability & Development
Ecotourism	
Study and Admiration	Stakeholders' Participation

The above figure shows the different aspects of Ecotourism.

Thenmala is one of the world's leading ecotourism destinations. It is first planned ecotourism project in India. The famous site is located about 72km from Thiruvananthapuram in Kerala at the foothills of Western Ghats. This project is aimed at protecting the local endangered species of flora which has many medicinal values and also to protect other species of flora. The project also ensures emanating education for the ecotourism and conservation of nature. It also has many advantages for the community and the local people because of its commitment for their development through active participation in all means. This project has won many international and national awards and inspiring others to develop such kinds of ecotourism destinations.

Laws and Acts Conducive for the Conservation of Wild-life- Environment and Development of Ecotourism

The Union government of India possesses all the rights to exercise to enact the laws and acts to safeguard the environment from depletion and to conserve the wildlife habitats. There are some very important laws and acts mentioned below which were enacted by the government of India time to time. And they proved very handy in the conservation of wildlife and its habitants. The laws range covering different constituents of environment like land, water, forests etc. Some of the Acts which were passed by the Government of India for the conservation and protection of wildlife, nature and its inhabitants are as follows:

- The Wildlife (Protection) Act, 1972 and Wildlife (Protection) Amendment Act, 1991

  The Wildlife (Protection) Act governs wildlife conservation and protection of endangered species. The Act prohibits trade in rare and endangered species. The centre provides financial assistance to states for:

  1. Strengthening management and protection of infrastructure of national parks and sanctuaries
  2. Protection of wildlife and control of poaching and illegal trade in wildlife products
  3. Captive breeding programmes for endangered species of wildlife
  4. Wildlife education and interpretation and
  5. Development of selected zoos etc.

- The Environment (Protection) Act, 1986

  The Environment (Protection) Act was passed by the parliament on 23rd May, 1986. By virtue of this Act, the Union

Government has armed itself with considerable powers deemed necessary for the prevention, control and abatement of environmental pollution. The powers include:

1. Coordination of action by states
2. Planning and execution of nationwide programmes
3. Laying down environmental quality standards specially those governing emission or discharge of environmental pollutants
4. Placing restrictions on the location of industries etc.

   The powers claimed are indeed comprehensive; the coverage includes handling of

   Hazardous substances, prevention of environmental accidents, research, inspection of

   Polluting units, establishment of laboratories, dissemination of information, etc.

- Forests Act, 1927
  1. Setting up and managing Reserved Forests, Village Forests and Protected Forests
  2. Protection of non-government forests and lands
  3. Control of movement of forest produce
  4. Control of grazing or trespass by cattle in forest land etc.
- Forest (Conservation) Act,1980

  Prohibiting or restricting non-forest use of forest lands etc.
- Prevention of Cruelty to Animals Act, 1960
  1. Restrictions on cruel treatment of animals including use, transportation and trade
  2. Restrictions on use of animals for purpose of experimentation and performances etc.
- Fisheries Act, 1897
  1. Prohibition on use of explosives for fishing
  2. Prohibition on use of poisons for fishing
  3. Regulation on fishing in private waters with the consent of owners/right holders etc.

- The Insecticide Act, 1968

  Pesticides are toxic chemicals and uncontrolled use brings hazards and ecological consequences. To protect the environment, its flora and the health of the citizens the Government of India enacted this Act. This Act was enforced from 1971 to regulate import, manufacture, sale, transport, distribution and use of insecticides with a view to preventing risk to human beings and animals. Several agencies such as the Central Insecticide Board, The Pesticide Registration Committee, The Pesticide Environment Pollution Advisory Committee, The Central Insecticide Laboratory, The committee to Ban/Restrict the use of Pesticides, were created for effective enforcement of this Act.

- The Water (Prevention and Control of Pollution) Act, 1974

  The Water Act defines water pollution, prescribes penalties and establishes administrative machinery called the Water Pollution Boards at the central and State level in order to control and prevent pollution of water. The coverage of the Act is quite comprehensive in that it includes streams, river water courses, inland waters, subterranean waters, and sea and tidal waters under state jurisdiction.

- The Air (Prevention and Control of Pollution) Act, 1981

  The Act was passed to mainly regulate and control emissions from automobiles and industrial plants. The Central Boards for the Prevention and Control of Water Pollution is authorized to implement and enforce the Act.

  Apart from the above Acts there are numerous Acts which were passed by the Government of India to conserve and protect the environment and its constituents from degradation and depletion. These Acts proved very conducive in the restoration of environment, its flora and fauna.

  (From Conservation of Biological Diversity in India: An Approach, Ministry of Environment and Forests, 1974)

  Ecotourism therefore is closely association with these Acts and laws. All the tourism activities which are directed at any place or point of time are governed through the regulations provided therein. The objectives of Ecotourism serve the needs of making these Acts and laws. Ecotourism activities are motivated towards making the visitors aware about the threats and problems which are being faced by the environment and its inhabitants. Ecotourism is about not only the conservation of natural resources but also the preservation of Cultural and Heritage resources. The visitors are told to stick to all rules and regulations which have been enacted to conserve and protect the environment or nature and its constituents by creating a sense of awareness and responsibility towards it. The visitors contribute in the management of the nature or environment by making significant contribution economically, hence the local community or the local people are benefited. And the local people are encouraged in the participation of Ecotourism and its activities.

Suggestions

To ensure responsible growth of Tourism without causing irreversible damage to the natural environment, activities relating to tourism should take care of the following:

- The volume and type of tourism activity must be balanced against the sensitivity and carrying capacity of the resources being used and developed.
- When developing Ecotourism, maintaining the quality of the environment is not only desirable but necessary for maintaining visitor satisfaction.
- Development of Tourism in harmony with the environmental conditions and without affecting the lifestyle of local people.
- Restriction on indiscriminate growth of Tourism and strict regulation of the tourist activities in sensitive areas such as hill slopes, islands, coastal stretches, National Parks and Sanctuaries.
- Visitors can contribute a lot in the Conservation of nature. And the attempts should be made to increase awareness, enlist support for environmental measures, alter personal behaviors and advocate for responsible development from the visitors.
- Public awareness must be generated.

- Environmental activists and organizations must be encouraged.
- More Ecotourism destinations need to be established.

Conclusion

Tourism is one of the fastest growing industry in the world. It is contributing a lot in socio-economic development of any region or place by generating revenue through tourism activities, generating employment for the local people to cater the needs of the tourists or visitors at a place and by giving opportunity to the people of different ethnic background to come close to one another and know one another's culture and heritage through tourism. Tourism in today's world is being given prime attention by the concern authorities and governments because of its far flung advantages. And every country and region is concentrating on the plans and policies to cash on the multifaceted benefits of tourism.

Tourism activities are of different types based on the nature and purpose of the visit. It is not always necessary that tourism contribute in positive sense. There are some situations when tourism can have adverse effect on the environment and the host community if it is not planned properly. So it become very crucial for the concern persons or authority to plan for such type of tourism which could benefit them in all senses. The tourism activity should contribute in the protection and conservation of their environment, benefit the local people through participation and disseminate education and training to the other people towards it. To fulfill these needs, Ecotourism is the best option and solution.

Ecotourism is widely accepted and implemented form of tourism in today's era which makes people aware about the environment of a particular place and its importance. The people and visitors are encouraged to protect the environment along with exploiting the benefit from its uniqueness, because every flora and fauna has its utmost importance in this world and these need to be conserved for the existence of the human beings. Therefore this form of tourism commonly known as Ecotourism has to be encouraged and planned in well manner.

References

Beaumont, N., (2001). Ecotourism and the Conservation Ethic: Recruiting the uninitiated or preaching to the converted?, Journal of Sustainable Tourism, Vol.9, No.4.

Benson, A. & Clifton, J., (2006), Planning for sustainable ecotourism: The case for research ecotourism in developing country destinations, Journal of Sustainable Tourism, Vol. 14, No. 3.

Blamey, R.K. & Braithwaite V.A., (1997), A Social values segmentation of the potential ecotourism market, Journal of Sustainable Tourism, Vol.5, No.1.

Boyd, S. W. & Butler, R. W. (1996).Managing Ecotourism: An opportunity spectrum approach, Tourism Management, Vol.17, No.8, pp. 557-566.

Buckley, R. (1994). Research Note, a framework for ecotourism. Annals ofTourism Research. pp. 21(3):661–669.

Campbell, L. M., (1999), Ecotourism in rural developing communities, Annals of Tourism Research, Vol.26, No.3, pp. 534-553.

Ceballos-Lascurain, H. (1996). Tourism, Ecotourism, and Protected Areas.

Ecology, Environment and Tourism,(2008). Indira Gandhi Open University, pp 29-50.

Environment and Conservation Ethics,(2008). Indira Gandhi Open University, pp 12-16

IUCN. The International Union for the Conservation of Nature. 301 pp.

Neto, F. (2003), A New Approach to Sustainable Tourism Development: Moving Beyond Environmental Protection. Natural Resource Forum, 212-222.

Nowaczek, A. "Ecotourism: Principles and Practices" Annals of Tourism Research 37.1 (2010):270–271.

Scheyvens, R., 1999, Ecotourism and the empowerment of local communities. Tourism management, 20: 245–249.

Stem, C.J., Lassoie, J.P., Lee, D.R., Deshler, D.D. & Schelhas, J.W.,

(2003), Community participation in ecotourism benefits: The link to conservation practices and perspectives, Society and Natural Resources,16, 387-413.

Swain, S. K. & Mishra, J. M. (2012). Tourism Principles and Practices, Oxford University Press, pp 502-514.

Weaver, D. B., (2005), Comprehensive and Minimalist dimensions of ecotourism, Annals of Tourism Research, Vol. 32, No.2, pp. 439-455.

Wight, P.A. (1993). Ecotourism: Ethics or Eco-sell. Journal of Travel Research.pp. 31(3):3–9.

https://www.ecotourism.org/

http://www.tourism.gov.in/

http://www.ecotourismsocietyofindia.org/

http://mfp.mpforest.org/eco/

ENTREPRENEURSHIP IN TOURISM AND HOSPITALITY INDUSTRY: PREVIEWS, VIEWS AND REVIEWS

Prashant Kumar Gautam

Assistant Professor

University Institute of Hotel Management and Tourism, Panjab University, Chandigarh

Prashant.k.gautam@gmail.com

Abstract

Present paper is an attempt in having an insight of entrepreneurial opportunities in tourism and hospitality industry. The paper reaches on the conclusions that the recent emphasis on entrepreneurship has been coupled with developments in education and teaching. The growth and diversity of the hospitality, leisure, tourism and sports industries along with increases in consumer expectations of their leisure time and experiences has placed greater demands on providers. Consequently graduates with entrepreneurial abilities, good technical, business and interpersonal skills are increasingly being sought by employers. In this paper author has attempted to discuss the core issues related with the entrepreneurship for the tourism and hospitality industry.

Key Words: Tourism and Hospitality Industry, Entrepreneurship.

As tourism sector is one of the major component of the service sector in India, its growth targets has to be linked to the targeted growth of service sector during the 12th Five Year Plan. Indian economy is expected to grow at the rate of 9%. To achieve this, services sector as well as the tourism sector has to grow at the rate of 12 % per annum. The current rate of growth in tourism sector is about 9 %. For improving the growth in tourism sector, persistent and concerted efforts have to be made during the 12th Plan. (Working Group on Tourism for 12th Five Year Plan)

Table 1: Key Targets and Focus for Tourism Sector

Key Target	Focus on Tourism
Foreign Tourist Arrivals (FTAs)	• Number of FTAs in 2016 is estimated to be 11.24 million. • Increase India's share of International Tourist arrivals to at least 1 % by end of 12th Plan - requiring an annual growth of 12.38% during 2011- 2016.
Domestic Tourism	• Number of Domestic Tourist Visits (DTVs) in 2016 are estimated to be 1451.46 million
Foreign Exchange Earnings(FEEs)	• The Foreign Exchange Earnings from Tourism will increase from Rs. 64889 crore (US$ 14.19 Billion) in 2010 to Rs. 134383 crore (US$ 30.3 Billion) in 2016. • Additional FEE from Tourism during 2010-16 are estimated to be Rs. 69494 crore (US$ 15.7 Billion).
Employment Generation	• Using the data on share of tourism in the total jobs in the country available from Tourism Satellite Accounts (TSA) for 2002-03 and estimated for years till 2007-08, the total number of jobs (direct and indirect) in the tourism sector in 2016 are estimated to be 77.5 million as compared to 53 million in 2010. • Therefore, an additional employment of 24.5 million (direct and indirect) is likely to be created during in 2010 to 2016.
Manpower Requirement in Hospitality Sector	The total employment in Hospitality Sector (Hotels-classified and unclassified, eating outlets, Tour Operators, Travel Agents and Medical & Wellness units) in selected years are estimated to be as follows:- Table-1 A • In year 2011-12 : 43.84 (Lakhs Employment) • In year 2012-13 : 47.26 (Lakhs Employment) • In year 2016-17 : 63.79 (Lakhs Empolyment)
Accommodation Units	• The existing accommodation units may not be sufficient for the targeted number of FTAS and DTVs in 2016. The availability of number of rooms in 2010 and requirement of additional rooms in 2016 for the targeted growth of tourism during the 12th Five Year Plan are given in Table-1B

Table 1 A: Manpower Required in Hospitality Sector

Year	Requirement (Lakhs)	Supply (Lakhs)	Gap (lakhs)
2011-12	5.83	0.52	5.32
2012-13 (estimated)	6.26	0.56	5.70
2016-17 (estimated)	8.29	0.75	7.54

Table 1 B : Accommodation Units

Availability of Hotel Rooms 2010	Classified	128771
	Unclassified	2583519
	Total	2712290
Requirement of Hotel Rooms 2016	Classified	310523
	Unclassified	4661807
	Total	4972330
Additional Requirement in 2016	Classified	181752
	Unclassified	2078288
	Total	2260040

How to meet the challenges?

Entrepreneurship is the answer

To meet the immediate as well as long term challenges of industry, increase and development of concept of entrepreneurship needed to be focused. This will serve three purposes:

- To meet the growing demand created by the increasing number of tourists.
- To deal with the relationship of skill-knowledge.
- To meet the challenges put forward by global economic environment.

Over the last two decades the business environment in India has undergone tremendous change. The result is a restructuring of economic and social systems in a way which has led to increased levels of business formation, innovation, new organizational forms, and more general shifts in attitudes and behaviour.

This mirrored a transition from a managerial to an entrepreneurial society which was evident in the USA in the 1970s, and was described by Naisbitt (1982) as an entrepreneurial explosion. Timmons (1994) views the transition as a silent revolution which may affect the twenty-first century as much as, and probably more than, the Industrial Revolution of the nineteenth century. This revolution is revitalizing economies, creating millions of jobs and forging new prosperity. It is built on the back of dynamic fast-track companies driven by ambitious entrepreneurs. Such entrepreneurs are willing to take risks on the road to success. Entrepreneurs are launching businesses which grow at well over 25 % per annum, and are operating in all industry sectors.

Embodied in this revolution is the process of entrepreneurship, central to which is the requirement for the personal initiative of the entrepreneur. Thus, the process of entrepreneurship is recognized as being at the heart of an economic development task and driven by the motivations of individuals, who are seeking to satisfy their personal goals. As such, the ultimate aim of economic development is to create opportunities for personal fulfilment through economic activity. This implies a partnership between policy-makers and entrepreneurs in order to achieve economic renewal and prosperity.

However, it is considered important to temper the exhilaration of the entrepreneurial revolution with the reality of why people are turning to entrepreneurial careers. Such people are, in fact, 'buying' personal independence and control through the process of new venture creation. In this respect, entrepreneurship may be seen as an aspect of the theory of choice, where people are pulled towards entrepreneurship. The universal truth of this interpretation in a situation of substantial change in labour markets is questionable. Such restructuring has effectively forced some to choose entrepreneurship, as the only alternative is not to have a job.

In this scenario individuals may also be pushed into entrepreneurship through the lack of alternative employment opportunities. This moves discussion of entrepreneurship into a choice between earning money or not having gainful employment. Thus, it is important to recognize that the route towards entrepreneurship may be varied - a response to a crisis situation or exploitation of a market opportunity, or both.

The entrepreneur and Entrepreneurship

It is often seen that the issue of entrepreneurship always comes to the fore and is a popular area of debate. This is natural as it enables an entrepreneur to see the light at the end of the tunnel. So many admire, and aspire to be an entrepreneur. It is easy to admire those that possess courage and conviction. It is natural for everyone to want their lives to have a positive impact.

So what is an entrepreneur?

Whenever anyone talks about entrepreneurship, the image that appears in most people's minds is that of people starting their own businesses. Although that image is compatible in part with the concept of sustainable entrepreneurship, we prefer to work with a different meaning. So, entrepreneurship is nothing more than the power to make things happen. According to this concept, an entrepreneur is anyone capable of generating results in any area of human activity.

According to the Merriam-Webster Dictionary, an entrepreneur is "One who manages and assumes the risks of a business or enterprise". Entrepreneurship always includes, risk, novelty and reward. It can apply to small tasks and to large enterprises; it can apply across all industry sectors and to every person, however, it is most relevant to managers and proprietors.

Entrepreneurship is the dynamic process of creating incremental wealth. This wealth is created by individuals who assume major risk in terms of equity, time, and career commitment of providing value for some product or service. The product or services itself may or may not be unique but value must somehow be infused by the entrepreneur by securing and allocating the necessary skills and resources.

So what does it require?

Lot of thought provoking and insightful has been written over the years about entrepreneurship. There is an old belief that 90% of people are frightened of failure which is huge barrier to the road to real success. Thus it can be said that entrepreneurs stand in the remaining 10% bracket. What is so special about them? There are many people who possess natural talent but are unable to turn that into something meaningful. Why? The bitter truth is that they do not have the necessary character traits that allow them to reach the pinnacle. We can easily aspire to the qualities required but very, very few are able to achieve this status as it requires some very exceptional qualities.

Answer to the questions posed above lies within the mindset and approach that individuals bring into their business. So many entre¬preneurs have a mental picture that other people just cannot see. Many times we have heard an entrepreneur make a statement 'other people might think it was a huge risk, but I thought there was an opportunity'. Marc Verstringhe (founder of Catering and Allied Services International) would often describe his role as being to stand at the top of a mountain and have a clear vision across the valley below so that he could guide his team. Others in the team would stand at various points lower down on the mountain and their views would be naturally more impaired.

It has recently become a cliché that successful people in all fields are able to adapt to changing markets and conditions. They are able to handle setbacks and find a way forward. They possess a clear vision of the destination that they are trying to reach and do not take their eye of their goal.

An entrepreneur needs to possess a positive mentality that allows them to handle difficult situations as they are psychologically prepared. But this kind of metal preparedness is not very common.

Entrepreneurs need to foresee the situation, favorable or unfavorable, to become successful. However, it is not just about visualisation and positive mental attitude. Often very talented individuals are not able to fulfil their potential for the reason that they do possess the most important inner traits viz. courage, conviction, or work ethic.

Now the question is to what to do. Young entrepreneurs need to take inspiration from the existing successful entrepreneurs. One should try to find the stories that stand behind success¬ful entrepreneurs and what can be learnt from their stories? The hospitality industry is an excellent forum for reviewing this question, as a lot are self-made and have built great careers from humble beginnings.

Entrepreneurship typically focuses on identifying new opportunities for creating value for customers or users and commercially developing those opportunities to establish a profitable business. The opportunities identified can be for new products or services, new markets, new production processes, new raw materials, or new ways of organizing existing technologies. While Schumpeter recognized that entrepreneurs can be driven by non-economic motives such as a desire for creativity or power, economic theories of entrepreneurship generally emphasize the role of profit as one of the major underlying goals of entrepreneurs and investors in developing a new venture opportunity.

To put it very simply, it means making things happen in a way that takes into consideration the short, medium, and long-term. From one point of view, the expression can be contrasted to the concept of "selfish entrepreneurship," in which people seek advantages only for themselves and often at any cost. On the other hand, the expression can also be contrasted to "unconscious entrepreneurship," in which a non-sustainable way of life is produced—a destructive way of living that generates imbalances of all kinds.

Definition of entrepreneurship

In clarifying what is meant by the term, it is necessary to address some fundamental misconceptions, for instance:

- "Entrepreneurs are always small business people and small business people are entrepreneurs"
- "Entrepreneurship and innovation are the same thing"
- "Beyond business management and planning, entrepreneur skills cannot be developed"
- "Entrepreneurial behaviour cannot be learned, you either have it or you don't"
- "Entrepreneurship can be dealt with by just adding some units of competency to the Training Package"

Defining entrepreneurship

Drawing on extant definitions of entrepreneurship, we propose a definition for the concept of sustainable entrepreneurship. While there are probably hundreds of definitions for entrepreneurship in the literature, we find Venkataraman's

(1997) definition of a multi-level domain for entrepreneurship research particularly appropriate. He broadly encompasses both the diverse contemporary research and early economic thought: entrepreneurship as a scholarly field seeks to understand how opportunities to bring into existence future goods and services are discovered, created, and exploited, by whom, and with what consequences (Venkataraman, 1997).

This definition is useful for several reasons. It focuses attention on opportunities and (1) their sources, (2) the agents of their exploitation, the entrepreneurs, and (3) the consequences of their exploitation.

According to the Merriam-Webster Dictionary, an entrepreneur is:

One who manages and assumes the risks of a business or enterprise

From the Business Dictionary online2 there is a more comprehensive definition:

Entrepreneurship is the capacity and willingness to undertake conception, organization, and management of a productive venture with all attendant risks, while seeking profit as a reward. In economics, entrepreneurship is regarded as a factor of production together with land, labor, natural resources, and capital. Entrepreneurial spirit is characterized by innovation and risk-taking, and an essential component of a nation's ability to succeed in an ever changing and more competitive global marketplace.

Entrepreneurship always includes, risk, novelty and reward. It can apply to small tasks and to large enterprises; it can apply across all industry sectors and to every person, however, it is most relevant to managers and proprietors. While the term is often associated with small business operators, in reality entrepreneurs can be found in big business, in the social sector or in any field of endeavour.

Key Personality traits of entrepreneurs

- Self-confident and optimistic
- Able to take calculated risk
- Responded positively to challenges

- Flexible and able to adapt
- Knowledge of markets
- Independent minded
- Versatile Knowledge
- Energetic and diligent
- Creative and innovative
- Dynamic leader
- Responsive to Suggestions
- Take Initiatives
- Perceptive and foresight
- Responsive to criticism.
- Risk taker

Entrepreneurship and small business

Not every cafe owner/manager or any small business owner is an entrepreneur. However because of the nature of small business—the slim margins, the risk of failure, the need for agility—it is assumed that successful small business owners have applied some level of entrepreneurship. However, a small cafe which is stable, routine and not growing would not be described as entrepreneurial, even though it may be described as successful. On the other hand a person working in a large organisation, for example, the head office of a chain of cafes may well be entrepreneurial in seeing the opportunity for and implementing a new venture, taking the risks and creating value.

Entrepreneurship, Creativity and innovation

Austrian economist Joseph Schumpeter, who in the 1930s succinctly identified the characteristics of an entrepreneur and the emerging role within an industrial economy, regarded innovation as central to the notion of entrepreneurship. He identified as essential:

- New products
- New markets
- New forms of organisation

- New production methods.

Entrepreneurship implies novelty, which is also central to the concept of innovation. Peter Drucker identified innovation as critical to the concept of entrepreneurship, but also identifies amount of wealth creation, speed of wealth creation and risk.

Entrepreneurship emerged as a concept with the industrial revolution, when there was increasing opportunity to create wealth through ideas and new enterprises. It is one of the four mainstream economic factors: land, labour, capital, and entrepreneurship.

Innovation and entrepreneurship often go hand in hand, but are not necessarily at the same time. Innovation exists when there is a new idea or the new use of an old idea which creates value and can apply to products, processes, and services. It might be radical or incremental and can often change the ways we behave (e.g. take away food has changed the way we eat).

An entrepreneur, on the other hand, may take the innovation and sell it to the community. They create the business model, the market and the profit or value. The innovator and entrepreneur can be the same person or they may be different people.

Relationship between Idea, Creativity, Innovation

1. An idea has little value until they are converted into new products, services or process.
2. Innovation, therefore, is the transformation of creative idea into useful application.
3. But creativity is prerequisite to innovation.
4. If creativity is the seed that inspires entrepreneurship, innovation is the process of entrepreneurship.

Creative process

STEP -1: IDEA GEMINATION

- Seeding process
- Individual's interest or curiosity about a specific problems or areas of study

STEP -2: Preparation

◈ Conscious search for knowledge

◈ Rationalization

STEP -3: Incubation

◈ Mulling it over

STEP -4: Illumination

◈ "Oh! I see"

STEP-5: Verification

Application or test to prove ideas has value.

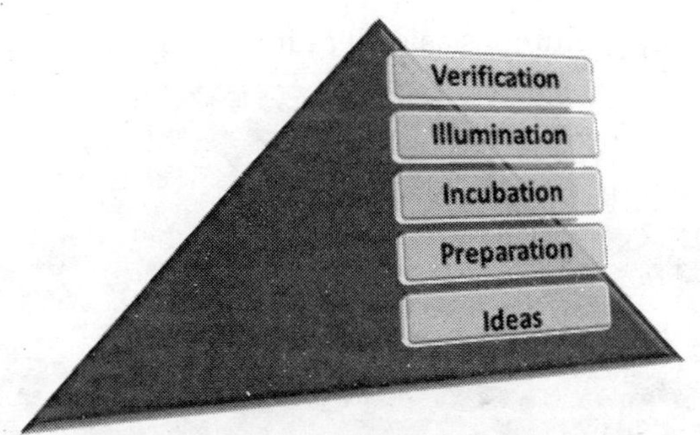

Figure: Creative Process

Entrepreneurship in the Service Industries

Entrepreneurial activity and innovation in the service industries may take many forms.

It typically involves any of the following:

- Starting a new enterprise in a new context;
- Creating a new business model for an enterprise;
- Creating new services, products to be offered to customers;
- Creating a new customer experience;
- Creating new workplace strategies;
- Hotels introducing quicker check-in and check-out technologies;
- Creating new marketing strategies, and so on.

Increasingly service industry innovation is not just about more effective and productive products, processes and services—it is also about ways to create competitive advantage through enhancing the whole customer experience. For instance, a hairdresser salon may offer foot massages and pizza, or a fitness studio may team up with a health food shop to create cross-patronage. A cluster of establishments may form a precinct and team up to market the whole area. A group of enterprises may collaborate and put together an integrated tourist program.

Therefore, an entrepreneur in the service industries not only needs skills and behaviors to help think through ideas, but—most particularly—needs to be externally focussed to look for collaborative opportunities as well as internal innovations.

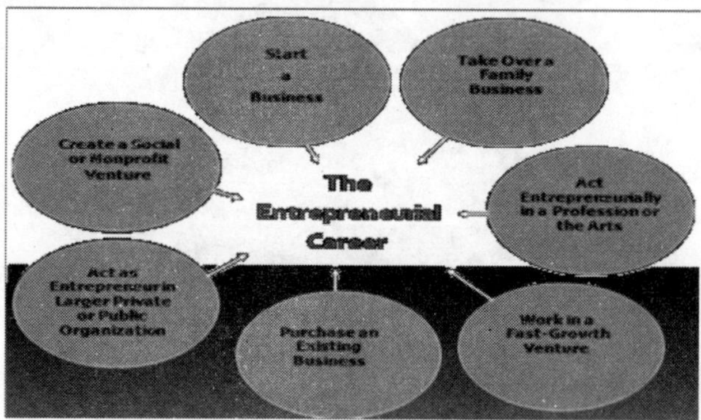

Figure: The Entrepreneurial Career

Opportunities for entrepreneurs in Tourism Industry

Business opportunity for entrepreneurs in tourism market sector may be in anywhere along the tourism supply chain. It could be a conventional tourism business or an unconventional business idea or just a subsidiary or secondary activity. When working for a business a business opportunity, it is important to know the difference between businesses based on products versus those based on services and then appropriate type that suited your interest. Business can sell physical product such as curious, cold drink, where tourist actually take an item away or consume it or businesses can provide a service like transport , booking, guiding which tourist are willing to pay for although they do not receive something concrete and touchable in return. There is a long list of exciting, new and unique services and product to select from for the type of tourism related business you may wish to get involved in.

Business opportunity in tourism market sector may be in anywhere along the tourism supply chain. It could be a conventional tourism business or an unconventional business idea or just a subsidiary or secondary activity. When working for a business a business opportunity, it is important to know the difference between businesses based on products versus those based on services and then appropriate type that suited your interest. Business can sell physical product such as curious, cold drink, where tourist actually take an item away or consume it. Or businesses can provide a service like transport , booking, guiding which tourist are willing to pay for although they do not receive something concrete and touchable in return. There is a long list of exciting, new and unique services and product to select from for the type of tourism related business you may wish to get involved in.

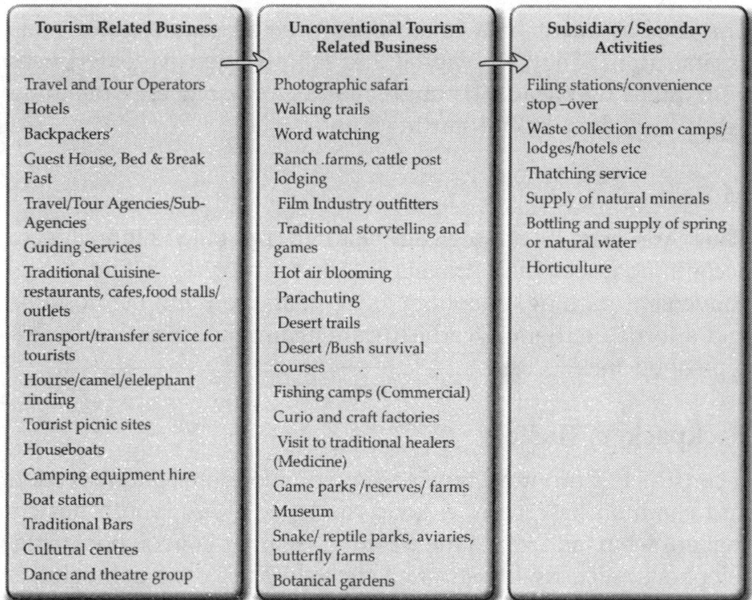

Figure: emerging business opportunities in Indian tourism market

Conventional Tourism Related Business Ideas

There are a number of conventional tourism business ideas which can still be sustainable given the demand supply gap at many destinations. Differentiated strategies can create new and exciting product for the customer.

Travel and Tour Operation

The operator organises and conducts tours locally or even regionally and these are usually vehicle-based. Some companies specialise in day trips. They work closely with other for instance, they may sub contract their service to a large hotel or to another tour operator. In this case, the operator's company may be hired by the hotel or safari operator to provide transport services, but not necessarily on a full time basis. This is different from the individual being employed by the safari operator.

Hotels

The establishment of a hotel, even a small one, require huge capital input. They are capital and labour intensive enterprises with huge overhead. Through market research and planning needs to be done before starting a hotel.

Motels

They are usually strategically located on busy highways to accommodate passing travellers are to provide facilities like convenient parking, telephone/fax/e-mail, food and comfortable and affordable room. Overheads are again high to maintain this type of business.

Backpackers Hostels

It consists of dormitory type accommodation for separate section and common bathroom. A good model is YWCA youth hostels that are set up all around the world. A swimming pool, pool table, telephone, security lock-up and tuck shop are essential facilities at these hostels. A good atmosphere has to be created these places i.e. if you get the formula right then you will get on to the back-packer circuit. This is a reasonably good business to invest in if there is a large influx of tourists coming to the place where you would like to start it.

Guesthouse/Bed & Breakfast

The provision of this type of accommodation is a popular choice amongst small business owners. The target market is usually self-drive tourists including domestic tourists and business traveller.

Travel/Tour Agencies/Sub-Agencies

These are usually situated in larger cities where there is an influx of tourist arrival or at tourist centres like Jaipur and Orchha. They could either do booking for local, regional or international destination. They network with other agents and sometimes do the marketing and booking for safari companies. These agencies generally serve as good tourist information centres.

Guiding Services

They could be provided in conjunction with travel and tour operations or independently. They provided could maintain/ retain a pool of professional guides/camp managers, interpreters. They would be commissioned during the peak tourist season, when there is demand for such services. They could temporarily replace manager/guides who go extended holidays.

Transport/Transfer Service for Tourists

It could either be provided to take tourists from point A to point B or hired out for a fee. There are many forms of transportation to choose from in India.

Tourist Camp Sites, Picnic Sites

These are typically cleared and fenced off area that have shady tree, demarcated camping and caravan sites, common toilets with hot and cold water, water stand- pipes and wash bins. This is probably one of the easier forms of tourism business that can be established by communities as well as individuals. There are many suitable and attractive spot in and around cities along primary roads, at national dams and other scenic places around country.

Houseboats

This is not a novel idea in India as one businessman has already applied to conduct houseboat safaris along the backwaters in Kerala and also in lakes in Kashmir and other hill station.

Camping Equipment Hire

The hiring of tents and other camping equipment is a good idea, because it saves the traveller having to carry heavy and bulky equipment. Tents are also commonly hired for social events like wedding and party so there will be no shortage of business even during low tourist seasons.

Boat Station

There is a great need for efficient and reliable ferry service across the Brahmaputra, in Daman and across the Ganges in Benaras. However, a proper, secure mooring site for boats with a filling station and supply store is required. Boat cruises or hire of boats and canoes from the boat station could be the main business activity at many destinations.

Traditional Cuisine

India offers a wide variety of cuisines. Indian cuisine varies every 300 km. Both vegetarian and non-vegetarian specialties have great potential to attract domestic and foreign tourists. They are always keen to try out the local cuisine and will pay to get value for money. The capital outlay for small food outlet is not high and people are encouraged to use their cooking skill to start small businesses. From dhabas to tea stalls, a wide range of eating joint can be offered.

Traditional Bars

Entertainment is a big money spinner if it is provided at the right time and at right place. Foreign tourist enjoys visiting traditional bars, mixing with locals and listening to, preferably, live music by social artist. If the decor of the bar is done in true local style it will take be a major action. Many visitors would also like it taste authentic local beverage.

Cultural Centres

They could be huge places housing and marketing the wares of curio and craft maker, painters and sculptors, other local artists and even hosting live music and dance shows. This type of business would suit a cooperative arrangement.

Dance and Theatre Group

These groups could perform at cultural centres, major national events, and special function at hotel.

Unconventional Tourism Related Businesses

It has developed because of special requirement of customer or because of some creative option being offered to them.

Photographic Safaris

The photographic safaris are a great attraction to photographers, amateurs as well as professionals. This area is quite untapped and only a few companies are into organising such tours and expeditions.

Walking Trails

These could be places in natural areas surrounding or in the vicinity of settlements. Guided tours can be done in small reserves.

Bird Watching Tours

Bird watching tours are boon for bird lovers. There is a dearth of entrepreneurs who are into organising such activities.

Horse Riding

Horse riding is an activity which is enjoyable and good for health as well. This is done generally in stud farms or may be started at some local small place with even one or two horses.

Hot Air Ballooning

It is a capital intensive and technical business that appears to be doing reasonably well in countries like South Africa and

Zimbabwe, but has been tried a little in India. The ballooning club of India organises international balloon festival and demonstration flight annually.

Parachuting

It will be probably be restricted to a very small market. This activity needs specialised equipment, technical expertise and a major capital input.

Dessert/Bush Survival Courses

These courses appeal to large business corporations who want their executive to learn leadership qualities and team spirit. The recent exercise where India hosted armies from several countries which participated in dessert survival courses for elite paratroopers, may very well put India on the map as a future destination for this activity.

Fishing (Commercial) Camps

Privately owned fishing camps along with Cauvery River are presently extremely popular with local and regional sport anglers. Opportunities exist for enterprising people to set up such camps along with lakes, river and at large dams around the country.

Film Industry Outfitters

Professional film makers and photographer are always looking for good local assistants to provide logistical support area knowledge and act as interpreter. They also need material support on form of fully self contained vehicles and camping equipments.

Traditional Storytelling and Games

Tourists visiting remote community areas enjoy listening to folklore participating in traditional games and knowing about the local people. In fact, the modern tourist is sometimes referred as an educated traveller. Storytelling is a popular performing art in India. Each religion has developed its own style and tradition of storytelling in various regional languages combining musical composition between narrations.

Traditional Music

It has always been very popular with tourists. Small groups can perform at all possible venues such as hotels, lodges and airports. Management contract can be signed with these establishments to provide entertainment on certain days or night.

Curio and Craft Factories

Many tourists would like to take home souvenirs from their visit to India, but they also want to see how these are manufactured. They could be charged a small fee for visiting your factory, but the real idea is to sell them.

Visit to Traditional Healers

Foreigners find traditional healers and witch doctors extremely intriguing and will pay to see them in action.

Botanical Gardens

Natural spots at some of the national dams lend themselves extremely well to the establishment of botanical garden. Expert advice would be needed to set these up and only indigenous plant should be propagated at these sites. It is a good idea to have a kiosk providing refreshments and an attractive spot for people to sit and relax.

The importance of entrepreneurship to hospitality industry

An entrepreneurial approach is just as relevant and important in hospitality, leisure, sport and tourism as in other sectors, if not more so. The hospitality, leisure, sports and tourism industries can be regarded as archetypal entrepreneurial industries employing people in food service outlets, guest houses, health and fitness clubs, hotels, visitor attractions - ranging from gardens to local museums and many other types of outlet. The vast majority of these are small independent owner-managed businesses with outlets which opened having taken advantage of low barriers to entry. They tend to be highly flexible to changing customer demands and offer personal and localised service. This is typified in the sports and exercise industry where many small businesses offer coaching and fitness services. These small businesses are the fabric of local society.

The hospitality, leisure, sports and tourism industries are areas where discussions related to change, development, innovation and management are increasingly being couched in terms of entrepreneurship. Entrepreneurship is a driver of change, innovation and employment in these industries and is crucial to meeting the rapidly changing demands of hospitality, leisure, sports and tourism consumers. Within established businesses the concept of intrapreneurship is key to enabling new markets to be developed for these changing consumer demands and to facilitate new concept development. Rob Bailey (Senior Manager, KPMG - Tourism and Leisure Advisory Services, March 2005) supports this view stating that:

'Entrepreneurship is critical to the hospitality, leisure, sports and tourism sectors, as with rapidly changing consumer demands and expectations, constant innovation by businesses is vital to meet and, hopefully, exceed these evolving demands and expectations.'

Entrepreneurship is an important force behind success in any industry. This is particularly so in the dynamic and rapidly evolving hospitality, leisure, sport and tourism industries throughout the world. These entrepreneurial industries are major contributors to national economies and their growth, and are guaranteed to grow both in terms of their quantity and quality. There are challenges though related to reaching growth targets and these relate to capacity, availability and skills of the workforce, developing new products and services, and ways of delivering these to the customer, and so on. Entrepreneurial activities generally develop newly combined means of production, new products, new markets, new methods of manufacturing or distribution, new sources of material, or new forms of organisation (Schumpeter, 1934). Hence, entrepreneurship is necessary for overcoming these challenges in these industries and in achieving this, the outcomes are the various forms of innovation. For businesses innovation has the potential to boost productivity and increase the ability to price discriminate and enhance profits. Entrepreneurship then, is key to gaining competitive advantage and, as a result, greater financial rewards. Entrepreneurship and innovation in these industries would therefore seem key contributors to economic development, not only in India but elsewhere, as the following quotes demonstrate:

'The role entrepreneurship plays in African economies and society particularly in the hospitality, tourism, sport and leisure industries, is enormous and cannot be over-emphasized in the provision of employment, wealth creation and in terms of innovation. The primary goal of entrepreneurship is profitability and growth.....' (E. I. Babagbale, General Manager, Yola International Hotel, Yola, Nigeria, March 2005).

'Unique touches and experiences that 'wow' are becoming tomorrow's expectations in the hospitality industry. Marriott and other leading brands are competing in a global market. Entrepreneurship in the development of new concepts and initiatives to gain a competitive edge is a key strategy as companies realign their brand vision and identity. Whether it is Marriott with their new bedding package, high speed wireless internet packages, new pre-arrival concierge service, or simply state of the art design at entrepreneur Ian Schrager's hotels, providing a unique experience will set the company apart from the rest.' (Nicola Roberts, Director of Revenue Analysis, Marriott Hotels, Miami Beach Cluster, March 2005). Often, external consultants are employed to advise businesses on entrepreneurial ideas and activities:

'In many cases, our tourism and leisure sector clients engage us to provide innovation, creative thinking and problem-solving to assist them in optimising the financial performance of their businesses. We are also engaged by clients to provide a 'sense check' of their entrepreneurial ideas, some of which may at first glance appear 'risky' commercially, but upon closer examination have significant potential.' (Rob Bailey, Senior Manager, KPMG - Tourism and Leisure Advisory Services, March, 2005).

While having its economic benefits, entrepreneurship in the hospitality, leisure, sport and tourism industries can also prove hugely beneficial in social terms, as the following indicates:

'Much in the same way that men of science have pushed back the boundaries of our physical world, entrepreneurs, in the hospitality and leisure industries, have influenced and pushed back the boundaries of our social world; for example, imagine not being able to take a low cost flight, stay in a budget hotel, or eat a cheap meal. Entrepreneurs are the life blood of the hospitality and leisure industries, trail blazers who take calculated risks, not unnecessary ones, to bring to the masses something new and unique, adding interest and colour to our lives.

As an entrepreneur, there is a need to be aware of the environment, and above all, one must have strength in your convictions and the courage to follow them through. One needs to be pragmatic; willing to lead by example, and able to recognise in others, traits that complement of one's weaknesses. Although fortune favours the brave, one should also be prepared for failure. Nevertheless, when one's take a risk it should be calculated, after all, the better part of valour knows when to walk away from a fight, and one needs to learn from every experience that life throws. Essentially an entrepreneur is an individual with vision, someone who works hard and has the courage to try something new - even if it means failing...' (Leslie Bailey MSc MHCIMA, Division Manager m.a.x. concepts, Hong Kong, March 2005).

Social entrepreneurship is an important aspect of entrepreneurship in the hospitality and related industries. Catering and tourist attractions are often important elements of economic development and regeneration initiatives. The revitalisation of inner cities is often linked with, and heavily reliant upon, ethnic minority entrepreneurship which has traditionally been concentrated in the catering, retailing and clothing industries, but is increasingly associated with the emergent industrial sectors (Deakins and Freel, 2003:89).

Critique on Entrepreneurship

The dominance of small, owner-managed tourism and hospitality businesses in many countries has 'led to recognition of the significance of entrepreneurship'. Despite this, it is argued that the field has not received the level of attention it deserves. Furthermore, it has been dominated by that derived from developed economies, with a paucity of studies focusing on lesser developed or transition economies. Some points of similarity across economies have been identified, for example, relative ease of entry into the sector, and financial and human resource poverty, but the majority of conventional wisdom remains indoctrinated by Western developed economies ideology. It has been observed that there are broadly two different models of entrepreneurship among small tourism and hospitality businesses. The first comprises those owners who have moved into a tourism destination for some non-economic reasons, usually combined with a lack of business experience. This group is categorised as 'non-entrepreneurs'. The second consists of 'constrained entrepreneurs'. These are mostly young people with a greater level of economic motives drawn from more professional but mainly non-business background. They are constrained by a lack of business skills and capital. However, a number of these studies have been conducted in the context of developed economies to explain these types motivations of small businesses. But the model of a continuum moving from strong profit and growth orientation at one end through to a tenacious focus on the social orientation of 'business' can prove to be a successful model. This has some utility as it recognises that there exist under the umbrella of the tourism and hospitality industries multiple manifestations of 'entrepreneur' and their individualized motivations. However, it does not address or explain the source of different world views within literature, and limited understanding within the context of transition economies.

Conclusions

In conclusion then, an awareness of the importance of entrepreneurship in hospitality, leisure, sport and tourism is not new, with evidence of entrepreneurial activity in these industries centuries ago. However, interest in entrepreneurship has heightened more recently as its importance has become increasingly recognised. 'Entrepreneurship' has become the battle-cry of recent governments in their pursuit of a variety of economic, social and other objectives. This cry acquired a new sense of urgency in the 1990s as economic growth started. Thus, entrepreneurship is often seen as an economic function. But, it is also viewed as a way of explaining business ownership and organisational structure, a means of improving social and individual well being, a means of analysis of industry structure, a rationale for government policy, and an approach to education. The motives of the young entrepreneurs entering into the business are not very clear to these entrepreneurs only, whether they are entering into the business for economic or some non-economic purposes.

References

Baum, T. (2001). Education for tourism in a global economy. In S. Wahab & C. Cooper (Eds), Tourism in the age of globalisation (pp. 198-212). London: Routledge.

Bennett, O. (1999). Destination marketing into the next century. Journal of Vacation Marketing, 6(1), 48-54.

Beugelsdijk, S., & Noorderhaven, N. (2004). Entrepreneurial attitude and economic growth. The Annals of Regional Science, 38, 199–218.

Birley, S., and Westhead, P. (1990b). Private Business Sales Environments in the United Kingdom. Journal of Business Venturing, 5, 349-373.

Breckler, S. J. (1984). Empirical validation of affect, behavior, and cognition as distinct components of attitude. Journal of Personality and Social Psychology , 47 , 1191-1205.

Brüderl, J., Preisendörfer, P., and Ziegler, R. (1992). Survival Chances of Newly Founded Business Organizations. American Sociological Review, 57, 227-242.

Buhalis, D. (2000). Marketing the competitive destination of the future. Tourism Management, 21, 97–116.

Bygrave, W. D., and Hofer, C. W. (1991). Theorizing About Entrepreneurship. Entrepreneurship Theory and Practice, 16, 13-22.

Caldwell, N. & Freire, J. (2004). The difference between branding a country, a region and a city: Applying the brand box model. Brand Management, 12(1), 50-61.

Charney, A.H., & Libecap, G.D. (2003). The contribution of entrepreneurship education: An analysis of the Berger Program. International Journal of Entrepreneurship Education, 1(3), 385–418.

Chaudhary, M. (2010). Tourism Marketing. Oxford University Press, New Delhi

Daye, M (2010): Challenges and Prospects of Differentiating Destination Brand : The Case of Dutch Carribbean Islands, Journal of Travel & Tourism Marketing, 27(1),1-13

De Chernatony, L. & MacDonald, M (2001). Creating powerful brands in consumer, Service, and Industrial Markets. Oxford: Butterworth-Heinemenn

Durie, M. (1998). Whaiora: Māori Health Development (2nd ed.). Auckland, New Zealand: Oxford University Press.

Entrepreneurship Summit, Executive Summary, Kauffman Foundation, the International Economic Development Council, September. 2008.

Gartner, W. B. (1990). What Are We Talking About When We Talk About Entrepreneurship? Journal of Business Venturing, 5, 15-28.

Gillespie, C.H., & Baum, T. (2000). Innovation and creativity in professional higher education: The development of a CD-Rom to support teaching and learning in food and beverage management. The Scottish Journal of Adult and Continuing Education, 6(2), 147-167.

Hankinson, G. (2004). Relational network brands: Towards a conceptual model of place brands. Journal of Vacation Marketing,10(2), 109-121.

Hanna J. (2008), Encouraging entrepreneurs: Lessons in Government Policy, HBS

Hanna J. (2008), Getting Down to the Business of Creativity, HBS.

Hanna, Julia- Encouraging Entrepreneurs: Lessons for Government Policy, HBS, March 10, 2008

Hawes, D. K., Taylor, D. T., & Hampe, G. D. (1991). Destination marketing by state. Journal of Travel Research, 30(1), 11–17.

Katrin, B (2005).Tourism destination marketing – A tool for destination management? A case study from Nelson/Tasman Region, New Zealand, Asia Pacific Journal of Tourism Research, 10(1), 45-57

Keasey, K., and Watson, R. (1991). The State of the Art of Small Firm Failure Prediction: Achievements and Prognosis. International Small Business Journal, 9, 11-29

Loucks, K.E. (1988) Training Entrepreneurs for Small Business Creation: Lessons from Experience, Management Development Series No. 26, Geneva: International Labour Office.

Marsh, C. J. & Willis, G. (2003). Curriculum: Alternative approaches, ongoing issues. (3rd ed.). Upper Saddle River, NJ: Merrill Prentice Hall.

Martinez, A.C., Levie, J., Kelley, D.J., Saemundsson, R.J., & Schott, T. (2010). Global Entrepreneurship Monitor Special Report. A global perspective on entrepreneurship and training. Babson Park, MA: Babson College.

Matlay, H. (2005). Researching entrepreneurship and education: Part 1: What is entrepreneurship and does it matter? Education and Training Journal, 47(8/9), 665–678.

Matlay, H. (2008). The impact of entrepreneurship education on entrepreneurial outcomes. Journal of Small Business Development, 15(2), 382–396.

McMullan, W.E. and Long, W.A. (1990) Developing New Ventures: The Entrepreneurial Option, San Diego, CA: Harcourt Brace Jovanovich. (A general reference text on entrepreneurism and entrepreneurial education.

Mitchell & Co. (2006) 'Entrepreneurship education in South Africa: a nationwide survey', Education and Training, 48 (5), 348-359

Morris, Michael H.Dr. and Chair, Mitchel Mallone (2009), Entrepreneurship as Driver of B School and University Transformation, Dept. of Entrepreneurship, Academy of Management Meetings, Oklahoma State University, Chicago

Phipps, S and Prieto, L (2012), "Knowledge is power? an inquiry into knowledge management, its effects on individual creativity, and the moderating role of an entrepreneurial mindset", Academy of Strategic Management Journal, 11 (1), 43-57

Ritchie, J. R. B. & Crouch, G. I. (2000). The competitive destination: A sustainability perspective. Tourism Management, 21(1), 1–7.

Robbie, K., and Wright, M. (1996). Management Buy-Ins:

Active Investors and Corporate Restructuring. Manchester: Manchester University Press.

Saarinen, J. (1997). Tourist destinations and the production of touristic space: Lapland as an ethnic landscape. Nordia 26:38–45.

Sharma, A. (2008) Trained Manpower, Hotel Business Review. 3(6).

UNWTO Report, Tourism Highlights, 2012

Wright, M., Robbie, K., & Ennew, C. (1995). Serial entrepreneurs. In W. Bygrave, et al. (Eds.), Frontiers of entrepreneurship research. Wellesley, MA: Babson College.

WTTC (2012) Travel and Tourism Economic Impacts, India.

NEW AGE TOURISM: ISSUES & CHALLANGES

Prateek Agrawal

Associate Professor, Institute of Tourism & Hotel Management, Bundelkhand University

Jhansi (U.P.) – 284128, e-mail: prateek_ithm@yahoo.co.in

Abstract

Recent years have seen a general recognition of the adverse impacts of tourism development. Much of the blame for the current situation has been attributed to the demands of mass tourism. Tourism practitioners, the media and many academics are now advocating 'new age tourism', otherwise known as soft, green, eco, gentle, appropriate, responsible, sustainable, (etc) tourism.

New age tourism is increasingly regarded as a key to sustainable development. The rationale is that contrary to mass tourism with its commonplace negative effects on receiving areas, new age tourism promotes a balanced growth form more in tune with local environmental and socio cultural concerns. Yet, academics are becoming increasingly skeptical as to whether new age tourism can be truly sustainable. Certain forms of tourism, known as new age or integrated tourism, are often proposed as solutions to the problems of mass tourism. Views on the viability and suitability of new age tourism diverge, partly because the concept of new age tourism is unclear.

An attempt has been made by critically reviewing the various aspects of the concept of new age tourism by looking at the motivations of the alternative tourists, the common characteristics of the practitioners of alternative tourism, the destinations visited, the types of accommodation used, the travel organizers specializing in this field, and the manner of implementation into the host community.

Keywords: New age Tourism, Sustainable Development, Old Tourism, E-marketing, Social & Cultural changes

Introduction

In the last decade the global challenges such as environment, health, employment, education, disparity and social mobility have multiplied and intensified. Priorities have shifted from "eco" to "socio". Institutions and instruments for managing change have evolved rapidly. These changes continue at an accelerating pace in an increasingly globalizing world. But there are some constants:

- Triple bottom line (environmental, social and economic) sustainability is being continuously reaffirmed, with the social dimension uppermost.
- Poverty remains the single most important cause of inequality and suffering.
- Local community needs must be factored early into global and regional development patterns.
- Public-private partnerships are an essential ingredient of constructive change.

Tourism has emerged in this decade as a central pillar of the services economy, and it can uniquely help society respond to global challenges, if its growth is managed prudently, with emphasis on ethics, poverty alleviation, the specific interests of developing nations and sustainable development.

The dynamic past and projected growth of the tourism sector, its broad direct and indirect impact across all economies - particularly those of developing countries make it particularly well suited as a development tool. It is particularly effective in economic terms in respect of:

- Job Creation
- Investment Attraction

- Economic growth
- External debt reduction
- Social welfare
- Foreign Exchange Earnings
- Re-distribution of economy
- Environmental fortification
- Creating Awareness
- Youth Employment
- Community Enrichment
- Gender Equality
- Cultural Preservation
- Diversification of economy
- Heritage conservation

Why New Tourism?

Now a day, New Tourism or Alternative Tourism has become a fashionable idea among those who are dissatisfied with the nature of mass tourism. Consumers are demanding newer forms of products and services and this has presented the opportunity and need for the tourism industry to respond to this market led approach. Many youth tourists who had rejected the conventional tourism consider their style of travel as 'New Age Tourism'. This type of idea has encouraged the emergence of tour operators and various non-commercially oriented projects offering a variety of 'Newer forms of travel'. New tourism has emerged as one of the most widely used and abused phrases of the last decade. But, the idea of new tourism has not yet been critically analyzed by the social scientists. So systematic examination of this appealing idea becomes imperative, and can be studied by reasoning and examination of what appear to be major effects resulting from tourism development are as follows:

- Price rises (labour, goods, taxes, land)
- Change in local attitudes and behaviour
- Pressure on people (crowding, disturbance, alienation)

- Loss of resources, access, rights, privacy
- Denigration or prostitution of local culture
- Pollution in various forms
- Lack of control over destination's future
- Problems of vandalism litter and traffic
- Less Government Control and Problems of Seasonal employment.

In general, there is remarkable ignorance and inaccurate perception of the dimensions, nature and power of tourism. At present there is a little evidence of any real ability to determine level of sustainable development i.e., capacity, as well lack of ability to manage and control tourism at international level. It is not possible to determine optimal visitations. Tourism behaves like most of the industries it causes imports and development can be self-sustaining and not easily reversible. Tourism is also extremely dynamic constantly changing and causing changes as well as responding to change. There is considerable Lack of agreement over developments, control and directions of development. All these elements combine to produce in many areas, virtual anarchy in co-ordination and planning of tourism (Butler 1990).

In Search of Appropriate Tourism

The last three decades have witnessed emergence of numerous critical studies that have challenged the necessity of tourism as a vehicle for national development. The response has been mixed, but largely hostile to mass tourism. If any thing is labeled 'New' its understanding revolves upon our comprehension of what is New for. An examination of the use of the idea of this phrase reveals that it is meant to be an alternative of several things.

A form of tourism may be categorized as New Tourism, which is more environmentally friendly in both its physical and cultural aspects, than the conventional mass tourism that went before it. It also represents the form of tourism that will make its development sustainable, through minimizing damage to resources and allowing for their future replenishment. Under this generic form, we can introduce a number of tourism terminologies including

Ecotourism, Green tourism, Rural tourism, Farm tourism, Urban tourism, Sports tourism, Adventure tourism, Indigenous tourism, Nature tourism, Wildlife tourism, Mountain tourism, Beach tourism, Responsible tourism, Soft tourism, Cottage tourism, Community Based Tourism (CBT), Highway tourism, Urban tourism, Appropriate tourism, Voluntary tourism, Just tourism, Special-Interest tourism and so on.

Within them, there seem to be an implicate assumption that such forms of tourism offer a better social and environmental balance than the existing models of main stream tourism. The implication is that by promoting such forms or calling ourselves "New tourists' we are encouraging a type of tourism that is better and more sustainable than what has gone before it.

Most of the characteristics of New tourism are in direct contrast to those of Conventional / Old / Mass / Main-stream tourism. Activities are likely to be a small scale, locally owned with consequently low impact, leakages and high proportion of profits retained locally. Ecotourism and sustainability have become a buzz word of the current scenario as a form of tourism which countries should pursue as being more environmental friendly and minimizing the negative environmental impacts of tourism.

Ecotourism has been defined by the Ecotourism society as: purposeful travel to natural areas to understand the cultural and natural history of the environment, taking care not to alter the integrity of the ecosystem, whilst producing economic opportunities that make the conservation of natural resources financially beneficial to local citizens.

Similarly, "Sustainable Tourism Development meets the needs of present tourists and host regions while protecting and enhancing opportunities for the future. It is envisaged as leading to management of all resources in such a way that economic, social and aesthetic needs can be fulfilled while maintaining cultural integrity, essential ecological processes, and biological diversity and life support systems." (WTO).

Poon observes the evolution of a new tourism typology with different behavior, values and expectations than the tourists before them. His presentation perhaps projects something of a stereo typical version of the two sets of tourists; it does display movement of attitudes of increasing numbers of tourists from those of believed supremacy, in tolerance and transience to those acceptances, tolerance, understanding and a wish to be educated.

Old Tourist	New Tourists
Search for the sun	Experience something new
Follow the masses	Want to be in charge
Here today, gone tomorrow	See and enjoy but do not destroy
Show that you have been	Just for the fun of it
Having	Being
Superiority	Understanding
Like attractions	Like sport and nature
Precautions	Adventurous
Eat in the hotel dining room	Try out local fare
Homogeneous	Hybrid

Eric Cohen (1991) has adopted a different approach mentioning the different conceptions of new tourism, same may be stated as:

New tourism as a reaction of modern mass consumerism: Many authors have criticized the modern establishments' for robbing the tourist of the authentic experience of travel of the past and offering instead spurious and contrived attractions, while inducing him to consume these like any other commodity. In their opposition to the conventional world, the travelling people even reject the label of 'tourist' and see themselves as 'travellers' or 'globe trotters', while others have labeled them as 'back packers', 'drifters' or 'hippies'. They seek to avoid itineraries, amenities and sites offered by tourist establishment, and travel off—beaten tracks, where they believe they can establish contact with locals.

New Tourism as a reaction to the exploitation of third world: It is a common belief that the developed countries exploit the people, cultures and amenities of the third world countries for the pleasure of rich tourists. Economic exploitation and cultural pollution are seen as the principal consequences of touristic penetration. The MNC' take away the major share of profits back to the developed world (i.e. their home countries) as a result the conventional tourism becomes an undesirable phenomenon.

'Concerned westerners however, rather rejecting it altogether set out to seek a form of alternative tourism', which while safeguarding the experience of travel, would also further enhance mutual understanding between people, prevent environmental and cultural degradation and most of all, exploitation and dehumanization of the local population this will there be 'just tourism' (Holden 1984).

'Counter Cultural Alternative Tourism: Counter Cultural Alternative Tourism inverts the values, motives, attitudes and practice of conventional mass tourism which are rejected together with the whole of established society. The conventional tourist is seen as seeking mere entertainment, recreation o relaxation. He is considered too lazy, uninterested bored, or over bearing to seriously try to experience the world beyond the home environment of the tourist establishment' They travel alone or in small groups, in a unhurried manner, they tend to change their plans suddenly according to their interest, disposable time, money and opportunities. The 'ideal traveler' is self reliant and enterprising an adventurer who does not shun dangers and is prepared to take risks if necessary, travelling alone through jungles, accepting the hospitality of local peasants and tribal people, eating their food and drinking the water without concern for comfort or health.

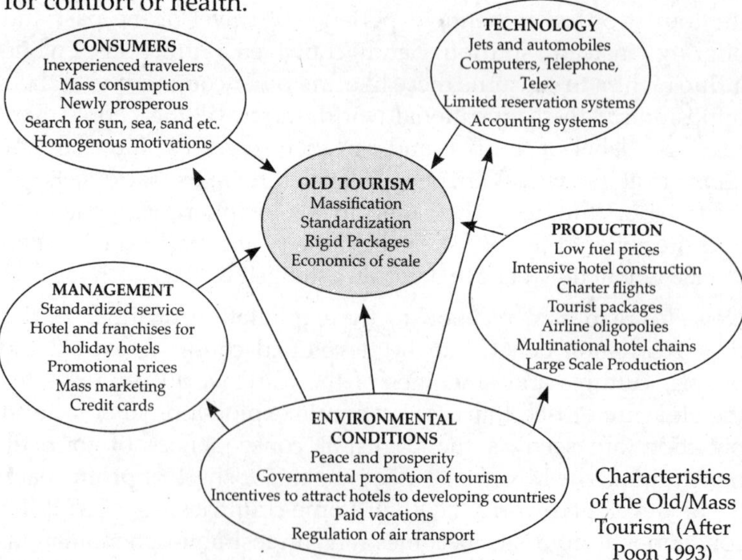

Characteristics of the Old/Mass Tourism (After Poon 1993)

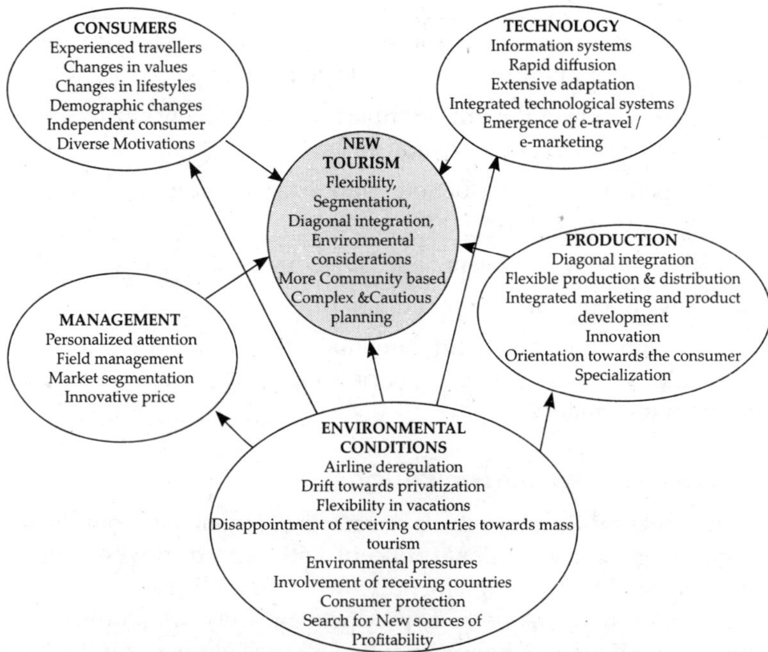

Characteristics of the New Age Tourism (After Poon 1993)

The Prevailing Circumstances of Market and New Entrepreneurial Model

With the rapid growth of tourism sector, the industry has began to offer standardized products to unseasoned tourists whose motives were very basic - search for the sun, sand and surf - in a moderately exotic atmosphere and at a competitive price. The model of large scale production of the industrial sector was emulated in tourism; rigid packages were created with better economies of scale and offered to tourists with low costs and not greatly varied expectation. Technologic advances in passenger transportation and communications made it possible to create mass markets of an international nature in various regions of the world. The New Age of Tourism is characterized primarily by the niche marketing, super segmentation of demand, flexibility of supply and distribution channels, and achieving profitability through the integration and subsequent system economies and integrated values, instead of economics of scale. The new age tourism model should permit the tourism sector to offer products adopted to the increasingly complex and diverse needs of demand, while being competitive with the old standardized products.

Flexibility is one of the important factors in the New age tourism. Flexibility is pertinent in several areas, like;

- Organization, production and distribution of tourism products & services,
- Reservation, purchasing and payments systems and
- Ways of consuming the tourism product.

New technologies are fundamental in this respect, and in particular, in the expansion and development of new systems of tourism information.

Issues for New Tourism Policy

In the new millennium, there seem to be reasonable grounds for redefining the conventional concept with regard to who should be responsible for implementing tourism policies, surely the complexity of infrastructure, products and services required for quality tourism experiences is sufficient reason for rising beyond this temporary perception of tourism policy that aims to confine absolutely to the public sector. Also, it would also be unfeasible to suggest that public sector intervention can be ignored from the specific requirements of tourism enterprises. For achieving total quality management and efficiency in tourism enterprises and regions, in the context of greater socio-economical gains the need for a partnership of the private, public and voluntary sectors seems binding to evolve and execute new tourism policy programmes.

The private sector in tourism, which is to a large extent made up of small and medium sized business, has risen to technological challenges with concentration and/or voluntary association strategies. The increasing complexity of tourism marketing action in terms of market information, the design and management of products and particularly, promotion has already triggered few joint ventures with the public sector across the globe.

Special attention should be given to the imperative role of the so called voluntary sector (NGOs), made up of non profit making organisations, of people or private entities. The NGOs have carried out important work in terms of tourism policy in association with the private and public sectors. In this respect, there is a need to identify and highlight their work in the field of information and promotion, the management of tourism excellencies plans (environment and ecology), the provision of auxiliary services that improve the competitiveness of tourism regions (information, after sales services etc.) and their collaboration with enterprises in terms of training and manpower development.

'Alternative Tourism' Policy

The spectacular changes that tourism markets are undergoing have provided enough reasons for the emergence of the New tourism. Owing to which several nations have incorporated strategically changes in their policies. This strategy changes has led to some traditional tourism policy objectives being given less importance (e.g. generating record tourist arrivals and receipts) and to the targeting of specific new and objectives, such as making tourism enterprises and regions competitive and meeting social, economic objectives. The Spanish Framework plan for competitiveness in Tourism (Plan Futures) approved in 1992 by the Central Government, and the 17 Autonomous Communities, like the Australian National Tourism Strategy, also approved in 1992, establishes competitiveness as the aim of tourism policy, in the Krippen-dor-fian frame work of appropriate social economic and environmental conditioning factors. Other advanced tourism policies are being developed in a similar benchmark scenario. Globally the Policy makers, Planners and the opinion makers are working of Models and Frameworks envisaging to incorporate judicious blend of both Old and Newer forms of Tourism. Haryana Tourism has set up an exemplary example in the country, having had used various forms of Tourism in right perspective. Pilgrimage among the oldest and conventional forms of activities is being promoted along side Highway; Adventure; Farm tourism; Craft Mela of Surajkund attracts several domestic and Foreign tourists. Proper policy designs have to be researched and developed based upon various possibilities in terms of Geographic Location, Resources, Socio-Religious-Cultural values & attractions etc., for individual destinations on case to case basis, no single paradigm successful at a place may be effective at different places or even at the same destination in different situations.

Infact, Tourism has emerged as an important tool for Poverty eradication and for distribution of income, WTO has initiated research and consultation on the interrelation between tourism and poverty. In recent years this focus has intensified as it has become apparent that this sector has immense potential to help the global fight against poverty.

- In the world's developing countries and particularly the less developed countries (LDCs), tourism is almost universally the leading source of economic growth, foreign exchange, investment and job creation.
- It is one of the few areas of potential comparative advantage common to all of these countries.
- It has unique potential to generate trade and investment directly at the local level as tourists and entrepreneurs seek new destinations.
- It can contribute significantly to rural development, agricultural transformation, community enrichment and social empowerment, particularly for women.
- It can preserve cultural and heritage traditions
- Most developing countries are well positioned to benefit from natural and cultural heritage tourism, provided that transport, infrastructure and sustainability criteria are effectively assured.
- Several development models can be cautiously adapted for intra- and interregional contexts.
- Developed states, agencies, enterprises and travellers themselves must adopt a proactive approach to tourism as a catalyst for poverty alleviation at the destinations.

Impact of Technology on New Tourism

The future technological changes in transportation are likely to be extensions of existing technologies in the form of bigger jumbo jets, faster trains etc., for travel. Technology can be used to create smaller air tunnels than the existing Air Corridors. Booking and Reservation system are likely to be more sophisticated, globalized and more widely available, like, SABRE, AMEADUS, GALILEO etc. The increase in use of Internet shall be much wide-spread and same in turn may pose some threat to Travel Agents. Use of Netscape Navigator, Internet Explorer to access the web makes home use and straight forward. The multimedia revolution offers the prospects of sophisticated home-based leisure and enhancement of attractions away from home. Digitized movies can be stored and accessed easily that shall definitely have positive impact on the extended tourism experiences. Computer games, Virtual Reality, or cyber space is an extension of technology which too shall have far reaching impact on the new age tourism, for instance, SEGA has developed theme park in Japan with interactive attractions which will let people shoot and steer their way through Adventures, and DISNEY utilizes virtual reality in its heritage park at Washington DC so that visitors can experience life as soldier, or as a slave.

E-ticketing

The International Air Transport Association (IATA) claims that penetration of e-tickets is already 93 per cent.

"In 100 days, the paper ticket will find a place in a museum. On June 1, 2008, we will achieve 100 per cent electronic ticketing," IATA Director General and CEO Giovanni Bisignani said in a statement. "While a paper ticket costs $10 to process, e-ticketing reduces that cost to $1. The industry will save over $3 billion each year by offering the passenger a better service. This is a win-win proposition." Sunil Chopra, IATA's country manager for India, pronounce that "In India, the penetration of e-tickets is 91 per cent, including foreign airlines,".

E-Marketing in Tourism

E-marketing approaches have been the major evolution—and revolution—in the hospitality industry in recent year. More and more customers are using online tools, and online tools are no longer exclusive to large hotel chains. The challenge of any tourism supplier is to generate traffic to its website, create demand and stimulate customer interest. Today, even with a limited budget and a little bit of creativity, small entities can also gain online presence simply by using their office tools more efficiently and effectively.

The Electronic Commerce has strong impact on the development of strong tourism destination brands. Electronic media have the potential to create strong direct links between individual tourism suppliers and their customers, thereby possibly undermining collective efforts to create strong destination brands. In addition, electronic media may have the potential to strengthen the process of destination brand creation, by facilitating interaction and cross-selling between complementary producers within a destination.

Conclusion

The spectacular growth of tourism trends in recent decades has given rise to a qualitative transformation of the markets. Standardized tourism products geared to a homogeneous demand are being replaced by a new age tourism i.e., the Alternative tourism, which should respond to the super segmentation of demand, the greater flexibility of supply, distribution and consumption, and the search for new sources of profitability in system economies and integrated values. In this context, the focus of the objectives and instruments of tourism policy has been progressively shifting from the simple maximization of visitors and tourism receipts to the creation of conditions for the competitiveness of tourism enterprises and destinations and from the primary use of promotional instruments to the application of specific models of tourism competitiveness that require the use of total quality management and process reengineering methods. The usage of technological advances is increasing, but, despite the growing importance of the Internet as an information source for international travellers, as a marketing tool and as a way of doing business, there is a general lack of information on how these travellers use the Internet for information, booking and purchase of travel products and services.

Indeed the New Tourism imbibes in itself a form of tourism activity which is more environmentally friendly, socially compassionate and aims at exploiting tourism with minimum negative impacts and maximizing the positive impacts. It envisages ensuring that the socio-economic benefits are percolated down to the lowest levels of society, and hence, proper policies may be worked out for effectively promoting Newer forms of tourism for mitigating poverty among lesser developing economies.

References

Blangy Sylvie 1991, Ecotourism and minimum impact policy, The role of guidelines and codes of ethics.

Butler R.W., 1991, Tourism, environment and sustainable development.

Cohen Erik 1984, The sociology of tourism, approaches, issues & findings.

Dietvorst, A.G.J. 1993, Tourist recreation development and spatial transformations.

Gunn Clare A. 1988 A Tourism planning, second edition.

Gunn Clare A. 1988 B Vacation Scope : Designing Tourist Regions second edition.

Guru, Lal Prasad 1989, Socio-Cultural, economic & Physical impacts of tourism in the southern part of Annapurna region, Nepal.

Fayos-Sola Eduardo (1996), Tourism Policy; A Mid-summer night's dream. Tourism Management 17(6).

Hass H. (1984), A Decade of Alternative Tourism in Sri Lanka. Alternative Tourism with a focus on Asia. Ecumenical Coalition on Third World Tourism, Bangkok.

Holden P. (ed) (1984), Alternative Tourism with a focus on Asia. Ecumenical Coalition on Third World Tourism, Bangkok.

Krippendorf, J, (1982), Towards new tourism: The importance of environmental and social factors. Tourism Management.

Kaur, Jagdish (1984) Himalayan Pilgrimage & New Tourism

Kumar, Bijender, "Tourism in Haryana : Need for Effective Training", Third world impact.

Lal Muni, Haryarna : On High Road to Prosperity (1974)

Lindberg Kreg, 1991. Policies for maximizing nature tourism's ecological and economic benefits.

Mishra S.K. "Haryana Tourism, Harbinger of Prosperity Back of the Beyond" (1980)

Ohja B.S. "Haryana Tourism Progress over the years, Haryana Review (1985)

Pahwa Ashok, "Resources are not: They become" (1979)

Poon (1993), A Tourism, Technology and Competitive Strategies CAB, Oxford.

Rosenow & Grreld Tourism Good, Bad, Ugly (1979)

Turner, L. and J. Ash, (1975), The Golden Hordes; International Tourism and the Pleasure Periphery, London; Constable.

COMMUNITY PARTICIPATION IN CULTURAL FESTIVALS AND ITS ROLE IN DESTINATION DEVELOPMENT

Ravinder Dogra

Assistant Professor, Indian Institute of Travel and Tourism Management, Gwalior

rdmtm9@gmail.com

Neelika Arora

Assistant Professor, Department of HRM and OB, Central University of Jammu

a_neelika@yahoo.com

Abstract

Community based tourism has become an important tool in promoting rural tourism. One of the emerging forms of community based tourism is the regional festivals or festival tourism, which is directly related with the local destination. The purpose of this study is to measure the impact of community awareness and perceived benefits on the participation of communities in the festivals and its impact on destination development. A survey, using a structured bilingual questionnaire, was conducted during the festival held in a rural destination (Mansar) of Jammu and Kashmir. The findings indicate that awareness regarding the tourism festivals and the benefits perceived by the local residents have a significant positive relationship with the community participation which further influences the destination development through events. This research provides insights about the importance of community awareness & perceived benefits in motivating local community to participate in the destination development process.

Keywords-Cultural Festivals, Community Participation, Destination Development, Rural Tourism

Introduction

Tourism as an industry is showing a tremendous growth and is proving itself as a most promising sector in terms of growth and development. It has been seen that tourism can do positive exploitation of economies of scale in national firms (Fagance, 1997; Liu, 2003; Andriotis, 2002; Croes, 2006). Tourism industry is spreading its arms and touching every aspect of human growth and giving its contribution in the growth of local economies, job creation and sustainable development of destinations (Williams & Shaw, 1998; Yu, Chancellor, & Cole, 2011). As the total international tourist arrivals increased from 25 million in 1950 to 277 million in 1980, 439 million in 1990, 684 million in 2000, 922 million in 2008 and international tourist arrivals grew by over 4% in 2011 to 982 million (UNWTO, 2012). UNWTO also forecasts a growth in international tourist arrivals of between 3% and 4% in 2012, so many Governments from different regions are working on tourism related projects to promote their economies from ground to top level. Economies of some small island countries are totally dependent on tourism and there tourism sector is getting full support from their governments (Louca, 2006). Tourism increases competition by encouraging new entrants in the market places, which provides a positive impact on the price level of goods and services (Croes, 2006).

Stronza & Gordillo (2008) pointed out that in long run tourism can destroy and disturb local communities. To avoid any negative consequences, the concept of sustainable tourism came into existence and it started involving local community participation in the development of destinations (Choi & Sirakaya, 2005; Hung, Sirakaya-Turk & Ingram, 2011). Sustainability in tourism can only be achieved by involving local communities in the development and decision making process (UNWTO,2005). There is a need to formulate a symbolic or mutual relationship between tourists and the community members (Wearing & McDonald 2002). Community participation is a fundamental requisite in decision making to achieve sustainability and absence of community participation in decision making for tourism development, leads to letdown in empowering the local communities (Miranda, 2007; Moscardo, 2008). Community participation in tourism planning and management is also supported by Neopopulist theory (Scheyvens, 2002). According to Mehmetoglu, (2001) community based tourism has become an important tool in promoting rural traditional industries as tourism generates large economic benefits for a destination. Aref & Redzuan (2009) pointed out that in absence of community partnership, the development and any kind of partnership cannot sustain in a destination.

Considering the need of community participation in tourism, different kinds of tourism like; eco, cultural, spiritual, business, and many others are promoted by the local governments and the destination planners by involving the local communities of tourist destinations in the planning and decision making processes. One of the emerging forms of community based tourism is the regional festivals or festival tourism, which is directly related with the local destination. Festival tourism is an emerging giant (Getz & Frisby, 1988) and it is accepted that it can be used as a tool for marketing of a destination and it creates opportunities for the community residents to work in a coordinated way to attract tourists in their destination for the success of the festival. Fairs and festivals are very economical kind of tourism product where not too much budget or resources are required for its organising and other positive point in its characteristic is its short duration, which motivates local residents to participate in these events with full energy and enthusiasm. Performing arts and other festivals are now a universal tourism trend (Getz, 1991; Rolfe, 1992; Chacko and Schaffer, 1993). There is a rise in number of festivals celebration worldwide, because of its multidimensional supplies like culture, heritage, local performances, local cuisines and local tradition. The demand factor also plays an important role as the demand of diverse kind of tourism product has changed and a huge segment of tourists prefer festivals as a tourism product (Hughes 1995; McCrone, Morris & Kiely 1995). Growing publicity of festivals is making it one of the fastest growing types of tourism attractions (Crompton & McKay, 1997; Getz, 1997). According to O'Sullivan, 2010, Festival tourism is a complex phenomenon and can be categorized into sociological perspective (Manning, 1983; Tomlinson, 1986; Van Esterik, 1982; Wilson & Udall, 1982); leisure participation (Getz, 1988; Pearce, 1982); community development (Getz & Frisby, 1988; Janniskee, 1996) and from a tourism industry perspective (Mitchell and Wall, 1989; Mules, 1998; Mules & McDonald, 1994; Smith& Jenner, 1998; Syme, 1989). Some of the festivals are so much powerful that they act as brand ambassador of their destinations and tourists visit these destinations just to witness these festivals. By organising festivals, communities also promote their culture, art, heritage and other touristic products. During the time of festivals, local residents get involved in various activities related to the embellishment and management of their locality (Janniskee, 1996).

By seeing the success of festivals in tourism promotion, community upliftment, economic gains and socio-cultural benefits, Government of India adopted a policy of promoting local regional festivals in different states and Union territories of the country. Under the scheme of festival promotion, ministry of tourism provides financial and technical assistance to State and Union Territory Government from the year 2007 and funds are sanctioned under this scheme for the upliftment and proper management of local traditional festivals. In 2007, Rs. 411 lakhs were sanctioned for the promotion of regional festivals covering Andhra Pradesh, Arunachal Pradesh, Assam, Chandigarh, Delhi, Haryana, Himachal Pradesh, Jammu and Kashmir, Madhya Pradesh, Manipur, Mizoram, Nagaland, Puducherry, Sikkim, Tamil Nadu, Tripura, Uttar Pradesh, Uttarakhand and West Bengal. In the financial year 2011-2012, the budget for the festivals promotion by the ministry of tourism was raised to 634.110 lakhs (MOT-GOI, 2012). Even the Department Of Tourism, J&K government has adopted the strategy of promoting destinations through fairs and festivals. Tourism department of Jammu and Kashmir has identified some festivals from the three different regions of the state namely Kashmir, Jammu and Ladakh (DOT-J&K, 2012). The various festivals getting support of tourism department of J&K have been listed out in table no. 1

Table No. 1:LIST OF FESTIVALS

S.No	Name of the Festival	Region of The State	Time of Occurrence
1	Lohri	Jammu	January
2	Baisakhi	Jammu/ Kashmir	April
3	Bahu fair	Jammu	Mar- April & Sept- Oct
4	Bhaderwah Festival	Jammu	June
5	Baba Chamliyal fair	Jammu	June
6	Jhiri fair	Jammu	Oct- Nov
7	Jammu Festival	Jammu	April
8	Navratra Festival	Jammu	Sept or Oct
9	Hemis festival	Ladakh	June
10	Ladakh Festival	Ladakh	Sept
11	Losar	Ladakh	Jan
12	Snow Festival	Kashmir	Jan or Feb
13	Saffron Festival	Kashmir	October
14	Kheer Bhawani festival	Kashmir	June
15	Tulip festival	Kashmir	April

Source- DOT-Jammu and Kashmir Government.

Literature Review

Festival Impacts and Perceived Benefits

Festivals have a positive impact on destination development as also on the community empowerment, as the festival extends the tourist season, generates revenue for the development of destination (Ritchie & Beliveau, 1974), support existing businesses and encourage new establishments (Mitchell & Wall, 1986). The negative impacts of festivals on the destination development and community are nominal as per the impact on environment is concerned, the transportation contributes a major impact. But due to the short duration of festivals, the negative impacts on the destination do not last last for a long term (Bramwell & Lane,

1993; Mathieson & Wall, 1982; Stewart, 1998). So it is would be apt to say that festival tourism promotes destination development in a sustainable way. In 1995 the British Tourist Authority promoted some 1000 cultural events under the banner of the festival of Arts & Culture which resulted in 150 million pounds extra spending by overseas visitors alone (Smith and Jenner, 1998). Due to ability of casting long lasting impacts on the minds of the tourists, these festivals are gaining greater popularity. As the festivals are directly related with the joy, happiness, enjoyment and fun, these festivals create a special place in the minds of the visitors attending these festivals .These kinds of festivals create the feeling of unity among the local residents and provide them the opportunity to present their cultural and heritage assets to the visitors. These events provide stage to the local communities to show their unique art and traditional assets to the visitors (Copley & Robson, 1996). The link between tourism and environmental conservation has been recognized (Mathieson & Wall, 1982; Bramwell & Lane, 1993; Stewart 1998) and as the short duration of festivals cause minimum harm to the atmosphere, so these short duration festivals are considered as eco-friendly tourism products.

Awareness and Involvement

Inskeep (1991) states that the host communities must be included in the planning process and participation should be in large sense so that there will be maximum socio-economic benefits to the local communities. Involvement of local communities is crucial in a tourism development process, as local community is the nucleus of a tourism product in a tourist destination. Lack of awareness is among one of the factors that act as barriers to the community participation and affect the tourism development process in a destination (Jamal and Getz, 1995). Ryan and Montgomery (1994) pointed out that there is a need to educate community about the benefits of tourism, and that how their participation can eradicate or solve their problems. Due to the considerable income generating properties and its ability to provide jobs, tourism is considered as a valuable asset in economic development (William & Shaw, 1998). Local residents should be involved in the planning decision regarding tourism development, as they are the people who live in communities in tourist destinations and enjoy or suffer the main impacts of tourism (Lea, 1988; Murphy, 1985).

It is hard to get public support and co-operation if the policy makers make the plan for a destination by ignoring local communities. Participation in tourism shares two main perspectives namely participation in decision making process and tourism benefits sharing (Timothy 1999). Choi and Sirakaya (2005) pointed out that local residents should be included in the decision making process of a destination, so as to make them feel part of the developmental process. Festivals are like special events which activate the spirit and energy of the local community, result in the active and positive participation by the local community residents. Policy makers and destination planners often use some famous and popular festivals to attract tourist towards the tourist destination. The entire process of tourism expansion at a destination depends on the vigorous and self-motivated support of the local residents, without which the sustainable development of a destination is not possible. Van Harssel (1994) pointed out that any efficient plan cannot be successful without involving local community in it. It simply proves that success of tourism development in a destination depends on strong community support (Getz, 1983). The level of local tolerance to tourism can be increased through resident participation and by increasing social carrying capacity in a destination (D'Amore, 1983; Tosun, 2002). On the basis of literature review, following hypothesis has been generated-

H1. The level of participation is positively related to the awareness and perceived benefits of the local community. Higher the level of awareness and perceived benefits, higher is the level of participation.

Participation and Destination Development

Tourism is basically a participatory approach and the participatory approach motivates the local community to create a reasonable consensus between tourism and the host community. Tourism planning may create a sense of ownership among residents- that it was their own decision to develop tourism in its present form (Wood, 1994). The role of community in destination development cannot be ignored and similarly community participation also helps in the development of a destination. It is essential to involve local communities in the development of destinations (Cook, 1982), as it is noted that community involvement represents a technique for limiting negative social impacts (Pearce, 1994). Tosun (2000) commented that the community should be made aware about the future benefits and impacts of tourism in their destination so that they can participate in tourism development process. The participatory approach leads to a greater sense of empowerment in addressing community issues as also solving destination related issues. Regional festivals promote community participation, engaging and motivating local communities to participate in the festival with vigor and absorption.

Choi and Sirakaya, (2005) states that the community should be the focus point of all the decision making process taken regarding the tourism development in the tourist destination. According to Tosun & Timothy (2003), community participation can change the attitude of local people from passivity to responsibility and can create a new positive relationship in the form of sharing power and decision making between the individual and the destination. Murphy (1985) puts it; tourism relies on the goodwill and cooperation of local people because they are a part of its product and where development and planning do not fit in with local aspirations and capacity, resistance and hostility can destroy the industry's potential altogether. Ying and Zhou (2007) gave two perspectives of community participation in tourism; first, the decision making process, a). Allowing residents to become empowered in tourism development. and b). Expressing their concerns and desires; and secondly the tourism benefits.

Hollnsteiner, (1977) argued that local residents should be involved in the decision making as it effects their lives from several aspects. Participation of local communities stimulates the formulation of implementable policies, with the assumption being that if local residents believe that they have a say in a fair and open process of policy and plan development they may be willing to accept the outcome of that process (Timothy, 1999). UNWTO, (2005) pointed out that there is a need to recognise that tourism should benefits the local community and the local residents should be involved in the decision making. Pearce (1994) supported the importance of community participation by arguing that it is a technique which limits negative social impacts in the community and in the destination.

White (1982) supported the necessity of community participation by outlining nine different arguments, which includes; i. More will be accomplished, ii. Services can be provided at lower cost, iii. Participation has an intrinsic value for participants, iv. It is a catalyst for further development efforts, v. Participation leads to a sense of responsibility for the project, vi. It guarantees that a felt need is involved, vii. Participation ensures things are done in right way, viii. It uses indigenous knowledge and expertise, ix. It frees communities from dependence on professionals. Boaden, Goldsmith, Hampton & Stringer (1982) identified four main reasons from public administration point of view that have made community participation necessary as an alternative strategy and that are i. Functional fragmentation of public administration, ii. Centralization of local government, iii. Professionalization of service provision and the increasing remoteness of government from people.

H2. Development of destination depends on the community participation. Higher the participation higher will be the development.

The study aims to test a community based on model to explain how the community benefits and community awareness can effect community participation also how the community participation effects the destination development.

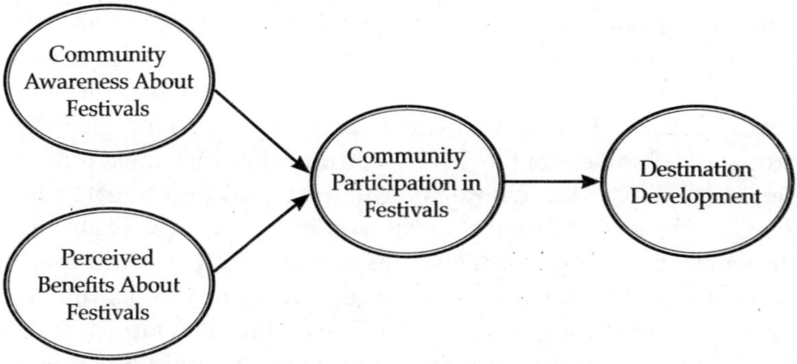

Fig. 1: Model for Community Participation and Destination Development

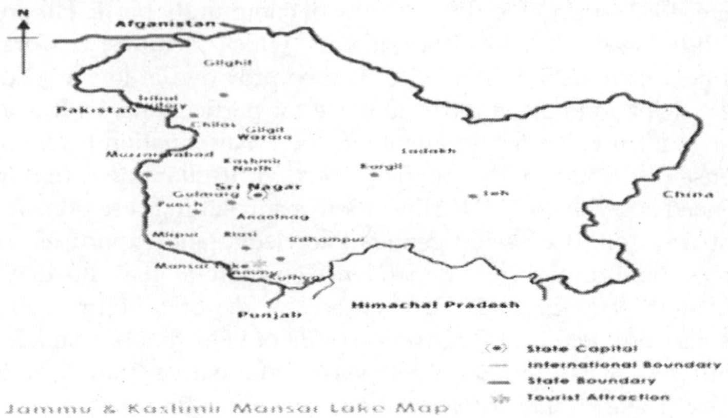

Jammu & Kashmir Mansar Lake Map

Study Area

A tourist destination Mansar was selected for this study as the destination is a popular tourist attraction in Jammu and Kashmir. Mansar is known for its lake, which is beautiful. This destination is situated on the national highway connecting Jammu to Kashmir region and is easily accessible to nearby destinations. The other nearby tourist destination is Surinsar and Manwal temples, which are also very popular in terms of tourism. Surinsar is a sister lake of Mansar and at a distance of 16 kms. Mansar believed to have link with the Mahabharata period as it is believed that Arjun's son Babor shot an arrow in Surinsar to reach Pataal (Hell) and came back from Mansar with Mani to cure his father Arjuna. The wildlife sanctuary located in the outskirts of Mansar is under development and it is stretched to Surinsar from Mansar. The nearby railway station Manwal is at around 12 kms. For the proper development of the destination an authority named SMDA (Surinsar Mansar Development Authority) has been created by the Government of Jammu and Kashmir. Nag temple is also an attraction of this place which pulls a large number of devotees to this place. Mansar witnesses large number of visitors during vacations and during festivals like Diwali and Navratras. From the last four years, department of tourism is organising baisakhi festival at this destination and this year also Department of tourism organised baisakhi festival in Mansar. This year department of tourism organised a cultural show along the lake premises and a large number of people, both local residents and the tourists were gathered there to witness the festival. SMDA has started many works for the development of destination which includes construction of Toilets, parking space, parks, eating point and accommodations for the tourists.

Research Methodology

The study was conducted at Mansar tourist destination of Jammu and Kashmir. A focus group interview was conducted with the local residents of Mansar and responses were recorded. A questionnaire was prepared and pilot tested on a sample of (n=20) local residents of Basohli (in J&K), during the famous Ramleela festival. Changes in the questionnaire were made according to feedback received from the respondents. For the purpose of this study a visit was made to the Mansar Lake during Baisakhi (13-15 April) and Meetings with Villagers, Shopkeepers and Small vendors were conducted. One hundred and fifty five (n=155) in-depth interviews were conducted with different local stake holders including shopkeepers, artists, panchayat members, students, government employees and senior citizens. A convenience sampling method was used because of shortage of time as the festival was for a limited time period. For all constructs measured in the study, a ten point likert scale was used. Questionnaire was prepared in both Hindi and English languages. The measurement scales used in the current study were developed from past studies. Local residents' awareness was measured on the basis of Tosun & Timothy's (2003) argument on community participation. Community participation was measured by Pretty's (1995) typology of participation. Perceived community benefits were measured by the motivation part of MOA model developed by the Hung, Sirakaya and Ingram (2010). The reliability of each factor was determined using Cronbach's alpha. The low value of alpha suggests the item has a low contribution to its construct (Churchill 1979).

Findings

The descriptive statistics (mean and standard deviation) related to each of the items measured is presented in Table 2. The findings suggest that expected for economic benefits and community involvement in festival planning, the mean scores for all the items are high. Further the Cronbach Alpha scores for each of the construct under study is greater than 0.7 indicating reliability in measurement.

Table 2: Descriptive Statistics of Constructs under Study (n=155)

S. No.	Construct / Item	Mean	Standard Deviation	Cronbach Alpha
	AWARENESS			
1	Festival can be used as a tool for tourist destination promotion.	8.23	1.62	0.831
2	This is one of the biggest festivals of your destination	8.26	1.31	
3	This festival provides opportunities to interact with people of other cultures	5.0	2.47	
4	Festival can be used as a tool for tourist destination promotion	8.23	1.62	
5	This is one of the biggest festivals of your 1destination.	8.24	1.31	
6	This festival provides opportunities to interact with people of other cultures	5.70	2.47	
	BENEFITS			
7	This festival generates employment opportunity in your area.	6.26	2.32	0.843
8	This festival is helping in raising the income of shopkeepers.	8.09	1.39	
9	This festival is increasing the income of villagers in your area	5.70	2.44	
	DESTINATION DEVELOPMENT			
10	This festival helps in raising the reputation of your destination.	8.60	1.33	0.822
11	This festival is promoting development in your destination.	7.37	1.86	
12	This Festival attracts large number of tourists.	7.70	1.68	
	This festival is promoting tourism in your area	8.37	1.25	

S. No.	Construct / Item	Mean	Standard Deviation	Cronbach Alpha
	PARTICIPATION			
13	Locals are also participating in this festival.	6.79	3.07	0.891
14	Locals of this destination are feeling themselves as a part of this festival	8.00	1.84	
15	Tourism agencies include our representatives in the planning and functioning of this festival.	6.74	2.09	

All items measured on 10 point Likert Scale

To test the first hypothesis i.e. impact of community's awareness regarding the festivals and perceived benefits from festivals on the community participation in festivals a regression analysis was done using SPSS and it was found that there is a positive significant relationship between community awareness and perceived benefits on community participation (see Table 3)

Table 3: Regression Results of Relationship between Awareness, Benefits and Community Participation

	Coef-ficient	SE	t	p	VIF
Constant	-1.267	1.594	-0.79	0.41	
Community Awareness	0.7104	0.3016	2.36	0.023	2.789
Community Benefit	0.3991	0.2071	1.93	0.041	2.789
	R- Square = 0.536				
	R- Square (Adjusted) = 0.512				

Dependent Variable: Community Participation

The regression results clearly indicate that there exists a significant relationship between community awareness (CA) & Community participation (CP) [$\beta = 0.71$, $p<0.05$] and between Perceived Community Benefits (CB) – Community participation (CP) [$\beta = 0.39$, $p<0.05$]. The direction of relationship is positive, so we accept the hypothesis that community awareness and perceived community benefits has a positive impact on the community participation.

The second hypothesis i.e. development of destination depends on the community participation tests the impact of community participation in festivals on the destination development. Regression analysis was done using SPSS and it was found that there is a positive significant relationship between community participation and destination development (see Table 4)

Table 3: Regression Results of Relationship between Community Participation and Destination Development

	Coefficient	SE	t	p	VIF
Constant	4.09	0.57	7.19	0.000	
Community Participation	0.50	0.08	6.57	0.000	1.000
	R- Square = 0.513				
	R- Square (Adjusted) = 0.501				

Dependent Variable : Destination Development

The regression results clearly indicate that there is a significant relationship between Community Participation (CP) and Destination Development (DD) [$\beta = 0.50$, $p<0.05$]. The direction of relationship is positive, so we accept the second hypothesis that community participation has a positive impact on the destination development.

Findings show that the community awareness and community benefits are having a significant impact on the community participation. People believe that they should be made aware about the impacts of tourism. It has been observed from different studies that awareness about the tourism impacts increases the participation level of local communities. There should be a share of local community in the benefits obtained. There is a significant impact of community participation on the destination development. Finding shows that the local community believes that they should be involved in the destination development planning and implementation. The findings shows that local community of Mansar agrees on a fact that a tourist destination can be promoted through organizing festivals and the role of festivals in the development of a destination cannot be ignored. Locals believe that Baisakhi festival acts like a catalyst to attract tourists in Mansar and it has been observed that their destination registers good number of tourist during this event. Event provides opportunities for villagers to earn some monetary benefits and raise the income of shopkeepers by many folds. Results depicts that the locals believe that Baisakhi is an important festival of their destination and this festival is helping in the promotion and development of their destination. Almost every respondent agreed on the fact that such festivals should be promoted in their destination.

Conclusion & Future Research

Festivals are the emerging form of travel attractions and such events are getting popularity because of short duration and are a blend of cultural heritage, energy, fun and enjoyment. The best thing about the festival is the involvement of local community in the functioning of the festival related activities. So a festival as a tourism product also helps in the empowerment of local communities by creating opportunities like employment, small business opportunities, good infrastructure and better civic amenities.

This study reached to the conclusion that people of Mansar destination took Baisakhi festival as one of the main occasion of their destination. This festival adds happiness and energy in the life of local residents and provides them a stage where they can celebrate this festival with natives as well as with the tourists. The remarkable finding came out from the study is the awareness of the local residents about their destination and the festival's importance in attracting tourists towards the destination. The festival holds special place in the hearts of local residents of Mansar and the residents from both Hindu and Muslim religions participated in it with full enthusiasm. Local residents believe that this festival holds the enough potential to attract tourists towards Mansar and this festival should be promoted and celebrated every year. In accordance with the classification given by Sullivan and Jackson (2002), this festival falls in the category of 'Tourist Tempter' festivals but this needs to promoted up to the level of 'Big Bang' festival.

The other noteworthy characteristic about the festival is that it requires very limited resources as compare to other forms of tourism. So for developing countries this is a very economical kind of tool where they can generate income from tourists and can also empower local communities by motivating them to get involved in the activities related with the organising of the festivals. Country like India, which is known for its culture and festivals is having a great potential to tap large number of tourists and simultaneously is having a chance to make its rural population self dependent. It has been found that mostly due to the lack of awareness; people of rural areas remain separated from the benefits of tourism. In case of festivals the locals are more aware regarding their cultural roots and cause of the festivals and can generate good income by passing this information to the visitors of their festivals.

Despite its contributions, this study has several limitations that should be addressed in future research. Present literature studies the role of festivals in community empowerment and destination development in developing countries but it lacks the aspect of studying the barriers in the destination development and community participation. As Tosun (2000), mentioned that conditions in both developing and developed countries are different and these both kinds of developing and developed countries requires different kinds of perspectives to understand the concept of community participation in tourism related issues. Tosun (2000), pointed three major kind of barriers in the community participation process in Turkey, which includes operational, structural and cultural barriers. Future research can be done in finding of some more kinds of barriers which may exist in developing countries regarding the community participation in events related to the tourism. Similarly research can be done in finding out the level of involvement of local communities in different kind of festivals and the impact of community participation on the success of a festival or event.

References

Andriotis, K. (2008). "Integrated resort development: The case of Cavo Sidero, Crete". Journal of Sustainable Tourism, Vol. 16 No. 4, pp. 428–444.

Aref, F., & Redzuan, M.B. (2008). "Barriers to Community Participation Towards Tourism Development in Shiraz, Iran". Pakistan Journal of Social Sciences, Vol. 5 No.9, pp. 936-940.

Aref, F., & Redzuan, M.B. (2009). "Assessing the Level of Community Participation as a Component of Community Capacity Building for Tourism Development". European Journal of Social Sciences, Vol. 8 No. 1, pp. 68-75.

Bramwell, B., & Lane, B. (1993). "Interpretation and sustainable tourism: The potential and pitfalls". Journal of Sustainable Tourism, Vol. 1 No.2, pp. 71–80.

Chacko, H.E., & Schaffer, J.D. (1993). "The evolution of a festival: Creole Christmas in New Orleans". Tourism Management. Vol. 1 No.46, pp. 475-482.

Choi, H.S., & Sirakaya, E. (2005). "Measuring Residents' Attitude toward Sustainable Tourism: Development of Sustainable Tourism Attitude Scale". Journal of Travel Research, Vol. 43, pp. 380-394.

Churchill, G.A. (1979). "A Paradigm for Developing Better Measures of Marketing Constructs". Journal of Marketing Research, XVI (February): 64-73.

Cole, S. (2006). "Information and empowerment: The keys to achieving sustainable tourism". Journal of Sustainable Tourism, Vol. 14 No.6, pp. 629–644.

Cook, C.C. (1988). "Components of neighbourhood satisfaction: Responses from urban and suburban single-parent women". Environment and Behaviour, Vol. 20 No.2, pp. 115–149.

Cook, K. (2000). "Charting futures for sociology: Structure and action". Contemporary Sociology, Vol. 29, pp. 685–692.

Cooke, K. (1982). "Guidelines for Socially Appropriate Tourism Development in British Columbia". Journal of Travel Research, Vol. 21 No.1, pp. 22–28.

Copley, P. & Robson, I. (1996). "Tourism, arts marketing and the modernist paradox. In M. Robinson, N. Evans and P. Callaghan (eds) Tourism and Culture: Image, Identity and Marketing", pp 15-44. Sunderland: Centre for Travel and Tourism, British Education Publishers.

Croes, R.R. (2006). "A paradigm shift to a new strategy for small island economies: embracing demand side economics for value enhancement and long term economic stability". Tourism Management, Vol. 27, pp. 453-465.

Crompton, J. L., & McKay, S. L. (1997). "Motives of visitors attending festival events". Annals of Tourism Research, Vol. 24 No.2, pp. 425–439.

D'Amore, L. (1983). "Guidelines to planning in harmony with the host community". Murphy (Ed.), Tourism in Canada: Selected issues and options (pp. 135-159). Victoria, BC: University of Victoria, Department of Geography.

Department of Tourism, Jammu and Kashmir.(2012). Events and Festivals 2012. Available from http://www.jktourism.org.

Dillman, D. A. (1978). "Mail and Telephone Surveys: The Total Design Method". New York: Wiley-Interscience.

Dillman, D. A. (2007). "Mail and Internet Surveys: The Tailored Design Method", 2nd edition. Hoboken, NJ: Wiley.

Dogan, H.Z. (1989). "Forms of adjustment: Social cultural impacts of tourism". Annals of Tourism Research, Vol.16, pp. 216-236.

Fagence, M. (1977). "Citizen participation in planning". Oxford : Pergamon.

Garrod B., & Fyall A. (1998). "Beyond the rhetoric of sustainable tourism". Tourism Management, Vol. 19, No. 3.

Getz, D. (1984). "Tourism, community organisation and the social multiplier". Leisure, Tourism and Social Change. Edinburgh: Centre for Leisure Research.

Getz, D. (1986). "Tourism and population change: Long-term impacts of tourism in the Badenoch and Strathspey District of the Scottish Highlands". Scottish Geographical Journal, Vol. 102 No.2, pp. 113–126.

Getz, D. (1993). "Festival and Special Events". In Khan, Olsen, & Var (Eds), Encyclopedia of hospitality and tourism, pp. 789-810. New York, NY: Van Rostrand Reinhold.

Getz, D. (1997). "Event Management & Event Tourism". New York: Cognizant Communication.

Getz, D. & Frisby, W. (1988). "Evaluating management effectiveness in community-run festivals". Journal of Travel Research (Summer), pp. 22–9.

Gursoy, D., & Rutherford, D. G. (2004). "Host attitudes toward tourism - an improved structural model". Annals of Tourism Research, Vol. 31 No.3, pp. 495-516.

Harrison, D. (1992). "International tourism and the less developed countries". In D. Harrison (Ed.), The social consequences of tourism in less developed countries (pp. 1–18). London: Bellhaven.

Harssel, V. (1994). "Tourism – An Exploration (Third Edition)". Prentice Hall Career & Technology, New Jersey.

Hollnsteiner, M.R. (1977). "People power: Community participation in the planning of human settlements". Assignment Children, Vol. 43, pp.11-47.

Hong, E. (1985). "The third world while it lasts: The social and environmental impact of tourism with special reference to Malaysia". Penang: Consumers' Association of Penang.

Hughes, G. (1995). "The cultural construction of sustainable tourism". Tourism Management, Vol. 16 No. 1, pp. 49–59.

Hughes, G. (2002). "Environmental indicators". Annals of Tourism Research, Vol. 29 No.2, pp. 457–477.

Hung, K., Sirakaya-Turk, E., & Ingram, L. J. (2011). "Testing the efficacy of an integrative model for community participation". Journal of Travel Research, Vol. 50, pp. 276–288.

Inskeep, E. (1991). "Tourism planning, an integrated and sustainable development approach". New York: Van Nostrand Reinhold.

Inskeep, E. (1988). "Tourism planning". Journal of the American Planning Association, Vol. 54 No.3, pp. 360-371.

Inskeep, E. (1991). "Tourism planning, an integrated and sustainable development approach". New York: Van Nostrand Reinhold.

Inskeep, E., & Kallenberger, M. (1992). "An integrated approach to resort development". Madrid: World Tourism Organisation.

International Institute of Tourism Studies (1991). "Global assessment of tourism policy". Washington, DC: The George Washington University.

Jamal, T.B., & Getz, D. (1995). "Collaboration theory and community tourism planning". Annals of Tourism Research, Vol, 22, pp. 186-204.

Jamal, T.B., and Getz, D. (1999). "Community Roundtable for Tourism Related Conflicts: The Dialectics of Consensus and Progress Structures." Journal of Sustainable Tourism, Vol. 7, pp. 290-313.

Janniskee, R. (1996). "Historic houses and special events". Annals of Tourism Research,Vol. 23, No.2, pp. 398–414.

Jurowski, C., Uysal, M., & Williams, D.R. (1997). "A Theoretical Analysis of Host Community Resident Reactions to Tourism". Journal of Travel Research, Vol. 36 No.2, pp. 3-11.

Lea, J. (1988). "Tourism and development in the third world". London: Routledge.

Likert, R. (1968). "The method of constructing an attitude scale". In M. Fishbein (Ed.), 'Readings in Attitude Theory and Measurement. New York: Wiley.

Liu, Z. (2003). "Sustainable tourism development: A critique". Journal of Sustainable Tourism, Vol. 11, No. 6, pp. 459–475.

Louca, C. (2006). "Income and expenditure in the tourism industry: time series evidence from Cyprus". Tourism Economics, Vol. 12 No. 4, pp. 603-617.

Mathieson, A., & Wall, G. (1982). "Tourism: Economic, Physical and Social Impacts". London: Longman.

Manning, F. (1983). "The Celebration of Society: Perspectives on Contemporary Cultural Performance". New York: Bowling Green Popular Press.

McCrone, D.,Morris, A., & Kiely, R. (1995). "Scotland—the Brand: The Making of Scottish Heritage". Edinburgh: Edinburgh University Press.

Mehmetoglu, M. (2001). "Economic scale of community-run festivals: a case study". Event Management, Vol. 7, No. 2, pp. 93-102.

Mehmetoglu, M., & Ellingsen, K.A. (2005). "Do small-scale festivals adopt "market orientation" as a management philosophy?". Event Management, Vol. 9 No. 3, pp.119-132.

Ministry of Tourism, Government Of India. (2012). "Festival schemes and sanctioned projects", available from http://www.tourism.gov.in.

Miranda, J.F. (1997). "The impact of tourism on community development". Unpublished graduation thesis, University of Costa Rica, San Pedro, Costa Rica.

Moscardo, G., & Pearce, P. (1999). "Understanding Ethnic Tourists". Annals of Tourism Research. Vol. 26, pp 416–434.

Mowforth, M., & Munt, I. (1998). "Tourism and sustainability: New tourism in the third world". London: Routledge.

Mules, T., & McDonald, S. (1994). "The economic impact of special events: The use of forecasts". Festival Management and Event Tourism, Vol. 2, pp. 45–53.

Mules, T. (1998). Events tourism and economic development in Australia. In D. Tyler Y. Gurrier and M. Robertson Managing Tourism in Cities: Policy, Process and Practice. Chichester: John Wiley.

Murphy, P.E. (1985). "Tourism: A community approach", Methuen, New York, NY (1985).

Okazaki, E. (2008). "A Community-based Tourism Model: Its Conception and Use." Journal of Sustainable Tourism, Vol. 16, No. 5, pp. 511-29.

O'Sullivan, D. and Jackson, M.J. (2002). "Festival tourism: A contributor to sustainable local economic development?". Journal of Sustainable Tourism, Vol. 10, No. 4, pp. 325–42.

Pearce, D. G. (1991). Challenge and change in East European tourism: A Yugoslav example. In M. T. Sinclair, &M. J. Stabler, The tourism industry: An international analysis (pp. 223-240). Wallingford: CAB International.

Pearce, P. (1995). "From Culture Shock and Culture Arrogance to Culture Exchange". Journal of Sustainable Tourism, Vol. 3, pp.143–154.

Pearce, P. (1982). "The Social Psychology of Tourist Behaviour". London: Pergamon.

Prentice, R. (1993). "Community-driven Tourism Planning and Residents' Preference". Tourism Management, Vol.14, pp. 218-27.

Pretty, J. (1995). "The Many Interpretations of Participation." In Focus, Vol. 16, pp. 4-5.

Reed, M. (1997). "Power relations and community-based tourism planning". Annals of Tourism Research, Vol. 24, pp. 566-591.

Ritchie, J.R.B. (1988). "Consensus policy formulation in tourism: Measuring resident views via survey research". Tourism Management, Vol. 9, No.3, pp. 199-212.

Ritchie, J.R.B. (1993). "Crafting a destination vision: Putting the concept of resident-responsive tourism into practice". Tourism Management, Vol. 14, pp. 379-89.

Ryan, C., Scotland, A., & Montgomery, D. (1998). "Resident Attitudes to Tourism Development: A Comparative Study between the Rangitikei, New Zealand and Bakewell, United Kingdom". Progress in Tourism and Hospitality Research,Vol 4, pp. 115–130.

Rolfe, H. (1992). "Arts Festivals in the UK", London, Policy Studies Institute.

Scheyvens, R. (2002). "Tourism for development: Empowering communities". Harlow, UK: Prentice Hall.

Simpson, M. C. (2008). "Community benefit tourism initiatives: a conceptual oxymoron?". Tourism Management, Vol. 29, pp. 1-18.

Sirakaya, E., T. Jamal, & Choi, H.S. (2001). "Developing Indicators for Destination Sustainability." In The Encyclopedia of Ecotourism, edited by D. B. Weaver. New York: CABI, pp. 411-32.

Sirakaya-Turk, E. (2007). "Concurrent Validity of the Sustainable Tourism Attitude Scale." Annals of Tourism Research, Vol. 34, No. 4, pp.1081-84.

Sirakaya-Turk, E., Y. Ekinci, & Kaya, A.G. (2008). "An Examination of the Validity of SUS-TAS in Cross-Cultures". Journal of Travel Research, Vol. 46, pp. 414-21.

Smith, C. & Jenner, P. (1998). "The jimpact of festivals and special event tourism". Travel and Tourism Analyst, pp. 4.

Stewart, E.J. (1998). "The place of interpretation. Tourism Management". Vol. 6, No.1, pp. 44–52.

Stronza, A., & Gordillo, J. (2008). Community views of ecotourism. Annals of Tourism Research, 35(2), 448–468.

Syme, G., Shaw, B., Fenton, D. and Mueller, W. (1989). The Planning and Evaluation of Hallmark Events. Oxford: Avebury.

Timothy, D. J. (1999). "Participatory Planning: A View of Tourism in Indonesia." Annals of Tourism Research, Vol. 26, No. 2, pp. 371-91.

Timothy, D. J., and C. Tosun (2003). "Appropriate Planning for Tourism in Destination Communities: Participation, Incremental Growth and Collaboration." In Tourism in Destination Communities, edited by S. Singh, D. J. Timothy, and R. K. Dowling. Cambridge, MA: CABI, pp. 181-204.

Tomlinson, G. (1986). "The staging of rural food festivals: Some problems with the concept of liminoid performances". Paper presented to the Qualitative Research Conference on Ethnographic Research, University of Waterloo, Canada.

Tosun, C. (1999). "Towards a Typology of Community Participation in the Tourism Development Process". Anatolia: An International Journal of Tourism and Hospitality Research, Vol. 10, No. 2, pp. 113-34.

Tosun, C. (2000). "Limits to Community Participation in the Tourism Development Process in Developing Countries". Tourism Management, Vol. 21, pp. 613-33.

Tosun, C. (2001). "Challenges of Sustainable Tourism Development in the Developing World: The Case of Turkey". Tourism Management, Vol. 22, pp. 289-303.

Tosun, C., and D. J. Timothy (2003). "Arguments for Community Participation in the Tourism Development Process". Journal of Tourism Studies, Vol. 14, No. 2, pp. 2-15.

Tosun, C. (2006). "Expected Nature of Community Participation in Tourism Development". Tourism Management, Vol. 27, No. 3, pp. 493-504.

United Nations World Tourism Organization. (2004). "National and regional tourism planning: Methodologies and case studies". Madrid, Spain: UNWTO.

United Nations World Tourism Organization. (2005). "Making tourism more sustainable: A guide for policy makers". Madrid, Spain: UNWTO.

United Nation World Tourism Organization (UNWTO). (2009). "Guidelines for policymaking and planning". http://www.unwto.org/sdt/fields/en/policy.php.

Van Esterik, P. (1982). "Celebrating ethnicity: Ethnic flavour in an urban festival". Ethnic Groups. Vol. 4, pp. 207–27.

Wall, G., & Mathieson, A. (2006). "Tourism: Change, impacts and opportunities". Harlow, UK: Prentice Hall.

Wall, G. and Mitchell, C. (1989). "Cultural festivals as economic stimuli and catalysts of functional change". In G. Syme, B. Shaw, D. Fenton and W. Mueller The Planning and Evaluation of Hallmark Events. London: Avebury.

Wearing, S., & MacDonald, M. (2002). "The development of community based tourism: The relationship between tour operators and development agent as intermediaries in rural and Isolated communities". Journal of Sustainable Tourism, Vol. 10, pp. 191–206.

White, P.(1974). The Social Impacts of Tourism on Host Communities: A Study of Language Change in Switzerland. Research Paper 9. Oxford: School of Geography, Oxford University.

Williams, A., and G. Shaw (1995). "Tourism and Regional Development: Polarization and New Forms of Production in the UK". TESG, Vol. 86, pp. 50–63.

Williams, A. and Shaw, G. (eds) (1998). Tourism and Economic Development: European Experiences (3rd edn). Chichester: John Wiley.

Wilson, J. and Udall, L. (1982). "Folk Festivals: A Handbook for Organisation and Management". Tennessee: Tennessee Press.

Wood, M.E. (1998). "Meeting the global challenge of community participation in ecotourism: Case study and lessons from Ecuador. Arlington: The Nature Conservancy".

WTTC. (2009). "Travel & Tourism Economic Impact: South Africa. 2009 Travel & Tourism Economic Research". (London: World Travel & Tourism Council).

Yeing, T., & Zhou. Y (2007). "Community, Governments and External Capitals in China's Rural Cultural Tourism: A comparative study of two Adjacent Villages". Tourism Management, Vol. 28, pp. 96-107.

Yin, R. (1994). "Case Study Research: Design and Methods (2nd edn)". London: Sage.

Yu, C. P., Chancellor, H. C., & Cole, S. T. (2011). "Measuring residents' attitudes toward sustainable tourism: Are-examination of the sustainable tourism attitude scale". Journal of Travel Research, 50, 57–63.

Zikmund, W.G. (1997). "Business research method (5th ed.)". Orlando, FL: The Dryden Press, Harcourt Brace College Publishers.

ROLE OF TOUR GUIDES TOWARDS THE PROMOTION OF SUSTAINABLE TOURISM- A STUDY WITH SPECIAL REFERENCE TO PROTECTED AREAS

Sandeep Paatlan

Assistant Professor, School of Management, Maharaja Agrasen University, Baddi- sandeep_966@yahoo.com

Promila Raita

Assistant Professor, Humanities, Maharaja Agrasen University, Baddi promila77raita@gmail.com

Sustainable tourism and natural resource management is incompatible in today's world. Sustainable tourism itself means to promote and protect the environment and tourism, as vacations and outdoor recreation require a healthy environment. A tourists resort with clean environs- air, water and scenery is most sought after by leisure seekers. In this perspective the role of Tour guides participation is impinged. It can help in glorifying, protecting, conserving and sustaining our flora and fauna. Tour guides participation is helpful in enriching and enlightening the tourists in protected areas effectively and efficiently through manifestations of deep rooted cultural, historical, natural interpretations of various attractions depending on the significant interest of the people at the grass root level. In order to develop sustainably there is a dire need to redefine and rethink the role of Tour Guides in a broader spectrum. In today's scenario initiative towards encouraging Local Tour Guides and their self recognition is highlighted in order to conserve and safeguard our scarce resources with unlimited means, Sustainable Development – development of natural resources in a manner that ensures economic, social and cultural needs are met while maintaining ecosystem integrity and biological diversity and without compromising the ability of future generations to meet their needs. In this research paper we are trying to identify the crucial role of tour guides and their contribution towards sustainability of natural resource in protected areas.

Keywords: Sustainable Tourism, Tour Guides, flora and Fauna, Protected Areas

Introduction

Tourism offers a privileged means of raising environmental awareness among the general public. It represents a valuable opportunity to support traditional economic activities and to improve the quality of life. It aims to prioritize the quality of environment through tourism while taking into account the conservation and sustainable development objectives of the area. It guarantees the best possible integration of tourism within the natural, cultural, economic, and social environment, and its coherent development in time and space.(FEDERATION, 2010).

The new emerging trend is to represent tourism as a major part of natural resource management that can substantially contribute to the conservation of nature and biodiversity, as it helps to evaluate it economically as a commodity that has no market price do it otherwise.(Igor Jurincic, 2009) There is a dire need to assess and to become conscious of the sensitivity towards natural, historic and cultural heritage and in this regard tourism has a major role to play effectively and economically considering issues of capacity, need and potential opportunity. According to the World Tourism Organization, sustainable tourism is tourism that leads to the management of all resources in such a way that economic, social and aesthetic needs can be fulfilled while maintaining cultural integrity, essential ecological processes, biological diversity and life support systems. The strategic objectives such as conservation of the environment, enriching our heritage, economic and social development are incompatible with the development and management of tourism and specifically in this regard role of tour guides in visitor management and enhancement of the quality of tourism offered and preservation and improvement of the quality of life of local residents.

Tour Guides can act as assets in the development of national park or other protected areas towards conserving wildlife, protection of biological resources and maintain natural areas, finding out ways and means to eliminate negative environmental impacts of tourism such as improper disposal of waste, air pollution from transportation, wildlife habitat and destruction. Successfully addressing the challenges of tourism in protected areas requires strong co-operation among all parties, including those operating within and outside protected area boundaries, as well as those that can promote effective management of protected areas by ensuring that the appropriate planning and management tools are adopted. Weiler and Davis (1993), examines the potential role and stated that kayak tour guides can play in shaping the experience of visitors in marine area, the Pacific Rim National Park. It uses two approaches to explore the perceptions of clients about the role of kayak guides using: (1) a pre- and post-trip questionnaire and (2) participant observation. Results indicate that five of the six roles were rated high in importance, but one role, the communication role, was not as important. These findings are discussed within the ecotourism paradigm, and their implications for protected area management and for visitor behavior modification are considered.(Rollinsb, May 2009).

Tour guides play a central role in the tourism industry. As intermediaries between tourists and tourism service suppliers, tour operators can influence the choices of consumers, the practices of suppliers and the development patterns of destinations. This unique role means that tour guides can make an important contribution to furthering the goals of sustainable tourism development and protecting the environmental and cultural resources on which the tourism industry depends for its survival and growth.(Tour Operators' Contributions to Sustainable Tourism in Protected Areas)

Rationale and Justification

This paper tries to explores the potential of tour guides towards the contribution towards the protection of natural areas by educating their visitors through interpretation and modeling environmentally appropriate behaviors. The present study has been persuaded with a view to increase the awareness and deeper understanding of sustainable tourism and also to acknowledge manifold problems related to tour guides that visitors face and to highlight the potentialities of tour guides towards enhancement of sustainable tourism.

Objective:

- To study the scope of tour guides in the contribution of sustainable development.
- To check the role of tour guides in the preservation of protected areas.
- To acknowledge manifold problems related to tour guides that visitors face.

Research Methodology:

Nature of the Data Used:

Both primary and secondary data has been used in order to collect the required information about the role of tour guides in particular has been able to enhance sustainable tourism.

Statistical Tools and Techniques Applied:

A survey was conducted in Protected Areas of Madhav National Park and Kahna National Park, M.P. Sample size consists of 60 visitors and through the process of random sampling a questionnaire method has been adopted and filled up by the tourists and tourist guide were interviewed.

Data Analysis

S. No	Statement	Strongly satisfied	satisfied	Neutral	Dissatis-fied	Strongly Dissatis-fied
1.	Do you think that the tour guide in-fluenced you in the preservation of the natural resources	20 (33.33%)	8 (13.33%)	12 (20%)	10 (16.66%)	10 (16.66%)

S. No	Statement	Strongly satisfied	satisfied	Neutral	Dissatis-fied	Strongly Dissatis-fied
2.	In your opinion please state that was the tour guides able to communicate the culture of the host community?	20 (33.33%)	5 (8.33%)	10 (16.66%)	10 (16.66%)	15 (25.00%)
3.	Were you satisfied with the activities arranged by the tour guides?	12 (20%)	6 (10.00%)	12 (20.00%)	20 (33.33%)	10 (16.66%)
4.	Are you satisfied with the interpretation skills of the tour guide?	10 (16.66%)	10 (16.66%)	13 (21.67%)	10 (16.66%)	17 (28.33%)
5.	Were you satisfied with the knowledge level of the tour guide towards natural habitat	25 (41.66%)	12 (20.00%)	8 (13.33%)	5 (8.33%)	10 (16.66%)
6.	Do you think environmental education should be necessary for tour guides	30 (50.00%)	12 (20.00%)	7 (11.67%)	8 (13.33%)	3 (5.00%)
7.	Do you think there is a dire need to provide extended training courses for tour guides	20 (33.33%)	20 (33.33%)	5 (8.33%)	8 (13.33%)	7 (11.67%)
8.	Were the tour guides able to address the positive impacts of the tourism?	10 (16.66%)	10 (16.66%)	12 (20.00%)	9 (15.00%)	19 (31.66%)

Field Survey 2014

Result:

There is a dire need to increase the knowledge of the protected areas through involvement of tour guides and thereof tour guides should be facilitated with focused and specialized training programmes. In order to glorify and sustain the environment active participation of tour guides is impinged towards promotion and protection of natural environment through incorporation of sustainable tourism initiatives:

- Tour guides needs to present local specific features and should focus manifest the old tradition.
- Well information should be provided about the natural and cultural features of visited and protected sites and their roles in the conservation of local ecosystems.
- Special financial contributions and assistance should be provided to sensitive protected areas.
- Initiative undertaken and opportunities provided to customers to pro- actively support protected areas.
- Creating awareness on how to avoid negative impacts while visiting sensitive areas for example by maintaining appropriate distances from wildlife etc.
- To add new eco friendly tourist products in the way that does not burden the environment and the local population and encouraging the visitors to use non-renewable energy and avoid unnecessary waste and noise in protected areas.
- Supporting database to check and improve the quality of facilities and services. To communicate effectively to visitors and representing well the special qualities of the area and providing educational facilities and services that interpret the area's environment and heritage to visitors and local people.
- Ensuring that the promotion of the area is sensitive to needs and capacity of natural habitat.

On the whole it can be said that tourism activities in and around protected areas can have both positive and negative impacts on local people and the environment and in this context there is a need to monitor and sensitize tourists and tour guides towards preserving the flora and fauna and role of tour guides through activities can only be sustainable if implemented with common understandings on 'green initiatives' and 'consensus-based approach'.

Bibliography

FEDERATION, E. (2010). European Charter for Sustainable Tourism in Protected Areas, Charter.

Igor Jurincic, A. P. (2009). SUSTAINABLE TOURISM DEVELOPMENT IN PROTECTED AREAS ON THE PATTERN OF STRUNJAN LANDSCAPE PARK. p. 178.

Rollinsb, C. R. (May 2009). Visitor perceptions of the role of tour guides in natural areas. Journal of Sustainable Tourism , May 2009, 357–374.

Tour Operators' Contributions to Sustainable Tourism in Protected Areas. UNEP. United Nations Environment Programme – Division of Technology, Industry and Economics.

INNOVATIVE CAPABILITIES AND ENTREPRENEURIAL ORIENTATION OF PROFESSIONALLY QUALIFIED AND NON PROFESSIONALLY QUALIFIED TRAVEL AGENTS: A COMPARATIVE ANALYSIS

Sandeva Khajuria

Research Scholar, School of Hospitality and Tourism Management, University of Jammu, Jammu and Kashmir, Email: sandeva_khajuria@yahoo.co.in

Nidhi Pathania

Research Scholar, School of Hospitality and Tourism Management, University of Jammu, Jammu and Kashmir, Email: nidhi_1_5@yahoo.com

Abstract

Innovative Capability is not just an ability to be successful at running a business new - stream, or to manage mainstream capabilities but is also about synthesizing these two paradigms (Australian Bureau of Statistics, 2005). Innovation by itself is not enough for business success, as it needs to be combined with an entrepreneuriaal approach to recognize opportunities that can be exploited through innovation to provide a financially successful outcome. (Balan P Noel L., 2010). Studies like Jogaratnam & Tse (2006); Tajeddini (2010); Figueiredo, Gomes & Farias (2010); have been carried out on the hotel industry by taking into consideration the innovative capability and entrepreneurial orientation but not too much work has been done on the tourism entrepreneurs. The present research is about the comparative analysis of innovations and entrepreneurial orientations of travel agents with tourism professional and non-tourism professional background. The study has included various aspects of these tourism entrepreneurs such as knowledge of trends in business environment, understanding of technologies and regulations which are conducive for the company, knowledge about costumers, workplace culture, organization structure etc. The statistical tools used in the study includes Percentage method, t - test, ANOVA etc.

Keywords: Innovation, Capability, Entrepreneur, Orientation, Tourism

Introduction:

Innovative Capability is the ability to continuously transform knowledge and ideas into new products, systems and process for the benefit of the business and its stakeholders (Lawson & Samson, 2001), while entrepreneurial Orientation can be related to the ability of a business to operate in an entrepreneurial manner. These two qualities are proven to make a major contribution in the success of an Entrepreneur. Entrepreneurship means different things to different people. While for some people it can be a way to make money, for others it can be a lifestyle. For some, it can be a one man show and for others it can be a team effort. But what hold universally true to run an enterprise successfully is to recognize, catch, utilize the prevailing opportunities and generate new opportunities. And enterprise is an industry which is blooming very fast and is a pool of opportunities, in particular, tourism industry, the role of entrepreneurs become much more important. Also as tourism is a service oriented industry, quite contemporary career, and a very competitive business, ample efforts are required in communicating and building trust between the various players in tourism. The stake holders need to do their best for their long term survival. This industry has been considered as a key industry for economic development in developing countries. This industry sells intangible products to the customers whose demands are entirely different from each other.

Where one customer may want to travel to a particular destination with his family to have leisure time in luxury budget, the other customer may want to travel to the same destination with his friends to have adventure in a very limited budget.

Thus the tourism service provider has to prepare customized services unlike many other industries like telecom, banking etc which have almost fixed services, allowing a very slight flexibility. Also due to a large number of small firms which work on very low margin are mushrooming very fast in this industry. This enforces the entrepreneurs to sell the services at best possible or lowest rates, which sometimes make tourism enterprise a low profit industry. The growing competition also calls for selling the same product over and over again with new ideas and concepts. Hence we can say that the marketing challenges faced by this business are unique and this businesses cannot be operated in isolation from their competing and complementary products. Thus the entrepreneurs of tourism need to develop and practice some key competitive skills like Entrepreneurship quality,, market and marketing orientation, entrepreneurial leadership risk taking, management, relationship building, innovation etc so as to make successful development in the business. These skill have been seen to have a positive impact on business performance of an tourism enterprise. Innovation being one among these skills and an eminent quality has transformed to a need of the present time. New ideas and ways of setting and improving the product helps in keeping the business going and sometimes leads to inventions as well. It is also an important driver of performance (Guan & Ma 2003). But innovation itself is not enough for an organization, enterprise or an individual. It needs to be adopted, combined with an entrepreneurial approach and practiced. Only then it can be utilized to recognizing opportunities that can then be exploited to provide a financially successful outcome. Thus the present paper aims to study the impact of these two factors ie Innovative capabilities and Entrepreurial Orientations on performance of an Entrepreneur. There have been few studies of innovation capability in the services sector, and these have addressed large government organisations (O'Connor, Roos & Vickers-Willis 2007). Dimensions of entrepreneurial orientation have also been studied across many different industry sectors, and these have generally identified a positive relationship between entrepreneurial orientation and firm performance (Rauch, Wiklund,Frese & Lumpkin 2005; Rauch, Wiklund, Lumpkin & Frese 2009), but no empirical study has investigated the impact of both on the performance of a business and also a comparative analysis of Innovative Capabilities and Entrepreneurship Orientation of Professionally and Non Professionally qualified Travel Agents has been made.

Review of Literature

Entrepreneurship

Entrepreneurship plays a crucial role in creating a platform for employability for communities and provide self-employment to those who have the potential to create something and capability to sell it. Though the developed countries identified the significance of entrepreneurship in bringing innovation, employment change, growth in economic activity and technical progress, and new venture (Baumol, 1986; Kirby, 2002; Schumpter, 1934), the case was not the same with countries with socialist economies. They rather believed in eliminating all major institutions and conditions for entrepreneurial development which included market competition, private ownership, and freedom of individuals to establish private enterprises (Kovac, 1990). However, a common feature of all was the position of the entrepreneur, being a deviant individual, vested with Western ideology, and a threat to a communist society (Bateman, 1997; Franicevic, 1990). The growth of tourism and hospitality businesses in many countries (Morrison et al., 1999; Tinsley and Lynch, 2007; Thomas, 2000, 2004; Shaw, 2004; Shaw and Williams, 2002) has 'led to recognition of the significance of entrepreneurship' (Shaw & Williams, 2004) in this field. Yet it is argued that the field has not received the level of attention it deserves (Ateljevic & Page, 2009; Ioannides & Petersen, 2003; Li, 2008; Morrison & Teixeira, 2004. Shaw & Williams (1998) identified some motivations like relative ease of entry into the sector, and financial and human resource poverty etc. among developing as well as matured economies.

Innovative Capability

The changing demands of the customers and dynamic nature of the market has pushed the sellers to make innovations. And this has gained a considerable attention in the field of research as well. Various models and theories regarding innovation have been developed which include institutional theory, cognitive theories, transaction cost economics, socio technical approaches, market orientation (MO) and resource-based view. Evidence suggests that a number of core elements and processes exist which aid effective innovation outcomes (Tidd, Bessant & Pavitt, 1997). The theory of Resource Based View (RBV) is one of the most effective theories in strategic Management. It suggests that organizations or firms compete not on new products, but on a much intense dimension of the capacity or potential to develop new products (Prahalad & Hamel, 1990). Thereafter, in 1994, Teece & Pisano developed the dynamic capabilities theory which was the subset of the competences/capabilities and helped in developing new products according to the changing trends of the market. Fuchs, Mifflin, Miller & Whitney (2000) also worked on Innovative Capabilities and proposed Innovation capability as a higher-order integration capability, that is, the ability to mould and manage multiple capabilities. The concept of higher-order integration capabilities in developed Organisations possessing this innovation capability have the ability to integrate key capabilities and resources of their firm to successfully stimulate innovation. Many researchers and practitioners suggested that innovation could be sector or industry specific, if not firm specific. (Lawson & Samson , 2001)

Entrepreneurial Orientation

Number of researchers have gained interest in studying the concept of entrepreneurial orientation (EO) making it central in the area and proving it a considerable theoretical as well as empirical attention. (Covin, Greene & Slevin,2006). According to Miller (1982) an entrepreneurial firm is "one that engages in product-market innovation, undertakes somewhat risky ventures, and is first to come up with "proactive" innovations, beating competitors to the punch. Entrepreneurial Orientation roots back to strategy making process literature (e.g., Mintzberg, 1973). Miller (1983) gave the most commonly accepted definition of Entrepreneurial Orientation, which was further evolved by Covin & Slevin (1989), and later discussed by Lumpkin & Dess (1996) . EO refers to the strategy making processes that provide organizations with a basis for entrepreneurial decisions and actions (e.g., Lumpkin & Dess, 1996; Wiklund &Shepherd, 2003. With the backdrop of earlier research on Strategy Management, measurement scales for Entrepreneurial Orientation have been framed (Covin & Slevin, 1989) and used. The relationship of EO with other dimensions like business performance (Grant & Bush, 1995; Balan & Lindsay,2010) growth (Casillas, Moreno & Barbero, 2010), Time Orientation (Revista da Micro e Pequena Empresa, Campo Limpo Paulista,) have also been examined. Studies like Balan & Lindsay (2010) have also explored the relationship between Entrepreneurial Orientation, Innovative Capability and performance of the business. Entrepreneurship orientation and Innovative Capability has been seen to have a positive impact on business performance.

Objectives

The main objective of the present research is to evaluate the factors related to innovation capabilities of the Professionally and Non-Professionally qualified travel agents along with determining the entrepreneurial orientation of the travel agents. The study also finds out the significant difference in the innovative capabilities and entrepreneurial orientation of Professionally and Non – Professionally qualified travel agents.

Hypothesis:

Entrepreneurship though anciently believed to be a family trend. People use to start their business only in shortage of job and earning. But now the scenario has changed. People are getting into entrepreneurship not because of any need but because of their interest and passion. Undoubtly, Entrepreneurs have certain innate traits which motivate them to set up their business. These traits are further enhanced when supported with concrete knowledge about the trade. Many researchers have worked upon the entrepreneurial skills and their role in business performance (Rauch et al, 2009; Casillas, Moreno & Barbero, 2010), Being in particular with Innovative Capability Entrepreneurial Orientation, their contribution in business performance has been discussed in various studies. (Guan & Ma 2003; O'Connor, Roos & Vickers-Willis 2007; Lumpkin & Dess 1996; Rauch,Wiklund,

Frese & Lumpkin 2005; Rauch, Wiklund, Lumpkin & Frese 2009). Few studies have also focused to examine the entrepreneurial orientation of hotels, working upon larger hotel chains (Jogaratnam & Tse 2004). Mercy Mureithi (2010) in her work upon tourism entrepreneurs and students observed that students find tourism an attractive sector due to the job opportunities available and expanding scope of business. She also observed lack of professional experience as a major barriers to entrepreneurship. Difference in perception of barriers between existing and aspiring entrepreneurs was also observed in her study. Anjan Kumar Bordoloi (2012) also discussed adequate education and training, certification, training programs, community awareness programs, facilitation of technological and skills transfer as a guideline for tourism planning including tourism business. Marija Ivaniš (2011) in his work upon the general model of small entrepreneurship Development in tourism destinations advocated the importance of educational background. Thus with this backdrop and assuming that different people with different background have difference in the qualities they possess, the hypotheses framed is:

H1: There is a significant difference in the innovative capabilities and entrepreneurial orientation of Professionally and Non – Professionally qualified travel agents.

Methodology

The present study is empirical in nature. The sample unit selected for research purpose was Tourism entrepreneurs. A Total of 51 PATA recognized Travel Agents from Delhi and NCR were approached with a structured questionnaire. The questionnaire used was taken from a study carried on Australian hotels by Peter Balan and Noel Lindsay (2010) and which was further refined to include the statements about IC and EO only. It comprised of three parts where first part represented Demographic Profile, Second Part consisted of 45 Statements regarding 'Drivers of Innovation' and the third Part had 20 Statements regarding 'Drivers of Entrepreneurship' were taken for the research. The respondents were given 5 point likert scale with '1' being 'Strongly Disagree' to '5' being 'Strongly Agree' to response their opinion. Out of the 51 approached Travel Agents, 31 responded back providing with a response rate of approximately 61%.

Analysis and Interpretation

Table 1. Demographic Profile

Demographic Variables		Frequency (N)	Percentage
Age of the Entrepreneur	20 -40 years	27	87%
	41-60 years	4	13%
	Above 60	0	0%
Tourism Professionally Qualified	Yes	17	55%
	No	14	45%
Education	Under Graduate	1	3%
	Graduate	6	19%
	Post Graduate	24	78%
Operational since	below 5 years	21	68%
	5 to 10 years	6	19%
	above 10 years	4	13%

Source: self-study

In table 1, the demographic profile of the respondents is given. It is found that approx. 88 % of respondents were between the age group of 20 to 40 years, while approx. 12 % were from the age group 40 to 60 years. None of the respondent was above 60 years of age. While 55% were professionally quailfied with some Degree/Diploma or Certificate in Tourism, the rest 45% did not had any qualification in tourism. Approximately 78% respondent were post graduate, 19% were graduate and the rest 3% were under graduate. Also 68% of the enterprises were operational for less than 5 years, 19% had an operation period between 5 to 10 years while the rest 13% were operational for more than 10 years.

Table 2. Dimension wise mean score of Innovation Capabilities of Travel and Tourism Enterprise

S. No	Dimensions	Mean Score
1	Environmental Awareness	3.581
2	Alliances	3.751
3	Customer Intelligence	3.935
4	Experimentation	3.806

S. No	Dimensions	Mean Score
5	Strategy to Planning	4.011
6	Manager Attribute	4.139
7	HR Human Capital	3.516
8	Resource Awareness	3.817
9	Operation	3.693

Source: self-study

Table 2. provides the information about the levels of various dimensions of Innovative capabilities possessed by the surveyed entrepreneurs. The highest dimension found among the entrepreneurs is "Manager Attribute" with a mean value of 4.139. Resource awareness holds a mediocre position with the mean value of 3.817. Among the nine dimensions studied, Environmental Awareness with the mean score of 3.581 is the lowest dimensions found, which implies that Entrepreneurs consider this dimension of least importance

Table 3. Dimension wise mean score of Entrepreneurial Orientations of Travel and Tourism Enterprise

S. No	Dimensions	Mean Score
1	Innovativeness	3.567
2	Risk Taking	3.494
3	Pro –activeness	3.473
4	Competitive Aggressions	3.720
5	Autonomy	3.524

Source: self-study

Table 3 shows the mean score of various dimensions of Entrepreneurial Orientation studied in the research. Among the 5 dimensions viz: Innovativeness, Risk taking, Pro-activeness, Competitive Aggressions and Autonomy, Competitive Aggressions with a mean score of 3.720 is the highest quality observed. Likewise the least observed quality here is Pro-activeness with mean score of 3.473. Other dimension including Innovativeness, Risk taking and Autonomy scored a mean value of 3.567, 3.494 and 3.534 respectively.

Table 4. Significant difference in Professional and non Professional Travel Agents on the basis of Dimensions of Drivers of Innovation (t-test)

S. No	Dimensions	Mean for Professionals	Mean for Non- Professionals	T-test
1	Environmental Awareness	3.431	3.0476	1.882*
2	Alliances	3.867	3.607	1.0789*
3	Customer Intelligence	4.34	3.809	1.2018*
4	Experimentation	3.705	3.928	-0.859*
5	Strategy to Planning	4.058	3.925	0.525*
6	Manager Attribute	4.098	4.190	-0.646*
7	HR Human Capital	3.264	3.821	-1.863*
8	Resource Awareness	3.980	3.619	1.872*
9	Operation	3.6176	3.785	-0.735*

Source: self-study

*Significance level at 0.05% (Table value= 1.96)

Table 4 shows the difference of the studied parameters between professionally qualified and non professionally qualified travel agents. The calculated value of t test for the two different set of data is less than the table value ie 1.96, so our hypothesis "there is a significant difference in the innovative capabilities of Professionally and Non – Professionally qualified travel agents" is proved to be true. As expected, Some qualities like Environmental awareness, Alliances, Customer Intelligence, Strategy to planning and Resource awareness were found to be higher in Professionally Qualified agents as they have gained theoretical knowledge about these qualities and while into entrepreneurship, they use their knowledge in practical terms. But in contrary to the general perception, qualities like Operations, HR Human Capital, Managerial Attribute and Experimentation were found to be higher among the Non professionally qualified agents. This may be due to the reason that due to lack of professional qualification, the non professionally qualified agents use their practical experience and have objective and realistic approach to the prevailing trends and issues and thus have better managerial and Operational skills. Also this is possible that non professionally qualified agents get into the tourism business due to their innate affinity, interest, knowledge, skills or experience of the trade and thus in some aspects of the trade, they do better than their professionally qualified counterparts.

Table 5. Significant difference in Professional and Non Professional Travel Agents on the basis of Dimensions of Entrepreneurial Orientation

S. No	Dimensions	Mean for Professionals	Mean for Non-Professionals	T-test
1	Innovativeness	3.494	3.657	-0.976*
2	Risk Taking	3.549	3.428	0.650*
3	Pro –activeness	3.4313	3.523	-0.370*
4	Competitive Aggressions	3.764	3.666	0.781*
5	Autonomy	3.455	3.607	-0.838*

Source: self-study

*Significance level at 0.05% (Table value= 1.96)

Table 5 shows the difference of the dimensions of Entrepreneurs Orientation between professionally qualifies and Non professionally qualified agents. Here again as seen in the table, there is a difference in each dimensions in the two sets of data (mean of professionals and mean of non professionals) for every dimension. Also the calculated value of t test is lower than the table value of 1.96 at 0.05% level of significance. Thus it can be concluded that the hypothesis "there is a significant difference in the entrepreneurial orientation of Professionally and Non – Professionally qualified travel agents" is accepted. The difference shown in the mean values can be interpreted as dimensions like Risk taking and Competitive aggression being higher in professionally qualified agents while other dimensions like Innovativeness, Proactiveness and Autonomy being higher in Non professionally qualified agents. The reason behind this result could be that changing trends of the market and urgency to bring innovation for a long term survival of the enterprise make the entrepreneurs possess innovativeness regardless of their educational background. Even after not having any professional education, this set of the respondents know and understand the requirements of the markets on practical grounds and thus are more Innovative, proactive and believe in self decision making.

They also give their employees a leverage to take decisions on their own to some extent and with swiftness as their emphasis is on profitable long term existence of the enterprise.

Conclusion

The results of the study shows that there exists a significant difference in the innovative capabilities and entrepreneurial orientation of professionally and Non – Professionally Qualified Travel Agents. Though both these factors are inevitably important for a successful enterprise and help the entrepreneurs to perform more, not all the qualities related to Innovation capabilities and entrepreneurial Orientation are found to be at par in all the travel Agents. The two sets of travel agents under study, viz: professionally qualified and non professionally qualified travel agents differ in the various qualities studied. Some qualities are found to be higher in professionally qualified set where as some qualities are higher in the non professionally qualified set. Qualities like Environmental awareness, Alliances, Customer Intelligence, Strategy to planning and Resource awareness, Risk taking and Competitive aggression are observed higher in professionally qualified Agents. At the same time qualities like Operations, HR Human Capital, Managerial Attribute, Experimentation Innovativeness, Proactiveness and Autonomy are higher in Non professionally. This leads to the conclusion that professional education contributes to many qualities and skills required by an entrepreneur to be successful but not all the required skills are learnt from a professional course. The role of strong educational background to implement the learnt theories and procedures to cater to the requirement of the dynamics of the trade cannot be avoided. But some qualities are gained from life experience, observations and understanding of the market, belief in quality production, commitment to the customers etc and play a crucial role even in the absence of professional educational background.

Limitations of the Study

The undertaken research has few limitations like smaller study area, smaller sample and low response rate. Only PATA approved travel Agencies of Delhi & NCR were considered for research. A total of 51 Agencies (owners of the agencies) were approached and out of them only 31 responded. There is scope to expand the research to their regions of North India and the other parts of the country and include more Travel Agencies in the survey. The sample size could be increased to at least 150 in future.

Future relevance

The study brings out the levels of various dimensions of Innovative Capabilities and Entrepreneurial Orientation among the two sets of travel agents: Those who have some or other kind of Tourism educational background and those who do not possess any tourism educational background. While certain qualities are found to be higher in first set, others are higher in the second set. This research will help the entrepreneurs to know what they are lacking in, to identify their shortcomings and will help them to cope up with their shortcomings and evolve further. This study is a contribution to understand and thus bridge the existing gap between the two sets of population surveyed. Also the study would help the professional Institutes to develop the curriculum in such a way that leads to the development of such qualities in budding entrepreneurs.

References:

Ateljevic, J.& Page, S. (2009). Introduction. In J. Ateljevic and S. Page (Eds) Tourism and Entrepreneurship: International Perspectives. Oxford, Butterworth- Heinemann: 1-6.

Bardoloi, A., K. (20120. Creating Entrepreneurial Environment through Eco- Tourism for

Women Entrepreneurs: A Strategic Framework, Indian Journal of Applied Research. 2(2), 98-101.

Bateman, M. (1997). Comparative analysis of Eastern European business cultures. In: M. Bateman(Ed) Business Cultures in Central and Eastern Europe. Oxford: Butterworth-Heinemann, pp.197-231.

Baumol, W. J. (1986). Entrepreneurship and a century of growth. Journal of Business Venturing, 1(2), 141-145.

Balan, P. and Lindsay, N. (2009) Developing an innovation capability in the Australian Hotel industry, Research Report, Sustainable Tourism Cooperative Research Centre.

Casillas. J., C., Moreno A., M., & Barbero, J.,L. (2010). A configurational approach of the relationship between entrepreneurial orientation and growth of family firms. Family Business Review 23, 27–44.

Covin, J. G., Green, K. M., & Slevin, D. P. (2006). Strategic process effects on the entrepreneurial orientation - sales growth rate relationships. Entrepreneurship Theory and Practice, 30(1), 57-81.

Covin, J.G & Slevin, D.P (1989). 'Strategic management of small firms in hostile and benign, environments. Strategic Management Journal, 10, 75–87.

Franicevic, V. (1990) Poduzetnistvo kako politicki projekt. In: D. Njavro and V. Franicevic (Eds) Poduzetnistvo: teorija, politika, praksa. Zagreb: Privredni vjesnik, pp.95-104.

Fuchs, P.H., Mifflin, K.E., Miller, D. & Whitney, J.O. (2000) Strategic integration: Competing in the age of capabilities. California Management Review, 42(3).

Grant, E. S., & Bush, A. J. (1995). Entrepreneurial orientation in the salesforce: Development of the EOS Measure. Proceedings of the Southern Marketing Association, November 8-11, 1995

Guan, J. ,C . & Ma, N. (2003). Innovative capability and export performance of Chinese firms, Technovation. 23(9), 737–747.

Ioannides, D. and Petersen, T. (2003). Tourism 'non-entrepreneurship' in peripheral destinations: a case study of small and medium tourism enterprises on Bornholm, Denmark. Tourism Geographies, 5(4): 408-435.

Ivaniš, M. (2011). General Model of Small Entrepreneurship Development in Tourism Destinations in Croatia. Tourism & Hospitality Management, 17(2).

Jogaratnam, G., and Tse, E.C. (2004). The Entrepreneurial approach to hotel operation: Evidence from the Asia-Pacific hotel industry. Cornell Hotel and Restaurant Administration Quarterly, 45(3), 248-259.

Kirby, D. (2002). Entrepreneurship. Maidenhead: McGraw-Hill. Kovac, B. (1990). Politicko-ekonomska uloga poduzetnistva. In: D. Njavro and V. Franicevic (Eds) Poduzetnistvo: teorija, politika, praksa. Zagreb: Privredni vjesnik, pp.69-93.

Li, L. (2008). A review of entrepreneurship research published in the hospitality and tourism management journals. Tourism Management, 29(5), 1013-1022.

Lawson, B. & Samson, D. (2001). Developing Innovation Capability in Organisations: A Dynamic Capabilities Approach. International Journal of Innovation Management, 5(3), 377–400.

Lumpkin, G.T. & Dess, G.G. (1996). Clarifying the entrepreneurial orientation construct and linking it to Performance. Academy of Management Review, 21(1), 135–172.

Morrison, A., Rimmington, M. and Williams, C. (1999) Entrepreneurship in theHospitality, Tourism and Leisure Industries. Butterworth-Heinemann: Oxford.

Mercy, M. (2010) , Barriers and facilitators of youth entrepreneurship. Gordon Institute of Business Sciences, University of Pretoria.

Morrison, A., Lynch, P., & Johns, N. (2004). International Tourism Networks. International Journal of Contemporary Hospitality Management,16(3), 198 – 204 .

Nunes, K., & Ferreira , L., C., (2010). Revista da Micro e Pequena Empresa, Campo Limpo Paulista, 4(1)

O'Connor, A., Roos, G., & Vickers-Willis. (2007). Evaluating an Australian public policy organisation's innovation capacity. European Journal of Innovation Management, 10(4), 532–558.

Rauch, A, Wiklund, J, Frese, M & Lumpkin, GT 2005, 'Entrepreneurial Orientation and Performance: Results from Two Meta-Analyses', paper presented at the Regional Frontiers of Entrepreneurial Research, Melbourne,10–11 February 2005.

Rauch, A., Wiklund, J., Lumpkin, G.T., & Frese, M. (2009). Entrepreneurial Orientation and Business Performance: An

Assessment of Past Research and Suggestions for the Future. Entrepreneurship Theory and Practice, 33(3), 761–787.

Schumpeter, J. A. (1934). The Theory of Economic Development. Cambridge: Harvard University Press.

Shaw, G. and Williams, A. (2004) From lifestyle consumption to lifestyle production: changing patterns of tourism entrepreneurship. In: R. Thomas (Ed) Small Firms in Tourism: International Perspective. Oxford: Elsevier, pp.99-113.

Shaw, G. (2004). Entrepreneurial cultures and small business enterprise in tourism. In A. Lew, M. Hall and A.M. Williams (Eds) A Companion to Tourism. Oxford: Blackwell, pp.122-134.

Shaw, G. and Williams, A. (2002) Critical Issues in Tourism: A Geographical Perspective. Oxford: Blackwell Publishing.

Thomas, R. (2004). International perspectives on small firms in tourism: A synthesis. In R. Thomas (Ed) Small Firms in Tourism: International Perspective. Oxford: Elsevier, pp.1-12.

Tinsley, R. & Lynch, P. (2007). Small business networking and tourism destination development: A comparative perspective. The International Journal of Entrepreneurship and Innovation, 8(1), 15-27.

Thomas, R. (2000). Small firms in the tourism industry: some conceptual issues. International Journal of Tourism Research, 2(5), 345-353.

Shaw, G., and Williams, A. (1998). Entrepreneurship, small business, culture and tourism development. In: D. Ioannides and K. Debbage (Eds) The Economic Geography of the Tourist Industry:A Supply-Side Analysis. London: Routledge, pp.235-255.

Teece, D.J. & Pisano, G. (1994). The dynamic capability of firms: An introduction. Industrial and Corporate Change, 3(3), 537–556.

Tidd, J., Bessant, J. & Pavitt, K. (1997). Managing Innovation: Integrating Technological, Market and Organisational Change. Great Britain: John Wiley & Sons Inc.

Prahalad, C. & Hamel, G. (1990). The core competencies of the corporation. Harvard Business Review, 68(3), 79–91.

Miller, W.L. & Morris, L. (1999) 4th Generation R&D: Managing Knowledge, Technology and Innovation. New York: John Wiley & Sons

Miller, D & Friesen, P.H. (1982). Innovation in conservative and entrepreneurial firms: two models of strategic momentum. Strategic Management Journal, 3, 1–25.

Lumpkin, G.T. & Dess, G.G. (1996). Clarifying the entrepreneurial orientation construct and linking it to Performance. Academy of Management Review,12(1), 135–172.

Mintzberg, H. (1973). Strategy-making in three modes. California Management Review, 16(2), 44-53.

Miller, D. (1983). The correlates of entrepreneurship in three types of firms. Management Science, 29(7), 770-791.

Lumpkin, G. T., & Dess, G. G. (1996). Clarifying the entrepreneurial orientation construct and linking it to performance. Academy of Management Review, 21(1), 135-172.

Wiklund, J., & Shepherd, D. (2003). Knowledge-based resources, entrepreneurial orientation, and the performance of small and medium sized businesses. Strategic Management Journal, 24, 1307-1314.

APPLICATION OF PUBLIC PRIVATE PARTNERSHIP MODEL FOR TOURISM GROWTH

U.N Shukla

Associate Professor,Deptt. of Travel & Tourism Management,Dr.B.R.Ambedkar University, Agra, e-mail:shukla.ithm@gmail.com

Ambar Vishal

Research Scholar,Deptt. of Travel & Tourism Management, Dr. B.R. Ambedka University, Agra, e-mail:ambarvishal@gmail.com

Abstract

Development in any field through Public Private Partnership process is globally recognized and practiced;tourism is not the exception in such a case. Throughout the world, tourism and hospitality industry got their pride because of coordinative efforts of public and private sectors. It is functioning as social mechanism along with the financial instrument progressively. This process plays a significant role in improvising the tourism concern facilities and other development projects whethereconomic, social, cultural or environmental concerns. The growth of any system can be seen in multiple forms by the application of PPP model.

No doubt,responsible participation of all the stakeholders through PPP gives the strength to sustainable tourism development and has an opportunity for government and private players to work together for creating infrastructure/superstructure in an innovative manner with advance technologies. This model has been adopted for development of amenities at the destination with its marketing and promotion too.

The PPP model in tourism field can increase the quality of services and facilities with optimum use of existing resources keeping in mind its uses for future generation. Thus, for the sustainable growth in tourism and allied sectors this model is highly applicable.

In this paper, our efforts will be to study the meaning and concept of PPP model, process, significance in tourism, Key benefits, its role in destination development and promotion, conservation of historic sites, sustainable tourism development and challenges faced in applicability of this model with the help of primary and secondary data.

Keywords: Public Private Partnership, Sustainability, Tourism Development.

Introduction

Meaning and concept of PPP

Applicability of Public private partnership (PPP)model in tourism industry is increasing day by day. There is hardly any field in which PPP model is not incorporated, starting from bottom to top. PPP model is essential for improving eco and environmental conditions, maintaining historical and archaeological sites, sustaining indigenous culture of tribes, rural and urban areas, in providing the basic amenities and other kind of infrastructure&superstructure development and of course in organizing national and/or international events, etc. Public private partnership comprises association between public and private sector to accomplish a long-standing goal.

The meaning of public private partnership can better be understood with the agreement between government authorities and the private stakeholders for public welfare projects. The predefined responsibilities, accountabilities and risks are the central concern of PPP model.

Definitions

The basic purpose of PPP model in relation to tourism sector is to increase the efficient working hands for executing, running and completing the tourism projects for the welfare of society in long term.

The term public-private partnership (PPP)is not defined at Community level. Ingeneral, the term refers to forms ofcooperation between public authorities andthe world of business which aim to ensurethe funding, construction, renovation,management and maintenance of aninfrastructure of the provision of a service. (Green Paper, April 2004)

The PPP can be defined as an association of public and private sectors with the aim of completing the assignment of government by managing the optimum resources of both the sectors with the best utilization of funds. PPP includes human resource management with their technical expertise and entrepreneurial skills in the development projects.

PPP model can be defined as cooperative activitiesby public and private sectors involving their expertise, resources and risks to achieve a particular public assignment.

The fields of promotion & marketing, development of tourism products, infrastructure/superstructure, education & skill development, financing, investment, etc. are the most frequent areas of PPP collaboration.Apart from these, environmental concerns, conservation and protection of cultural and historical heritage are also in focused through PPP. The destination development and destination management are also major components for joint venture of public and private sector (WTOBC, 2000:58)

According to WTO, the role of the public sector is to provide a stable infrastructure, legal, tax and social framework of the entrepreneurial initiative of the private sector in tourism, while the private sector should provide financial and other concern support in the planning, promotion, education and other activities related to tourism. (WTO, 1996)

There are basically two components of PPP model. Firstly the expertise and efficiency of private sector are applicable in the work of public sector. Secondly a PPP is structured in such a manner so that for any kind of arrangement or investment public sector should not seek the borrower from rest of society.

Evolution of PPP

The history of recorded PPP models is unable to tress outbut it is evident that this model is in used from the beginning of democratic system throughout the world. Following is the coded history of applicability of PPP models in various fields ofIndian context. (GoI & ADB, 2006)

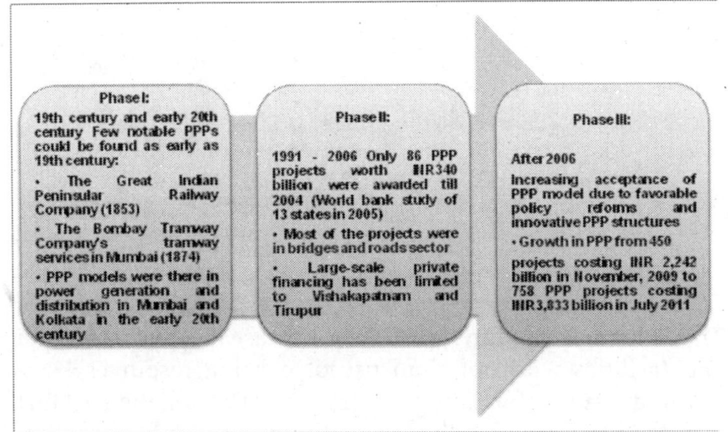

Current status of PPPs in India

The PPP India database (Department of Economic Affairs, Ministry of Finance) indicates that 758 PPP projectscosting INR3,833 billion3 is awarded/underway status (i.e., in operational, constructional or in stages wherein atleast construction/implementation is imminent). There exists significant untapped potential for the use of the PPPmodel in e-governance, health and education sectors. Karnataka, Andhra Pradesh and Madhya Pradesh are the leading states in terms of number and value of PPPprojects. At the central level, the National Highway Authority of India (NHAI) is the leading user of the PPP model. (FICCI, 2012)

Following is the status of some important sector in which PPP model is practiced in India:

Brief account of tourism industry

The growth of any economic system can be seen in multiple forms by the application of PPP model. Public private partnerships have positive effects in tourism and hospitality sector in all concern whether the economic, social, cultural or environmental.

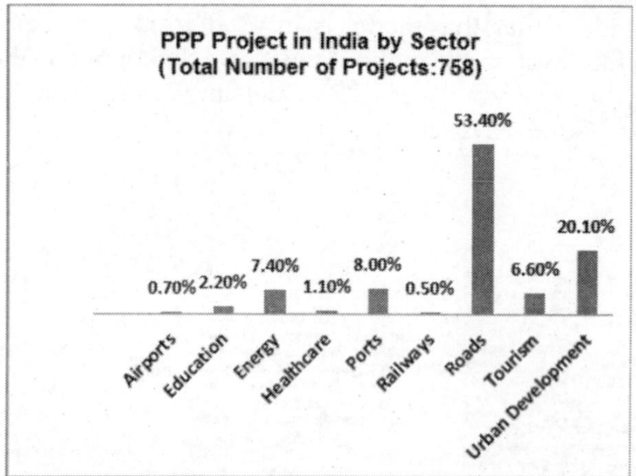

The PPP model in tourism field can increase the quality of services and facilities with optimum use of existing resources keeping in mind its uses for future generation. Thus for the sustainable growth in tourism and allied sector this model is highly applicable.

The government should frame the tourism policies and planning for promoting the involvement of the private sector in tourism concern projects. The PPP model in tourism can play a key role in developing countries like India.

The Government of India (GoI) has been focusing on the development of enabling tools and activities to encourage private sector investments in the country through the PPP format. Private investments amounting to US$150 billion is expected to bridge the infrastructure gap of US$500 billion over the period 2007-2012. (Accelerating PPP, 2012:7)

The Government of India recognizes that there is significant deficit in the availability of physical infrastructure across different sectors and that this is hindering economic development. The development of infrastructure requires large investments that cannot be undertaken out of public financing alone, and that in order to attract private capital as well as the techno-managerial efficiencies associated with it, the Government is committed to promoting Public Private Partnerships (PPPs) in infrastructure development; and Whereas the Government of India recognizes that infrastructure projects may not always be financially viable because of long gestation periods and limited financial returns, and that financial viability of such projects can be improved through Government support.

To identify the area for public-private partnerships (PPP) is one of the one of the biggest challenges on national and international level. Public private partnership (PPP) plays a crucial role in the development of any economic as well as social system.

These partnerships have beneficial effects in health and medical, infrastructure and superstructure, travel and tourism, airlines and other investment sectors etc.

There is no doubt that PPP model will be beneficial in removing regional imbalances and unemployment problems.

Thus, there will be a chain increase in demand for the touristic and health product and India will be able to become known and recognized as a true tourism destination that meets all requirements.

The policy of creation / development of PPPs should be a policy of national interest, meaning that it should be oriented on branches and sub-branches considering the real needs.

Research Methodology

Objectives

Theresearches have various identified and unidentified objectives, besides which it's difficult to give proper direction to the study and also to obtain final result. Following are some basic objectives of this study:

- To recognize the significance of PPP model.
- To identify the Challenges faced in applicability of PPP model.
- To analyze the role of different partners in PPP model.
- To study Functioning and Applicability of PPP model

Collection of Data

The data have been collected through various primary and

secondary sources. The primary data have been collected through interviews of top executives of Private investors and government officials. The sources for collecting the secondary data are; publications of Ministry of Tourism, Government of India, India Tourism Department, Uttar Pradesh Tourism, Central Library of Dr. B.R. Ambedkar University Agra along with the published research/case studies of various publications of central and state governments. Many websites have also been searched during the study. The subject matter has been collected through research articles, journals, magazines, newsletters, books and others.

Review of Literature

Green Paper on Public- Private Partnerships and Community Law on Public Contracts and Concessions, presented by the European Commission (2004).

This paper describes the concept and nature of public private partnership with its area of operations. The writer has given legislative recommendations with the reference of Europe. The Green Paper promotes a public consultation to ensure the development of PPPs under conditions of effective competition and legal clarity.

Turina, N, Diana Car-Pušić, overview of PPP models and the analysis of the Opportunities for their application, university of Rijeka, faculty of civil engineering, Croatia.

The article gives the explanation, that the being consumer oriented market and services, the public sector adopted association with the private sector to bring skills, finances and other resources on the common platform. The author has taken the examples of Republic of Croatia and the City of Rijeka, for successful implementation of PPP process and the methods adopted.

WTOBC, 2000, 58; FTHM, 2008). WTOBC (2000) Public-private Sector Cooperation: Enhancing Tourism Competitiveness, WTO Business Council, Madrid.

The significance of PPP in tourism industries has been described in this article of WTO. Tourism marketing, promotion and the budget constrains taken on priority and increased private sector funding in tourism industry is growing every year. WTO mentioned about the changing the role of government in the promotion of tourism and the new global tourism environment.

WTO (1996) Towards New Forms of Public Private Partnership, World Tourism Organisation.

This publication of WTO gives major credit to the private sector for sustainable tourism although the key role for tourism development and its promotion in the country is played by the government department. The changing political and socio-economic conditions is are described well with the significance of increased participation of private sector at all the levels.

Asian Development Bank (ADB), 2010Bulletin 3P: Sharing Knowledge on PPP Projects, Events and Activities, Issue.

This bulletin described the association of GoI and ADB. The document describes about present scenario of PPP in India with framework, cross-learnings, policies of GoI, actions and reviews of activities under PPP implementation. This document emphasizes more investments in PPP process and its rationales.

Ministry of Finance & Asian Development Bank, December 2006. Facilitating PPP for Accelerated Infrastructure Development in India.

This report describes about knowledge management and capacity building required in PPP. The views presented in it do not necessarily reflect the views and policies of the ADB. Accelerated infrastructure development in India, relevance of PPPs in the current Indian context and new initiatives undertaken by the central government, strategic and practical significance of PPP are included in the document. According to the document the PPPs do not mean reduced responsibility and accountability of the government.

FICCI-E&Y Report on Accelerating PPP in India, released at the India PPP Summit 2012 organized by FICCI.

This report focuses on development of PPPs in India over the years, the challenges and frame work, role of PPP at state level development, areas of PPP implementation, practices followed in other countries, funding opportunities and recommendations. The case studies of Andhra Pradesh Gujrat, Jharkhand, Karnataka, UK, Australia, Brazil, Philippines etc. are included in the document with inclusion of twelfth five year plan.

Turina, N, Diana Car-Pušić, overview of PPP models and the analysis of the Opportunities for their application, university of Rijeka, faculty of civil engineering, Croatia.

This article reflects the need of PPP and its adoption globally, especially in developing countries and the significance of active participation of all the stakeholders at all level. The key conditions and risks with clearly defined the responsibilities and accountabilities of all the partners, defined well. The paper gives an overview of PPP models and the most significant European Commission's documents related to the PPP.

Bogheanu, M. Public-Private Partnership, Development Alternative for Health Tourism,University of Craiova.

The document gives an overview on development in Romania through PPP with the advantages. Focusing on health tourism wellness, prevention and proper health care services can be adopted through PPP process. This article recommend the doption of PPP in rehabilitation of roads, mineral springs, rehabilitation of urban infrastructure, construction of tourist accommodation resorts, entertainment centers, adventure parks, better marketing of touristic destinations, etc.

Harrill R. and Bender B., State Tourism Funding: Equity, Consensus, And Accountability Models (2007), Department of Hotel, Restaurant, and Tourism Management, Columbia, University of South Carolina, USA.

This article uses narrative, case study analysis to investigate three major alternative models to state tourism funding. The arisen of PPP, characteristics of PPP and their implications for the tourism industry, defined well. The article suggests new hybrid models for PPP in tourism.

Nature, Scope and Significance of PPP un Tourism Industry

Some common characteristics can be seen in different type of PPP models, comprising contract between the private and public entities for achieving the pre decided task. PPP take place for the delivery of services, infrastructure development and management with risk controlling for reducing their impact and consequences.

Adopting PPP model can multiply the efficiency of delivery of services, financial management, facing risks, project management and operations. In any condition, the PPP model cannot replace the public sector or act as a controller. It works with the rational profit for private sector with strong political will in the country.

From Tourism point of view, PPPs model needs to be developed in following areas:

- Infrastructure and superstructure development
- Safety and security systems
- destination development
- Medical and Health
- Social and Cultural activities
- Economic stimulation or recovery
- Education / Skills Development
- Mega-event activation
- Marketing and promotion of the destination.
- And a variety of other destination specific needs

It is suggested that PPP will enhance the competitive advantage of tourism industry in a particular destination ordestinations.

The advantages of public-private partnership

The importance of Public-Private Partnership can be observed at multitudes in concern with the tourism industry. Now a days government, private players and the communities have started joining hands to share subject matters in cultural, ethnic and most important fiscal partnerships for identified project with the long term associations. The consequence of such partnerships is decentralization of decision making and planning so that each ally has focused concerns with responsibilities and accountabilities. "Efficient use of PPP schemes in delivering necessary services in travel and hospitality sector; the PPP investments can help ease the pressure on public finances and deficits as well as contribute to more stable economic growth and increased transparency of public spending; by maximizing the value of public money, more can be built and operated with given amounts of public resources." (Kazatsay Z, 2005)

With the various benefits, PPP model allow the private and public sectors to work together with complimenting the strength of each partner for attainingthe common goal.

Followings are some key benefits of PPP model:

- Private investors supplement the public funds in completion of the project and facilitate it in running too.
- Through this model the liabilities of whether fixed assets or working capitals are shared, therefore, the project is looked after in effective manner as pros and cons all goes together for the both sectors.
- Since all agreements and conditions are laid down in advance before implementing the PPP model so liabilities are fixed in better and effective way to meet the target.
- It is noticed that since in private sector, the investors are directly affected with profit and loss so they provide highly efficient services, which are quality and time bound and public sector are more acquainted with government policies and regulations,thus through PPP approach the output are achieved more accurately and effectively.
- Strengthen the hands of communities in decision making and profit gaining as financial burden and liabilities are shared by both the sectors
- Gives recognition to private investors along with the public contributor.
- Spread awareness in the community as they themselves are the handler of situations.
- Least developed and developing countries get more advantages from such joint venture of both the sectors because their rich ethical and social values along with indigenous culture.
- Through multi-facets and opportunities, both the sectors are directly benefited as this model is working for; the fast implementation of policies and planning, flexibility in way of implementation, applicability of new techniques and innovative ideas, change and alteration of rules and regulations, marketing based research and allocation of funds

and profits, sharing of risks, trading and other incentives with professional approach and common goals.

- Ensure the transparency in system in both cases whether gain or loss, as it is the main pillar of the PPP model.
- PPP model approaches for sustainable development as it comprises of the opportunities and challenges to both the parties on equally shared bases.

Functioning and Applicability of PPP Model

FICCI-E&Y Report on Accelerating PPP in India to be released at the India PPP Summit 2012 suggested the following steps in the PPP model:

PPP	Development stage	Procurement stage	PPP contract
Identification stage Consists of strategic planning, project prefeasibility analysis, Value for Money analysis, PPP suitability checks, and internal clearances to proceed with PPP development	Consists of project preparation (including technical feasibility and financial viability analysis), project structuring, reparation of contractual documents and obtaining of project clearances and approval	Consists of procurement and project award	Management and monitoring stage Consists of project implementation and monitoring over the life of PPP project

In the operational process of a PPP arrangement, private organization and its team has to deal with many government regulations of different states.

The PPP model is a financing tool. The public sector is the source of funding in PPP projects or the finances comes directly from the user group against availing the facilities or services, provided by private sector. These types of projects majorly involve direct revenue generating sources such as tolls,for making the balance between the profits and the cost of the facility utilization. Through this procedure the burden of funding moves towards the user group from government side.

The concept of PPP has much scope for public sector for finding innovative quality solutions to address social needs and ability to raise financial capital and opportunities to deliver the assignments to the private sector to claim the performance of assignment cost effectively.

The private players have wide range of business opportunities through PPP with the long term contracts, which were previously in the hands of public sector exclusively.

The major areas in which PPP model act or apply are as such:

To improve facilities at existing destination and to develop new sites:

In the developing countries, governments lack in generating the resources, required for developing infrastructure, financial managements, skilled manpower, etc. For coping-up this situation, various countries have started joining hands with private sector to develop new regions to tourism and other concern opportunities.In the PPP project, the private organization provides a public service and undertakes significant technical, financial, and operational risk. The PPP approach can be used to revitalize heritage buildings. The government can support efforts to improve infrastructure or superstructure by promoting PPP opportunities to foreign investors.

The tourism development zones can be created with the support of PPP model, focusing all the tourism concern facilities within these zones, (e.g. water supply, electricity,telecommunications, roads etc.)

Provide basic amenities:

The PPP model can be applicable extensively in ; water and sewage, power production and distribution industry, transportation services, infrastructure/superstructure development, waste management, medical and health concern services, education, heritage conservation, environmental concerns, IT services etc.The implementation of public-private partnership became successfully popular in recent years and given very good outcomes in social, economic and environmental aspects at national and global level.

The government of India has launched a PPP model based scheme called PURA (Provision of Urban Amenities to Rural Areas), during the eleventh five year plan. This concept was given by former president of India;Dr. A.P.J. Abdul Kalam.The ministry of rural development, government of India implemented this scheme focusing the concept of PPP between local executive bodies such as Gram Panchayats and private players.

With the rich cultural and historical heritage, Uttar Pradesh has wide opportunities in tourism;Government of Uttar Pradesh has decided to promote tourism through PPP model.According to the press release of Empowered Committee on Public Private Partnership, Infrastructure & Industrial Development Corporation Government of Uttar Pradesh, the procedure of approval for issuance of Request for Qualification (RFQ) document is under process, for setting up Helium Balloon Ride facility at three places, viz. Agra, FatehpurSikri, Varanasi and restarting of Light & Sound show at Residency, Lucknow. Further, Consultant for preparing Detailed Project Report (DPR) for setting up Ropeways at three places was selected along with in principle approval to encourage development of roadside amenities by private developers. In the first phase, Helium balloon Ride facility is proposed at Shilpgram-Agra,RahiGulistan TouristComplex-FatehpurSikri and Sant Ravidas Ghat-Varanasi.

Decision was also taken to encourage private players to create new public amenities along theroads routinely used by travelers and tourists and developing and maintaining facilities like hygienic public toilets, clean drinking water, and signage on either along theroads side.etc.

Preservation, conservation and promotion of cultural and historical sites:

The culture, values, customs and traditions are not considered as a source resulted in the decay or decline of both the tangible and the intangible cultural heritage. The public investments and attention have radically reduced in favour of cultural concern promotions and conservations. The active participation and support of communities and private organizations, located in and around historical places can act as catalysts in the conservation and revitalization of their cultural heritage, and its promotion through PPP model. This process can lead towards social and economic development.

There are huge unexplored opportunities and potential for partnership in the cultural sector.

Partnerships in the area of culture can provide remarkable investment opportunities to the private sector and fund arrangements for public sector.

Here the example of Vaishno Devi temple can be coded successfully as a joint venture of government efforts and Vaishno Devi Shrine Board.

Promotion and marketing of destinations:

In India there are many states, in which main sources of economy are tourism or allied industries. There is no doubt, Government has initiated in all such states for the promotion of domestic and inboundtourism, but it is quite true that without the efforts of local artisans, craftsman, and key persons from the destination; no promotional activities can be successful. In fact if the private person are the originator and sustainer of any destination than the public sector adding the services for the maintenance, management and beautification of it.

Promotional campaign through joint venture procedure, multiply the output as compare to individual stakeholder. The higher level of promotion and marketing with combined efforts of public and private sector can attract the tourist to a low profile destination too and this procedure becomes more effective in progressively competitive environment.

During the PPP project implementation;all the involved partners becomes inter-dependent for achieving their objectives more effectively. The private sector cannot be successful in strategic planning, without taking inputs from public sector.

The PPP model has become important as a strategic tool for tourism development, in recent years. Tourism needs diversified services and supplies at the destination to make thye product that satisfy the visitors' need and experience. The PPP model has been widely recognized for such type of prohibitions. Partnerships between the public and the private sectors have a strong and established position among the various forms of associations.

Sustainable development through PPP model:

In nature, the development of any step should not be considered in isolation. This is quite true that all living organisms are interdependent and even they are dependent upon non-livings. The same principle is applied in man-made environment too for the sustainable growth of it. The PPP model act on this principle, therefore, for the involvement of whole community in any kind of maintenance or development it is required not only for the current uses but also to sustain it for the future generations. For social, cultural, economic and environmental purposes, the sustainability in growth and development can only be maintained through the partnership or coordination of all beneficiaries. The growth of tourism industry is basically depends upon infrastructural and superstructure development, which is not the work of public sector alone. Throughout the world it is noticed that this development is mainly on public-private partnership bases, which is the main source of its sustainability.

Challenges Faced in Applicability of PPP Model

Considering the PPP model, the respondents must recognize the consequences also. There may be circumstances whenpublic and private both have to exercise together for the cautions. After selecting the PPP, public authorities may face significant challenges or difficulties to overcome. Some challenges in the application of PPP model are as follows:

- Adopting the PPP model for the development process creates a typical situation of maintaining the quality at lower cost, because the process of selection of tender by authorities is very competitive. During the agreement partial risk comes in the domain of private sector
- There may be the situation in which the cost and complications can overshadow the expected outcome of PPP.
- Delaying of funds disbursement by the public sector may hamper the task.

- In many areas of travel, hospitality it is very difficult to apply PPP model as there is a monopoly of public sectors in specific field and all the powers are in the hand of government.
- In many sectors huge investment with huge risks are involved, initially private sector is not in a position to invest without thinking about benefits for a long time. Therefore, PPP model can only be applicable if either government invest on such projects or give liberty to the investors from the taxes levied.
- In many areas where the involvements of local citizens are much for producing the local products, there are always threats to the PPP authorities to work in collective way, as local citizens considered this practices the interference of public sector in their jobs or with working hands.
- For taking the healthy involvement of local citizens, the public sector should form the policies foe securing the local residents, as the source of livelihoods gets hamper out of infrastructure projects.In most of the cases, the local vendors face problems, when any infrastructure development project takes place.
- Due to red-tapism, PPP model becomes more time taking and complexity occurs some times. The implementation process becomes very difficult as it involves the participation of many departments of public and private partners.
- The lack of technical, communicable skills among public authorities, to deal with private partners is hampering the proper functioning of the PPP model. In huge development projects like construction of bridges, roads, installation of power projects etc. the private contractors work with government authorities, in which generally the bureaucrats are lacking the technical skills but as they are authorities through whom all projects will be sanctioned. Thus they create hindrances in the installation and functioning of overall project. Similarly communication gap between public and private respondents delay the completion of project.
- In the selection process of tender it is noticed that always tender of that contractor is selected, who is supplying their material or services at lower cost rather to check that whether the contractor is technically sound or not.

Suggestions and Conclusion

The applicability of PPP model for the tourism growth is beneficiaries on the one side than it is also true that it has complexity in its functioning. To overcome from such situations following are some key suggestions for the effective functioning and applicability of this model, especially in service sector like tourism and hospitality:

- The public authorities should consider all the consequences of PPP model while forming the guidelines. In this way the balance between cost, complications and expected outcome can be maintained up to the end of the project.
- The selection process of the private partners should be based on the technical skills, commitment to work and efficiency to bear the risks. The lower cost concepts should not be always on priority for the final selection of the tender.
- A separate committee comprising the officials of different departments, apart from PPP partners, can be formed for the monitoring of the project. This committee can evaluate the progress work, funds disbursement and other quality measures on regular bases. Finally, this will improvethe quality of result within stimulated time span.
- The PPP model should be formed in such a way, which can boost up the good environmental conditions for the private partners.
- The implementation of project through PPP model, should involve local residents and other stakeholders, apart from public and private partners because the local residents and society are affected by the consequences of the implementation and development of the projects and they are the beneficiaries too.
- PPP models need to incorporate the prohibitions of skill development trainings of all the involved stakeholders on the regular intervals. This will help all the partners in understanding each other and technicalities & complications of progress.
- The capacity building programmes should be effectively run by model institutionsto develop the innovative skills of

private partners as well as public authorities. This kind of programmes should run on regular bases.

- Each partner and society, involved in PPP model, have multiple effects. All the responsibilities and accountabilities with clearly defined criteria should be incorporated carefully during the formation of PPP model.

In most of the countries of the world, public sector supersedes the private sector. But this is not the overall principle throughout the world. For the development point of view, the whole world can be classified in to three categories, namely; developed, developing and undeveloped countries. The economic system in these countries varied with different aspects but there is no doubt that in all economic system uses of PPP model is beneficial as onthe one side it reduces the cost of the project and time taken in its completion than on the other, it gives more responsible hands for the overall development of any country.

The PPP model increases the number of enterprises in different field. It also develops the platform for local business by adding innovative ideas from the communities. Cost reductions, effective management of resources are some other key benefits of the applicability of this model. Last but not least, it is true that the success of any enterprise in any area is not the effort of any individual but it is through the joint effort of private and public ventures.

Bibliography

African Journal of Hospitality, Tourism and Leisure Vol. 3 (2) - (2014).

Asian Development Bank (ADB), 2010Bulletin 3P: Sharing Knowledge on PPP Projects, Events and Activities, Issue 1.

Bogheanu, M. Public-Private Partnership, Development Alternative for Health Tourism,University of Craiova, Page 40

Brookings-Rockefeller | Project on State and Metropolitan Innovation | December 2011, Emilia Istrate Senior Research Analyst Metropolitan Policy Program Brookings Institution, US

Campos, M. J. Z & Hall, M.C. (2012). Public–private collaboration in the tourism sector: balancing legitimacy and effectiveness in local tourism partnerships, Journal of Policy Research in Tourism, Leisure and Events, 4:1, 61-83.

Elliott, James. 1997, Tourism: politics and public sector management, Routledge, New York.

European Investment Bank, The EIB's role in Public-Private Partnerships, July 2004.

FICCI-E&Y Report on Accelerating PPP in India, released at the India PPP Summit 2012 organized by FICCI

Geo Journal of Tourism and Geo sites, no. 1, vol. 3, 2009, 63-69.

Green Paper on Public- Private Partnerships and Community Law on Public Contracts and Concessions, presented by the European Commission (2004) 327.

Harrill R. and Bender B., State Tourism Funding: Equity, Consensus, And Accountability Models (2007), Department of Hotel, Restaurant, and Tourism Management, Columbia, University of South Carolina, USA.

http://delhi.gov.in/wps/wcm/connect/doit_shahjahanabad/DoIT_Shahjahanabad/Home/About+Us/

http://en.wikipedia.org/wiki/Public%E2%80%93private_partnership

http://en.wikipedia.org/wiki/Tourist_Resorts_(Kerala)

http://englishfrombasics.wordpress.com/2013/08/20/ppp-model-in-india-understanding-its-pros-and-cons-2/

http://pura.net.in/Home

http://timesofindia.indiatimes.com/city/goa/Experts-focus-on-role-of-PPP-in-tourism/articleshow/10469126.cms

http://www.business-standard.com/article/economy-policy/up-mulls-ppp-model-for-tourism-development-112061402010_1.html

http://www.centrum-ppp.pl

http://www.governancenow.com/news/regular-story/now-ppp-model-boost-tourism

http://www.incredibleindia.org/trade-product/products/promotion-of-caravan-tourism-and-caravan-camping-parks/about-the-product#sthash.wnVthwmq.dpuf

http://www.investopedia.com/terms/p/public-private-partnerships.asp

http://www.pppinindia.com/Defining-PPP.php

http://www.tourism.gov.in/TourismDivision/AboutScheme.aspx?Name=Tourism%20Infrastructure%20Development&CID=67&INO=6

IMF (2004), Public-Private Partnerships, the Fiscal Affairs Department, World Bank.

International Journal for Responsible Tourism – Vol. 2, No. 1, Paper.

Investment Advisory Series, Series A, number 5, United Nations Conference on Trade and Development, Promoting Foreign, Investment In Tourism, 2010, UNCTAD publication.

Investment in Infrastructure in India," Article base website, http://www.articlesbase.com/investing-articles/investmentin-infrastructure-in-india-4585328.html, accessed)

Jose, A. and Ibanez G., Regulating infrastructure: Monopoly, Contracts and Discretion Cambridge, MA: Harvard University Press, 2003); OECD, 2008;

Kim, D.K., Kim, C., Lee, T.H. (2005) Public and Private Partnership for Facilitating Tourism Investment in the APEC Region, APEC Tourism Working Group & Ministry of Culture and Tourism, Republic of Korea.

Leonard C. Gilroy and others, Building New Roads through Public- Private Partnerships: Frequently Asked Questions, Reason Foundation Policy Brief No. 58, 2007

Menon,S. and Edward,M.Public private partnerships in tourism-a case study of Kerala Travel Mart, 2.

Ministry of Finance & Asian Development Bank, December 2006. Facilitating PPP for Accelerated Infrastructure Development in India.

National Public Private Partnership Policy – Draft for consultation, Ministry of Finance, September 2011

Palmer, A., &Bejou, D. (1995). Tourism destination marketing alliances. Annals of Tourism Research, 22(3), 616-629.

Perić,M.Quality Models and Public-Private Partnerships in Croatian Tourism, (project no. 116/1162459-2456), conducted with the support of the Ministry of Science, Education and Sport of the Republic of Croatia and University of Rijeka, Opatija,

Proceedings of conference, The International Congress "Culture: Key to Sustainable Development" was held in Hangzhou (China) from 15 May to 17 May 2013. organized by UNESCO

Proceedings of Public Management Committee 32nd Annual meeting of Working Party of Senior Budget Officials, 6-7 June, Luxembourg.

Roseau, P. Villancourt: The Strenghts and Weaknesses of Public-Private Policy Partnerships. The MIT Press Cambridge Massechussets. London 2002.

Taraszkiewicz, T. Improving Quality of Tourist Traffic Service by Public-Private Partnership In Hong Kong, Department of Tourism and Recreation, Poland80-336.

Tomasz T., (2009), Improving Quality Of Tourist Traffic Service By Public-Private Partnership In Hong Kong, Department Of Tourism And Recreation Poland.

Turina, N, Diana Car-Pušić, overview of PPP models and the analysis of the Opportunities for their application, university of Rijeka, faculty of civil engineering, Croatia.

UNWTO. (2012). Tourism Success Stories and Rising Stars (World Tourism Conference Proceedings). Kota Kinabalu, Sabah, Malaysia, 4 – 6 October 2010,

VerkehrB.für, Bauen and Wohnen, German PPP Task Force, German Transport, Construction and Housing Ministry.

WTO (1996) Towards New Forms of Public Private Partnership, World Tourism Organisation.

WTOBC, 2000, 58; FTHM, 2008). WTOBC (2000) Public-private Sector Cooperation: Enhancing Tourism Competitiveness, WTO Business Council, Madrid., 58

ZoltanKazatsay, Deputy Director General, DG TREN, European Commission at the 2005 PPP Transport Summit.

EXPLORATION OF BUDDHIST TOURISM POTENTIAL IN HIMACHAL PRADESH (INDIA)

Suneel Kumar

Assistant Professor, Department of Commerce, Shaheed Bhagat Singh College, University Of Delhi, India drsuneel.sbsc@gmail.com

Abstract

The ancient name of Himachal Pradesh is "Dev Bhumi" the sacred land of gods and goddesses-seems appropriate today also. It has beautiful and fertile valleys, snowcapped mountains, temples and other religious places. In this research paper, an attempt has been made to analyses the perception of tourists regarding the Buddhist points of attractions and to explore the neglected and concealed Buddhist tourism potential in the state of Himachal Pradesh. Special emphasis has been given to the Buddhist circuits, Buddhism, famous places for Buddhism in order to make people acquaint with the Buddhist culture, tradition, His Holiness Dalai Lama, Buddhist religion, and monks and monasteries. The present study is based on multi stratified sampling. At the first stage with the help of convenience and purposive sampling four districts i.e. Shimla, Kullu, Kangra, and Kinnaur have been selected. At the second stage, twenty tourist places from these four districts with the help of simple random sampling have been selected. At the third stage, 300 tourists (200 domestic and 100 foreign) @ 15 tourists from each tourist destination are selected conveniently.

After that the chi square test has been applied on the collected data and proves the hypothesis. It is clear from the study that very low proportion of tourists visited the state due to monks and monasteries and around fifty percent of total respondents opined that they don't have any idea about the Buddhist tourism. More than sixty percent tourists have not visited the Tabo monastery, did not have any knowledge about other places which were famous for Buddhism, and opined that the Buddhist circuits are remain hidden and concealed.

Keywords: -Dev Bhoomi, Buddhist Circuits, Buddhist Religion, Monks and Monasteries, Tabo Monastery, Holiness Dalai Lama

Introduction

Tourism is an ever expanding service industry with talent growth potential and has therefore, become one of the crucial concerns of national and international community as a whole. It is largely examined of its ample potential to give rise to changes in the economic, ecological, social and cultural edifice of a country. However, two aspects of tourism; 1) its capacity to generate employment and 2) its potentiality to earn international currency for the host country have made this industry greatly desirable for people in general and government, planners and entrepreneurs in particular. Tourism is the second largest economic activity in the world and is the main element in the economy of many countries. It paves the way for economic growth and is essential for the development of under developed economies (UNWTO Reports). However, there are certain hindrances in the development of this industry. It requires heavy investment for development of infrastructure of the place and provision of other facilities like good food, lodging, transport, entertainment etc. hence the longer gestation period to get returns.

Secondly while putting the tourism industry in a wider developmental context; one may have to spend to make available the leakage including income going outside the destination to those goods and services, which are not available locally.

The proper growth and development of tourism in Himachal is faced with problems like financial constraints, limited tourist season, high cost of constructions/production and limited modes of communication. In-depth knowledge of tourism industry is of utmost importance for this development. Himachal Pradesh Government has however declared tourism as an industry and provides financial aid to promote it (Tourism Policy of HP).

Critical Issues and Review of Literature

A set of studies conducted Dutta (1980), Singh (1985), Tayal and Motwani (1986) and Kumar (1995) observed that India has vast potential for the development of tourist spots. They predicted that India's enormous tourism potential is destined to attract an increasing number of tourists every year. Mishra and Panwar (1993) laid stress on the application of marketing concepts to tourism industry. They mainly focus on the marketing of cultural tourism; there is a need to take care of our culture and tradition.

Soni (1990) studied the role of religion in Nepal for the promotion of tourism industry and pointed out that the valley has valley has potential for promoting tourism especially pilgrimage and adventure tourism. Jackson and James (1997) concluded that the growth of tourism in Western China is because of distinctive religious groups and their unique landscape which attract tourists. Negi (2002), Chauhan (2006) and Sara (2008) suggested that Eco tourism has been accepted as a new approach as it provides decentralized opportunities for community development, stress on appropriate use of limited resources and focuses on community development in order to meet the social, economic and cultural needs of a community.

A domestic tourism survey conducted by the Indian Ministry of Tourism in 2002 reported that more than 100 million visitors travelled for 'religious purposes and pilgrimages' and eight of the top-ten ranking domestic tourist destinations were pilgrimage sites.

According to the Ministry's Tourism Satellite Accounts, religious tourism segment contributed almost 20% towards the total domestic tourism consumption (approximately INR 2.8 Billion) and this contribution is likely to increase annually. Such figures, often based on estimates from formal components (such as travel costs, accommodation in registered places, etc.), should be considered only as partial indicators of the volume of religious tourism market.

After the thorough and critical review of relevant literature indicates that the bulk of studies conducted so far only analyze the performance of tourism development. Serious attempts to study the religious tourism in general and Buddhist tourism in particular are however missing in the state of Himachal Pradesh. So, there is a need to undertake an empirical study, which could identify and develop the Buddhist tourism potential areas in Himachal Pradesh. There remain certain unanswered questions with regard to Buddhist tourism in Himachal Pradesh:

1. What is the status of religious tourism with special reference to Buddhist tourism in the state?
2. What is the perception of tourists regarding the Buddhist points of attraction in state of Himachal Pradesh?
3. Are there famous places for Buddhism in the state?
4. Do the Buddhist Circuits remain neglected and concealed from tourism point of view?

In view of the above stated questions, there arises an urgent need to study; 1) the perception of tourists regarding the Buddhist points of attraction in state of Himachal Pradesh, 2) to explore the neglected and concealed Buddhist tourism potential areas in the state. In order to examine the objectives of study, following hypotheses have been formulated.

Ho. There is no significant difference in the opinion of tourists, their sex, income, and occupation regarding the Buddhist points of attraction.

Ha. There is a significant difference in the opinion of tourists, their sex, income, and occupation regarding the Buddhist points of attraction.

Ho1. There is no significant difference in the opinion of domestic and foreign tourists regarding the Buddhist tourism, visit to Tabo monastery, other places famous for Buddhism, and neglected Buddhist circuits.

Ha1. There is a significant difference in the opinion of domestic and foreign tourists regarding the Buddhist tourism, visit to Tabo monastery, other places famous for Buddhism, and neglected Buddhist circuits.

Data Base and Research Methods

The present study is mainly based on primary data. It includes the information about tourism values attached with Buddhist religion, their points of attractions, and the potential areas liable to be developed further. A total of 19 field visits have been made to 20 tourists destinations of four districts of Himachal Pradesh, i.e., Shimla, Kullu, Kangra, and Kinnaur. Of which, four visits were the pilot study visits made to each district. Each tourist destination has been visited once to do the questionnaire survey. The sample respondents have been selected with the help of convenience and purposive sampling from four districts. A total of 300 tourists (200 domestic and 100 foreign) have been selected from 20 tourists destinations of selected districts, thereby taking 15 samples from each destination. While selecting the samples, special care has been taken to ensure the representation of different regions, age groups, educational levels, sex and income levels. Tourist's response has tabulated and further interpreted by calculating the simple percentage. In view of the large size of sample (300), hypotheses have been tested by using chi square test at 5 % level of significance.

Results and Disscussion

The responses of domestic tourists indicate that majority of them visit Buddhist points of attraction to know about their art and culture, traditional values and also to enjoying the scenic beauty with 19% falling in each category. Thirteen percent of domestic tourists visit for monks and monasteries. However some tourists visit such places since they are influenced by Buddhists religion and His Holiness Dalai Lama (Table 1). In case of foreign tourists, a large number of tourists visit Buddhist spots to know about the traditional values (24%) and art & culture (20%). About 16% of foreign tourists are attracted towards monks and monasteries and a few also visit these spots as they are fascinated by the Buddhist religion and by their teaching. The chi square value (6.36) is insignificant at 5% level of significance, hence there is no significant difference in the opinion of domestic and foreign tourists so null hypothesis (Ho) is accepted.

Table 1 Tourists perception about Buddhist points of attraction (%)

Buddhist Points of Attraction	Nationality		Total
	Indian	Foreigner	
Monks and Monasteries	13	16	14
Historical places	8.5	12	9.7
Art & culture	19	20	19.3
Traditional statues	19	24	20.7
Scenic beauty	19	14	17.3
Peaceful and good climate	11	5	9
Dalai Lama	7	5	6.3
Buddhist religion	3.5	4	3.7
Total	100	100	100

Source: Primary Probe

The data signifies that most of the male tourists visit such places to know about traditional values (23%) followed by those who want to know about the Buddhist art and culture (18.8%). About 16% of male tourists visit these spots for their scenic beauty and 12.4% to know about monks and monasteries (Table 2). On the other hand in case of female tourists, it can be inferences that above 20% female visit these spots due to their interest in art & culture followed by those visiting to witness the scenic beauty. It is observed that 17% of female tourists visit such spots for monks and monasteries and further 17% for traditional values. After applying the chi square test it is evident that value (4.45) is insignificance. It means there is no significant difference in the opinion of male and female tourists hence null hypothesis (Ho) is accepted at 5% level of significance.

Table 2 Gender wise perception about Buddhist points of attraction (%)

Buddhist Points of Attraction	Sex		Total
	Male	Female	
Monks and Monasteries	12.4	17.3	14
Historical places	10.4	8.2	9.7
Art & culture	18.8	20.4	19.3
Traditional statues	22.3	17.3	20.7

Buddhist Points of Attraction	Sex		Total
	Male	Female	
Scenic beauty	16.3	19.4	17.3
Peaceful and good climate	9.9	7.1	9
Dalai Lama	6.9	5.1	6.3
Buddhist religion	3	5.1	3.7
Total	100	100	100

Source: Primary Probe

The analysis indicates (Table 3) that more than 20% tourists from private sector have shown high preference for art & culture and 18.3% show their interest in traditional statutes. An equal proportion of tourists visit for reasons, like peaceful and good climate and historical places (13.4% each). Above twelve percent of them visit for reasons like monks and monasteries and scenic beauty. The main reason cited by students for their visit is to explore about traditional statutes, art & culture and monks and monasteries.

While looking at business class tourists, it is observed that they visit such sites to know about art & culture, traditional statutes and monks and monasteries. But tourists from public sector show variations as above 50% visit, such spots because of scenic beauty, traditional statutes and monks and monasteries. In case of professionals, there is very small difference in the number of tourists falling in different categories like traditional statutes, art & culture, scenic beauty etc. The chi-square test result shows that there is a significant relationship between occupation of tourists and Buddhist points of attraction hence alternate hypothesis (Ha) is accepted at 5% level of significance.

Table 3 Occupation wise perception about Buddhist points of attraction (%)

Buddhist Points of Attraction	Occupation						Total
	Public Sector	Private Sector	Business-man	Pension Holders	Stu-dents	Profes-sional	
Monks and Monasteries	10.4	12.2	15.7	55.6	14.5	9.8	14
Historical places	6.3	13.4	13.7	-	7.2	7.3	9.7
Art & culture	12.5	22	27.5	-	17.4	19.5	19.3
Traditional statues	14.6	18.3	23.5	33.3	23.2	22	20.7

Buddhist Points of Attraction	Occupation						Total
	Public Sector	Private Sector	Business-man	Pension Holders	Stu-dents	Profes-sional	
Scenic beauty	41.7	12.2	7.8	11.1	14.5	17	17.3
Peaceful and good climate	6.3	13.4	2.0	-	10.2	12.2	9
Dalai Lama	4.2	7.3	3.9	-	5.8	12.2	6.3
Buddhist religion	4	1.2	5.9	-	7.2	-	3.7
Total	100	100	100	100	100	100	100

Source: Primary Probe

The relationship between annual income of tourists and Buddhist points of attraction has been layout that the tourists with annual income of 3 to 4 lakhs visit such spots due to their inclination towards scenic beauty (21.1%), followed by traditional statutes, art & culture (19.3% each) and above 11% of tourists from this group showed interest in monks and monasteries (Table 4).

Tourists with negligible income visit due to different reasons like monks and monasteries, art & culture, traditional statutes and scenic beauty. In case of tourists with annual income of 4 lakhs and above, about 50% are influenced by the reasons like monks and monasteries and traditional statutes. Tourists with income level varying between 1 to 3 lakhs are mostly influenced by traditional statutes, art & culture and monks and monasteries.

The study also reflects that only 10% of respondents visit due to their interest in Buddhist religion and His Holiness Dalai Lama. The outcome of chi-square test shows (33.96) that there is no significant relationship between annual income and Buddhist points of attraction, hence null hypothesis (Ho) is accepted.

Table 4 Income level of respondents and their perception about Buddhist Points of Attraction (%)

Buddhist Points of Attraction	Annual income						TO-TAL
	Nil	Below 1,00,000	1,00,000-2,00,000	2,00,000-3,00,000	3,00,000-4,00,000	4,00,000 and above	
Monks and Monasteries	15.3	-	20.0	7.5	11.4	24.4	14
Historical places	10.2	-	13.3	7.5	12.3	4.4	9.7
Art & culture	16.9	33.3	23.3	20	19.3	15.6	19.3
Traditional statues	18.6	16.7	20	25	19.3	24.4	20.7
Scenic beauty	15.3	16.7	13.3	12.5	21.1	17.8	17.3
Peaceful and good climate	11.9	16.7	6.7	17.5	6.1	4.4	9
Dalai Lama	6.8	-	3.3	5	7	8.9	6.3
Buddhist religion	5.1	16.7	-	5	3.5	-	3.7
Total	100	100	100	100	100	100	100

Source: Primary Probe

The opinion of domestic and international tourist's exhibit that, 51% of domestic tourists did not have any idea about the Buddhist tourism followed by 26.5% refused to give their responses and 22.5% admitted that they have an idea about the Buddhist tourism (Table 5). While in case of foreign tourists, 43% did not have any idea about the Buddhist tourism followed by 32% refused to give their responses and 25% admitted that they have an idea about the Buddhist tourism.

The result clearly indicates that the Buddhist tourism is still neglected and concealed and there is a need to explore such type of tourism. Further the chi square value (1.74) is insignificant. It means there is no significant difference in the opinion of domestic and foreign tourists hence null hypothesis (Ho1) is accepted at 5% level of significance.

Table 5 Responses of tourists about Buddhist Tourism (%)

Nature of Responses	**Nationality**		**Total**
	Indian	**Foreigner**	
Yes	22.5	25	23.3
No	51	43	48.3
Can not say	26.5	32	28.4
Total	100.0	100	100

Source: Primary Probe.

It is depicted from table 6 that 65% domestic tourists did not visit the Tabo monastery. Almost equal percentage (66%) of foreign tourists did not visit the Tabo monastery.

Table 6 Tourists and their visits to Tabo Monastery (%)

Nature of Responses	Nationality		Total
	Indian	Foreigner	
Yes	21	20	20.7
No	65	66	65.3
Can not say	14	14	14
Total	100	100	100

Source: Primary Probe

Further the chi square (0.042) value is insignificant. It means the opinion of both the tourists does not vary significantly hence null hypothesis (Ho1) is accepted at 5% level of significance.

It is observed that in case of domestic tourists, 63.5% refused to give their responses followed by 16% who admitted that they have knowledge and 16.5% did not have any knowledge about the other places which are famous for Buddhism (Table 7). While in case of foreign tourists, 65% refused to give their responses followed by 21% who admitted that they have knowledge and 14% did not have any knowledge about the other places which are famous for Buddhism in the state.

Further the chi square value (0.33) is insignificant. It indicates that there is a similar perception of both the tourists regarding the famous places for Buddhism hence null hypothesis (Ho1) is accepted at 5% level of significance.

Table 7 Respondents and other places famous for Buddhism (%)

Nature of Responses	Nationality		Total
	Indian	Foreigner	
Yes	20	21	20.3
No	16.5	14	15.7
Can not say	63.5	65	64
Total	100	100	100

Source: Primary Probe

More than fifty percent domestic tourists confessed that the Buddhist circuits remained neglected and hidden followed by 31% refused to give their responses and 13% who did not believe that the Buddhist circuits are remained neglected and hidden from tourism point of view (Table 8). On the contrary 70% foreign respondents admitted that the Buddhist circuits are remained neglected and hidden followed by 19% refused to give their responses and 11% who did not believe that the Buddhist circuits remained neglected and hidden in the state of Himachal Pradesh. Further the chi square value (5.90) is insignificant hence null hypothesis (Ho1) is accepted at 5% level of significance.

Table 8 Respondents and neglected Buddhist Circuits (%)

Nature of Responses	Nationality		Total
	Indian	Foreigner	
Yes	56	70	60.7
No	13	11	12.3
Can not say	31	19	27
Total	100	100	100

Source: Primary Probe

Conclusion

It is concluded that majority of the respondents visit the Buddhist points of attraction due to traditional statutes, scenic beauty, monks and monasteries. It seems that most of the visited tourists participate in the site seeing activities, walking and evening entertainment. Further, it is evident from the analysis that the fairs and festivals, historical monuments, culture and heritage play a vital role in the development of tourism but these are still untapped from tourism point of view in the state

It is also observed that majority of the visited tourists did not have any idea about the Buddhist tourism; even they don't know about the other places which are famous for Buddhism. It can also be concluded that the Buddhist circuits including the Tabo monastery are remained neglected and concealed from tourism point of view and can be tapped with the help of local fairs and festivals, tourist information center, proper marketing mix and by the exploration of culture and traditions.

References:

Chauhan, P. 2006. Eco-Centric - The Thrust is now on Adventure and Eco-Tourism. The Tribune, Chandigarh, Dec. 23.

Jackson, R. H. & James, D. A., 1997. Religion and Tourism in Western China, Tourism Recreating Research, Vol. 22(1) pp. 3-10.

Kumar, M. 1995. Tourism in Himachal Pradesh, Retrospect and Prospect, and Tourism Management: A Global Prospective. New Delhi: Deep and Deep Publication.

Panwar, J. S., 1993. Strategic Marketing to Develop Tourism in India. International Journal of Management and Tourism, Vol. 1(4), pp. 446-457.

Religious Tourism in Asia and the Pacific ISBN-13:978-92-844-1380S UNWTO pp 295

Sara, D. & Leisch F., 2008. Selective Marketing for Environmentally Sustainable Tourism. Tourism Management, vol. 29, pp.672-680.

Singh, T. V. & Kaur J., 1985. In Search of Holistic Tourism for the Himalayas in Integrated Mountain Development. New Delhi: Himalayan Books.

Soni, B., 1990. Development Tourism in South Asia (A case study of Tourism in Nepal, Tourism in 21 century), New Delhi: Anmol Publisher.

Tayal, N. D. & Matwani M., 1986. Tourism Development and Mountaineering in Himalayas. New Delhi: Neeraj Publisher.

TRENDS OF TOURISM IN INDIA: A PARADIGM SHIFT

Vishal Kumar

Associate Professor, Maharaja Agrasen School of Management, Maharaja Agrasen University, Baddi (H.P.)

vkfzr@hotmail.com

Savita

Assistant Professor in Commerce, Dev Samaj College for Women, Ferozepur City (PB)-152002

dhawansavita@hotmail.com

Abstract

Tourism is one of the fastest growing industries of the world. It plays vital role in the economic development of a country. India is one of the popular tourist destinations in Asia. Bounded by the Himalayan ranges in the north and surrounded, on three sides by water (Arabian sea, Bay of Bengal and Indian Ocean), India offers a wide array of places to see and things to do. The enchanting backwaters, hill stations and landscapes make India a beautiful country. Historical monuments, forts etc. add to the grandeur of the country. They attract tourists from all over the world. Tourism is the second largest foreign exchange earner in India. The tourism industry employs a large number of people, both skilled and unskilled. Hostels, travel agencies, transport including airlines benefit a lot from this industry. Tourism promotes national integration and international understanding. It generates foreign exchange, promotes cultural activities, the traditional handicrafts sector etc. The present paper focuses on the growth of tourism in India for the last one and half decades and tries to highlight some facts by using the trends of tourism in India.

Keywords: Tourism, Trends in Tourism, Paradigm Shift in Tourism, Foreign Collaborations, Tourism Policy.

Introduction

Tourism is the world's largest and fastest growing industry. It is an invisible export, which earns valuable foreign exchange without any significant or tangible loss of internal resources. It is a source of revenue and employment. There are countries in the world whose main source of revenue is tourism. India is a country with a great potential for tourism including ancient historical and archaeological interests, wild life sanctuaries, beach resorts and winter sports which attract tourists from all over the world. Tourism is the second largest foreign exchange earner in India. The tourism industry employs a large number of people, both skilled and unskilled. Hostels, travel agencies, transport including airlines benefit a lot from this industry. Tourism promotes national integration and international understanding. It generates foreign exchange, promotes cultural activities, the traditional handicrafts sector etc.

The diverse geographical locales of India delight the tourists. The monuments, museums, forts, sanctuaries, places of religious interest, palaces, etc. offer a treat to the eyes. Every region is identified with its handicrafts, fairs, folk dances, music and its people. Tourism is not only a growth engine but also an employment generator. According to the Economic Survey 2011-12, the sector has the capacity to create large scale employment both direct and indirect, for diverse sections in society, from the most specialized to unskilled workforce. It provides 6-7 per cent of the world's total jobs directly and millions more indirectly through the multiplier effect as per the UNs World Tourism Organization (UNWTO)[1]. The importance of tourism as a creator of job opportunities can be understood from the fact that in India every one million invested in tourism creates 47.5 jobs directly and around 85-90 jobs indirectly. In comparison, agriculture creates only 44.6 jobs and manufacturing a mere 12.6 jobs. Moreover

1 www.incredibleindia.org

tourism is the third largest foreign exchange earner after gems and jewellery and readymade garments[2].

Objectives of The Study

The main objectives of the study are:

1. Trends of Tourism in India since 1997 and its interpretation
2. To understand the impact of tourism on the growth of India.
3. To measure the policies of Indian Government about Tourism.

Sources and Methods of Data Collection

This research is a descriptive study in nature. Only secondary data has been used in the present study. The secondary data has been collected from research papers in journals, articles in magazines, reports in newspapers and various websites from internet. The additional required information has been collected from the concerned reports of the Ministry of Tourism etc. The study is based on the time period from 1997-2013. We have used the Secondary data from:

- Websites of Ministry of Tourism
- Journals like journal relates with tourism
- Books and magazines
- Reports and publications of various associations connected with tourism business and industry, Tour and Travelling Agencies etc.
- Historical documents and other sources of published information.

Trends of Tourism in India

Tourism is an important sector of Indian economy and contributes substantially not only in growth of the country but also contributes in the country's Foreign Exchange Earnings. A statement giving FTAs (Foreign Tourist Arrivals) in India and FEEs (Foreign Exchange Earnings) from tourism, from the years 1997 to 2013 is given below:

2 Kurukshetra, May 2012, Vol.-60, No.7, p.1

Foreign Tourist Arrivals in India
During the years 1997-2013 (Till June)

Year (million)	Foreign Tourist Arrivals	Percentage Change Over Previous Year
1997	2.37	3.8
1998	2.36	-0.7
1999	2.48	5.2
2000	2.65	6.7
2001	2.54	-4.2
2002	2.38	-6.0
2003	2.73	14.3
2004	3.46	26.8
2005	3.92	13.3
2006	4.45	13.5
2007	5.08	14.3
2008	5.28	4.0
2009	5.17	-2.2
2010	5.78	11.8
2011	6.31	9.2
2012	6.58	4.3
2013 (June)	3.31	2.6

Advance Estimates *Revised Estimates

Source: -Bureau of Immigration, Govt of India, 1997-2012

-Ministry of Tourism, Annual Report 2012-13

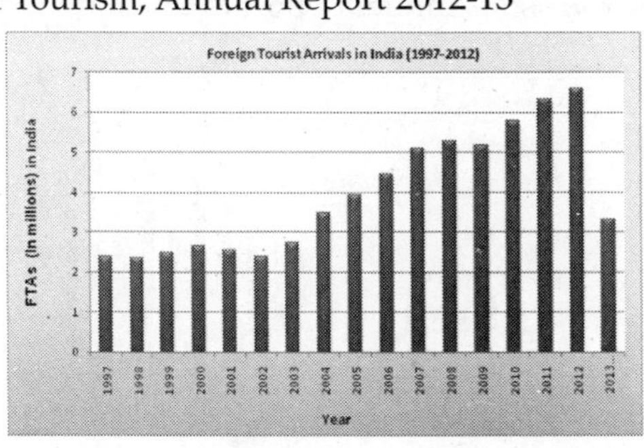

Foreign Exchange Earnings (FEE)(in US $millions) From Tourism in India

During the years 1997-2013 (Till June)

Year	FEE from Tourism in India (in US $millions)	Percentage Change Over Previous Year
1997	2889	2.0
1998	2948	2.0
1999	3009	2.1
2000	3460	15
2001	3198	-7.6
2002	3103	-3.0
2003	4463	43.8
2004	6170	38.2
2005	7493	21.4
2006	8634	15.2
2007	10729	24.3
2008	11832	10.3
2009	11136	-5.9
2010	14193	27.5
2011	16564	16.7
2012	17737	7.1
2013 (June)	9201	8.8

Advance Estimates *Revised Estimates

Source: -Bureau of Immigration, Govt of India, 1997-2012

-Ministry of Tourism, Annual Report 2012-13

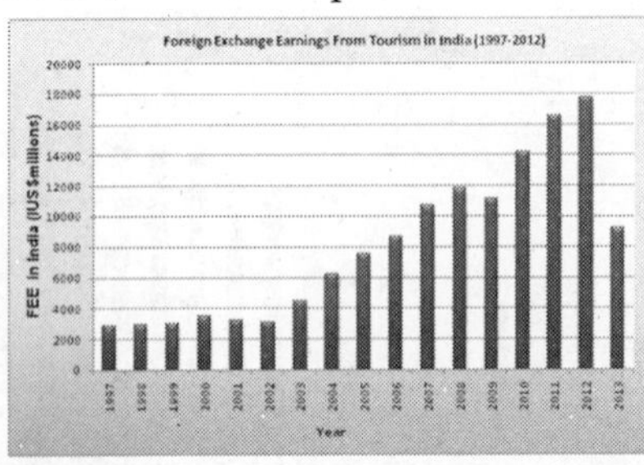

As tourism is highly relative to social, cultural, political and economical environment of the country, therefore it keeps on changing every year. But the trend of the Foreign Exchange Arrivals shows that how important the tourism is for the growth of the country. The above trend shows during 2011 FTAs in India were 6.31 million with a growth of 9.2% over 2010. FTAs during 2012 were 6.65 (provisional) million with a growth of 5.4%, as compared to the FTAs of 6.31 million during 2011. Foreign Exchange Earnings (FEEs) from tourism, in rupee terms, during 2011 was Rs.77,591 crore (provisional), with a growth of 19.6%, as compared to the FEEs of Rs.64,889 crore (provisional) during 2010.

During 2012, the Foreign Exchange Earnings (FEEs) from tourism registered a growth of 21.8% from Rs.77,591 to Rs.94,487 crore (provisional) when compared to FEEs during 2011. The summarised information about Indian Tourism is given below:

Important Facts About Indian Tourism

India

- No of Foreign Tourist Arrivals 6.58 millions
- Annual growth rate 4.3%
- No of Indian Nationals departure from India 14.92 millions
- Annual growth rate 6.7%
- No of Domestic Tourist visit to all States/UTs 1036 millions
- Annual growth rate 19.9%
- Foreign Exchange Earnings from Tourism:
  - i. INR Terms 94,887 Crore

    Annual Growth Rate 21.8%
  - ii. In US $ Terms US $ 17.74 Billion

    Annual Growth Rate 7.1%

World

- No of International Tourist Arrivals 1035 million

  Annual growth rate 4%
- International Tourism Receipts US $ 1075 Billion

  Annual Growth Rate 3.2%

Asia & the Pacific Region

• No of International Tourist Arrivals	233.6 million (P)
Annual growth rate	7%
• International Tourism Receipts	US $ 322.8 Billion (P)
Annual Growth Rate	8.1%

India's Position in the World

• Share of India in International Tourist Arrivals	0.64%
• India's rank in the World Tourist Arrivals	41
• Share of India in International Tourism Receipts	1.65%
• India's rank in International Tourism Receipts	16

P : Provisional

A : Advance Estimates

India's Position in Asia & Pacific Region

• Share of India in International Tourist Arrivals	2.82%
• India's rank in the World Tourist Arrivals	11
• Share of India in International Tourism Receipts	5.50%
• India's rank in International Tourism Receipts	7

P : Provisional

A : Advance Estimates

Interpretation:

- The number of Foreign Tourist Arrivals (FTAs) in India during 2012 increased to 6.58 million from 6.31 million in 2011. The growth rate in FTAs during 2012 over 2011 was 4.3% as compared to 9.2% during 2011 over 2010. The growth rate of 4.3% in 2012 for India was better than the growth rate of 4% for the International Tourist Arrivals in 2012.
- The share of India in international tourist arrivals in 2012 was 0.64%, India's rank in international tourist arrivals declined to 41 , in 2012, from 38 in 2011. India accounted for 2.82% of tourist arrivals in Asia and the Pacific Region in 2012, with the rank of 11.
- About 91.7% of the FTAs entered India through air routes followed by 7.6% by land routes and 0.7% by sea routes.

Delhi and Mumbai airports accounted for about 54.9% of the total FTAs in India. The top 15 source markets for FTAs in India in 2012 were USA, UK, Bangladesh, Sri Lanka, Canada, Germany, France, Japan, Australia, Malaysia, Russian Fed., China(Main), Singapore, Nepal and Republic of Korea. These 15 countries accounted for about 71.37% of total FTAs in India in 2012.

- Tourism continues to play an important role as the foreign exchange earner for the country. In 2012, foreign exchange earnings (FEE) from tourism were US$ 17.74 billion as compared to US$ 16.56 billion in 2011, registering a growth of 7.1%.
- Number of domestic tourist visits in India during 2012 was 1036.3 million (Provisional) as compared to 864.53 million in 2011, with a growth rate of 19.9 %.
- Number of Indian national departures from India during 2012 was 14.92 million as compared to13.99 million in 2011, registering a growth rate of 6.7%.

Role of The Government

The role of the Government in tourism development has been redefined from a regulator to that of a catalyst. Apart from marketing and promotion, the focus of tourism development plans is now on integrated development of enabling infrastructure through effective partnership with various stakeholders. Tourism development in India has passed through many phases. The development of tourist facilities was taken up in a planned manner in 1956 coinciding with the Second Five Year Plan. The approach has evolved from isolated planning of single unit facilities in the Second and Third Five Year Plans. The Sixth Plan marked the beginning of a new era when tourism began to be considered a major instrument for social integration and economic development.

However, it was only after the 80s that tourism activity gained momentum. A National Policy on Tourism was announced in 1982.In 1992, a National Action Plan was prepared and in 1996 the National Strategy for Promotion of Tourism was drafted. In 1997, a draft New Tourism Policy in tune with the economic policies of the Government and the trends in tourism development was published for public debate. The draft policy is now under revision. The proposed policy recognizes the roles of Central and State Governments, Public Sector Undertakings and the Private Sector in the development of tourism. The need for involvement of Panchayati Raj institutions, local bodies, non-governmental organizations and the local youth in the creation of tourism facilities has also been recognized[3].

As per the working strategy for the 12th Five Year Plan, the Ministry of Tourism has adopted a "pro-poor tourism approach which could contribute significantly to poverty reduction. More than half of Tourism Ministry's Plan budget is channelized for funding the development of destinations, circuits, mega projects as also for rural tourism infrastructure projects. The Ministry also ensured that 10% and 2.5% of its total Annual Plan (2012-13) outlay went to the tourism projects in the North-Eastern region and the tribal areas respectively.

The other major development that took place was the setting up of the Indian Tourism Development Corporation in 1966 to promote India as a tourist destination and the Tourism Finance Corporation in 1989 to finance tourism projects. Altogether, 21 Government-run Hotel Management and Catering Technology Institutes and 14 Food Craft Institutes were also established for imparting specialized training in hoteliering and catering.

Initiatives by The Government for Tourism Promotion

'Hunar se Rozgar' Programme

A special initiative was launched in 2009-10 for the creation of employable skills among youth belonging to economically weaker sections of the society in the age group of 18-25 years (upper age limit raised to 28 years in November, 2010) with the basic objective to reduce the skill gap affecting the hospitality and tourism sector and to ensure the spread of economic benefit of tourism to the poor. The programme offers short duration courses of 6 to 8 weeks which are fully funded by the Ministry of

3 Govt. of India, Press Information Bureau release, dated 8.5.2000

Tourism. Initially covering two courses viz. (i) food and beverage service; and (ii) food production, courses in Housekeeping, Utility, Bakery and Patisserie were added subsequently. With the growing acceptability of the initiative more trades/training areas were added like- to bring up drivers, golf caddies, stone mason, security guards and tourist facilitators etc. For the year 2012-13, 21,175 persons have been trained under the initiative upto 31 January 2013.

Visa on Arrival (VoA)

Considering the importance of Visa facilities in enhancing tourist inflow, the facility of „Long Term Tourist Visas◎ of five years duration with multiple entry, carrying a stipulation of 90 days for each visit, has been introduced on a pilot basis for the nationals of the 18 selected countries. The findings of an evaluation study conducted by this Ministry have reinforced the belief that the presence of the facility of "Visa on Arrival" (VoA) significantly influences the tourists◎ travel plans to any country. During 2012, a total number of 16,084 VoAs (Visa on Arrival) were issued as compared to 12,761 VoAs during the corresponding period of 2011, thereby showing a growth of 26%. Efforts are on to extend the VoA facility for the nationals of more countries.

Publicity and marketing strategy

As part of its domestic and global publicity and marketing strategy to promote tourism and create social awareness through the print and electronic media, the Ministry of Tourism launched campaigns on Clean India, Atithi Devo Bhava and Hunar Se Rozgaar through radio channels. Campaigns highlighting the tourism potential of North-East and J&K were also carried out through Doordarshan. Campaigns were also taken up for "Incredible India" branding on TV during 2nd Formula Grand Prix and London Olympics, 2012, during the International Film Festival of India (IFFI) held in Goa, and during the International India Film Academy (IIFA) Awards 2012 in Singapore.

The Ministry had participated in major international Travel Fairs and Exhibitions in important tourist generating markets the world over, as well as in emerging and potential markets, to showcase and promote the tourism products of the country. These included

Arabian Travel Market (ATM) in Dubai, International Trade Business (ITB-Asia) in Singapore, World Travel Market (WTM) in London, International Meetings Exhibitions (IMEX) in Frankfurt, International Tourism Trade Fair (FITUR) in Madrid, etc.

To showcase and project the Buddhist Heritage of India, an International Buddhist Conclave was organized by the Ministry of Tourism in Varanasi in September 2012 and attended by 132 international delegates from around 30 countries. The delegates were taken for a visit to Sarnath and Bodh Gaya. For the first time, an International Tourism Mart was held at Guwahati in January, 2013 to showcase the largely untapped tourism potential of the north-Eastern region in the domestic and international markets.79 International Buyers and media delegates from 23 countries and hundreds of tour operators from different parts of India participated in the Mart and engaged in one-to-one meetings with sellers from the North East Region and West Bengal. The international delegates were taken on Familiarization Tours of the North Eastern Region.

Niche Tourism Products

The Ministry of Tourism has also taken the initiative of identifying, diversifying, developing and promoting the nascent/ upcoming niche products of the tourism industry. This is done in order to overcome the aspect of „seasonality◎ to promote India as a 365 days destination, attract tourists with specific interests and to ensure repeat visits for the products in which India has comparative advantage. Accordingly, the following Niche Products have been identified by the Ministry of Tourism for development and Promotion:

- Cruise
- Adventure
- Medical
- Wellness
- Golf
- Polo
- Meetings Incentives Conferences and Exhibitions (MICE)
- Eco- Tourism
- Film Tourism

Conclusion

To sum up, Indian tourism has vast potential for generating employment and earning large sums of foreign exchange besides giving a flip to the country's overall economic and social development. Much has been achieved by way of increasing air seat capacity, increasing trains and railway connectivity to important tourist destinations, four-laning of roads connecting important tourist centres and increasing availability of accommodation by adding heritage hotels to the hotel industry and encouraging paying guest accommodation. But much more remains to be done. Since tourism is a multi-dimensional activity, and basically a service industry, it would be necessary that all wings of the Central and State governments, private sector and voluntary organizations become active partners in the endeavour to attain sustainable growth in tourism if India is to become a world player in the tourist industry

References:

Books

Tourism Environment: Nature Culture Economy, New Delhi. Inter-India Publications, 30-38

Indian Tourism Statistics, 2012

Cook, W. Jr. (1992), Compatibility of Tourism and Wilderness

Tewari. S.P : Tourism Dimensions

Singh. R.D : Tourism Today (3rd Volume)

Sinha. P.C : International Encyclopedia of Tourism Incredible India

Babu Sutheeshna (2008), Spatial Dimensions of Tourism in India.

Tourism Development Revisited: Concepts Issues and Challenges, Response books, New Delhi, Sage Publishers pp285-305

Articles/Journals/Reports

Anand T (2006) "Incredible India Finds Its Way to Times Square." agencyfaqs!,February 15. Available at: http://www.afaqs.com/advertising/story.html (accessed 7 August 2011)

Dictionary of Travel, Tourism, and Hospitality (3rd edition) by S. Medlik Location: REF G 155.A1 M397 2003

RNCOS Report, Media Reports, Ministry of Tourism, Press Releases Department of Industrial Policy and Promotion (DIPP)

Websites

www.Incredibleindia.org

www.tourism.gov.in

ROLE OF RURAL TOURISM IN SUSTAINABLE DEVELOPMENT A CASE STUDY ON RURAL TOURIST DESTINATION RAJGARH, DIST. SIRMOUR, HIMACHAL PRADESH

P.K. Yadav

Ex. Pro. V.C. Head and Dean Faculty of Management, M.J.P. Rohilkhand University, Bareilly

Vivek Mittal

Dean, Faculty of Management, CGC-Technical Campus, Mohali

Anurag Agarwal

Associate Professor, Department Of Commerce S.S. PG College Shahjahanpur

Divya Khanna

Guest Faculty, Deptt. of Business Administration, MJP Rohilkhand University, Bareilly

Gireesh Kumar

Guest Faculty, Deptt. of Business Administration, MJP Rohilkhand University, Bareilly

Abstract

Tourism growth potential can be harnessed as a strategy for Rural Development. The development of a strong platform around the concept of Rural Tourism is definitely useful for a country like India, where almost 69% of the population resides in its 7 million villages. Across the world the trends of industrialization and development have had an urban centric approach. Alongside, the stresses of Urban lifestyles have led to a "counterurbanization" syndrome. This has led to growing interest in the rural areas. At the same time this trend of urbanization has led to falling income levels, lesser job opportunities in the total areas leading to an urbanization syndrome in the rural areas. Rural Tourism is one of the few activities which can provide a solution to these problems. Besides, there are other factors which are shifting the trend towards rural tourism like increasing levels of awareness, growing interest in heritage and culture and improved accessibility, and environmental consciousness. In the developed countries, this has resulted in a new style of tourism of visiting village settings to experience and live a relaxed and healthy lifestyle. This concept has taken the shape of a formal kind of Rural Tourism. In the present paper author has tried to find out the role of rural tourism in increasing the level of income of rural India.

Keywords: Home Stay, Occupancy, Tourist, Rural Destination, Employment

Tourism growth potential can be harnessed as a strategy for Rural Development. The development of a strong platform around the concept of Rural Tourism is definitely useful for a country like India, where almost 69% of the population resides in its 7 million villages. In true sense India means villages as per 2011 Census Of the 121 crore Indians, 83.3 crore live in rural areas while 37.7 crore stay in urban areas. As per Registrar General of India and Census Commissioner Mr. C. Chandramouli the rural-urban distribution is 68.84 per cent and 31.16 per cent respectively. The rural economy is based on Agriculture and The share of agriculture and allied sectors in India's GDP is 14.1% in 2011-12. (Business Standard, May 13, 2014). This clearly shows that 68.84% population share the 14.1% of GDP.

Without increasing the share rural income in National GDP we cannot think of sustainable development, else we have to shift the rural population to urban area. In India has a small holdings as it 2 hectare per head (Agriculture Land) thus there is limitations to increase the level of income through agriculture.

Literature Review

Sustainable Development

There are many definitions of sustainable development, including this landmark one which first appeared in 1987:"Development that meets the needs of the present without compromising the ability of future generations to meet their own needs." (from the World Commission on Environment and Development's (the Brundtland Commission) report Our Common Future (Oxford: Oxford University Press, 1987)" The same conference identified three pillars of sustainable development that is :- Economic Development, Social Development and Environment Protection. We cannot imagine sustainable development of India without the Economic and Social Development of rural India and for that we have to develop alternative sources of income for our villages. Development of rural tourism can be one of them.

Rural Tourism

The definition of rural tourism has been the subject of many debates in the literature without arriving at any firm consensus (Pearce 1989; Bramwell 1994; Seaton et al. 1994). Ministry of Tourism , Govt. of India has defined it as "Any form of tourism that showcases the rural life, art, culture and heritage at rural locations, thereby benefiting the local community economically and socially as well as enabling interaction between the tourists and the locals for a more enriching tourism experience can be termed as rural tourism . Rural Tourism is essentially an activity which takes place in the countryside. It is multi-faceted and may entail farm/agricultural tourism, cultural tourism, nature tourism, adventure tourism, and eco-tourism. As against conventional tourism, rural tourism has certain typical characteristics like; it is experience oriented, the locations are sparsely populated, it is predominantly in natural environment, it meshes with seasonality and local events and is based on preservation of culture, heritage and traditions." (Ministry of Tourism Government of IndiaRural tourism scheme for infrastructure development Scheme guidelines, as revised on 9-12-11)

Butler et al. (1998) note economic and social forces operating at the global level are determining both the nature and form of the rural landscape and how we value and use it. These changes, coupled with new ideas and approaches to leisure and recreation time are encouraging tourism development in rural areas at an ever increasing pace (Williams 1998: Reid et al.2000). Gannone and Klaze has defined Agri Tourism as "A range of activities, services and amenities provided by farmers and rural people to attract tourist to their area in order to generate extra income for their businesses". (Gannon, 1988 in Klaze, 1994).

Rural Tourism Includes :-

1. Agri Tourism
2. Heritage and Cultural Tourism
3. Eco –Tourism

Rural Tourist Destination – A Product

There are some critical factors responsible in the evaluation and development of rural tourism as a product.

Dr. R. Gopal, Ms. Shilpa Varma and Ms. Rashmi Gopinathan has described following factors for Rural Tourism Destination product –

- Changes in the preferences and needs of visitors.
- Destination of the natural and manmade environment.
- Change or disappearance of those attractions, which brought tourists to the area.
- Identification of potential consumer.
- Understanding the rural tourists buying behaviour.

To be competitive rural tourism destination must possess basic tourist requirements

- Such as hygienic accommodation and catering.
- It should be connected with the farm accommodation.

About Rajgarh :- Popularly known as the Peach valley, Rajgarh is located in the heart of Sirmaur district in a lush green valley. Rajgarh lies on the Solan - Nahan route It is the biggest subdivision of Sirmaur with a population of 76,509. Rajgarh has two subdivisions, one is Rajgarh itself and the other is Sarahan, another beautiful valley of Sirmaur. The total geographical area of Rajgarh is 810 sq km and 30 per cent of the total area is under forest. It has potential for Rural Tourism. Though data particular of the tourist arrival in Rajgarh is not available. Though it is available for the District according to it in 2011-12 total domestic tourist arrival is as 445260 and foreign tourist arrival is 2513. (Ministry of Tourism Survey by AC Neilsen ORG Marg Survey)

Objectives of the study

The Key objectives of this paper are:-

1) Examines the key issues involved in the development of Rural-Tourism.
2) The challenges faced by Rural- Tourism industry in general and Rajgarh in Particular.
3) Suggest recommendations for the success of Rural Tourism at Rajgarh, Himachal Pradesh

Research Methodology

The research methodology involved both the desk research and the field research. The Research Design is Exploratory and Descriptive. At first stage it is exploratory as it tries to find out understand the concept of Rural Tourism, its scope in Rajgarh and various stakeholders of rural tourism at Ragjarh. Further field research was done. A Questionnaire was used collect information. The questionnaire comprises of both open-ended as well as close-ended questions. Researcher has also taken in-depth interview of the owners of Home Stays at Rajgarh and visitors at Rajgarh. Additionally discussions were also held with the officials of the district and other taluka levels to understand the government policies etc. The subject being vast, we have limited the study to Rajgarh, District Sirmour.

Sample Size :-

1. Home Stays :- 7, At Rajgarh there were 7 home stays and I interviewed all of them thus whole universe is interviewed.
2. Tourist :- 60 Tourist were interviewed who were staying at these Home Stays, or had stayed in these home stays. Of these 50 were domestic and 10 were foreign tourist.

Questionnaire was administered by researcher himself. 18 Domestic Tourist and 8 Foreign tourist were interviewed personally and questionnaire was emailed to 32 respondents and further they were administered through telephone. The details of these 32 respondents were given by these home stays owners.

Findings:- The research has following findings:-

Table 1:

Total number of rooms/accommodation available at Rajgarh at Home Stays :-

Sl No	Number of Home Stay	Rooms Available at Accommodation Unit	Number of Beds Available per day
1	Yatin Home Stay	02	08
2	Romi Chauhan Home Stay	02	08
3	Satyam Shivam Sundram Home Stay	04	15
4	Thakur Home Stay	03	12
5	Shivlok Home Stay	04	14
6	Joginder Home Stay	03	12
7	Ram Lal Home Stay	02	08
	Total	20	37

At Rajgarh there are seven home stays belonged to local people. These home stays are registered with the Tourist Department and have a total capacity of 37 persons. The main occupation of the owners of these Home Stay is agriculture. They have converted 2 to 4 room of their house in home stays.

Table 2 :- Room Rent and other service

Sl No	Home Stay	Rent (Per Room/Per Day)	Room Service	Food/ Limited Choice	Profes-sional Cook
1	Yatin Home Stay	1000	Yes	Yes	No
2	Romi Chauhan Home Stay	500	Yes	Yes	No
3	Satyam Shivam Sun-dram Home Stay	2200	Yes	Yes	Yes
4	Thakur Home Stay	800	Yes	Yes	No

Sl No	Home Stay	Rent (Per Room/Per Day)	Room Service	Food/ Limited Choice	Profes-sional Cook
5	Shivlok Home Stay	500	Yes	Yes	No
6	Joginder Home Stay	1200	Yes	Yes	No
7	Ram Lal Home Stay	750	Yes	Yes	No
	Total				

All the home stays provide room service, housekeeping and food service. Though most of them precisely 6 out of 7 don't have any professional cook. Only one stay that is Satyam Shivam Sundaram has a professional cook and it provides multi - cuisine food. Else all other provide only traditional food and fast food. Most of them have hired one person permanent for housekeeping and room service and during season time (April-July) they hiıe one or two more person for the same.

Table 3:- Occupancy (Per Quarter, in Percentage)

Sl No	Home Stay	January-March	April-June	July -September	October-December	Total
1	Yatin Home Stay	23	52	15	12	25
2	Romi Chauhan Home Stay	29	48	23	18	30
3	Satyam Shivam Sundram Home Stay	36	78	27	22	50
4	Thakur Home Stay	31	59	13	11	29
5	Shivlok Home Stay	36	62	26	18	36
6	Joginder Home Stay	28	45	19	13	26
7	Ram Lal Home Stay	17	58	11	9	24
	Total	29	57	19	15	30

Position of occupancy is not very good at home stay. The annual average occupancy is 30% and it is not normally distributed on the one hand it is as high as 57% during April-June and on the other hand it as low as 15% during October –December. These means that during most part of the year the home stay remains vacant. And the basic purpose of generating income gets futile. Even it is not generating employment for full year. At peak season also it is not more than 57%. It is a crucial issue. We have to find out ways to increase the number of visitors.

Table 4 Age Distribution of Sample Visitors in the Rajgarh

Age Group	% of Domestic Visitors	%age of Foreign Visitors
15-24	10	8
25-34	50	54
35-44	36	34
45-60	4	4
	100	100

Most of the domestic visitors are of the age group of 25-34 as 50% belong to that group. Among foreign visitors 54% are of the age group of 25-34. Followed by the age bracket of 35-44 as 36% of domestic visitors are of this age group same is with foreign visitors.

Table 5: Occupation Sample Visitors in the Rajgarh

Occupation	% of Domestic Visitors	%age of Foreign Visitors
Industrial/Trader/ Shop Owner	4	0
Self Employed Professional	6	32
Government Service	46	18
Private Service	16	28
Business	24	18
Student/Researcher	4	4
Agriculture	0	0
	100	100

Table 6: Purpose of Visit

Purpose of Visit	% of Domestic Visitors	%age of Foreign Visitors
Excursion	92	91
Research	1	9
Official	0	0

Purpose of Visit	% of Domestic Visitors	%age of Foreign Visitors
Health	3	0
Honeymoon	4	0
Office Training	0	0
Total	100	100

Perhaps purpose of visit is the most important factor of any tourism research. Rajgarh is a small mountain hamlet most people come here for excursion and peace. They come here to leave in peace as 92% of domestic and 91% of foreign visitors come at Ragjarh for this reason. 9% foreign visitor come for research purpose and only 1% domestic visitor came for research purpose. Most important finding of this table is that only 4% couple came here for honeymoon purpose among domestic visitors and 0 in case of foreign visitors. This percentage can be increased. For health reason 3% of domestic visitor came.

Table 7: Duration of Stay

	Domestic Visitor	Foreign Visitors
Average Stay in Days	5	17

The average stay of the domestic tourist is very low. If we increase the average stay of visitor the occupancy rate will automatically increase.

Table 8: Tourist Accompanied with

Accompany	% of Domestic Visitors	% of Foreign Visitors
Friends	17	77
Spouse	27	23
Spouse and Childeren	35	0
Relatives	23	0
Office Collogues/ Sponsored by Employer	0	0
	100	100

Table 8 explains that with whom people prefer to go for Rural Tourism. In the above table we find that 35% domestic tourist came to home stay with their children and spouse and 35% came with their spouse thus in total 62% of the total domestic tourist came with their immediate family this can be concluded in way Rural Tourism should be marketed to the whole family. Among foreign tourist 77% of foreign tourist came with their friends.

Table 9: Popular Source of Information of Tourist Destination

	% age of Domestic Visitor	**% of Foreign Visitors**
Newspaper/Magazine	8	4
Television	0	0
Newspaper and Television Both	2	0
Internet	44	59
Reference	35	18
Tour and Travel Consultant	11	19
Total	100	100

The above tally is very important as it indicate the suitable mean of communication with the target segment. Above table clearly indicates that the most widely used mean of communication to get the information is Internet as 44% visitor has used it, followed by references. These references are those persons who have already visited the place. Thus it shows that in case of rural tourism a satisfied customer is of utter importance. In case of foreign visitors the importance of internet is more. As 59% of foreign visitor used the internet to get the information. In case of foreign tourist the role of Tour and Travel consultant is also important as 19% of foreign tourist took the help of Tour and Travel Consultant to manage their trip though in case of domestic tourist the role of Tour and Travel is less.

Table 10: Medium of Booking of Home Stay

	Internet	Tourist Agent	Govt. Agency	Self/On the Spot	Total
Domestic	48%	32%	14%	6%	100
Foreign	70%	10%	-	20%	100
	59%	21%	7%	13%	

Table 6 clearly indicates that 59% visitors use internet to book to book the home stay. Though in case of Domestic visitors it is very low as only 48% used the internet. 70% of the foreign tourist used Internet for booking. In case of booking, tourist agent also plays a important role as 32% of domestic visitor preferred tourist agent for booking. In case of booking tourism department of Himachal Tourism also plays a role as 14% customer booked their home stay through them.

Table 11: Satisfaction Level of Service by Visitors

Services	% of Domestic Visitors		% of Foreign Visitors	
	Satisfied	Unsatis-fied	Satisfied	Unsatis-fied
Availability of Tour Operator	44	56	33	67
Availability of Transportation	78	22	54	66
Availability of Tourist Guide	49	51	64	36
Quality of Accommodation	71	29	53	47
Accommodation Tariff	66	44	69	31
Public Convenience	31	69	19	81
Eating Places	94	6	86	14
Information Center	74	26	51	49
Upkeep of Tourist Sites	55	45	43	67
Behavior of Local People	92	8	83	17
Security	86	14	78	22
Quality of Roads	91	9	81	29
Entertainment Places	32	68	14	86
Quality of Information	53	47	22	78

Table 11 discusses the satisfaction of customer regarding various services during their stay at Home Stay. Above table clearly shows that tourist are most satisfied with the behavior of local people and domestic tourist are most dissatisfied with the availability of entertainment places and for same factor the dissatisfaction level of foreign tourist was 86%. It is most crucial thing but to arrange places of entertainment in rural area is difficult. Another area of concern is Public Convenience as 81% of foreign tourist are dissatisfied with it and 69% of domestic tourist are dissatisfied with it. Otherwise in most other factors some up gradation is required to increase the tourist arrival at home stays.

Table 12 Expectation Level of Visitors

Expectation Level	% of Domestic Visitors	% of Foreign Visitors
Much Better than Expectation	5	4
Somewhat better then expectation	80	85
As per Expectation	11	12
Worse than Expectation	4	0
Much Worse than Expectation	1	0

If in totality we see the satisfaction level of tourist then we find that 80% domestic tourist expressed that they somewhat felt better than expectation and in case of foreign tourist it was 85%. When discussed in detail they revealed they have never expected such a hospitality by the owners of home stays. The rooms were very clean and local people helped a lot. Thus it can be said one reason of going with this statement is the expectation level of tourist were not so high.

Recommendation and Suggestions

A complete tourism package can be provided through initiation by the local government bodies of activities such as beautification campaigns, sponsorship of special events that tie in with local tourist attractions and participation of all businesses in the area.

To increase the number of tourist, more reasons to go should be given to target customer to go for rural tourism. These reasons can be :-

-Corporate T&D:- Share of Outdoor Training and Development sessions of corporate is increasing in total tourism pie and Rural Tourism could also share it by proper marketing and approaching the Corporate sector.

-Share of Honeymooners was very less in rural tourism as in the case of Rajgarh we found that of total only 4% of total tourist came for honeymoon. Honeymooners can be a very attractive segment as they are spenders , their average stay is very high and they need aloofness. And most important it that big number of marriages takes place in the month of October, November and December thus occupancy will increase in the off season.

-Internet : The role of internet is very high in getting tourist for rural tourism. Table No. 9 shows that 44% of domestic customer and 59% of foreign tourist got the information regarding rural tourism from internet. Thus the Govt. and Promoters should use internet in more professional way to get tourist. And it is most economical way of communication with prospective tourist.

-CRM:- Customer Relationship Management is very important as we have seen that references also played a critical role in getting tourist as far as rural tourism is concern as it is not very popular type of tourism.

-We have seen that 47% of domestic customer are from Govt. service this shows that Govt official are big market and it is easy to target them as their location and mean of communication can be easily identified. They can be targeted direct at their offices through literature and internet.

-Support and participation of local government; The role of local government is especially important in the following areas; funding for tourism development and promotion, creating and maintenance of infrastructure necessary for tourism, zoning and maintenance of the community so that it looks clean and appealing to tourists and educational support for farmers.

In the finding we have seen that 90% tourist went for rural tourism for excursion only

- Sufficient funds for tourism development; Most of the rural communities depend on public funds that are very often insufficient to cover all the needs of the rural community; private funds are something that most often can't be reached since local people do not have sufficient incomes by themselves to invest; therefore it is very important to explore for other sources of funding and assistance.

-Coordination and cooperation between rural tourism entrepreneurs; Tourism requires different types of businesses to work together because, by its nature; tourism has intertwined relations between different types of business such as shops, accommodation facilities, restaurants and tourist attractions. They may create different types of networks, both formal and informal.

Conclusion

Development of agri-tourism in Himachal rural areas is still in its nascent stage. Himachal Pradesh has perfect opportunities to enhance its agri-tourism offer and it also represents one of the few states, which has such a pleasant climates, natural characteristics and socio-cultural entities. Though there has not been much initiative by the state government for rural-tourism development, it has been successfully initiated through the farmers' efforts. Rural tourism can bring wealth directly in hands of farmers. It not only increase the income level of owners of home stay rather it gives employment to local people without their displacement and it generate revenue for other stakeholders in the village as kirana shops, tea shops etc. Rural Tourism does not have any negative impact on environment. Thus rural tourism can prove to be a good tool of economy for sustainable development.

References

Bramwell, B. (1994), Rural Tourism and Sustainable Rural Tourism, Journal of Sustainable Tourism 2 (1-2), pp.1-6

Butler, R.W., (1980), The concept of a tourism area cycle of evolution; implications for management of resources, Canadian Geographer Vol. XXIV (1), pp.5-12.

Butler, R.W., Hall, C.M. Jenkins, J. (eds) (1998), Tourism and Recreation in Rural Areas, John Wiley & Sons, Toronto.

Getz, D. Carlsen, J., (2000), Characteristics and Goals of family and owner operated businesses in the rural tourism and hospitality sectors. Tourism management, 21, pp.547-560.

Gopal,r.,Varma,S.,Gopinath,R., (2008), Rural Tourism Development: Constraints and Possibilities with a special reference to Agri Tourism, Conference on Tourism in India – Challenges Ahead, 15-17 May 2008, IIMK

Murphy P.E. (1985; Tourism; A Community Approach.

Journals 'Indian Economic Growth: Can it Translate into Rural Prosperity?' The Analyst, Special Issue on Agri-Business, August 2007.

'Social Entrepreneurship: The Alicia Polak Way, The ICFAI Journal of Entrepreneurship Development, Vol IV No. 2, June 2007.

Share of Agriculture in National Income of India : ijsr - International Journal of Scientific Research, Volume 2, issue 9 Journal of ATDC, Various volumes.

Report : Tourism Survey for the state of Himachal Pradesh by AC Neilsen-Org Marg

'Rural economy is key to growth', Business Standard, 30.07.07, Pg 3.

Internet Sources:

http://europa.eu.int/comm/agriculture/rur/leadership/index_en.htm

http://www.ecovast.org/indexe.htm.

http://www.hgk.hr.

http://www.biznet.hr.

http://www.ruraltourism.org.uk/index.php?s=4&p=Informal_Tourism_activities.

http://www.xomba.com/agri_tourism_growing_in_india

http://www.thehindubusinessline.com/2006/11/16/stories/2006111602532100.htm

http://cities.expressindia.com/fullstory.php?newsid=242580

http://www.agritourism.in/index.htm

http://www.agritourism.in/faq.htm